PRAISE FOR

Royal Affairs

"Carroll . . . has a true talent for weaving fascinating narratives. Her entertaining writing style makes this one book you do not want to put down. Entertaining, impeccably researched, and extremely well written, it will appeal to all readers with an interest in British history." —*Library Journal*

"There are lots [of] royal romps cataloged in this entertaining, enormously readable book." —*Las Vegas Review-Journal*

"Carroll offers . . . insight behind the closed doors of the last thousand years of England's busiest bed-hopping and head-lopping kings and queens." —Book Fetish

"An eminently readable, lusciously lascivious smorgasbord of the lewd, bizarre, and sometimes illegal sexual behavior of past and present members of royalty . . . a voyeuristic thrill that not even the best of today's erotica can top." —Curled Up with a Good Book

ALSO BY LESLIE CARROLL

Royal Affairs

Notorious Royal Marriages

A JUICY JOURNEY THROUGH
NINE CENTURIES OF
DYNASTY, DESTINY, AND DESIRE

LESLIE CARROLL

 NEW AMERICAN LIBRARY

New American Library
Published by New American Library, a division of Penguin Group (USA) Inc.,
375 Hudson Street, New York, New York 10014, USA
Penguin Group (Canada), 90 Eglinton Avenue East, Suite 700, Toronto,
Ontario M4P 2Y3, Canada (a division of Pearson Penguin Canada Inc.)
Penguin Books Ltd., 80 Strand, London WC2R 0RL, England
Penguin Ireland, 25 St. Stephen's Green, Dublin 2, Ireland (a division of Penguin Books Ltd.)
Penguin Group (Australia), 250 Camberwell Road, Camberwell, Victoria 3124,
Australia (a division of Pearson Australia Group Pty. Ltd.)
Penguin Books India Pvt. Ltd., 11 Community Centre, Panchsheel Park,
New Delhi-110 017, India
Penguin Group (NZ), 67 Apollo Drive, Rosedale, North Shore 0632,
New Zealand (a division of Pearson New Zealand Ltd.)
Penguin Books (South Africa) (Pty.) Ltd., 24 Sturdee Avenue, Rosebank,
Johannesburg 2196, South Africa

Penguin Books Ltd., Registered Offices: 80 Strand, London WC2R 0RL, England

First published by New American Library, a division of Penguin Group (USA) Inc.

First Printing, January 2010
10 9 8 7 6 5 4 3 2 1

 REGISTERED TRADEMARK—MARCA REGISTRADA

LIBRARY OF CONGRESS CATALOGING-IN-PUBLICATION DATA
Carroll, Leslie.
Notorious royal marriages: a juicy journey through nine centuries of dynasty, destiny, and desire/Leslie Carroll.
p. cm.
Includes bibliographical references.
ISBN 978-0-451-22901-4
1. Marriages of royalty and nobility—Europe—History. 2. Kings and rulers—Sexual behavior—History. 3. Queens—Sexual behavior—History. 4. Europe—Politics and government. I. Title.
D107.C29 2010
940.09'9—dc22   2009030451

Set in Sabon
Designed by Jessica Shatan Heslin/Studio Shatan, Inc.

Printed in the United States of America

PUBLISHER'S NOTE
While the author has made every effort to provide accurate telephone numbers and Internet addresses at the time of publication, neither the publisher nor the author assumes any responsibility for errors, or for changes that occur after publication. Further, publisher does not have any control over and does not assume any responsibility for author or third-party Web sites or their content.

For my darling and devoted husband, Scott,

From "Kleines Fraüchen" with "ein Kuss"

"I love you, those three words have my life in them."

Contents

The State of Princes . . . in matters of marriage [is] far of worse sort than the condition of poor men. For Princes take as is brought them by others, and poor men be commonly at their own device and liberty.

—Anthony Denny, Member of the King's Privy Chamber and chief body servant to Henry VIII, 1540

Foreword

Everyone loves a royal wedding. Except, perhaps, the bride and groom. Throughout history, most royal marriages were arranged affairs, brokered for diplomatic and dynastic reasons, and often when the prospective spouses were mere children. The perfect royal marriage brought territorial gains to the ruling dynasty's side (usually the groom's) and cemented alliances between families and regions. It was of little consequence that the spouses often didn't meet until their wedding day. Or that they had been in love with someone else and were now compelled to abandon all hope of the personal happiness or emotional fulfillment that might have come from nuptial bliss with another. There is no *I* in *dynasty*.

In general, there was one primary goal of a royal marriage: to beget an heir. And for a good part of the past millennium, when much of Western Europe was embroiled in perpetual warfare, it was believed that only a *male* heir would be able to defend and hold the throne, although a female could legally inherit the throne in England and Scotland. During more martial eras, royal wives who managed to produce only daughters—Katherine of Aragon and Anne Boleyn, for example—were disposed of by their autocratic spouse, powerless to challenge his authority. If execution was no longer an option to ending a problematic or infertile marriage, there was always divorce. Napoleon Bonaparte divorced his first wife, Josephine de Beauharnais, because she failed to bear him a son.

With so many marriages being little more than dynastic alliances, how did these royals manage to survive their arranged nuptials and make their peace with the world into which they were born? Or did they? Precious few of the notorious royal marriages profiled in this book began as love matches—although they didn't necessarily stay that way. And for several centuries, if things weren't working out, the monarch might play the all-purpose, get-out-of-marriage-free card known as a papal dispensation on the grounds of consanguinity. In other words, plenty of unions were sundered after cousins who had received a dispensation to marry in the first place suddenly decided to become appalled and repulsed by how closely they were related when it became expedient to wed another.

With so many intriguing relationships, choosing whose stories to omit was nearly as difficult as selecting which ones to include. Within this volume are some of the world's most famous royal unions, as they affected and were affected by the historical and political events of the times; it is not intended to provide an overview of world history, to probe with great depth the wars and revolutions that gripped Europe for centuries, or to present full biographies of the principals.

Comparing the selection of a marriage partner to fishing for an eel—that staple of Renaissance diets—Sir Thomas More's father commented that it was as if "ye should put your hand into a blind bag full of snakes and eels together, seven snakes for one eel."

In these pages are the snakes as well as the eels—the disastrous unions and the delightful ones; the martyrs to marriage and the iconoclasts who barely took their vows seriously; the saintly and the suffering; the rebels and the renegades—all of whom took the phrases "I do" and "I will" and ran as far as they could go with them, exploring and embracing the broad spectrum of passion, power, and possibilities far beyond the royal bedchamber.

Notorious
Royal Marriages

LOUIS VII
1120–1180
RULED AS CO-KING OF FRANCE: 1131–1137
RULED AS KING: 1137–1180

and

ELEANOR OF AQUITAINE
1122–1204

married 1137–1152

"I thought I married a king, but I find I have married a monk."

—Eleanor of Aquitaine, on her husband, Louis VII of France

WHAT'S IN A NAME? WELL, WHEN YOUR MATERNAL GRAND-mother's is the Countess Dangerosa, one might easily speculate that you, too, could spell Trouble.

The Countess Dangerosa was the mistress of Eleanor of Aquitaine's grandfather the lusty Duke William IX of Aquitaine, whose bawdy ballads garnered him the reputation as the first known troubadour. Eleanor was the eldest daughter of the duke's son (also named William) and Dangerosa's daughter Aenor, by her first husband. After Duke William X died of dysentery on Good Friday, April

9, 1137, the fifteen-year-old Eleanor became Europe's richest heiress, inheriting much of what now comprises western and southern France—including the regions of Poitou, Aquitaine, and Gascony.

According to Richard de Poitevin, writing in the 1170s, Eleanor was "brought up in delicacy and reared in abundance of all delights, living in the bosom of wealth." She was quite the catch, even if she'd been a bit spoiled as a girl. Headstrong, willful, high-spirited, and exceptionally intelligent, she was also an acknowledged beauty. Although no physical description of her survives, Eleanor's father and grandfather were both redheads.

Twelfth-century Western Europe was a feudal society. The king was the ultimate overlord, at the apex of a pyramid of power. Dukes and counts were his vassals, but had vassals of their own in the local barons, whose vassals included knights, and so on down the social food chain. It was also an era in which might made right. If a count or baron could take a neighboring castle—or county—or dukedom—by force and hold it, it became his.

Things weren't much different where women were concerned. Marriage by abduction was a popular way to get a bride. Aenor, about whom little is known, died when Eleanor was only eight years old, so the orphaned teen was at the mercy of predatory nobles who would think nothing of rape as a substitute for an engagement ring. But Eleanor's father left her lands in trust to his own overlord, King Louis VI of France, until such time as she married, with the tacit understanding that Eleanor would be wed to Louis's heir.

However, Louis VI's firstborn son had died at the age of fifteen when his horse shied at a runaway pig and threw him. So the king was compelled to recall his second son, Louis, from the monastery of St. Denis, where he was being groomed to enter the church. The elder Louis had determined that marrying his son to an heiress who would quadruple the size of his kingdom with a simple "I do" beat marrying God any day, so the sixteen-year-old Louis the Young was sent to Bordeaux to wed Eleanor.

Not too many weeks after her father's death, on Sunday, July 25, 1137, the teens were married at the Romanesque Cathedral of

St. André in Bordeaux, followed immediately by their coronation as Duke and Duchess of Aquitaine. A few days later, they were also crowned Count and Countess of Poitou at the region's capital, Poitiers.

Although his father was the actual ruler until his death, the youth had become King of France in 1131, in accordance with the French custom of royal heirs being crowned during the older king's lifetime. Louis the Young, as he was called—to differentiate him from his father, Louis the Fat—was a tall blond stripling with the personality of a permanent penitent.

The meek bridegroom, who had spent much of his life as a "child-monk," was shy and awkward in company, and at his own wedding reception he was both shocked and appalled by the merry dancing and ribald songs, not to mention his new wife's unchecked vitality and exuberance during the festivities. Luckily, the couple enjoyed a mutual physical attraction—and Louis remained smitten with Eleanor's looks until the day they divorced. However, their temperaments could not have been more dissimilar.

As Louis was both quiet and spiritual, Eleanor often took the lead in their relationship, although such aggressiveness defied what was considered the natural order of things. But Aquitanian women were more forthright than most and Eleanor had learned how to manage estates, as well as people from all walks of life, having accompanied her father as he rode through his vast territories collecting his vassals' tithes and tributes.

Her new husband, on the other hand, although he was considered quite intelligent, wasn't quite ready for prime time when his father died of dysentery on August 1, 1137, just seven days after the royal marriage. In the space of a single week the sensitive, untested Louis became both bridegroom and king.

And although her formal coronation did not take place until Christmas Day, Eleanor was now Queen of France. Her lands, inherited from her father, became Louis's domains, although they would revert to her if she became widowed or divorced.

Trusted vassals were placed in control of Eleanor's provinces and seneschals, or stewards, maintained her castles and estates, while the new queen, uprooted from her beloved south, moved to her husband's damp and dreary capital, Paris. Although it was the greatest center of education in Western Europe, the noisy, filthy city of 200,000 souls, densely concentrated on the tiny Ile de la Cité, offered Eleanor a disappointing welcome. The stench of sewage was everywhere, and beyond the crenellated walls that encircled the fortress-like palace many people lived cheek by jowl in dust and mud.

Her family's castles in the south had boasted airy rooms and a sultry atmosphere with lush gardens and sparkling fountains. The bleakness of Paris proved a startling contrast. So Eleanor immediately set to redecorating, endeavoring to transform the castle and her own suite of rooms into a sophisticated re-creation of her childhood homes. Her improvements, including the tapestries commissioned from Bourges, shutters fitted over the drafty arrow slits, and a startling innovation—a fireplace and chimney built directly into the wall—cost Louis a fortune and earned Eleanor the immediate enmity of her mother-in-law.

Adelaide, the Dowager Queen of France, had little use for this medieval Martha Stewart who dared to question her own interior design sense while running up impressive bills for her extravagant wardrobe and the care and feeding of the troubadours she imported to the conservative north to entertain her entourage. Eleanor required tablecloths to be spread over the dining boards in the Great Hall, ordered the servants to wash their hands before serving meals, and insisted on attention to table manners—and Adelaide felt insulted that what had been good enough for the Capets, France's ruling family for centuries, wasn't acceptable to her spoiled and decadent daughter-in-law. What probably galled the dowager queen the most was that her timid son indulged his fifteen-year-old bride in her every whim, and sought, even deferred to, Eleanor's opinion in everything, including matters of governance—in which, Adelaide conceded, the vivacious Aquitanian girl had more experience than Louis did.

Adelaide blinked first, moving to another castle. But her démenage had little effect on an ever-widening rift within the royal marriage. Odo de Dieul, Louis's secretary, and later his chaplain, described the king's life as "a model of virtue," noting "worldly glory did not cause him sensual delight." While his queen entertained the age's greatest musicians and poets, the pious Louis spent much of the day on his knees in prayer. Eleanor bedecked herself in silks and furs, painted her face, and adorned her neck, wrists, and ears with gold, while Louis felt most at home in a hair shirt.

Their world was a violent one, despite her efforts to civilize it in even the smallest of ways. Many of Louis's vassals were both ambitious and ruthless and he was not a decisive ruler. At every turn, Eleanor endeavored to toughen up her husband and turn him into a strong sovereign. A contemporary chronicler, William of Newburgh, described Louis as "a man of warm devotion to God and of extraordinary lenity to his subjects . . . but he was rather more credulous than befits a king and prone to listen to advice that was unworthy of him." It's not clear to whom William referred, but as it was considered unnatural for wives to offer political counsel, it's quite possible that the barb was aimed at Eleanor. Whenever Louis tried to impress her by acting like an authoritative overlord, the result was a complete turnaround from tyro to tyrant—unchecked outbursts of temper that invariably led to rash, ill-considered behavior, which he invariably regretted.

In the summer of 1141, Louis tussled with a vassal over the man's adulterous affair with Eleanor's sixteen-year-old sister, Petronilla, and had another disagreement with the vassal's equally powerful brother over the appointment of a bishop. As a result of the latter dispute the Pope excommunicated Louis; and during a turf war between the king and his rebellious vassals, an entire village of innocents was slaughtered inside the church at Vitry-sur-Marne. Mortified by the carnage he had unleashed, Louis underwent an even stricter course of penance, replacing his regal garb and flowing blond tresses with a monk's coarse robes and the circular fringe of a tonsure.

The king's increasing asceticism immensely exacerbated the existing problems within his marriage. As it was, his raging physical attraction to Eleanor was more of a curse than a blessing; he felt guilty every time he went to her bed because it violated his fervent belief that copulation was supposed to be for the getting of heirs, an obligation and duty, not an eagerly anticipated act of enjoyment. The untoward stirrings within his loins therefore required more, and stricter, penance. His conjugal visits, already infrequent, grew even fewer. Religious holidays and feast days were taboo. So were Sundays. And like many men and women of his day, Louis was convinced that performing in anything other than the "missionary" position was punished by three years' penance; failure to follow any of these connubial rules would result in deformed babies or lepers.

Consequently, Eleanor wasn't able to uphold her end of the marriage contract, since it was her job to bring forth children. "I thought I married a king, but I find I have married a monk," she complained, frustrated sexually and dynastically.

And she wasn't the only one unhappy with the marriage.

Abbé Bernard of Clairvaux, as ascetic as Louis, began to question the union's validity, expressing his misgivings as early as 1143. Although Louis's mentor Abbé Suger had given them a dispensation, Eleanor and Louis were fourth cousins, related within the prohibited degrees of consanguinity. The unhappy Eleanor silently noted Bernard's doubts; they would bear fruit one day.

The following year, 1144, the twenty-two-year-old Eleanor received a scolding from the disapproving Bernard, who demanded that she "put an end to your interference with affairs of state." Eleanor's response took him utterly by surprise. The queen admitted, quite sincerely, that she delved into politics because her life was otherwise empty; in the seven years since her wedding, she had not been able to conceive a child.

Bernard softened immediately, and struck a deal with the distraught queen. According to the *Vita Tertia, Fragments of a Life of Bernard of Clairvaux*, by Galfredas Claras Valensis, the cleric told Eleanor, "My child, seek those things which make for peace. Cease to stir up the king against the Church and urge him to a better course of action. If you will promise to do this, I in my turn will promise to entreat the merciful Lord to grant you offspring." His words had an immediate effect on Eleanor. Later that day, Louis and his rebellious vassal Count Theobald of Champagne signed a peace treaty, quite possibly due to Eleanor's pressure on her husband. Soon, Eleanor became pregnant, bearing her first child, a daughter, Marie, in 1145. But because France was under Salic law, where only males could inherit the crown, Louis remained without a successor.

His soul was still tormented by the fiery debacle in the church at Vitry-sur-Marne. So, he seized his chance to make reparations when he received word that on Christmas Eve 1144, the Moslem Turks had captured Edessa, one of the four Christian states surrounding the Holy Land, comprising the region known to Europeans as Outremer.

Here was Louis's chance to become a Crusader. Ignoring Abbé Suger's advice to remain in France and continue trying to beget an heir, Louis took the Cross on Easter Sunday 1146. To the surprise of many, the adventurous Eleanor was right there with him. After a year of preparation, the Pope himself blessed this Second Crusade in June 1147, and God's army of 100,000 strong began its long march toward Jerusalem. Baby Marie was left safely behind in France.

On March 19, 1148, Eleanor and Louis arrived in Antioch, another of the Outremer Christian states. Antioch's prince was Eleanor's thirty-six-year-old cousin, the handsome and brave, if somewhat impetuous, Raymond of Poitiers. Eleanor and Raymond spent hour after hour alone together, and in public they were always head-to-head in animated laughter and conversation in *langue d'oc*, their native tongue—the dialect spoken in southern France.

Louis, who understood none of it, as his mother tongue was the northern *langue d'oeil*, grew jealous and assumed that they were flirting outrageously, quietly wondering whether anything untoward was transpiring right under his nose. It was partly Louis's envy that led to his refusal to aid Raymond in a preemptive strike against

Edessa so that the Turks would not be tempted to invade Antioch as well—a strategic disagreement that further increased the rift between Louis and Eleanor. Louis had vowed not to wage war before he had cleansed his soul in Jerusalem. So Eleanor resolved to support Raymond on her own, threatening to remain behind in Antioch with her numerous vassals.

Eleanor and Louis argued bitterly over this issue. Louis reminded his queen that she was not only his vassal, but as his wife she was his property. Eleanor, bristling, brought out the heavy artillery, insisting that their marriage was legally invalid anyway, as they were too closely related in the eyes of the Church. She demanded a divorce.

Louis was just as aware of their degree of consanguinity, but he could not bear to lose Eleanor. For one thing, her immense holdings of land would revert to her possession and control, which would reduce his kingdom to its previous puny size and jeopardize its security. That rationale was a predictable one. But the king had another argument for hanging on to his wife for dear life: according to John of Salisbury, writing a few months later, in 1149, Louis "loved the Queen almost beyond reason."

What to do, what to do? Once again, Louis listened to questionable counsel. His chaplains advised him to eliminate Raymond's undue influence on the queen and assert his rights as her husband by abducting Eleanor and carrying her off to Jerusalem. Louis agreed to the scheme, but it was *Eleanor's* reputation that suffered. The dramatic circumstances surrounding her hasty departure fueled rumors that would persist for centuries claiming that Louis had snatched her from an adulterous—and incestuous—affair with Prince Raymond of Antioch. Given their degree of consanguinity, the royal *marriage* was incestuous as well, although the couple had conveniently overlooked this detail for years!

Eleanor was infuriated by Louis's ignominious treatment of her, and from that point on resolved to have as little to do with him as possible.

In 1148, at Christmas, a heavy-hearted Louis wrote to Abbé

Suger from Jerusalem, informing him of his intention to seek a divorce from Eleanor as soon as he returned to France.

The royal estrangement dragged on into the spring. Louis's Crusade had so far yielded nothing but tremendous loss of life and precious equipment. But another life would be forfeited that would strain the marriage even further.

After spending Easter in Jerusalem, Louis and Eleanor set sail for home—in separate ships. Eleanor's vessel got caught in the middle of a naval battle between the Sicilians and the Byzantine Greeks, and for two months Louis had no news of his wife. When Eleanor landed safely in Sicily, she received news that the Turks had invaded Antioch after their departure and beheaded Raymond. Eleanor blamed Louis for his death.

On the Italian mainland, the royal couple met with the Pope, and each employed the pontiff as a personal marriage counselor. According to John of Salisbury, Louis told Pope Eugenius that he "loved the Queen passionately, in an almost childish way." And Eleanor privately confided her doubts about the marriage's validity because of the consanguinity issue, admitting to His Holiness that she and Louis no longer had sex. The Pope's response was not only to reiterate his sanction of the royal marriage but to escort Eleanor and Louis to a lavish, sensuously appointed bed and encourage them to heed nature's call. John of Salisbury wrote that the king was delighted, making amorous overtures to his queen "in an almost puerile fashion." By the time they returned to France on November 11, 1149, Eleanor was pregnant.

But the ugly rumors of Eleanor's alleged infidelity with Raymond preceded her, and not only did the French believe them, but they blamed *her* for the failure of the Second Crusade. Louis's chaplains then persuaded him to remove any governmental power and authority from her hands.

In the latter half of 1150, Eleanor gave birth to another daughter, Alix. It was a huge disappointment to Louis and, as far as the queen was concerned, offered further proof that God disapproved of their marriage. After fourteen years of wedlock and only two girls to show for it, surely there must be a greater plan at work. Eleanor's reiterated desire for a divorce was unwittingly aided by the French barons, who encouraged Louis to put her aside for the sake of the succession, and marry another (and less controversial) woman who would bear him sons.

The following summer, another catalyst for Eleanor's divorce appeared on the horizon—or, more specifically, at court—in the persons of the handsome Count Geoffrey of Anjou, known as Geoffrey le Bel, and his son, the stocky, redheaded Henry, now Duke of Normandy.

Evidently, there was an instant undercurrent of sexual tension between the twenty-nine-year-old Eleanor and the eighteen-year-old Henry—the man destined to become Eleanor's future husband and King Henry II of England. Days later, Eleanor obtained Louis's consent to a divorce and the first steps were taken to annul their marriage. They embarked on a final trip to Aquitaine, where Louis's officers were replaced by Eleanor's, although she would remain Louis's vassal.

Eleanor last saw Louis in September 1151. There were no tearful good-byes, even with little Marie and Alix, who, in accordance with French law, were left behind in Paris to be raised in their father's court. Eleanor had lost custody of them and would not see them again.

On March 11, 1152, a synod of bishops convened to debate the validity of the royal marriage, and ten days later, with the approval of Pope Eugenius, the union was annulled on the grounds of consanguinity. During the Middle Ages, it was exceptionally rare for a woman to seek and receive a divorce, and when a noblewoman, even a queen, received her decree, her ex-husband usually shoved her into a convent.

But Eleanor had beaten the system. She was a free woman, and though no longer Queen of France, governed lands far vaster than the little kingdom on the Seine. She was now mistress of her own destiny. Or was she? In reality, she was a prime target for kidnappers. If she were violated, she would have to wed her abductor and everything she owned from her body to her estates would become his, a dynamic that played itself out centuries later between Mary, Queen of Scots and the 4th Earl of Bothwell.

But Eleanor's cunning and political savvy prevented her from becoming a victim. And although their divorce redrew the map of France and significantly altered the balance of power in the realm, Louis—though not without regret—got what he wanted out of the annulment as well. He was now free to marry again, and in the grand scheme of things, his eagerness to have a successor outweighed the loss of Aquitaine, Poitou, and Gascony.

Louis married Constance of Castile in 1154, but she died on October 4, 1160, after giving birth to their second daughter, Alys. Alys would grow up to become the mistress of King Henry II of England, who was at the time married to Eleanor of Aquitaine. At long last, Louis's third wife, Adela of Champagne, bore him the son and heir he'd long desired on August 22, 1165. Fourteen years later, in 1179, the prince, who would rule France as Philip II Augustus, was crowned according to Capet tradition during his father's lifetime—but just barely. Louis had suffered a paralytic stroke on August 26, which had effectively ended his reign, and was too ill to attend Philip's coronation ceremony. He died on September 18, 1180, and was interred in the basilica of Saint-Denis outside Paris.

HENRY II
1133–1189
RULED ENGLAND: 1154–1189

❧ *and* ❧

ELEANOR OF AQUITAINE
married 1152–1189

"... with a glad heart ... now ... I am joined in wedlock
to Henry, Duke of Normandy."
>   —fragment of philanthropic charter granted by Eleanor
>   of Aquitaine in 1152

*I*T WAS A MEETING THAT WOULD CHANGE THEIR DESTINIES
and have a profound effect on the balance of power in Europe.
Henry Plantagenet, the eighteen-year-old Duke of Normandy, had
been remiss in paying his homage to Louis VII, his overlord, so that
his title could be formally recognized. So, in the summer of 1151,
Henry accompanied his father, Geoffrey Plantagenet, Count of
Poitou, to the French court.

Geoffrey had been summoned to Paris on charges of illegally
imprisoning a king's high officer, a crime for which Abbé Bernard
of Clairvaux had excommunicated him. To the cynical Count of

Poitou this ecclesiastical punishment meant nothing, but he was still expected to answer for his political actions to his sovereign lord. The unrepentant Geoffrey dragged his prisoner in irons through Louis's Great Hall, and hotly refused to release him. Abbé Bernard, who was present to adjudicate the matter, then launched into one of his own famously fiery tirades, prophesying that Geoffrey's blasphemy would condemn him to an untimely death.

During this heated exchange, Queen Eleanor grew intrigued by the restless pacing of Geoffrey's teenage son, the muscular, gray-eyed, bull-necked Henry. His legs were bowed from so much time in the saddle. Like his dashing father, he affected the sartorial quirk of garnishing his hat with a sprig of the yellow common broom plant, known in Latin as *planta genista*—the genesis of the family name Plantagenet.

Geoffrey of Anjou had invaded Normandy in 1141 and by 1144 the duchy was his. In January 1150, he ceded it to his son Henry. Louis VII correctly perceived the ambitious and energetic young duke as a greater threat to his crown than his father was. Henry would also become the greatest threat to Louis's marriage.

Eleanor found herself attracted on several levels to this freckled, testosterone-fueled teen who seemed to brim with promise and potential. Her desires were obvious and the chroniclers of her day were convinced that she had acted on them, and that they were the impetus for her divorce from Louis. William of Newburgh wrote that ". . . while she was still married to the King of the Franks, she had aspired to marriage with the Norman duke, whose manner of life suited better her own, and for this reason she desired and procured a divorce." According to Walter Map, Eleanor "contrived a righteous annulment and married him."

Giraldus Cambrensis was a bit more lurid, claiming that Eleanor "cast her unchaste eyes on Henry immediately on seeing him. . . . It is related that Henry presumed to sleep adulterously with the Queen of France. . . . How could anything fortunate, I ask, emerge from these copulations?" Giraldus recorded an even more sensational bit of news, adding that Geoffrey "frequently forewarned his son" to stay away from the queen, adding that Geoffrey had forbidden "him in any wise to touch her, both because she was the wife of his lord and because he had known her himself."

Although this claim has never been proven, Henry would give it credence when he considered divorcing Eleanor in the 1170s. True or not, it has certainly done much to enhance Eleanor's legend as a medieval Jezebel. But in the light of day, political considerations trumped any qualms of conscience: a few days after Geoffrey's theatrical stunt with his manacled prisoner and his subsequent showdown with Abbé Bernard, the count and his son returned to court absent all trace of their Plantagenet temper. They apologized for their former misbehavior and offense to their overlord, and contritely offered Louis the Vexin, a small but strategically placed territory on the border of France and Normandy. Louis, always anxious to increase his kingdom's boundaries, accepted this "gift," utterly ignorant of any behind-the-scenes passion or political machinations between Henry and Eleanor. He gave Henry the kiss of peace, which officially acknowledged him as Duke of Normandy, and the Angevin vassals departed Paris with a spring in their steps.

But within days, Geoffrey caught a chill en route to Anjou. Abbé Bernard's malediction proved true; Geoffrey died on September 7, 1151. Henry was suddenly Count of Anjou as well as Duke of Normandy.

On March 11, 1152, the synod of bishops reviewing the validity of Eleanor's marriage to Louis VII formally determined that the royals were indeed related within the proscribed degree of consanguinity. Eleanor had her divorce. And as soon as she reached Poitou, after successfully evading two different abductors, she sent word to Henry that she was now "available" and in effect summoned him to come and marry her.

That May, Henry rode to Poitiers and on the eighteenth of the month the couple were wed in the Romanesque Cathedral of Saint-Pierre.

One has to feel sorry for King Louis. Within weeks of a divorce he never really wanted, the woman he still loved gave herself to a younger, palpably virile man who happened to be his political archrival. By marrying Eleanor, Henry increased his holdings to an area roughly half the size of modern-day France. He also had a legitimate claim to the English throne through his mother, Matilda, the daughter and heir of the late Henry I.

However, the more land an overlord possessed, the greater the difficulty he had controlling it. This dynamic ended up benefiting Eleanor. Although he was perpetually on the road, Henry could not cover such a vast territory on his own, which permitted her to be a genuine coruler. Eleanor toured their lands collecting taxes, dispensing justice, granting charters, and using her own revenues to fund construction projects.

She was a happy newlywed. In reference to one of her philanthropic efforts, she wrote that she bestowed the funds "with a glad heart . . . now that I am joined in wedlock to Henry, Duke of Normandy." And by the end of 1152, she was pregnant.

However, her marriage to Henry was destined to be one of the most turbulent in history. The spouses were too much alike, possessed of strong-willed, formidable personalities, which made for numerous unpleasant clashes. Henry had inherited his father's legendary temper, which manifested itself in black rages and tantrums so intense that he was known to writhe on the floor and chew at the straw rushes.

He was also ostentatiously unfaithful to Eleanor. According to the contemporary chronicler Giraldus Cambrensis, "he was an open adulterer," indulging his vast sexual appetite whenever it suited him, siring bastards with more than one mistress. Eleanor's views regarding Henry's illegitimate children—whom she raised with her own offspring—have not survived. But her reaction to Henry's infidelities may have had something to do with the creation of her own court, where music and poetry abounded. Minstrels and troubadours composed love songs to highborn women, who, within Eleanor's miniscule civilization, were at the top of the food chain.

Henry, however, had little use for these frivolities. Raised in the north of France, he was unfamiliar with the cult of chivalry as a romantic ideal and felt threatened by Eleanor's court of love and the deliberately seductive, impassioned lyrics of the troubadours. He was particularly unnerved by the attentions that the most renowned of them, Bernard de Ventadour, paid to his wife, and sent Bernard packing at the first opportunity.

On August 17, 1153, Eleanor gave birth to William, her first child by Henry. He was on a military campaign in England at the time, but returned to France the following April with the triumphant news that King Stephen, cousin to his mother, Matilda, had formally acknowledged him as his successor. Henry did not have to wait long to become King of England. In November 1154, as he was at home in France busily reducing a rebel vassal's castle to rubble, Henry received news of Stephen's death.

Eleanor was a queen once more. Their realm would now stretch from the Scottish border all the way to the Pyrenees.

Henry and Eleanor were crowned at Westminster Abbey on Sunday, December 19, 1154. And as they toured their new realm, Eleanor received the greatest civics lesson of her life. She discovered that there was no uniform system of laws from shire to shire; the same applied to weights and measures. Trial by combat or by ordeal was still popular in many villages. Seated beside her husband, Eleanor absorbed the workings of his keen legal mind as Henry dispensed justice like a circuit judge and enacted reforms to standardize regional discrepancies regarding calculations of measurement. Henry's decisions were well considered and equally well respected, and during his reign trial by jury gradually replaced trial by ordeal. In time, Eleanor, too, gained a reputation as a learned and fair adjudicator.

As King of England, Henry's seat of government was located primarily at Westminster; he ruled his French territories long-distance, through the stewardship of trusted vassals. Nonetheless, medieval courts tended to be itinerant. Touring his kingdom was one of the only ways a monarch could gain an understanding of his subjects' concerns, and thereby maintain control of his realm. In Henry's frequent absences—during military campaigns or touring other parts of his vast holdings, including his French provinces—he often named Eleanor co-regent along with his justiciar, or chief minister. Thorough and pragmatic, she zealously upheld Henry's policies and implemented them in his stead, becoming an astute politician herself. Her vast responsibilities made her an anomaly among women of her era, and until 1163 Eleanor issued documents written under her own name and seal.

It wasn't all business, though. The royal couple enjoyed hawking and hunting together, and Eleanor had no trouble keeping up with her athletic, energetic husband. Once again she parlayed her talent for aesthetics into redecorating the palace at Westminster, importing upholstery silks, oil for her lamps, and spices for the kitchen. She insisted that her floor rushes be scented. And because she detested the taste of English beer, she also imported her own wines from Bordeaux.

As time went on and Eleanor began to lose her preeminence in the royal boudoir, undoubtedly resenting her husband's numerous paramours, she soon found her *political* role challenged as well. She had believed herself a full partner in Henry's governance of their sprawling kingdom, but the appearance of Thomas à Becket changed everything.

In 1152, Becket, the son of a London merchant, was archdeacon to the Archbishop of Canterbury when Henry made him chancellor of the realm. In short order, Becket became Henry's most trusted friend and adviser, and before long he assumed many of the administrative duties and responsibilities that had been Eleanor's purview, including acting as Henry's regent in his absence.

However, there was one role that could never be denied her. Eleanor was the mother of the future King of England. All told, she would bear Henry five sons and three daughters, and was forty-five years old when their last born, John, entered the world on Christmas Eve 1166. All but one child lived to adulthood, a remarkable record in an age of tremendous infant mortality.

On April 18, 1161, the Archbishop of Canterbury died, and Henry decided to replace him with Thomas à Becket, a highly irregular choice, since the chancellor was not even a cleric. Henry arrogantly assumed that appointing his best friend would put the management of both church and state in his pocket; but Becket warned the king that he would take his new ecclesiastical responsibility extremely seriously. When Becket refused to compromise canon law to satisfy Henry's political agenda, the friendship between the two powerful, brilliant, and excessively stubborn men was torn asunder.

The rift between Henry and Becket lasted six years and was never entirely repaired. In 1170, Eleanor and Henry were holding their Christmas court at Normandy when the king learned of the archbishop's most recent defiance of his aims. Henry unleashed the famous Plantagenet temper and in words he would come to deeply regret, exclaimed, "Will no one rid me of this turbulent priest?" Four of Henry's knights took him literally, and traveled to Canterbury. They murdered Becket in the cathedral on December 29, unwittingly martyring him—which turned Henry devoutly penitent, and catapulted Becket into the express lane for canonization.

With Becket in heaven, one might think the tarnished king's attentions would once again turn toward his queen, but Eleanor had already lost all hope in that regard. In 1166 Henry had met Rosamund de Clifford, the sixteen-year-old daughter of one of his Welsh marchers, or border earls. Although for eight years their passionate affair remained a secret to the outside world, and presumably to much of the court, Eleanor must have known of it or at least suspected what was going on. Henry made no secret that "the Fair Rosamund" was the great love of his life. Eleanor was middle-aged and pregnant when Henry and Rosamund commenced their affair, and by then the royal couple was already squabbling over which of their sons would inherit the crown, as the system of primogeniture (inheritance by the first-born son) was not yet established.

In 1168, two years after Henry met Rosamund, Eleanor initiated a marital separation, an event that was confirmed in an 1173 letter written by Rotrou of Warwick, the Archbishop of Rouen. But because they had lands to govern and conflicts to adjudicate, Eleanor and Henry endeavored to maintain a cordial working relationship.

The queen still took her place at royal ceremonial occasions and acted as Henry's deputy when necessary in Anjou and Normandy. Yet from then on, her focus became her children.

Eleanor did not exact her revenge against her straying husband by taking lovers of her own. She achieved it through their teenage sons, whom Henry continued to infantilize by ceding them some of his territories in France while denying the boys any authority to govern them. Feeling their oats, the three eldest princes complained bitterly to their mother, who utterly empathized with their want of power.

By 1172, seventeen-year-old Henry, fifteen-year-old Richard, and Geoffrey, age fourteen, were prepared to stage a revolt against their own father. Full-scale rebellion broke out in 1173. Discontented English barons joined forces with the young princes. At first Henry refused to believe it was his own flesh and blood who had betrayed him, nor did he suspect Eleanor of any complicity; in fact, he had left her at Poitiers to govern Aquitaine in his absence. Then he began to surmise that young Henry alone had been the instigator.

The chroniclers of the day formed their own opinions. Ralph of Diceto placed the blame for their sons' sedition squarely on Eleanor's shoulders. William of Newburgh and Gervase of Canterbury, who described Eleanor as "an exceedingly shrewd woman, sprung from noble stock, but fickle," shared Ralph's assessment. And Richard FitzNigel, who seemed to have a thorough comprehension of the teenage male psyche, was convinced that although Henry's sons "were young, and by reason of their age, easily swayed by any emotion, certain little foxes corrupted them with bad advice, so that at last his own bowels [meaning his wife, Eleanor] turned against him and told her sons to persecute their father."

What seems relatively clear is that the uprising was as much a wife's rebellion against her husband as the revolt of their sons; and Eleanor, who was a tremendous influence on their children, was willing to violate her marriage vows to achieve it. There was neither love, nor honor, nor obedience in her actions. And Henry finally began to realize it. He may even have had spies placed at her court who confirmed the worst. So he commanded the Archbishop of Rouen, Rotrou of Warwick, to persuade Eleanor to patch up the rifts—on threat of her excommunication.

According to the *Patrologiae Latinae: Recueil des historiens*, Rotrou, writing to Eleanor, was heartsick that "you, a prudent wife, if ever there was one should have parted from your husband. Once separated from the head, the limb no longer serves it. Still more terrible is the fact that you should have made the fruits of your union with our Lord King rise up against their father. . . . Before events carry us to a dire conclusion, return with your sons to the husband whom you must obey and with whom it is your duty to live. . . . Bid your sons, we beg you, to be obedient and devoted to their father, who for their sakes has undergone so many labours."

The archbishop's plea was ignored. Eleanor had no intentions of reconciling with Henry or reining in their sons. But she did fear that her husband might invade Poitiers, so she set out for Paris, where, ironically (albeit for political reasons), her former husband was obligated as her overlord to protect her. Her anxiety was justified. Eleanor's party was waylaid as they entered a forest near the border of France. Although she was dressed as a man and had ridden astride in order to avoid detection, her disguise was quickly unmasked. In Henry's name she was apprehended and escorted to Rouen, where she was "detained in strict custody."

The only person "punished" for their sons' uprising was Eleanor. Henry forgave the princes' rashness, attributing it to their youth. But he never again trusted them.

At midday on July 8, 1174, accompanied by Henry, Eleanor was bundled onto a ship bound for England—and further imprisonment—primarily at the wide-moated double-walled Sarum Castle near Salisbury. She was also kept under house arrest in Winchester Castle from time to time. In each location, Eleanor was permitted only a single waiting woman, her personal maid, Amaria; and her communication with the outside world was effectively severed, depriving her of the ability to influence her sons or to shape world events. Her custodians were men that Henry implicitly trusted. Divorcing Eleanor would have meant Henry's loss of Aquitaine and her other continental territories, so he offered a compromise: take the veil as abbess of Fontevrault Abbey and, contrary to the customary regulations governing a religious vocation, she would not have to relinquish her lands.

Eleanor staunchly refused. And for the rest of Henry's life—until 1189—she remained his prisoner, released on special occasions, such as Christmas and Easter, so the family could celebrate the holidays together. Henry also permitted Eleanor to travel on occasion, although under heavy guard, if such journeys concerned their daughters' betrothal or marriage plans.

With Eleanor imprisoned, Henry began to live openly with Rosamund de Clifford, although she never usurped the prerogatives or ceremonial duties of the queen. But Rosamund was soon out of the picture, entering Godstow Priory, where she died of unknown causes in 1176 at the age of twenty-six. However, Henry's bed had not remained cold during Rosamund's illness; Gervase of Canterbury alludes to the forty-two-year-old king's efforts in 1175 to annul his marriage to Eleanor because he wanted to marry a *different* mistress—Princess Alys of France—now in her mid-teens. Alys had been raised at the English court since she was nine years old, and was officially betrothed to Prince Richard. Richard would eventually refuse to wed Alys anyway—not because he was homosexual, as some twentieth-century historians, including A. L. Rowse, are fond of asserting (with scant proof to back it up), but because Alys had been his father's concubine, a relationship Richard disclosed with great discomfort to her half brother Philip after Philip became King of France.

Henry's affair with a French princess created enough of a scandal; seeking to divorce his wife compounded it. A primary argument for an annulment was consanguinity, even though their relation as third cousins hadn't bothered Henry and Eleanor when they married. Eleanor and Henry were even more closely related than she had been to Louis and *that* marriage had been sundered for reasons of consanguinity. Not only was it truly remarkable that for several centuries obtaining a Pope's permission to wed automatically validated an incestuous relationship, but that the reversal of such a papal sanction suddenly made the same legitimately solemnized marriage the sin everyone knew it already was!

Because Eleanor would still retain her lands after an annulment, Henry tried another loophole: incest. After all, his late father, Geoffrey, Count of Anjou, had admitted to an affair with Eleanor and had initially warned Henry to stay away from her. However, repudiation on *these* grounds at this stage in the game would make their numerous children bastards and leave Henry without a legitimate heir. Even in her deprivation, Eleanor appeared to be retaining the upper hand.

Tragedy struck the family in 1183 when their oldest son, Henry, died of dysentery. Three years later, Prince Geoffrey was unhorsed and trampled to death during a tournament. Only Richard and John, the respective favorites of their mother and father, remained to duke it out for the grand prize: succession to the English throne.

But while Henry was in England mustering men for another crusade, rebellion erupted once again in Normandy, led by Richard and backed by Philip of France. In 1188, Henry left England for the last time, hastening to the Continent to quell the uprising. After many of his knights had deserted him for his son, Henry, weak and ill, agreed to parlay with him. A formidable negotiator, Richard demanded that his father cede him all of his continental lands and acknowledge him as the heir to England's throne.

Henry died on July 6, 1189, at the age of fifty-six, and Richard was crowned King of England at Westminster Abbey on September 3, 1189, amid spectacular pageantry.

On hearing of Henry's death, Eleanor's custodians immediately released her. Having endured fifteen years of incarceration, she spent the rest of her life in the service of her sons, acting as regent for Richard while he was off on the Third Crusade and governing a kingdom that reached from the harsh borders of Scotland to the peaks of the Pyrenees.

In 1191, Eleanor even chose a bride for her favorite son. At the age of nearly seventy, she escorted young Berengaria of Navarre to Sicily to meet up with Richard, who was en route to the Holy Land. But during his return, Richard was captured by Duke Leopold of Austria and subsequently imprisoned by Leopold's cousin, the Holy Roman Emperor, Henry VI of Germany. Eleanor spent an entire year arranging for the collection of a ransom so immense it amounted to twice the sum of England's annual revenue.

Richard spent only a few months of his ten-year reign in England. He died in France in Eleanor's arms on April 6, 1199, after suffering an arrow wound in the process of besieging Charlus Castle, where he'd heard a treasure had been buried.

While Richard was on Crusade, Prince John usurped his throne. He pillaged the kingdom for his own ends, and Eleanor, who couldn't be everywhere at once, was powerless to curb much of his ambition. However, after Richard's death, she had no choice but to support him. John was her only surviving son, and he was now King of England.

But the Plantagenet family feud was far from over. Arthur of Brittany (the son of Eleanor and Henry's son Geoffrey and his wife, Constance of Brittany) allied himself with King Philip of France and set to besieging John's continental territories. In 1202, at the age of eighty, the intrepid Eleanor was imprisoned by Arthur's army at Mirabeau castle, where she had taken refuge from the ongoing strife between John and Philip. Eleanor cleverly played for time, allegedly negotiating with her rebellious teenage grandson from a castle window. She managed to get a message to John, who came to her rescue and defeated Arthur and his forces. Arthur was taken prisoner and never heard from again.

It was the dowager queen's last hurrah. Exhausted and ailing, she retired to the Abbey of Fontevrault, placed herself in the care of their nurses, and, according to abbey records, took the veil herself. She died there on April 1, 1204, at the age of eighty-two and was buried in the abbey church beside the tombs of her husband Henry and their son Richard. Her effigy depicts a serenely beautiful woman clasping a book.

Today, Eleanor's legacy—flinty and strong, courageous and tenacious—endures. When even a queen was expected to be little more than a walking womb, Eleanor of Aquitaine made history—not only as the wife of two kings, but as one of the most powerful and influential women of all time.

EDWARD IV
1442–1483
RULED ENGLAND: 1461–1470 AND 1471–1483

❊ and ❊

ELIZABETH WOODVILLE
1437–1492

married 1464–1483

"The most beautiful woman in the island of Britain [with]
heavy-lidded eyes like those of a dragon. . . ."
—Compliment paid to Elizabeth Woodville by a
fifteenth-century writer

*L*EGEND HAS IT THAT THEY "MET CUTE." THE WIDOWED
mother of two young boys, Elizabeth Woodville waylaid the tall,
dark, and handsome King Edward IV in the shadow of an oak tree
in Whittlebury Forest, and threw herself on his mercy. She'd become involved in a land dispute related to her first marriage and
urged him to intercede on her behalf.

In his prime, the six-foot-three-and-a-half-inch Edward was quite
an impressive sight, a snappy dresser with soft brown hair, hazel
eyes, and a straight nose. He was purportedly struck by Elizabeth's
"mournful beauty" and fell deeply in lust. It was evidently mutual.

So, His Majesty did what he always did when he saw an attractive woman: he propositioned her. But Elizabeth—described by Thomas More as "both fair, of a good favor, moderate of stature, well made and very wise"—wouldn't consent to be his mistress, "and so increased his passion by her refusals that he came to realize that he could not live without her." The tree was subsequently named "the Queen's Oak" and became a cult destination for diehard romantics. From meeting to marriage, Edward's courtship of Elizabeth Woodville had all the makings of a fairy-tale romance—a Cinderella story *avant la lettre.*

Elizabeth Woodville's parents had also made a socially mismatched marriage. She was the oldest of twelve children born to Jacquetta Woodville, the widow of Henry V's brother, the Duke of Bedford, as well as a descendent of Charlemagne and a member of the royal family of Luxembourg. Elizabeth's father was Sir Richard Woodville, a lowly but brave knight who had served in Bedford's train. Jacquetta had wed the middle-aged duke when she was a teenager, making her the second-highest lady in England for a time. After Bedford died in September 1435, a relationship between Jacquetta and Sir Richard began to flourish. The two wed without the king's permission and on March 1, 1437, Jacquetta had to pay a hefty fine of £1,000 (over $731,000 today) for her disobedience. However, the couple was pardoned that October, and Sir Richard Woodville proved himself a brave and gallant courtier. On May 8, 1448, Henry V elevated him to the peerage, creating him Baron Rivers.

It was the era of the Wars of the Roses, a series of violent skirmishes between the feuding aristocratic houses of York and Lancaster—each of which descended from King Edward III, and each of which believed they had a more legitimate right of succession. The Woodvilles fought for the Lancastrian cause, as did Elizabeth Woodville's first husband, Sir John Grey of Groby.

Elizabeth had wed Grey when she was most likely in her mid to late teens, and bore him two sons, Thomas and Richard. Grey was killed at the Second Battle of St. Albans in 1461, fighting on the Lancastrian side.

On April 30, 1464, Edward IV stopped at Stony Stratford en route to Grafton. There, by the great oak tree (or not), he encountered Elizabeth Woodville, and the following day they secretly wed in the presence of Elizabeth's mother, a priest (the Dominican Master Thomas Eborall), possibly two other unnamed witnesses, and "a young man who helped the priest sing." Although many historians believe their marriage probably didn't take place until August of 1464, May Day is traditionally ascribed to lovers, and the May 1 wedding date has long been part of the story's lore. Whatever the date, the velocity of the whirlwind romance stunned even the bride. Elizabeth Woodville was now the first English-born queen consort since the eleventh century.

Edward's union with Elizabeth Woodville was the ultimate mixed marriage. Elizabeth hadn't merely married a man from a different social caste, she'd wed the *sovereign*—and not only was she a commoner, but the Woodvilles were stalwart Lancastrians, while the king, the eldest surviving son of the late Duke of York, had deposed the reigning Lancastrian monarch, Henry VI.

It's said that Jacquetta initially kept the royal marriage a secret from her husband, Baron Rivers. No doubt she had her reasons, but even the *bridegroom* didn't feel obligated to mention it to anyone until his Privy Council met in Reading that September to discuss his wedding plans to Bona of Savoy, the sister-in-law to the French monarch—a dynastic alliance that was being brokered by the Earl of Warwick. The earl's martial prowess and political savvy had helped Edward win his crown (thereby gaining himself the moniker of "kingmaker"). And he was none too thrilled to end up with diplomatic egg on his face after the sovereign's admission that—oops, sorry!—he was now a newlywed, so it would be in everyone's best interests to put the kibosh on the Bona situation.

Once his union with Elizabeth Woodville was made known, criticism of Edward's lopsided marriage was swift and widespread.

A Venetian merchant reported that "the greater part of the lords and the people in general seem very much dissatisfied at this, and for the sake of finding means to annul it, all the peers are holding great consultations in the town of Reading."

The peers' or Privy Council's reaction to the king's admission that he couldn't marry Bona because he was already wed to Elizabeth Woodville is best summarized by the Burgundian chronicler Jean de Waurin: "They answered that she was not his match, however good and however fair she might be, and he must know well that she was no wife for a prince such as himself; for she was not the daughter of a duke or earl, but her mother, the Duchess of Bedford, had married a simple knight, so that she was the child of a duchess and the niece of the count of St. Pol, still she was no wife for him." Additionally, the council argued that their union served no foreign or domestic diplomatic purpose, and might anger or alienate the King of France.

Furthermore, Elizabeth was a widow with two young sons who would expect preferment commensurate with their new station. The royal marriage would be an expensive one, too, the councilors insisted. The new queen consort had eleven siblings (ten of whom survived to adulthood). They would become the crown's beneficiaries as well, their social standing elevated to a level appropriate for a king's in-laws. Brilliant marriages would have to be found for Elizabeth's sisters and positions at court secured for her brothers.

The Church had a problem with the sovereign's surprise marriage as well. It tended to be reluctant to bless a second union—even if one party was the king—on the grounds that such marriages were motivated by lust, which in the groom's case was particularly true. It was a popular theory at the time that death didn't automatically end a marriage because the spouses would eventually be reunited in heaven. The more pragmatic reason for the Church's view was that England was a land-based society and property was inherited upon the death of a spouse, so a remarriage threatened the inheritance of any issue from the previous union.

And speaking of children from a prior marriage, Edward's Privy Councilors also feared that when Elizabeth's two sons, Thomas and Richard Grey, matured, they might form a rival faction to her heirs by Edward.

Is it any wonder, therefore, that, in the words of the Tudors' historian Polydore Vergil, the union between Edward IV and Elizabeth Woodville was described as an "impolitic and unprecedented" marriage, motivated by "blind affection and not by rule of reason"?

And Edward's press hadn't been all that good to begin with. In 1461 he had taken the throne by force from the fanatically religious and half-mad Henry VI, defeating him in a skirmish at Mortimer's Cross, near Ludlow. While Henry and his warrior-queen, Margaret of Anjou, were campaigning in the north, Edward marched down to London, taking control of the capital and declaring himself king. That same year his Yorkist army wiped out the rest of the Lancastrian forces at the Battle of Towton, and the victorious Edward ascended the throne. By the time he met, wooed, and wed Elizabeth Woodville in 1464, Edward IV had worn the crown for only three years, and in the eyes of many Britons, remained a usurper.

Despite all arguments against the king's marriage, the fact remained that it was a fait accompli. By virtue of their little wedding ceremony in the woods, Elizabeth Woodville was Queen of England whether the Privy Council, the Earl of Warwick, or any number of scribbling monks who called themselves chroniclers of history liked it or not.

Elizabeth's coronation took place on Ascension Day, May 26, 1465. The lavishness of the extravaganza made up for the quickie wedding. Allegorical pageants greeted her state entry into the capital as she traversed London Bridge, which had been specially fumigated for the occasion. Edward created thirty-nine new Knights of the Bath in her honor; these men escorted her to Westminster from the Tower, where English queens traditionally spent the night before their coronations. Elizabeth was "clothed in a mantyll of purpull & a coronall upon hir hede." (Spelling was phonetic at the time and would not be standardized for centuries, which also accounts for alternative spellings of Elizabeth's maiden name as Wydeville and Widvile.)

At the north door of the monastery Elizabeth was met by the Archbishop of Canterbury. She shed her shoes, entering the abbey barefoot. Once the coronation began, she was given the scepter of the realm to hold in her left hand, and in her right, the scepter of St. Edward. About her was a carmine sea of humanity, with the duchesses and countesses clad in red velvet, and the baronesses attired in scarlet and miniver. After the ceremony, three thousand guests attended the coronation banquet.

At the time—and the bad press filtered down through the centuries—Elizabeth was soundly criticized for promoting the interests of her large family. Her father was made Treasurer on March 4, 1466; that May he was made an earl and the Constable of England for life. Her brothers were ennobled and received lucrative governmental appointments, and her sisters were wed into the highest echelons of the aristocracy. But none of this patronage was out of the ordinary. And the loyalty and competence of Elizabeth's relations was never called into question. The promotions elevated her family to a status more appropriately befitting a king's bride, but more important, they bound a number of aristocratic families to the throne. As a newbie who had not inherited the crown through primogeniture, Edward needed all the backing he could get.

Elizabeth spent the better part of the next fifteen years pregnant, bearing ten children—seven girls and three boys—seven of whom survived their father. The gaps in their birth years came when Edward was on the battlefield defending his crown, or on the run from those who sought to snatch it from him.

And such occasions were many. Not long after marrying Elizabeth, the man largely responsible for his attaining the throne grew disillusioned with Edward. The "kingmaker," Richard Neville, the 16th Earl of Warwick, was a relative of Edward's on his mother's side. In 1469 he joined forces with Edward's brother, the Duke of Clarence, to dethrone him, fomenting uprisings in Yorkshire that spring. Warwick captured Edward with the intention of ruling in his name, but was ill prepared for the minutiae of governing; and holding the king hostage proved to be spectacularly unpopular with the nobles. So Warwick released Edward and the two of them, plus Clarence, reconciled and joined forces to defeat the Lancastrians.

But Elizabeth's family suffered greatly during the dispute. On August 12, 1469, Elizabeth's father, Earl Rivers, and Sir John Woodville, one of her brothers, were captured by Warwick's men and executed outside Coventry. Elizabeth's mother was accused in absentia of using sorcery to make the king fall in love with her daughter, a charge that never stuck (but would surface again several years later). In any event, by the time Jacquetta Woodville was tried for witchcraft in January 1470, the political landscape had changed and Edward IV had regained his freedom.

However, the renewed partnership between king and kingmaker was short-lived. Clarence and Warwick began to plot anew. Edward and a handful of supporters fled to Burgundy, where they lived in exile. Back in London, a pregnant Elizabeth took sanctuary at Westminster Abbey with their three young daughters, where, on November 2, 1470, she gave birth to her first son, Edward.

Edward IV's predecessor, Henry VI, was released from the Tower and reclaimed his throne in a period that was known as the Readeption. Meanwhile, Elizabeth was described as "the Queen that was." But not for long. In the spring of 1471 Edward regained the crown. After the famous Battle of Tewkesbury in which Henry VI's son, Edward of Lancaster, was slain, Edward IV emerged victorious and triumphantly entered London on May 21.

He acted quickly to secure his position. The very night of his victory, he had Henry VI quietly killed in the Tower. On June 26, 1471, Elizabeth and Edward's infant son was created Prince of Wales. Twenty months later the boy was given his own household at Ludlow in Shropshire; his affairs were to be managed by a subcommittee empowered to make decisions "with the advice and express consent of the Queen."

In 1475, when Edward departed England to engage in a new

phase of the Hundred Years War, he appointed the four-and-a-half-year-old Prince of Wales as Keeper of the Realm; but the king wrote a will in which he named his "derrest and moost entierly beloved wiff Elizabeth the Quene" as his primary executor, and stipulated that she should keep the worldly goods he had not otherwise bequeathed to holy orders. Edward IV might have been a serial philanderer, but he did take excellent care of his wife and seemed to be very proud of her. Throughout their marriage, Elizabeth and Edward were very close and he evidently sought, and listened to, her counsel.

The fifteenth-century chronicler Dominic Mancini wrote that the king had fallen in love with her because of her "beauty of person and charm of manner." Edward respected Elizabeth tremendously and probably loved her deeply, but she was far from the only woman in his life. The chronicler Gregory remarked that even before his clandestine marriage to Elizabeth, "men marveled that [he] was so long without any wife, and were ever afraid that he had been not chaste of his living."

By all accounts Elizabeth always behaved with queenly dignity during her husband's frequent infidelities. It was a wise move. We can guess that there were few fusses and recriminations, because they surely would have been documented if people had been privy to them. Elizabeth's tolerance endeared her all the more to Edward, and in this way until his death she was able to maintain her hold over him where it counted. Evidently, her charms continued to attract him, since she gave birth to their tenth child in 1480 at the age of forty-three.

On April 9, 1483, after a brief unidentified illness, Edward IV died in his bed at Westminster at the age of forty. During the last years of his reign, he had grown monstrously obese and was a slave to every kind of gluttony and excess, or "fleshy wantonness," as his contemporaries graphically phrased it. They attributed his downfall as a monarch to his amorous temper—from his insistence on the marriage to Elizabeth Woodville to his bevy of mistresses, some of whom also bore him children. At the time of his demise the "goodly personage . . . princely to behold, of visage lovely, of body mighty, strongly and cleanly made," resembled Jabba the Hut.

His funeral was conducted at Westminster Abbey on April 17 and he was interred in St. George's Chapel at Windsor three days later.

Genial, but never gullible, Edward had gained political mileage from delegating authority to those he could trust regardless of rank, yet was swift to yank it away when it was abused. To some, he did the unthinkable by ordering the judicial murder of his brother, the Duke of Clarence, in 1478—but Clarence had twice raised an army against Edward and continued to plot against him with the intention of snatching the crown for himself.

Upon Edward's death, his oldest son, not yet thirteen years old, became Edward V; and by the terms of the late king's will, his younger brother Richard, Duke of Gloucester, once his ally and seneschal in the north, was named Protector. While ostentatiously assuring everyone of his fealty to the boy king, Richard immediately and ruthlessly began to eliminate anyone that stood between himself and the throne, creating phony treason plots and arresting the alleged perpetrators—among them, Elizabeth's brother, now Earl Rivers, and her younger son by her first marriage, Lord Richard Grey.

Richard conveyed Edward V to the Tower, ostensibly to await his coronation, and promised Elizabeth he would personally guarantee the safety of the boy's younger brother, ten-year-old Richard, Duke of York, if she would send the child to him. Elizabeth didn't trust Richard as far as she could spit, but she decided it was safer to acquiesce than to rebel.

Richard imprisoned both boys in the Tower. Then he executed Rivers and Grey. But in order to legitimately claim the crown, he had to delegitimize others. So he sought to have Edward IV's marriage to Elizabeth declared invalid on the grounds that before the late king met Elizabeth, he had entered into a precontract with a young widow named Lady Eleanor Butler. A precontract was considered as binding as an actual marriage, rendering any subsequent union bigamous unless the precontract was sundered. It was said that Lady Eleanor Butler had done the same thing as Elizabeth Woodville; that is, she held out for marriage before agreeing to sleep with Edward. Although Lady Eleanor Butler had died in 1478, Richard dredged up the cleric who had been present at the precontract and had him testify to its existence. Richard also renewed the charges of witchcraft against Jacquetta Woodville, who had died in 1472, claiming that she had used sorcery to enchant the late king into marrying her daughter.

The matter of the precontract with Lady Eleanor Butler was the only issue that was awarded any serious credence. Yet, during Edward's lifetime no one had ever questioned the validity of his marriage to Elizabeth or the legitimacy of their children, or doubted that their firstborn son was the true Prince of Wales. However, if the royal children were retroactively declared bastards, there would be only one Yorkist claimant to the throne still standing, and that was—surprise!—Richard, Duke of Gloucester.

On June 25, 1483, in a formal document issued by Parliament known as the *Titulus Regius*, Elizabeth's marriage to Edward IV was declared null and void—which meant that all of their children were illegitimate, and therefore barred from inheriting the throne. Elizabeth was deprived of the title of Queen Mother, to be known thereafter simply as Dame Elizabeth Grey.

Elizabeth had little choice but to pretend to back Richard. By now he had custody of her two sons, who were languishing in the Tower. Her efforts to covertly raise troops against him were unsuccessful. For a time she lived in sanctuary with her daughters, but Richard convinced her to return to court, assuring her that no harm would come to any of them and vowing to arrange for good marriages for the girls—provided everyone behaved themselves—which meant turning a blind eye to anything he chose to do.

On June 26, 1483, the Duke of Gloucester usurped the throne, proclaiming himself Richard III. Edward V and his younger brother Richard were "progressively removed from men's sight," according to Dominic Mancini, and by the autumn of 1483 they were never seen or heard from again.

For two years Richard managed to withstand all rebellions against him propagated by Lancastrian forces, but on August 22, 1485, he was defeated in the Battle of Bosworth, struck down by the Welsh-born Henry Tudor, Earl of Richmond, who claimed the throne as Henry VII. Henry had been a lifelong supporter of the Lancastrian claim to the throne. His subsequent marriage to Elizabeth and Edward's eldest daughter, Elizabeth of York—whom he relegitimized, along with her siblings—united the feuding houses of York and Lancaster and, with the denouement of the Battle of Bosworth, finally ended the Wars of the Roses.

Elizabeth Woodville spent the last five years of her life at Bermondsey Abbey, dying on July 8, 1492, at the age of fifty-four or fifty-five. On June 10, her body was conveyed by boat to Windsor, and her modest wooden coffin was interred on top of Edward's lead-encased one in St. George's Chapel.

She may not be a household name, but Elizabeth Woodville's fame is far-reaching—scant degrees of separation from some of the most famous royals in Britain's history. Not only was Elizabeth the first commoner in centuries to become Queen of England, she was the mother of the two princes in the Tower, whose purported remains now repose in Westminster Abbey; the sister-in-law of Richard III; the grandmother of Henry VIII (and his older brother, Arthur, to whom she stood as godmother); the great-grandmother of Mary I and Elizabeth I; and the great-great-grandmother to two beheaded queens, Mary, Queen of Scots and Lady Jane Grey. As grandmother to Henry VIII's older sister Margaret, who wed the King of Scotland, Elizabeth Woodville's blood infused the Stuart line, and eventually wended its way through the Hanovers down to the current ruling family of England, the Windsors.

The union of Edward IV and Elizabeth Woodville is one of the few in the sordid history of royal marriages to have begun as a love match. It survived numerous wars, incarceration, agonizing months of separation, the temporary loss of the throne, as well as Edward's frequent and flagrant infidelity; and yet their relationship remained fruitful and passionate until his death. A "happy" marriage? Who can say for certain? But it was undoubtedly a successful one.

FERDINAND II OF ARAGON

1452–1516

❧ *and* ❧

ISABELLA OF CASTILE AND LEON

1451–1504

CO-RULED CASTILE AND LEON: 1474–1504

CO-RULED ARAGON: 1479–1504

FERDINAND RULED ARAGON: 1504–1516

married 1469–1504

"It has to be he and absolutely no other."
—Isabella to her half brother, King Enrique IV of
Castile, regarding her choice of Ferdinand of
Aragon as her bridegroom

"Common people may look for handsome wives, but
princes do not marry for love; they take wives only to
beget children."
—Ferdinand of Aragon

SCHOOLCHILDREN SAY THEIR NAMES IN A SINGLE BREATH, as if they were one person: *FerdinandandIsabella*. Regardless of what may have transpired behind closed doors, including Isabella's feelings about the four illegitimate children her husband begot with as many lovers, the monarchs were the ultimate power couple in medieval Europe. They were careful to present an image of complete conformity—an indivisible unit and a united front, in person, and on coins and official seals. This strategy made their marriage, and their reign, unique in its day.

According to the *Crónica incompleta*, "Between the King and the Queen there was no discord . . . they ate together in the public hall, talking of pleasant things as is done at table, and they slept together . . . their wills coincided through intimacy born of love." And the royal chronicler Fernando del Pulgar wrote, "if necessity separated their persons, love joined their wills together." In fact, the sovereigns' royal motto was *Tanto Monto, Monto Tanto*, which has often been translated to "it amounts to the same thing." Although the motto's origin had nothing to do with joint sovereignty, being an allusion to the Gordian knot—"Cutting as Untying"—the monarchs did nothing to dispel the subliminal meaning.

According to Fernando, Isabella was seen as a good queen because she was "Catholic and devout." And the image of Isabella as the Queen of Heaven on Earth, a second Mary, as reflected in Spanish art and poetry of the day, is not coincidental. It was all part of a clever marketing strategy that underscored the concept of royal infallibility and helped Isabella—the rare medieval queen regnant—to maintain her subjects in a state of fear and awe during an age of institutionalized misogyny.

The rational, disciplined, and assertive Isabella, described by a contemporary as having "the heart of a man, dressed as a woman," wielded more clout than her husband did. Her kingdom of Castile, insular and aristocratic, covered a vast swath of the western part of modern-day Spain, stretching from the Bay of Biscay to the kingdom of Granada, the Iberian Peninsula's last Muslim stronghold. It was all Isabella's, but she'd spent the first few years of her reign fighting to hold on to it. After the death of her father, Juan II of Castile, in 1454, Isabella's half brother Enrique had inherited the throne. Isabella's mother, Isabella of Portugal, widowed at the age of twenty-seven, became a recluse, incapable of offering her daughter any guidance as she grew up. According to the court chronicler Alfonso de Palencia, she "closed herself into a dark room, self-condemned to silence, and dominated by such depression that it degenerated into a form of madness."

King Enrique IV, nicknamed "the Impotent," was believed to be homosexual; it was widely accepted that the real father of his daughter Juana was the queen's lover, a Castilian nobleman named Beltrán de la Cueva—earning the little girl the nickname of "Juana la Beltraneja."

In January 1469, Isabella of Castile willfully ignored Enrique's plans to marry her off to the King of Portugal, insisting that she would only wed the King of Sicily—Ferdinand, the son of King Juan II of Aragon. "It has to be he and absolutely no other," she told her half brother. And on October 12, she informed Enrique that her choice had not been guided by lust, but by pragmatically weighing her options; Ferdinand was the right husband for the good of the kingdom. Isabella affirmed that Ferdinand was also the first choice of the Castilian grandees—the nobility—who much preferred an Aragonese match to a Portuguese one. Additionally, Isabella believed that if *she* didn't marry Ferdinand, Enrique would disinherit her, after dynastically wedding Juana la Beltraneja to him instead.

But because Isabella and Ferdinand were second cousins, they were related within the proscribed degrees of consanguinity; therefore, a papal dispensation was necessary in order for them to marry. Both were descendants, through different wives, of a son of Edward III of England, John of Gaunt, the 1st Duke of Lancaster. And there are conflicting versions of events regarding the dispensation. Some scholars claim that the document was read aloud on October 18 by the Archbishop of Toledo, Alfonso Carrillo de Acuña. Yet another report claims that the royal couple lacked the appropriate exemption, and so they presented the priest with a phony document. Both accounts could be true if the Bishop of Toledo was reading a forgery.

Although Isabella had yet to meet Ferdinand when she made her decision to wed him, when they finally came face-to-face, the attraction was both powerful and mutual. At the time of her marriage Isabella was eighteen years old, plump and auburn-haired with fair coloring and intelligent blue-green eyes. Seventeen-year-old Ferdinand was well built, of medium stature, with straight dark hair, twinkling eyes, and a mile-wide charismatic streak. According to a contemporary, "He had so singular a grace that everyone who talked to him wanted to serve him." Among those devotees would have been the two mothers of his pair of bastard children, sired before his marriage to Isabella. His illegitimate daughter, Juana of Aragon, was born in 1469 (the same year he wed Isabella); and his natural son, Alfonso of Aragon, came into the world the following year.

Ferdinand was the heir to a kingdom in the northeast part of Spain that was about a quarter of the size of Isabella's vast realm of Castile, with one-tenth of Castile's population. From Isabella's perspective, she brought more to the marriage and from the outset she made sure that Ferdinand knew it.

At their first meeting a notary recorded Ferdinand and Isabella's promises to marry. And on the morning of October 19, 1469, they were publicly wed in Valladolid. Two thousand guests from all estates—the nobility, clergy, and commoners—attended the ceremony performed by a priest named Pero López de Alcalá.

The wedding festivities lasted all day and the union was consummated that night according to witnesses, who waited expectantly in the hall below for the opportunity to inspect the telltale stains on the bridal bedsheet.

Luckily, Ferdinand was accustomed to strong women. His headstrong and protective mother, Juana Enriquez, acted as her husband's regent while Juan II of Aragon was in his sister kingdom of Sicily. Ferdinand was five years old when his father ascended the Aragonese throne and immediately became embroiled in a civil war, leading his troops into battle, despite being half blind from cataracts. Juan II then became totally blind for three years, until a Jewish doctor performed an operation that restored his sight, which might have been one reason that decades later Ferdinand would favor conversion over expulsion of the Jews until his wife convinced him to agree with her.

But there were other points of divergence that surfaced early in their marriage. Although they deliberately gave their subjects the impression that they would be coequal rulers, Ferdinand's desire to be King of Castile, and Isabella's resolve to preserve her rights as queen regnant, was a perennial bone of contention between the spouses. Because Isabella brought more wealth and territory to their union, she adopted a "What's mine is mine, and what's yours is mine, too" philosophy regarding their marriage contract. To that end, Isabella would be entitled to jurisdiction in her own right in parts of Ferdinand's kingdom of Sicily, while it was Ferdinand who, at their wedding ceremony, vowed to observe Castile's laws and customs, appoint only Castilian officers, reside in Castile, and not remove Isabella from her sovereign territory except for brief visits elsewhere. In addition, while the pair would sign everything jointly and share all titles, Ferdinand was to make "no movement" in Castile without Isabella's counsel and consent. He would inherit his father's realms, of course, and if he predeceased Isabella she would rule them during the remainder of her lifetime. But when it came to the inheritance of Castile, Isabella did not name her husband as her immediate successor.

Their quarrel over Ferdinand's rights was eventually submitted to formal arbitration, which led to a co-sovereignty whether the couple was together or apart. The equality of the dual monarchs was rare enough in medieval Europe, but even more exceptional was that the administration of Castile was executed by the queen in her own right. And until she bore a son, she intended for her oldest daughter to follow in her footsteps.

The couple had five children—four girls (Isabella, Joanna, Maria, and Katherine) and a boy, Juan, who was born eight years after their first daughter.

Supporters of Juana la Beltraneja's claim to succeed Enrique IV on the Castilian throne were delighted that Isabella's first child, born in 1470, was a paltry girl. They became even more gleeful when they discovered that the valid papal dispensation relied upon to unite Isabella and Ferdinand had not been presented at the time of their marriage ceremony. The actual document did not arrive until June 18, 1472, when Cardinal Rodrigo Borgia, the future Pope Alexander VI, delivered the long-awaited papal bull absolving the pair from wedding without the proper dispensation. It still boggles the mind that incest was okay as long as the Pope said so.

By then, Ferdinand had been in Aragon since February, the first of many absences from Isabella. But when they were apart, he would send her romantic letters. During the War of Castilian Succession in the 1470s, in a letter conferring about military strategy, Ferdinand wrote to her, ". . . In getting together we help each other more than anything in life. . . ." And on July 14, 1475, on the eve of another foray, fearing he would never see his wife again, he sent her a passionate note from his camp: "God knows it weighs on me that I will not see your Ladyship tomorrow, for I swear by your life and mine that never have I so loved you."

The couple enjoyed a healthy sex life—but Ferdinand was not entirely faithful. According to Palencia's successor, Fernando del Pulgar, "Although he loved the Queen his wife greatly, he gave himself to other women." Needless to say, as with most royal marriages, extramarital dalliance was good for the gander, but the goose would have been roasted for trying it herself. During her husband's absences, Isabella slept in an all-female "dormitory," so there were always several witnesses who could attest that her marital fidelity had been preserved.

But as powerful as Isabella was, she was not immune to jealousy. Passionately in love with her husband, she kept an eagle eye out for signs that he was straying. If she thought he had a *tendre* for any woman at court, the queen found a way to remove her rival.

The early 1470s were a time of civil strife in both Castile and Aragon, but Isabella began to gain the allegiance of several Castilian cities and towns that preferred to see her—and not Juana—succeed

Enrique. He died on December 11, 1474, at the age of forty-nine, leaving no will, but allegedly declaring "my daughter [Juana] heiress of these kingdoms." His remark was still no proof that the girl was legitimate.

Isabella received the news on December 12. She immediately donned mourning garments of white serge and went to mass—after which she changed into a sumptuous gown accessorized with gold and glittering gems. At the portal of the church of San Miguel in Segovia, she mounted a hastily constructed platform and proclaimed herself Queen of Castile and Leon, since Enrique had recognized her rights of succession back in September 1468. Her power grab would spark the five-year War of Castilian Succession. Isabella finally emerged victorious in 1479, and Juana la Beltraneja was packed off to a convent for the rest of her life.

Ferdinand was amazed that he had to learn of Isabella's proclamation ceremony from someone else and was surprised to hear that it had taken place at all. He rode straight into Segovia with banners flying, not expecting his wife to hold him to his formal prenuptial *capitulaciones*. Palencia wrote that Ferdinand was confident "in conquering with patience and felt certain he would triumph through satisfying assiduously the demands of conjugal love, with which he could easily soften the intransigence that bad advisers had planted in his wife's mind." But Ferdinand was either very optimistic or very misguided if he thought that whispering a few sweet nothings in his wife's ear, followed by hot sex and a few more sweet nothings, would sway Isabella politically.

Part of Isabella's rationale in claiming the crown quickly—and alone—was that her only child was a daughter, and she wanted to forge a precedent for her. Although women could not succeed to the throne in Aragon, Castile did have a history of proprietary queens, and never would a spouse inherit his wife's throne if they had a legitimate daughter. Isabella patiently explained this law to Ferdinand, reminding him that her kingdoms would go to *their* children, adding that she had taken the crown alone because in the future, "should the Princess Isabel marry a foreign prince who wants to take over Castile's fortresses and royal patrimony, the kingdom would come into the power of a foreign dynasty, which would weigh heavily on their consciences and be a disservice to God."

Isabella managed to steer a delicate course between asserting her political supremacy and her traditional view of gender roles when it came to personal matters. She did not openly challenge the commonly held credo that the male should always be the dominant partner in a marriage, and assured her nobles—who worried about what information she might be persuaded to share with her husband during pillow talk—that the rights of matrimony had no bearing on the rights of lordship or of royal power.

"The instilled pride of the queen," in Palencia's words, was often at odds with the image of joint sovereignty that she and Ferdinand were so keen to maintain. In 1475 she returned documents for redrafting because her husband's name was written before hers. Accusing her of impugning his masculinity, Ferdinand sulkily threatened to leave for Aragon, to which, according to Palencia, Isabella protested "that she would never for any reason have wanted to cause the least humiliation to her most beloved consort, for whose happiness and honor she would sacrifice willingly not only the crown but her own health." She pleaded with Ferdinand "not to leave his beloved wife; for she would not or could not live separated from him."

And in 1479, the misogynistic Palencia wrote, "The queen had been preparing for a long time—since just after she was married—something that in the judgment of any prudent man was not fitting for the future succession in these kingdoms: reducing the influence of her husband, in case, as a result of her death, any contingency presented itself in the regular course of the inheritance, if she was survived by her husband."

Perhaps one reason Ferdinand had trouble understanding his wife's point of view on the subject of her royal authority was because they'd achieved their respective crowns in different ways. Although Ferdinand had to wait to inherit Aragon until his father died in 1479, he always knew the throne would be his. Isabella had to win her throne, or at least cement her claim to it, by the sword. But neither monarch ever questioned their divine right to rule.

Although their marriage was unique because of the way it impacted the sovereignty of Spain, the historical significance of several of their political achievements has earned the royal couple a double-wide niche in the pantheon of European monarchs.

Between 1390 and 1420 there had been a series of anti-Semitic riots or pogroms in Spain, after which many Jews chose to convert to Christianity as an act of self-preservation. These former Jews became known as *conversos*. On November 1, 1478, in response to a petition from Isabella complaining that the *conversos* were reverting to the beliefs and practices of their former religion, Pope Sixtus IV issued the bull that would become the foundation of the Spanish Inquisition. Although both Ferdinand and Isabella had ancestors who were Jewish *conversos*, cleansing Spain of its heretics became a cornerstone of their reign. Isabella had no second thoughts about consigning people to the flames. In her view, ridding Spain of "judaizers" was God's work.

By 1492 the sovereigns were determined that the only effective method for ridding Spain of its Jews and lapsed *conversos* and *marranos* (secretly practicing Jews, or "crypto-Jews") was expulsion. A decade later Ferdinand and Isabella would reach the same conclusion about Spain's Muslims and *moriscos* (the Muslim converts to Christianity) and expel them as well.

It was a tenet of the monarchs' marriage obligation to make war against the Moors. Beginning in 1481, in what became known as the Reconquest, Isabella and Ferdinand sought to annex the Andalusian lands that remained in Muslim hands, claiming them for Christianity. Ferdinand was the ace general, leading his soldiers into battle, while Isabella acted as a sort of managing director and quartermaster, drawing up military and financial plans, mustering and supplying the armies, and coordinating troop movements. Even when she was pregnant, the queen rode to the front lines to boost morale. The war against Islam was a matter of vital concern for Spain because of the increasing threat from the Ottoman Turks in the Mediterranean. If the Turks made it into Spain, they would undoubtedly try to reverse the land gains made by the Christians during the two previous centuries.

The Catholic Monarchs, as Pope Alexander VI would formally title them in 1496, viewed the Reconquest as a crusade or holy war. Isabella in particular believed that she served a divine purpose in recapturing the Muslim territories. But her ultimate goal was far more ambitious. Their unification of Spain would be the beginning of a new, Catholic empire that would spread southward onto the African continent, westward to the Caribbean, and eastward to the Indies and the Middle East, ultimately snatching the jewel in the imperial crown—Jerusalem—from its Muslim rulers, claiming it for Christendom.

After a decade of war, on November 25, 1491, terms were negotiated for a surrender of Granada. At dawn on January 2, 1492, Boabdil, the last emir of Granada, surrendered the keys of the Alhambra, the fortress enclosing the royal palace, to one of Isabella's retainers. Four days later, on the Feast of the Epiphany, the Catholic Monarchs made their official entry into Granada.

The reign of Ferdinand and Isabella also coincided with the great Age of Exploration, as Spain endeavored to beat Portugal for the discovery—and therefore, control—of lucrative trade routes to the Orient, and the colonization of whatever lay to the south and the west of Iberia. The Spanish conquests would result in a pattern of violence against the native populations of the Canary Islands and territories in Africa, the Americas and the Caribbean islands, and the Mediterranean. Resistance to Catholic conversion or refusal to accept the sovereignty of the foreign invaders too often resulted in slaughter.

Isabella and Ferdinand had a banner year in 1492, beginning in January with the achievement of the conquest of Granada. Finally, Spain was unified as a Catholic kingdom. Present for the January 2 celebration below the Alhambra was the navigator who had appealed to them to finance his voyage to the Indies. The queen had twice denied Christopher Columbus the funds because the ongoing holy war was sapping the royal treasury. But with their victory in

Granada, Columbus was green-lighted to equip a fleet of ships for his voyage to what he and the monarchs referred to as the New Jerusalem—another realm to conquer in the name of Christianity. Columbus's caravels hoisted anchor on August 2, the last day that Spain's Jews were allowed to remain in the kingdom, pursuant to the expulsion edict issued on March 31 of that year. He would eventually make four voyages on behalf of the Spanish crown.

But 1492 would bring catastrophe for the royal spouses as well. On December 12, Ferdinand narrowly survived an assassination attempt when the heavy gold chain he wore about his neck deflected the blow from a dagger. Nine days after the attack Ferdinand still burned with fever and his tongue was so swollen that he couldn't speak. According to Isabella, "the wound was so great . . . that I had not the heart to see it, so large and deep, of a depth of four fingers, of such size that my heart trembles in saying it. . . . But God made it with such compassion [that it was] in a place where it could be done without danger . . . the pleasure of seeing him get up was as great as had been the sadness."

Ferdinand survived the attack, remarkable enough in an age where infection might kill a man just as easily as a sword could do so; and during the ensuing years the couple continued to implement their grand plans for Spanish hegemony until 1504, when illness took its toll on the formidable queen.

During the last months of her life, Isabella remained bedridden, riddled with physical ailments, including a fever that started in July 1504 and never broke. On October 12, she made her will, naming her oldest surviving daughter, Joanna ("*Juana la Loca*"), heir to the throne of Castile. In the event of Joanna's incompetence to rule, Ferdinand was to act as governor of the kingdom during her lifetime, but the Castilian crown would pass to Joanna's son Charles.

Isabella died between eleven a.m. and noon on November 26, 1504, at the age of fifty-three. In 1972, the Vatican commenced the process of her "beatification," the first step on the road to sainthood. But because of her role in the Spanish Inquisition, which resulted in the torture and judicial murder of hundreds, if not thousands, of

Jews, Jewish groups have opposed it. Her sanctioned brutality against the native populations of Spain's "discovered" territories is also a bone of moral contention.

Yet according to Ferdinand and Isabella's court chronicler Fernando del Pulgar, "It was certainly a thing most marvelous that what many men and great lords did not manage to do in many years, a single woman did in a short time through work and governance." For this reason, Isabella's reign and her role within her marriage are groundbreaking. In the words of the Renaissance humanist Ambassador Pietro Mártire d'Anghiera, Isabella was "stronger than a strong man, more constant than any human soul, a marvelous example of honesty and virtue. Nature has made no other woman like her."

By the time Isabella died, her husband securely held the crown of Naples, thanks to a treaty with France, whose ambitions in Italy rivaled Spain's. Wishing for an heir of his own to "leapfrog" over Joanna's rights of succession to the Castilian throne, Ferdinand remarried the following October, taking for his bride Germaine de Foix, the teenage niece of King Louis XII of France. On May 3, 1509, she bore Ferdinand a son, Juan, Prince of Aragon, who died shortly thereafter.

From 1513 on, Ferdinand showed little interest in politics. He became testy and cantankerous, possibly due to the inefficacy of the bull's balls he'd been ingesting to enhance his virility. On January 23, 1516, Ferdinand's asthma and dropsy caught up with him. At the age of sixty-three, he died while traveling to Seville with the future Pope Adrian VI for the purposes of assembling a military expedition to be deployed in North Africa, or against France or Italy.

Having usurped his daughter Joanna's rights of succession in Castile, Ferdinand was succeeded by fifteen-year-old Charles, the oldest son of Joanna and Archduke Philip of Burgundy, who acceded to the Aragonese throne as well. In 1519, Charles would also become Holy Roman Emperor. Reigning as Charles V, he ruled most of Spain, as inherited from his mother and maternal grandfather; the Netherlands, inherited from his father; and huge swaths of Germany, inherited from his paternal grandfather, the previous Holy Roman Emperor Maximilian.

By then, Joanna was queen in name only, imprisoned by her son, ostensibly for her own good. Ferdinand and Isabella's other surviving child, Katherine, was Queen of England, the wife of Henry VIII.

A contemporary chronicler fudged the truth a bit when he wrote of the Catholic Monarchs that "King and Queen together, they were chosen by God, united by Him, who joined together in this way, ruled and governed thirty years, and although two in body, in will and unity they were only one."

FerdinandandIsabella indeed.

JOANNA OF CASTILE

("JOANNA THE MAD" OR "JUANA LA LOCA")
1479–1555
RULED SPAIN (THEORETICALLY): 1504–1555

and

PHILIP THE HANDSOME,

DUKE OF BURGUNDY/PHILIP I OF CASTILE
1478–1506

married 1496–1506

". . . it would be the total destruction and loss of these kingdoms due to her illnesses and passions, which are not expressed here for modesty."
—language from a 1506 secret treaty signed by Joanna's husband, Philip of Burgundy, and her father, Ferdinand II of Aragon

"HOW SHARPER THAN A SERPENT'S TOOTH IT IS TO have a thankless child!" So declares King Lear. But how much more painful and deadly it is to have a thankless husband and a thankless father as well!

Joanna the Mad, or *Juana la Loca,* as she is known in Spain, was the second daughter born to the Catholic Monarchs, Isabella of Castile y Lyon and Ferdinand of Aragon. From an early age, she demonstrated a fascination with the macabre. She once told her governess that she wanted to try on her skeleton and burst into tears when she was informed that it was already inside her. She collected talismans, was morbidly superstitious, and obsessed with death. Pretty and mild-looking, pale and serious, the auburn-haired Joanna had wanted to become a nun, but Isabella and Ferdinand couldn't afford to marry her to God; their empire had to be strengthened and preserved through strategic dynastic alliances.

In the late summer of 1496, a fleet of 133 ships carrying an entourage numbering between 15,000 and 22,000 accompanied the sixteen-year-old Joanna to Flanders, where she was to meet her eighteen-year-old bridegroom, Archduke Philip of Burgundy, the only son of the Holy Roman Emperor Maximilian I. At the time, it was the most lavish procession of its kind. But the vessel carrying Joanna's wardrobe and many of her personal possessions struck a sandbank and sank with all hands on board. Joanna's journey seemed even more ill-starred when her groom was not there to greet her as she stepped ashore, sending his sister Margaret instead.

The reason for Philip's absence was that some of his advisers were against the match with Joanna. In his day, the archduke was not known as "Philip the Handsome" but as *Philippe le Croit Conseil*—Philip the Believer of Counsel—because he was so malleable.

But Philip's advisers hadn't brokered his marriage and therefore could not prevent it, regardless of their opinions on the subject. So, on October 20, 1496, Philip and Joanna were married in Lier, Belgium, by the Bishop of Cambray. It was a double wedding; Philip's sister Margaret married Joanna's only brother, Juan, Prince of Asturias and heir to the thrones of Aragon and Castile. In accordance with the treaties signed by their parents, which twisted the rules regarding one of the most common marriage traditions, the two brides were awarded no dowries. Instead they were to receive a set amount of revenues from their husbands' respective lands. In other words, the two grooms were expected to pay their wives' dowries!

Philip's mother, Mary of Burgundy, had died when he was four years old and he was raised in a decadent court filled with diversions, sports, and banquets. Archduke Philip of Burgundy was a spoiled and rakish youth who had already earned a reputation as a ladies' man. But when he and Joanna laid eyes on each other, it was lust at first sight for both of them, and the randy teens urged the local priest to pronounce them man and wife as hastily as possible so that they could hotfoot it to the royal boudoir.

Coming from the sober and rigid court of Spain, Joanna, innocent of the ways of the world (and men), could not have known that her new husband considered her no more than another attractive and willing body. All the poor girl could tell was that the sex was terrific. And frequent. And she did fall in love with Philip. But the archduke did not equate sex with love, and he soon returned to the dissolute philandering of his bachelor days. Joanna was fanatically jealous of Philip's other women and felt betrayed by his abandonment and his numerous infidelities. But, at that point, anyway, she wasn't "mad"— she was angry.

A Burgundian chronicler described the young Archduchess of Burgundy as "illustrious and virtuous" and "of handsome bearing and gracious manner." But those qualities must not have been alluring enough to Philip, because Joanna went to extreme measures to keep her husband enticed, changing her sleeves and the trains of her gowns several times a day and wearing dresses with a thousand slits. The gentleman she had married preferred blondes, so she dismissed the fair-haired women in her retinue; when Philip found his yellow-tressed conquests somewhere else, Joanna lightened her own hair.

At the time of her wedding, Joanna was a dynastic cipher, with an elder brother who was the heir apparent to her parents' kingdoms (and whose offspring, it was expected, would continue the line). She also had an older sister. But just because Joanna was positioned a few rungs down on the ladder of succession, it didn't mean that her marriage to Philip of Burgundy was not politically or dynastically motivated; their union was intended to check French interests by forging an alliance between Castile and the Emperor Maximilian. However, when Joanna arrived in Flanders she was dismayed to discover that her new husband's advisers were all pro-French. Additionally, she had a hard time assimilating into the Flemish court; the only aspect she picked up with ease was the fashions. Part of her difficulty in adapting was financial. Joanna had no money to feed her starving Spanish entourage because Philip had not made her dowry payments, and her parents refused to ameliorate matters by sending her the funds to sustain them.

In October 1496, the same month as his daughter's marriage, King Ferdinand dispatched an ambassador to Flanders to insist that Philip pay Joanna her allowance. But the sums set aside in Joanna's name were paid into Burgundy's general treasury instead. And Philip emphatically refused to give her any funds for incidental expenses.

With no friends and no money, the high-strung Joanna grew lonely, which only increased her natural moodiness and irritability. Philip abused her mentally and physically. When they quarreled—often over his penchant for buxom blondes—he would punish her by avoiding her bedroom, which only sent Joanna spiraling further into depression. Weeping and railing, she would throw herself against the wall.

Joanna was also perpetually pregnant, bearing six children during the ten years of their marriage. Her first child, Leanor, was born in 1498; hormonal changes during or just after her pregnancy may have exacerbated her depression. Joanna even had a difficult time getting her husband to finance the expenses of the nursery. Philip maintained that because she had given birth to a daughter, the infant's care should be *her* responsibility, declaring, "Because this child is a girl, let the archduchess provide the estate, and then, when God grants us a son, I will provide it."

When their son and heir, Charles, was born on February 24, 1500, Joanna's status temporarily increased. Ever the politicians, her parents urged her to use that cachet to further Spanish interests in Flanders. But Joanna insisted that she could do nothing without her husband's favor, promising them she would win Philip's will when they were alone together, "because [she] knows that he loves [her]."

Joanna's moods rose and fell according to her husband's passions and his rejections. She both loved and feared him; and during the final two years of their marriage, she raged against Philip's indifference to her. More jailer than husband, he controlled Joanna's access to her own mother and tried to distance her from Isabella. When Joanna resisted, her conduct was branded as out of control. On many occasions her behavior was indeed excessive, even paranoid, but it was not without reason.

After their third child, Isabel, was born, Philip began asserting dominion over the nursery, choosing their offspring's governess and attendants. In October 1501 he sent all three children, under the supervision of his retainers, to visit their paternal grandmother in Mechlen.

Joanna's brother, Juan, had died in 1497, soon after his marriage to Margaret of Burgundy, and Joanna's older sister, Isabella, died in childbirth in 1498. Isabella's son, the Infante Miguel, never made it past his second year. When Miguel died in the summer of 1500, Joanna became the infanta—the heir to the crowns of Aragon and Castile.

In 1501 the royal couple traveled to Spain to tour their future kingdom; it was the first time that Joanna upheld her rights as the proprietary heiress of her parents' dominions. But Philip, who had signed a treaty with Louis XII in July of 1498, refused to alter his allegiance to France in preference to his Spanish in-laws. Joanna and Philip then visited the French court to hammer out the marriage negotiations of their son, Charles, to Louis's daughter Claude.

Before returning to Spain, Philip and Joanna stopped in Bayonne, where she began negotiations to wed their infant daughter, Isabel, to the heir to the King of Navarre. Far from being "mad," by arranging brilliant matches for her children, Joanna was doing everything that was expected of a royal mother.

In 1502, after Joanna gave birth to another daughter, she and Philip left their young brood in Flanders and returned to Toledo, where Joanna was proclaimed Princess of Asturias, the title held by the heir to the Spanish throne. Accordingly, both the Castilian and Aragonese Cortes, the national legislative assemblies, recognized Joanna as her parents' heir, but the Archbishop of Saragossa made it clear that the rights of succession could not be altered without a formal agreement between the Cortes and King Ferdinand. Offering Joanna an unfortunate taste of things to come, it was Ferdinand who shared the canopy of state with Philip, cutting Joanna—who was compelled to enter the city of Toledo behind them—out of the picture.

The young royals remained in Spain throughout 1502, but Philip made it increasingly clear that he hated it there. The climate during the summer was brutal, and the Spanish court too strict, meaning that it was too hard to seduce the ladies. He became even more miserable when he contracted measles. Toward the end of the year he and Joanna had another violent argument, possibly about Philip's desire to leave Spain. In any case, that's exactly what he did, departing for Flanders in December 1502.

Joanna wished to follow him immediately, but she was several months pregnant, so her parents refused to let her leave. In March 1503, after she gave birth to a son, Ferdinand, she reiterated her desire to join her husband, but her parents locked her up in the castle of La Mota. By now, new hostilities between Spain and France made travel risky. Thinking like a canny politician instead of a compassionate mother, Isabella also feared that Philip's pro-French advisers would try to influence Joanna if she were to return to him. So Isabella told her daughter that it was crucial for her to remain in Spain to prepare for the day when she would become queen.

Joanna's depression increased, although her despair was diagnosed as "lovesickness" by the court physicians. Finally, she received a letter from Philip and was determined to return to his arms. In November 1503, Joanna's orders for a ship to bring her back to Flanders were ignored. Unwilling to be thwarted, one windy and cold night, half-dressed and barefoot, she tried to escape from La Mota, but was halted by the guards, who closed the gate. Joanna threw herself against the iron bars and hurled abuse at everyone within earshot, including a bishop who tried to calm her down, threatening him with torture and death for keeping her confined. Refusing to go indoors, she stationed herself atop the ramparts "like an African lioness in a fit of rage" according to a contemporary chronicler. At two in the morning she finally retreated into a fruit shed and crouched under a table, which is where her mother found her and finally persuaded her to take shelter.

The exhausted Joanna was carried back to her chamber, flying into a hysterical rage. According to Isabella, Joanna "spoke to me with such severity and disrespect, so removed from how a daughter should speak to her mother that had I not seen the disposition in which she found herself, I would not have tolerated her words."

The queen assured Joanna that she had no intention *de la decasar de su marido*—"to separate you from your husband," promising her daughter that she could return to Flanders on March 1, 1504. But crossing her formidable mother proved to have been a mistake. In retaliation, Isabella requested Philip to give the leading Burgundians "full authority to hold" Joanna and "restrain her in the things that her passion can make her do," adding that they should deter her daughter from "anything that could endanger or dishonor her person" during the voyage.

Within a month of Joanna's arrival in Flanders that April, she suspected Philip of committing adultery with one of the noblewomen attached to the court. Joanna flew into a rage and exacted her revenge by ordering the woman's gorgeous blond hair to be cut off. Philip then raised his hand to his wife. Did he hit her in the face—or merely threaten to do so? The chroniclers aren't clear. Joanna fled to her room, remaining there for days, where she purportedly began mixing love potions from recipes provided by her Moorish serving maids. When Philip discovered her little laboratory, he dismissed the maids and confined Joanna to her chamber.

She retaliated by going on a hunger strike. A few days later the royal couple patched up their differences, but soon the cycle of abuse began anew.

On her deathbed, wily Queen Isabella checkmated her ambitious son-in-law, leaving a clause in her will that if Joanna were to "be unable or unwilling to govern," then Ferdinand would do so until Joanna's son Charles was old enough to rule. But Philip wasn't about to blithely accept his father-in-law's supremacy. If his wife was the queen, then he was going to claim the rights of succession, and the throne, on her behalf.

However, the Cortes was the legislative body charged with approving the monarch. And after hearing the testimony of Martín de Moxica, one of the principals of Joanna's household, regarding her allegedly unstable behavior—the "accidents, passions, and impediments that overcame the queen and had her outside her free will"— which therefore made her an unfit sovereign, the Cortes unanimously confirmed Ferdinand as guardian and governor of Castile. This created tension in the kingdom because the grandees, or aristocracy, preferred to support Joanna and Philip, who was a friend to the nobility.

Between 1504 and 1506, Philip and his allies enforced Joanna's silence. Wherever the couple dwelled, they kept her confined to her chamber, guarded by a dozen archers. When Philip and an elderly gentleman of honor visited her one day, she came after them with an iron bar. Philip ducked just in time, but the old man ended up clocked on the head. Then she brained her doorkeeper, "swearing she'd have them all killed."

Even taking into account her violent behavior, it still seems that Joanna wasn't necessarily "mad." What she *was*, was enraged.

Philip had Joanna's correspondence confiscated, laying the foundation for the legend of her outsized passion for him. A letter written by Pietro Mártire d'Anghiera, a humanist attached to the Castilian court, attests that Joanna was "lost in love" for her spouse. "Neither ambition for such kingdoms nor the love of her parents and other childhood companions would move her. Only attachment to the man whom they say that she loves with such ardor would draw her here."

It's wildly romantic. But when one looks at everything Joanna endured and her behavior as time went on, one has to assume it's simply not true.

On September 15, 1505, Joanna gave birth to Philip's fifth child, their daughter Mary. After all the mistreatment Joanna had endured at Philip's hands and all the cruel measures he had devised to ruin her in every way, did she still want him sexually? Or by that time was the exercise of conjugal rights a dynastic duty? *Was* Joanna "mad for love"?

In 1506, in Spain, Joanna and Philip were sworn in as the monarchs of Castile. It wasn't long before the clues to her true state of mind began to emerge. After the past two years of marital and political discord (not to mention incarceration), Joanna acknowledged that her differences with Philip were irreconcilable. Far from being senselessly devoted to him, she recognized that the only way to thwart his political agenda and preserve her kingdom as her parents intended it to be ruled was to enter into an alliance with her father.

In July the Cortes of 1506 refused to grant Philip a legal mandate for Joanna's imprisonment after she told them that she supported her father's right to rule Castile, agreed to dress in the Castilian manner, and refused to employ female attendants, "knowing the nature of her husband." Presumably the legislative body found her testimony sensible. Philip didn't much like the decision of the Castilian Cortes, so he went venue shopping and insisted that the decision be rendered from Valladolid. There on July 12, the Cortes declared both Philip and Joanna to be the true and legitimate rulers "of these said kingdoms and lands."

No better case can be made that Joanna's overweening passion for her spouse was merely mythological than the document Philip's supporters subsequently presented to Joanna for her signature, which stated that if she were mad, she authorized no one else but her husband to rule her kingdom on her behalf because of the great love she bore him.

Joanna crossed out that sentence.

So Philip's advocates stetted it and presented it to her again.

And Joanna deleted it.

Evidently Joanna, who was in frequent conflict with Philip by that point, objected strenuously to the word "love." But finally, after five rounds of the same two edits, Joanna's signature appeared on the document, ostensibly endorsing Philip's takeover.

However, the signature was probably forged; it does not match her acknowledged signature on forty-four other documents. It was also known at the time that Joanna supported her father's—and not Philip's—claim to the stewardship of the Spanish crown. One of her primary aims as queen was to restore the patrimonial lands and revenues to the crown that her husband had illegally distributed among the Spanish nobility in order to purchase their loyalty. So for obvious reasons, the grandees were not keen to enforce her orders. Consequently, measures were frequently dispatched without her signature or her approval.

Ferdinand suspected forgery and threatened to publish a list of grievances against Philip if he didn't start treating Joanna with more dignity. By this point the couple was back in Brussels and Joanna was once again being kept in isolation by her husband, who informed her father that she preferred not to receive visitors. It was a tactic that might have played well long-distance, but not in person. Philip must have acknowledged that it might be a tad inappropriate to imprison his wife in their own home, especially when company came to call, because on August 24, 1506, not too long after their return to Burgundy, he permitted Joanna to emerge from her enforced incarceration in order to welcome her father-in-law, Emperor Maximilian. During the emperor's visit, Joanna was highly social, attending jousts and other celebratory events, where the Venetian ambassador Vicentio Quirini noted that she was *"molto bella"* with the manner of "a wise and prudent lady." It would seem that Joanna only showed symptoms of "madness" when she was in captivity.

Or when Philip betrayed her.

But it had also been a mistake to have allied with her father after Queen Isabella's death, because Ferdinand proved just as capable of deceiving her.

Without consulting Joanna, Philip and Ferdinand negotiated an arrangement for the government of Castile. Their ultimate goal was to have her declared incompetent to rule.

Philip obtained the legal authority to govern in her stead, but his victory was short-lived. During their visit to Burgos that September Philip hosted a lavish banquet for one of his local supporters. After drinking a considerable amount of cool water he came down with a fever and chills. A few days later, he could barely speak, was sweating profusely, and was incapable of swallowing. One chronicler, referring to Philip's fondness for gaming and women, wrote, "through bad government, he passed from this life to the next." Joanna remained by his bedside, nursing him day and night, but the twenty-eight-year-old "Philip the Handsome" died of typhus fever on September 25. He had wished to be buried in the royal chapel in Granada; Joanna, pregnant with their sixth child, was determined to fulfill his final desire to inter him alongside the Spanish monarchs.

So, on December 20, Joanna traveled to the Convent at Miraflores, where her husband's body had been temporarily interred. She ordered his coffin opened and had some noblemen identify the putrefying remains. Satisfied that she had the right corpse, Joanna began the journey to Granada with Philip's coffin. A cortege of soldiers and priests accompanied the royal entourage. They traveled only by night. During the day, the lengthy procession stopped only at monasteries (Joanna refused to take refuge in convents), and though he had been dead for three months, she would not allow any women, whether lay or in orders, near her husband. She was described as being "lost, without any sense," although her secretary, Juan Lopez, insisted that Joanna was "more sane than her mother," a telling declaration, considering that Isabella of Spain had been one of the most pragmatic, capable, and respected women in Europe.

In January 1507, during her pilgrimage to Granada with Philip's corpse, Joanna went into labor. Shunning help from midwives, she delivered her daughter Catalina alone. Philip's coffin was placed for safekeeping before the altar in a nearby church. It remained there for four months until Joanna resumed her journey. When a storm forced the cortege to take refuge in a village, Joanna insisted on resting there for another few months before continuing on to Granada. Each time they stopped, Joanna purportedly had the coffin opened for a body check. But it was not love that motivated each of these "reveals." It was politics.

Perpetuating the myth that Joanna was mad for love, an anonymous Bulgarian chronicler wrote that she visited her husband's corpse every day and kissed its feet—a lurid narrative that assumed legendary proportions. The general belief was that Joanna's passion for her husband had made her so nuts that she couldn't function—which of course meant that she couldn't govern.

Joanna was crazy, all right—crazy like a fox. To paraphrase Hamlet, she knew a hawk from a handsaw. She refused to contradict the colorful rumors about her behavior because it was politically advantageous for her to let them spread. After Philip's death Joanna had two goals: to avoid a second marriage—which would have prejudiced her children by Philip—and to secure their children's inheritance. Only by sticking close to Philip's coffin could Joanna secure the succession for their oldest son, Charles, once Ferdinand died. From December 1506 to August 1507, Joanna made four nocturnal torchlight pilgrimages with Philip's coffin. She had it opened at each stop for the express purpose of showing his body to their subjects. It was all a giant display of sham devotion to reinforce the fact that young Charles was a direct descendant of Ferdinand, not just through Joanna, but through Philip as well.

In any case, the party was over when Ferdinand returned from a trip to Naples in August 1507. Warned that the Spanish nobles might withdraw their support from him, after Joanna deposited Philip's coffin in the Royal Monastery of Saint Clare he confined her to the adjacent palace at Tordesillas, a small town in central Castile.

Resisting her father's authority, Joanna refused to bathe or change her clothes and insisted on eating off the floor. Whatever her reasons, if she had any, the result was the widespread report that she was incapable of governing her own person, much less the kingdom. As the months wore on, Joanna became an ascetic, following the model of Saint Clare, "who never had a bed or a mattress or anything soft" and who "always went almost naked and barefoot." As this was conduct unbecoming a monarch, the Spanish nobles became suspicious of Ferdinand's motives. After all, he had once imprisoned her at La Mota.

Among those who dared to question the legitimacy of Joanna's insanity was the widowed Henry VII of England, who was mulling over the idea of asking Joanna to marry him. When the Spanish ambassador, Fuensalida, advised Henry that the young woman was probably in no mental condition to wed *anyone*, the English king replied, "Tell me, ambassador, is the Queen such as they say she is? If what they say is true, God defend that I should marry her for three kingdoms such as hers, but there are those who say it is your King who keeps her shut up and spreads this rumor about her. Indeed, I have reports from Spain that she listens and replies rationally and seems quite normal. When I saw her two years ago, her husband and some of his council were giving it out that she was mad, but at that time she seemed very well to me, and she spoke with a good manner and countenance, without losing a point of her authority. And although her husband and those who came with him depicted her as crazy, I did not see her as other than sane then, and I think her sane now." To this passionate and reasoned defense of Joanna's lucidity, Fuensalida could only stammer that the fifty-one-year-old Henry was too old to toy with thoughts of remarrying.

A veil of secrecy shrouded the events behind the thick stone walls of Tordesillas, and no one was permitted access to the twenty-seven-year-old queen. Joanna's older children remained in Flanders with Philip's sister, Margaret of Austria. Little Catalina, Joanna's last connection with her husband, was her sole source of comfort, confined with her mother and two female servants.

A 1509 accord officially deprived Joanna of the right to exercise any royal authority. She became ruler of Castile in name only. Until his death on January 23, 1516, Ferdinand autocratically ruled Spain. Not long after that, on March 14, Joanna's sixteen-year-old son, Charles, still in Brussels, assumed the titles of King of Castile y Leon, and Aragon.

Accompanied by his sister Leanor, Charles arrived in Spain in 1517, with the intention of ruling Aragon and Castile. However, this was technically impossible while his mother still lived. So he continued to keep Joanna imprisoned, preventing her from being seen in public, writing to her governor, the Marquis of Denia, "It seems to me that the best and most suitable thing for you to do is to make sure that no person speaks with Her Majesty, for no good could come of it." Her meals of bread and cheese were usually left outside her door because she refused to eat in the presence of anyone.

Charles even prevented his mother from evacuating the castle during an outbreak of the plague. To maintain her isolation during the pestilence, Joanna was told that the disease had ravaged and depopulated the outlying lands. In order to make the lie more convincing, Charles instructed the marquis to stage mock funeral processions around the palace several times a day.

What better device to *drive* a person crazy than solitary confinement, a starvation diet, and a systematic attempt to alter her reality?

For forty-seven years—from 1509 to 1555—Joanna of Castile, Queen of Spain, was locked away in a chamber with no natural light. Her jailers, guards hired by her own son and governed by the Marquis of Denia, were allowed to make use of "the strap" either to beat or bind her if they deemed it necessary. But if she were really mad—and dangerously so—to begin with, Charles and his minions would probably not have left his youngest sister in Joanna's care. Although Joanna was undeniably moody, prone to melancholy, and was capable of extreme fits of temper, her behavior does not appear synonymous with an incapacitating madness that deprived her of all reason.

On April 12, 1555, death took the seventy-five-year-old Joanna out of her misery. By that point, she was paralyzed from the waist down and her legs were covered with gangrenous ulcers. Technically, she had been Queen of Castile for more than fifty years. All of her six children had lived to adulthood—a Renaissance rarity—and each one had become a monarch. Charles of course became King of Spain and Holy Roman Emperor; his younger brother, Ferdinand, succeeded him as Holy Roman Emperor. The daughters of Philip and Joanna—Leanor, Isabel, Mary, and Catalina—became the queens of France, Denmark, Bohemia, and Portugal, respectively.

Joanna was interred beside the palace of Tordesillas at Saint Clare's, where her husband's corpse had rested for forty-eight years.

By a 1574 order of their grandson, Philip II of Spain, Philip's and Joanna's coffins were moved to the Royal Chapel at Granada, where they still rest beside the tombs of Ferdinand and Isabella. Poor Joanna was betrayed and/or abandoned by everyone who mattered in her life, beginning and ending with her family members; and if she wasn't "mad" to begin with, their cruelty would have been enough to destabilize her. Yet it's hard to imagine that she would ever want to lie anywhere else for all eternity except alongside them. "*Loca*," or merely livid, she was still a Queen of Spain.

ARTHUR, PRINCE OF WALES
1486–1502

✣ *and* ✣

KATHERINE OF ARAGON
1485-1536

married 1501–1502

"Willoughby, bring me a cup of ale, for I have been this night in the midst of Spain."
> —Arthur, Prince of Wales to his steward on the morning of November 15, 1501

". . . as intact and uncorrupt as when [she] emerged from [her] mother's womb."
> —Katherine of Aragon's assertion regarding the nonconsummation of her marriage to Arthur

AFTER TWO YEARS OF NEGOTIATIONS, BY THE TREATY of Medina del Campo ratified by Henry VII of England on September 23, 1490, his four-year-old son, Arthur, the Prince of Wales and heir to England's throne, was contracted in marriage to Catalina, or Katherine, the youngest daughter of Ferdinand and Isabella of Spain. Half of Katherine's dowry was to be paid upon her arrival in England and the balance upon her marriage—which left the Catholic Monarchs a lengthy gap of time before they would have to finance the second installment, as Katherine—thereafter styled as the Princess of Wales—was all of five years old.

Ferdinand expressed concern about *Arthur's* inheritance, however. The Tudor "dynasty" could hardly be termed as such; the prince was born the same year that his father, then the Earl of Richmond, snatched up the crown from where it lay on Bosworth Field after Richard III met the blade of a broadsword. With Richard's death the reign of the Plantagenets ended. After his victory at Bosworth, the Welsh-born Henry proclaimed himself Henry VII, and the Tudor era began.

But Henry and Ferdinand were both aware that in a world where might made right, nothing was a guarantee. The nephew of Edward IV, Edward, Earl of Warwick, had a strong enough pedigree to warrant a claim to the English throne and threaten Henry's successor—namely, little Arthur. Ferdinand needed to be certain that his daughter's future would be secured, so he stalled the negotiations until he was satisfied. Eager to move the talks along, Henry had Warwick killed. That little assassination accomplished, the royal marriage could take place—once the children came of age.

Finally, on May 14, 1499, twelve-year-old Arthur married Katherine (who was only thirteen) by proxy at Tickhill Manor. However, the bride's parents were still insisting that she not travel to England until her groom reached the age of fourteen. Further wrangling over the details of Katherine's dowry, as well as the composition of the entourage that would accompany her to England, continued through the following year.

After a Muslim uprising and storms at sea postponed Katherine's departure, her ship landed at Plymouth on October 2, 1501, surprising her future father-in-law, who hadn't expected her arrival until the seventh of the month. Eager to check her out, Henry intercepted her journey to London, meeting her in Hampshire on November 4. He flouted the Spanish protocol enforcing Katherine's seclusion until her wedding day, insisting that before he would introduce his son to her, he would see his future daughter-in-law "even if she were in her bed." Apparently satisfied with the package, the king departed with Arthur in tow and Katherine was left with her retinue to continue her progress into London.

There they were greeted on November 12 with a series of lavish pageants and spectacles. Two days later Katherine and Arthur, both clad all in white, were formally wed at St. Paul's Cathedral in a three-hour ceremony, which followed the exchange of the first installment of Katherine's dowry, and the reading of the formal terms of the marriage along with the appropriate papal dispensations, as Katherine was a third cousin of her father-in-law, Henry VII, and fourth cousin of her mother-in-law, Elizabeth of York.

A raised six-hundred-foot runway, covered in red cloth trimmed with gilt nails, had been erected from the west doors of the church all the way to the chancel, where the nuptial mass was conducted on a raised stage. The musicians were stationed in the soaring vaults, which gave the illusion that their resounding melodies emanated from on high.

The bride was considered a beauty, blessed with abundant auburn hair, gray eyes, dainty hands and feet, and the damasked pink-and-white complexion that was so prized in England. But the English had never seen an ensemble quite like her wedding attire. With her skirts stretched over her Spanish farthingale—a horizontal cage tied about her hips—Katherine resembled a ship of state as she sailed along the walkway, high above the crowd. Her white silk veil, or mantilla, fluttered to her waist, weighed down by a jeweled border two fingers wide.

Outside the cathedral the wine flowed freely from a conduit—royal largesse to the cheering throngs—as the bells of London pealed. After the ceremony the teenage newlyweds, "both lusty and amorous," were conveyed to Baynard's Castle in a grand procession, where a sumptuous feast awaited them, as did a public, though strictly ceremonial, bridal bed.

Preparing the actual bed of state was a production number involving several participants who were honored to get the assignment, including the yeoman of the guard, whose job it was to roll "up and down" the litter of straw that formed the bed's base layer. This brave soul was not merely matting the rushes; he was searching for hidden weapons.

After what amounted to a stag night, replete with bawdy songs to get the groom in the proper frame of mind to perform his conjugal duty, Arthur was escorted to the great bed, where Katherine was already waiting for him. The bishops blessed the couple and wished them many years of fruitful life together, then departed and left the newlyweds to nature.

Or not—depending on whom you asked. And depending on the circumstances in which you asked and how many days, weeks, or years it was from the wedding night itself.

Arthur's steward recalled his fifteen-year-old master boasting of his sexual prowess on the morning after the wedding night with the bawdy metaphor, "Willoughby, bring me a cup of ale, for I have been this night in the midst of Spain." Other witnesses heard this remark as well as Arthur's exhortation, "Masters, it is good pastime to have a wife." True, it could have been no more than macho swagger—but why? Those who saw the young couple together noticed a genuine attraction between them.

And Katherine had a rock-solid sense of duty. Her marriage negotiations had been long in the making; now that she was wed to the future King of England, her job was only half accomplished. To permanently cement Spain's alliance with England and fulfill her parents' diplomatic aims, she had to get pregnant and deliver an heir, an obligation made all the easier with a nice-looking husband. Two days after the wedding, she attended St. Paul's to formally witness her husband and father-in-law give thanks to God "that so prosperously His Goodness had suffered everything of this laudable [marriage] to be brought to its most laudable conclusion [the getting of children]." Now, it's possible that she could have been playing along, knowing what was expected of her, and if there had been a problem in the bedroom she would never have dared to disclose a word of it. However, it's equally conceivable that everything went just *fine* in the boudoir and the marriage was consummated, even enjoyably so, without a hitch.

Katherine's duenna Doña Elvira insisted—and Katherine reiterated as much years later—that the conjugal visits remained chaste. But Doña Elvira's assertion would seem to contradict the opinion of William Thomas, Arthur's Groom of the Privy Chamber and one of his most intimate body servants. Thomas was in charge of preparing the prince for his visits to the marriage bed. He "made [Arthur] ready to bed . . . and conducted him clad in his night gown unto the Princess's bedchamber door often and sundry times . . . and that at the morning he received him at the said doors . . . and waited upon him to his own privy chamber."

At the end of November Arthur wrote to his in-laws, informing them that "he had never felt such joy in his life as when he beheld the sweet face of his bride. No woman in the world could be more agreeable to him. [He] promises to be a good husband." This comment, too, would indicate that he fully intended to do his dynastic duty and become a father.

Yet the royal wedding still didn't mean that all was settled between Spain and England. Initially, Henry VII had not been keen to have the young couple set up their household and assume full marital relations. Doña Elvira, Katherine's duenna, agreed with him. But for Katherine, who had inherited her mother's iron will, time was of the essence and it was *she* who managed to change the king's mind. Additionally, Katherine's tutor and confessor, Alessandro Geraldini, persuaded Henry that "on no condition in the world should [he] separate them, but send her with her husband." Otherwise, Isabella and Ferdinand would be highly displeased and Katherine herself "would be in despair." So Arthur and Katherine set off for Ludlow, arriving on December 21, 1501.

In the spring of 1502 Arthur became ill, his ailment described by a herald as "the most pitiful disease and sickness that with so sore and great violence had battled and driven, in the singular parts of him inward, [so] that cruel and fervent enemy of nature, the deadly corruption, did utterly vanquish and overcome the pure and friend-ful blood." Many modern historians believe that the herald refers to the Sweating Sickness that was sweeping the West Country, or else to a bronchial or pulmonary infection, such as pneumonia or consumption. However, the phrase "the singular parts of him in-ward" may allude to testicular cancer.

An unknown witness recalled hearing one of Arthur's servants dating the onset of his illness to Shrovetide, February 8, 1502: "He had lain with the Lady Katherine, and was never so lusty in body and courage until his death, which [he] said was because he lay with the Lady Katherine." Arthur died on Easter Sunday, April 2, 1502.

The servants' accounts suggest that the Waleses enjoyed frequent and successful connubial visits. Katherine's confessor and tutor, Alessandro Geraldini—who was recalled to Spain not too long after Arthur's demise—concurred. But according to Katherine, between their arrival in Ludlow and the prince's death, the newlyweds had spent only seven nights together, and although they had shared a bed, they had never in fact consummated the marriage. Nearly thirty years later, during the hearings regarding the validity of her mar-riage to Henry VIII, the same contradictions about whether the union of Arthur and Katherine was consummated would emerge. Arthur's steward repeated his young master's boast on the morning after his wedding, to the effect that he "had spent the night in Spain," intimating that the couple had enjoyed intercourse, although Katherine would testify that she had remained "as intact and uncor-rupt as when she emerged from her mother's womb."

Arthur's body lay in state for three weeks before it was buried at Worcester Cathedral. Katherine, sixteen years old, nearly alone and friendless in a foreign kingdom, would remain in England for the next seven years in a state of political limbo. She was retired to Durham House to await whatever fate Henry VII and her parents decided for her. As her marriage portion had not been fully paid by Ferdinand and Isabella, Katherine was not entitled to claim her widow's dower of one-third of Arthur's lands. Additionally, be-cause several of Katherine's retinue vociferously insisted that her marriage to Arthur had never been consummated, Henry VII went so far as to assert that she was not in fact the Princess of Wales, and therefore, he was not obligated to provide for her. Katherine's debts mounted, and when she had to pawn her jewels and plate—a contested element of her dowry—to pay her entourage, she was accused of spending Henry VII's property.

Eventually, a marriage was brokered between Katherine and Henry's surviving son, the future Henry VIII, but her marriage to Arthur and the subject of its consummation would remain the elephant in the parlor—rearing its trunk and smashing breakables—for years. It was the subject of the papal dispensations required for her union with young Henry—a brief and a bull that either contradict or complement each other, depending on one's interpretation of the wording. The argument over whether Katherine's union with Arthur was a "true" marriage would be fought again when Henry chose to put her aside in order to wed Anne Boleyn. Katherine continued to avow that she had come to Henry's bed a twenty-three-year-old virgin.

By the time Henry's Great Matter was under debate in the late 1520s, Katherine's keen understanding of dynasty and diplomacy had made her more than a loving wife and devoted mother. She was Spain to Henry's England, an alliance that possibly overrode any qualms of conscience.

Perhaps Arthur had spent his wedding "night in the midst of Spain" after all.

Henry VIII
1491–1547
RULED ENGLAND: 1509–1547

and

KATHERINE OF ARAGON
("HUMBLE AND LOYAL")

married 1509–1533

"This twenty years I have been your true wife . . . and when ye had me at the first I take God to be my judge, I was a true maid without taint of man. And whether this be true or no, I put it to your conscience."

—Katherine to Henry and his council in open court,
June 21, 1529

EVER SINCE SHE CAME TO THE ENGLISH COURT IN 1501, the diminutive, round-faced Spanish infanta with the penetrating gray eyes and hip-length auburn hair had intrigued the boisterous and precocious Duke of York. Katherine had married his older brother, Arthur, that fall, but the prince had died on Easter Sunday 1502, after a brief illness, throwing Katherine's status into limbo while her father and father-in-law wrangled and carped and dithered over the outstanding payments on her dowry.

In 1503, extensive negotiations between Henry VII and the Catholic Monarchs resulted in a formal treaty to wed Katherine to Henry's younger son and namesake when the boy reached the age of fifteen, in June 1506. Yet before this treaty could be ratified a papal dispensation was necessary, on the assumption that Katherine had consummated her marriage to the youth's older brother. When Henry, Duke of York and Katherine of Aragon were betrothed on June 25, 1503, the paperwork was still in progress. Young Henry, who seemed game enough to wed Katherine, still had a way to go until his fifteenth birthday; perhaps that was the reason why Pope Julius II didn't bother to make a dispensation available until a document referred to as a papal brief was sent to Isabella shortly before her death in November 1504. This document bluntly stated that Arthur and Katherine *had* in fact consummated their union. The eventual papal bull was backdated to December 26, 1503, and covered all eventualities, granting dispensation for the marriage of Katherine and Henry *forsan*—"even if"—Katherine's previous marriage had been consummated.

However, during the intervening years between Arthur's death and Katherine's marriage to Henry, the shifting political landscape in Spain had an impact on England's foreign policy. After Queen Isabella's will named her daughter Joanna heir to the Castilian crown, appointing Ferdinand as regent if Joanna proved mentally unfit to rule, Spain quickly split into factions. Unsure of which way the wind would eventually blow, Henry VII became leery of allying himself too closely to Ferdinand. So, on June 27, 1505, the day before his son's fourteenth birthday, the king compelled the young Henry, now formally Prince of Wales, to privately repudiate his betrothal to Katherine, alleging that he had never given his consent to it. It was a political ploy, intended to buy the English some time until the situation in Spain sorted itself out.

For her part, Katherine remained adamant about going through with the marriage, keenly aware of the political importance of an alliance between Spain and England—the very reason she had been sent to marry Arthur. She got her wish when Henry VII died on April 21, 1509, and his seventeen-year-old son became King of England. He summoned Guitierre Gomez de Fuensalida, the new Spanish ambassador, and told him to make the marriage to Katherine happen—without further delays or negotiations. According to Henry VIII's biographer A. F. Pollard, the pair were wed "with almost indecent haste."

In contrast to the spectacle of her first royal wedding, Henry and Katherine were quietly married in the Franciscan Oratory in Greenwich on June 11, 1509, just six weeks after Henry's accession to the throne.

Though Katherine was six years Henry's senior, he was not at all unhappy about the match, cheerfully telling people that "he loved true where he did marry," informing his father-in-law that "if I were still free, I would choose her for a wife before all others." Katherine wrote to Ferdinand, "Among the many reasons that move me to love the King, my lord, the strongest is his filial love and obedience to Your Highness."

The newlyweds enjoyed a double coronation at Westminster Abbey on Michaelmas, June 24. Once they were married, Henry and Katherine spent several hours of the day together, enjoying lively discussions of statecraft, politics and religion, and sportive pursuits, such as hunting, and evening entertainments. Henry VIII's court was vibrant, filled with gallant courtiers and comely damsels intent on showing off their finery and having fun. One visitor in the early days of Henry's reign described the king as "young and lusty, disposed all to mirth and pleasure, nothing minding to travail in the busy affairs of his realm."

Katherine was a delighted and willing audience to Henry's jousts and the masques in which he would appear in some exotic disguise. He wore her favors in the lists; when he came across a new piece of music that he thought would please her, he couldn't wait for her to hear it. They shared a passion for literature and theology. Henry adored Katherine's high spirits and her grace, her dignity and nobility, and her penchant for fine gowns in colors rich as gemstones.

During the early years of his reign Henry was very much the warrior-king, and he trusted Katherine to act as his regent. In 1513, while he campaigned in France, Katherine had the authority to raise troops and make appointments, although much of the administration of the realm was done long-distance by Henry's council in the field. Under Katherine's regency, while Henry was in France, England achieved its most significant Tudor-era military victory until the vanquishing of the Spanish Armada in 1588. The queen led a reserve army north to meet her husband's troops, but it was disbanded in Buckinghamshire when word came of the English victory at Flodden and the death of the Scots king on the field. Katherine gleefully wrote to Henry, "In this your grace shall see how I can keep my promys, sending you for your banners a king's coat. I thought to send himself unto you, but our Englishmen's hearts would not suffer it." Katherine also acted (de facto) as England's key diplomat with Spain until her father died in January 1516.

Meanwhile, she was busy with her primary duty as consort: bearing an heir to her husband's throne. Katherine became pregnant soon after the wedding, suffering a stillbirth late in January 1510. However, the incident was kept a secret and Katherine was instructed to maintain the pretext of a pregnancy, including the acquisition of a lavish layette and the enduring of a lengthy and claustrophobic prenatal confinement. The Tudor spin doctors released the story that the queen had been pregnant with twins, and had lost one of them. Unfortunately, the Spanish ambassador blew Katherine's cover when he learned that her periods had returned and reported as much to his employer.

On New Year's Day 1511, after a decade of living in England, Katherine finally achieved what she was brought there to accomplish: she produced a male heir to the throne. The king hosted a spectacular tournament in their son's honor, and never had Henry, who dubbed himself "Sir Loyal Heart," been so in love with his wife as on those glorious days of pageantry and celebration. But the boy, named for his father, died some days later.

In the nine years between 1509 and 1518, Katherine was pregnant at least seven times. After suffering two more stillbirths, on February 18, 1516, at the age of thirty-one, she finally bore a healthy daughter, the Princess Mary—"a baby who never cries," Henry boasted. He remained optimistic about Katherine's fertility, telling the Venetian ambassador, "The queen and I are both young, and if it is a girl this time, by God's grace boys will follow."

But there would be no more children of either gender. And as time wore on, it was clear that Katherine's body had betrayed them both. Although there was nothing in English law to bar the succession of a female, in Henry's mind, daughters didn't count. His greatest desire was a legitimate son for the security and peace of the realm, and he began casting about for reasons to rid himself of Katherine and take a more nubile wife.

By 1519, when Henry's mistress Bessie Blount had given him a bouncing baby boy who was everything he desired (except legitimate), Katherine's influence with him was on the wane. So were her looks. Not only had she been replaced by Cardinal Wolsey as the king's chief confidant, but a Venetian visitor to the English court remarked that Katherine was "rather ugly than otherwise." Repeated pregnancies had thickened her waist. Her hair had darkened to a dull brown, losing its reddish luster. The queen retreated almost entirely from court life, rarely appearing in public beside her younger, taller, and still-handsome husband. She'd also become more overtly devout; under her garments she now mortified her tender flesh with the coarse habit of the third order of St. Francis.

Henry's myriad reasons for the annulment of his first marriage are more properly part of the story of his relationship with Anne Boleyn. But one cause, in a nutshell, was that Katherine failed to do her job, which was to bear a son and heir. Katherine went through menopause in 1524 at the age of thirty-nine and suffered from a mysterious "female ailment" as well—possibly leucorrhea, an infection with a smelly yellow vaginal discharge—which may have sent Henry, who was very particular when it came to his women's looks and hygiene, even further from her bed. Cardinal Wolsey cryptically wrote, "There are certain diseases in the queen defying all remedy, for which causes the king will never live with her."

In 1527, after her nephew Charles V, the King of Spain and Holy Roman Emperor, sacked Rome and took the Pope hostage, Katherine and Henry had a falling out. By then, he had decided that she was no longer politically useful to him. And that same year, when Anne Boleyn had told Henry she would consent to be his queen, but never his mistress, he conveniently expressed doubts about the legitimacy of his marriage to Katherine.

After eighteen years of marriage, based on a dispensation from the very situation he was now certain invalidated their union, Henry cynically conceived the idea of an annulment—by claiming that he and Katherine had never been legally wed because they had violated the word of God. Brandishing a Bible, he invoked the words of Leviticus 20: "And if a man shall take his brother's wife, it is an unclean thing: he hath uncovered his brother's nakedness; they shall be childless." Deciding that the Princess Mary was chopped liver, Henry chose to interpret "childless" as a reference to male offspring only, convinced that God had punished him for marrying Arthur's wife by denying them *sons*, and that it was also God's will that he be given the chance to have a boy. Getting rid of Katherine was the only way to break the curse.

However, the precept of Leviticus was violated frequently in dynastic royal marriages. King Manoel of Portugal had first wed Katherine's oldest sister Isabella; after she died, he married their sister Maria. Not too many years before Henry's crisis of conscience, the late King Afonso of Portugal had received a dispensation to marry his sister's daughter, Juana la Beltraneja. And Henry himself was seriously considering wedding Henry Fitzroy, his bastard son by Bessie Blount, to the boy's half sister, Princess Mary.

Nonetheless, Henry's older sister, Margaret, had managed to pull off a divorce that very year on similar grounds to the Leviticus argument, so Henry had high hopes of success.

Katherine had been blindsided by the news that Henry (through Wolsey) had secretly convened a commission to study the validity of their marriage. Not until several weeks after the hearings began on May 17, 1527, did Henry have the courage to confess what the Spanish ambassador had already disclosed to her. On June 22, the king informed his wife of his recent discovery "that they had been in mortal sin during all the years they had lived together, and that this being the opinion of many canonists and theologians whom he had consulted on the subject, he had come to the resolution, as his conscience was much troubled thereby, to separate himself from her *a mensa et thoro* [from board and bed] and wished her to choose the place to which she would retire."

Katherine's initial reaction was to be expected, "bursting into tears and being too agitated to reply." Henry ended up awkwardly comforting his wife, reassuring her that "All should be done for the best," before urging her to keep their conversation a secret and making an embarrassed exit from the chamber.

The queen felt betrayed, and she soon became embittered. But she was also well coached, garnering expert opinions to bolster *her* position. She countered Henry's Leviticus argument with the insistence that she had never consummated her marriage with Arthur, a claim substantiated by her ladies-in-waiting—although other courtiers would later testify that Katherine had lost her virginity to him. Cardinal Wolsey counterpunched, informing the queen's Almoner, Dr. Robert Shorton, that after Katherine's wedding night in 1501 the Spanish ambassadors "did send the sheets they lay in, spotted with blood, into Spain, in full testimony and proof thereof."

Tradition accepts Katherine's testimony, painting her in a saintly glow that modern historians still strive to reproduce. But in the 1860s, G. A. Bergenroth discovered documents in the Spanish archives that contest Katherine's assertion. Correspondence between her father, her nephew Charles, and the imperial ambassador Eustache Chapuys contains allegations that Katherine had not only lied about her virginity in order to remain in England, but that her pregnancy announced in February 1510, less than a year after her marriage to Henry, was also a sham. Bergenroth found a letter from Katherine's confessor Friar Diego that states she had a miscarriage that January. Yet on May 27, 1510, Katherine wrote to Ferdinand to inform him that she lost the child "a few days ago." In other words, for nearly half a year she kept the truth from her own father. Despite her genuine piety, Katherine was clearly capable of duplicity when it was politically advantageous to maintain a fiction. When all was said and done, she was the daughter of two powerful and highly manipulative monarchs and may have gleaned much from watching them in action.

To "divorce" Katherine, Henry sought a papal dispensation from Clement VII that would effectively overturn, or cancel, the previous dispensation issued by Pope Julius II. The earlier document dispelled with the prohibited degree of affinity, *permitting* Henry to wed his late brother's wife. Now, nearly a quarter century later, the king was demanding that Clement's dispensation uphold the nullity of his marriage to Katherine *because* she had been his late brother's wife.

Negotiations to legally divest himself of Katherine so he could marry Anne Boleyn and make her his queen dragged on for six years, from 1527 to 1533. Aware that public sympathy was on her side, Katherine proved to be as tough and shrewd an adversary as Henry had ever faced. As the Great Matter progressed, she continually thwarted Henry's desire for secrecy by broadcasting information regarding the events, and her feelings about them, to all the foreign ambassadors so that the entire international community would learn what was taking place in England. Although she claimed to be one woman alone against Henry's mighty legal machine, she was receiving information and advice every step of the way. And there was at least one mole inside Henry's private meetings with his lawyers and theologians who reported every detail to the queen.

One double agent risked his life to aid Katherine. Near the outset of the Great Matter, Wolsey had told her that only the original dispensation regarding her marriage to Arthur—which lay in Spain's archives—would be admissible as evidence, and that the document she had produced could be discredited as a forgery. Luckily for the queen, Thomas Abell, the envoy who had been handpicked by the cardinal to fetch the original document, happened to have a conscience. He procured a legally notarized copy of the papal bull, admissible in any court. For abetting Katherine's case, Abell spent the last six years of his life in the Tower; his body was tortured, his spirit was broken, and he was eventually hanged.

Nor was Katherine about to go quietly. Her retreat into religious devotions had made her stronger, rather than more malleable. Furthermore, she loved Henry, as a queen, as a wife, and as a woman. "She assured me that she would live and die in the estate of matrimony," averred Cardinal Campeggio, the papal legate who, along with Cardinal Wolsey, had been instructed by His Holiness to deliver an opinion on the Great Matter—as long as they took their sweet time about it.

One way that Pope Clement managed to make himself look like he was moving the matter forward was by granting Henry a papal dispensation that set aside the first degree of affinity with regard to Mary Boleyn. The document would have enabled Henry to marry Anne in the eyes of the Church, despite the fact that he'd bedded her sister. But without the decrees nullifying Henry's marriage to Katherine, it was as good as the parchment it was written on. So, in February 1528, two English envoys set out for Rome with the king's petition, bearing a letter from Cardinal Wolsey—which it must have choked him to write—extolling Anne's many virtues of character.

That summer, pro-Katherine sentiment ran so high in London that there were demonstrations in the streets against Henry's plan to divorce her. Realizing that he was losing in the court of public opinion, the king cast himself as the beleaguered party. He summoned as many subjects as he could into the great chamber at

Bridewell Palace, where he lay the case before them, then sanctimoniously declared, "If it be adjudged that the Queen is my lawful wife, nothing will be more pleasant or acceptable to me, both for the clearness of my conscience, and also for the good qualities and conditions I know her to be in . . . so that if I were to marry again, if the marriage might be good, I would choose her above all women. But if it be determined in judgment that our marriage is against God's law, then shall I sorrow, parting from so good a lady and loving companion."

His words couldn't have been further from the truth.

And Katherine was not fooled by them. She knew perfectly well that Henry hungered for the opposite verdict. And she also desired to know why, after so many years of living together as man and wife, Henry suddenly thought their marriage had been a sham, and therefore, the Princess Mary was a bastard. Katherine refused to accept Henry's compromise to take the veil (which might have saved Mary's legitimacy), because if she took his offer to enter an abbey, she would also be embracing the premise that she had broken God's law, acknowledging that her marriage to Henry had been invalid from the start. Sticking to her original story, on October 27, 1528, she swore under the seal of the confessional in the presence of Cardinal Campeggio that she and Arthur had shared a bed only seven times during their brief marriage, but that they had never enjoyed intercourse on any of those nights, and therefore, she had remained a virgin.

Henry's council, known as the legatine court, had commenced their hearings in June 1529. Katherine, more or less evicted by Henry, had by then taken up residence at Baynard's Castle, where her wedding reception to Arthur had been held.

On June 21, Katherine stunned the council by testifying in person. Stepping down from her raised dais, she slowly threaded her way across the room to Henry's platform, and dramatically knelt before her husband, remaining at his feet, although he twice tried to raise her up. Then, according to Campeggio, "in the sight of all the court and assembly, in broken English" she begged Henry "to consider her honor, her daughter's and his; that he should not be displeased at her defending it, and should consider the reputation of her nation and relatives, who will be seriously offended; in accordance with what he had said about his good will, she had throughout appealed to Rome, where it was reasonable that the affair should be determined, as the present place was open to suspicion and because the cause is already [begun] at Rome."

In her still-thick Spanish accent Katherine implored Henry, "I beseech you for all the love that hath been between us, let me have justice and right, take of me some pity and compassion, for I am a poor woman, and a stranger, born out of your dominion. I have here no assured friend and much less indifferent counsel. . . . I take God and all the world to witness that I have been to you a true, humble, and obedient wife, ever comfortable to your will and pleasure . . . , being always well pleased and contented with all things wherein you had any delight or dalliance, whether it were little or much . . . I loved all those whom ye loved, only for your sake, whether I had cause or no, and whether they were my friends or my enemies. This twenty years I have been your true wife, and by me ye have had divers children, although it hath pleased God to call them from this world, and when ye had me at the first I take God to be my judge, I was a true maid without taint of man. And whether this be true or no, I put it to your conscience."

The room itself seemed to hold its breath waiting for the king's reply. But Henry made no answer.

"If there be any just cause that you can allege against me, either of dishonesty, or matter lawful to put me from you," Katherine continued, "I am content to depart to my shame and rebuke, and if there be none, I pray you to let me have justice at your hands."

A week later, Arthur's steward was brought to testify before the council. He recalled his late master's wedding morning boast, "Willoughby, bring me a cup of ale, for I have been this night in the midst of Spain." Whether Arthur's words had been the truth or merely a macho pronouncement made by a scrawny adolescent, it didn't help Katherine's cause. Compounding matters, Katherine's former tutor and confessor, Alessandro Geraldini, supported the steward's testimony.

Anne Boleyn was elated at the possibility that Katherine had been lying about her chastity. But as far as Rome was concerned, the Great Matter remained unresolved, and it was in the papacy's interests to stall for time for several reasons. In 1527, Rome had been sacked and the Pope temporarily taken prisoner by forces under the command of Katherine's nephew Charles V of Spain. Consequently, it was a bad idea for the curia to do anything that might further anger Charles. It was vital to preserve the peace as well as the delicate balance of political power. And because the papacy also had grave doubts about Henry's argument for an annulment, it was more comfortable for them to accept Katherine's version of events.

Heartened by Rome's delays, Katherine had not given up, nor had her supporters. The queen's faction intended to reveal the real reason for Henry's petition. In 1529, seventeen of Henry's love letters to Anne Boleyn were stolen by an agent of Cardinal Campeggio, one of the papal legates charged with determining the Great Matter. The letters were brought to the Pope, and to this day they remain in the Vatican's archives.

One day that summer, after the legatine court had been adjourned on a technicality—which conveniently delayed a verdict until October at the earliest—Katherine flung herself at her husband's feet and begged him to take her back. She informed Henry that she refused to accept the decision of the biased English court and intended to appeal directly to the Pope. Appearing to be as concerned for Henry's religious apostasy as she was about his marital infidelity, Katherine wrote to the pontiff, passionately urging him to sanction Anne's champions:

> . . . Your Holiness had promised to renew the brief issued at Bologna, and to issue another commanding the King, my lord, to dismiss and utterly to cast away this woman with whom he lives . . . my complaint is not against the King, my lord, but

against the instigators and abettors of this suit. I trust so much in . . . the King's natural virtues and goodness that if I could only have him with me two months, as he used to be, I alone would be powerful enough to make him forget the past. But they know this is true, so they contrive to prevent his being with me. . . . Therefore, put a bit in their mouths! Proceed to sentence! Then their tongues will be silenced and their hopes of mischief vanish; then they will set my lord at liberty and he will become once more the dutiful son of Your Holiness as he always was.

But Henry never veered from his course. In July of 1531, he saw Katherine of Aragon for the last time. She spent her final four and a half years in various royal demesnes, each one draftier than the last, struggling to maintain the modest household Henry had permitted her. Even so, she was almost always in arrears.

Over the years Katherine had adopted the roles of warrior-queen and attorney in her own defense, but when she realized that nothing could persuade her husband to depart from his course, she donned the martyr's mantle. "Wherever the king commanded her, were it even to the fire," she would go—although she had no intent to relinquish either her title or her marital status, declaring "in this world I will confess myself to be the king's true wife, and in the next they will know how unreasonably I am afflicted."

Katherine was caught between Scylla and Charybdis. As a wife, her primary duty was to obey her husband. But as a queen consort, she was expected to maintain her dignity and to lead and rule. And as a devout Catholic, her conscience had to be obeyed. To that end, in 1531, when the Duke of Suffolk, Charles Brandon, was deputized to pressure Katherine to step aside, he reported to the king that Katherine was prepared to obey his command, "but she owed obedience to two persons first. . . . God was the first; the second was her soul and conscience."

By then she had endured approximately five years of "the pains of Purgatory on earth" at Henry's hands. She had also suffered routine assaults on her fertility by Henry's deputies who (conveniently forgetting the existence of the Princess Mary) tried to convince her that her marriage to the king was an abomination in the sight of God "by the curse of sterility." And she had endured the cruel separation from her daughter. Henry refused to allow Mary and Katherine to cohabit because he feared that the imperial ambassador Eustache Chapuys might spearhead an attempt to spirit Mary out of the country so she could rally the Spanish against him.

On May 23, 1533, after Henry had been married to Anne Boleyn for four months, the Archbishop of Canterbury Thomas Cranmer declared the king's marriage to Katherine null and void on the ground that she had consummated her marriage with his brother Arthur, and no dispensation could remove the impediment imposed by God in the words of Leviticus.

But even after Anne's coronation on June 1, 1533, Katherine insisted on being referred to as the queen, rather than accept the demoted title of Princess Dowager. Warned that her stubbornness might redound on Henry's treatment of their daughter, she replied that she would place her trust in his mercy. And when Katherine was threatened with prosecution for treason, she insisted, "if it can be proved that I have given occasion to disturb my lord, the king, or his realm in any wise, then I desire that my punishment according to the laws should not be deferred . . . but should I agree to your persuasions I should be a slanderer of myself and confess to have been the king's harlot these four and twenty years. . . . As long as the King, my lord, took me for his wife, as I was and am, I am also his subject, but if the King take me not as his wife, I came not into this realm as merchandise, nor yet to be married to any merchant. . . ."

On March 24, 1534, approximately fourteen months after Henry had wed Anne Boleyn, Pope Clement finally declared that the marriage between Katherine and Henry was valid in the eyes of God and Church. But by that time the judgment was moot. Henry had settled the matter by declaring himself Supreme Head of the Church in England, and as such he recognized no law made by Rome. Six weeks later, a deputation from the king visited Katherine at the damp and drafty Buckden, for the purposes of extracting from "the old Princess Dowager" and her remaining household staff the oath affirming on pain of treason that the king's first marriage was unlawful; that his union with Anne was good and valid; and their daughter Elizabeth was the legitimate heir to the throne. Katherine refused to take the oath, as did every one of her courageous attendants.

England was ripe for rebellion that year, with many of the most prominent and powerful nobles not only supporting Katherine's cause but deeming Henry's hijacking of the Church unlawful, and his conduct with regard to his marriage an offense to both God and reason. Meeting with them covertly, the imperial ambassador Eustache Chapuys was the secret link between all of these discontented men. Although he may not have been aware that his kingdom was a powder keg, Henry told his council in 1535, "The Lady Katherine is a proud, stubborn woman of very high courage. If she took it into her head to take her daughter's part she could quite easily take the field, muster a great array and wage against me a war as fierce as any her mother Isabella ever waged in Spain."

Luckily for the king, Katherine considered herself to be his loyal wife to the very end and refused to conscience any form of rebellion.

At the end of December 1535, Henry received the news that Katherine lay dangerously ill. Although he refused to see her, in her waning days, Katherine wrote one last letter to the king, forgiving him for his sins of casting her aside and averring her everlasting passion for him.

My most dear Lord, King and husband. The hour of my death now drawing on, the tender love I owe you forces me, my case being such, to commend myself to you, and to put you in remembrance with a few words of the health and safeguard of your soul, which you ought to prefer before all worldly matters and before the care and pampering of your body, for the which you have cast me into many calamities and yourself into many troubles.

For my part, I pardon you everything, and I wish and devoutly pray God that He will pardon you also. For the rest, I commend unto you our daughter Mary, beseeching you to be a good father unto her, as I have heretofore desired. . . .

Lastly, I make this vow, that mine eyes desire you above all things.

The letter was signed "Katherine the Queen."

In her final days Katherine had a crisis of conscience, debating whether her decision to maintain her status as queen, come hell or high water, had done the kingdom more harm than good. Standing her ground had compelled Henry to break with Rome, thereby allowing the new religion to take hold. If she had accepted the invitation to step aside and enter a convent, would everything have been different?

Yet perhaps there was a deeper reason for her feelings of guilt, as well as her motive for wearing the coarse order of the Franciscans beneath her gowns for the last years of her life. Katherine may very well have lied—to Henry, to his commissioners and delegations, and to God. The documents unearthed by the Victorian historian G. A. Bergenroth showed Katherine's historically honorable character to be somewhat less than saintly. If she had indeed consummated her marriage to Arthur, as the papers suggest, then her performance during the sham trial regarding the legality of her marriage to Henry was as farcical as the king's. And in that case, no wonder she felt the need to perpetually atone before the cross. As devout as she was, she must have believed that for this sin, she would surely roast in hell.

Katherine had never been averse to lying if it accomplished certain desirable diplomatic goals. In 1507 she had proudly told her father—a past master of dissembling—"I bait [the widowed Henry VII] with this [the possibility of a marriage to her sister Joanna]" in order to achieve better treatment from the English king. She also boasted to Ferdinand of her ability to manipulate the Spanish ambassador, de Puebla: "I dissimulate with him and praise all that he does . . . I say everything I think may be useful for me with the king, because in fact, de Puebla is the adviser of the king and I would not dare to say anything to him, except what I should wish the king to know."

In 1510, Katherine lied to two monarchs and an ambassador when she continued to maintain the illusion of a pregnancy, fooling an entire kingdom, except for a handful of people in the know.

So why wouldn't she have lied about consummating her marriage with Arthur? She kept her mouth shut after their wedding, giving every impression that the couple had enjoyed a normal sex life—fearing she'd be packed off to Spain, a failure in her primary mission. And immediately after Arthur's death (although her duenna told another story), Katherine could not contradict reports of their active sex life because she needed to maintain the image, fictional or otherwise, that she was legitimately the Princess of Wales, so she could remain in England.

But when her great hope became a marriage to Henry, the future king, she couldn't let that prospect slip away. So it became convenient to be a virgin again, precisely *because* of the Leviticus problem. *Then*, she had to maintain at all costs that she had *never* been Arthur's true wife, in order for the plans to go forward with as few hitches as possible.

So Katherine was a politician as well as a penitent. Not for nothing was she the daughter of those arch-pragmatists, Ferdinand and Isabella. If she deliberately lied about being a virgin on her wedding night to Henry, she chose to place that sin upon her conscience in preference to destroying Spain's vital diplomatic alliance with England—her raison d'être for coming to England in the first place. More important, Katherine chose to lie for the greater good of protecting her daughter Mary's rights of succession—which, in the long run, it did. And Katherine chanced a dance with the devil for the greater good of Catholicism as well. With Mary on the throne, Katherine knew that the true religion would be restored.

She could not have foreseen at what cost, and that it would not last.

On January 7, 1536, just days after her fiftieth birthday, Katherine died in the arms of her dear friend and former lady-in-waiting, Maria de Salinas, the Dowager Countess of Salisbury—mother-in-law to the Duke of Suffolk, Charles Brandon. It is generally accepted that a cancerous tumor on the queen's heart claimed her life. But the physician who examined her corpse suspected that "a slow and subtle poison" might have been put into the glass of beer that Katherine drank in her final hours because her heart tissue was black all the way through, as was the tumor on it, and Katherine's supporters were keen to believe the worst. The cause of her death has never been conclusively proved, but for centuries romantics have liked to say that one way or another she died of a broken heart.

Charles V donned black mourning and declared that he never understood how Henry could have put aside "so sage and virtuous and sainted a wife" for a whore. However, within a few months of his aunt's passing he was eager to resume diplomatic relations with England. Upon hearing of Katherine's demise Henry and Anne Boleyn donned ensembles of yellow; that night the king gave a ball in Greenwich, gaily displaying baby Elizabeth to his guests and jubilantly exclaiming, "God be praised, the old harridan is dead, now there is no fear of war."

As a result of Henry's desperation for an annulment of his marriage to Katherine, he ignored the opinions of the Pope at peril of his own excommunication, proclaimed himself head of the Church in England, and a reformed religion was born, which would eventually morph into the Church *of* England—but not without bloodshed, mass destruction, and threats of war. The monasteries were dissolved and their property absorbed by the Royal Exchequer. Many glorious medieval buildings were razed in the zeal to rid England of the Roman Church's corrupt influence. Dissidents were executed for speaking against the validity of Henry's marriage to Anne Boleyn.

Ironically, Katherine's death hastened Anne's downfall and demise. By the spring of 1536, Henry was sick of her, as she, too, had failed to give him a son; but he had dared not consider putting her aside while Katherine still lived.

Katherine of Aragon was buried with modest pomp at Peterborough. At her funeral the arms of England were ungilded and the chaplet she wore was the open circlet of a princess rather than the closed crown of a queen. The bishop who delivered the funeral sermon boldly lied, informing the bereaved that in a deathbed confession Katherine had admitted that she had never been England's rightful queen.

Nineteen-year-old Princess Mary, bastardized and stripped of her royal title, was insulted by the paltry trappings. And not until the twentieth century did Katherine's resting place receive the honors it deserved when Mary of Teck, the queen consort of George V, ordered the symbols of queenship to be displayed over Katherine's tomb. The two banners bearing the royal arms of England and Spain hang there still.

MARY ROSE TUDOR
1495/6–1533

QUEEN OF FRANCE: 1514–1515

and

LOUIS XII OF FRANCE
1462–1515

RULED FRANCE: 1498–1515

married 1514–1515

and

CHARLES BRANDON,
DUKE OF SUFFOLK

1484–1545

married 1515–1533

"How lovingly the King my husband dealeth with me. . . ."
—Mary Tudor, in a letter to her brother, Henry VIII,
soon after her marriage to Louis XII of France

". . . remembering the great virtues which I have seen and perceived heretofore in my Lord of Suffolk, to whom I have always been of good mind, as ye well know, I have affixed and clearly determined to marry with him . . ."

—Mary's letter to her brother, Henry VIII, February 1515

$\mathcal{J}$N GENERAL, THERE TEND TO BE TWO KINDS OF ROYAL marriages: those that are a fulfillment of duty and the ones that spring from desire. Mary Rose Tudor, the younger, and favorite, sister of Henry VIII, is one royal who experienced both types of unions.

From her mother, Elizabeth of York, who died in 1503 when Mary was seven or eight, she inherited the fair coloring and blue eyes of the Woodville women. But Mary was also a Tudor through and through, from her red-gold hair to her stubbornness and pride, her passion for luxury, her impatience and desire to impress, her willfulness, and her quick temper.

Mary grew to be tall, graceful, and fine-boned—one of Europe's most beautiful princesses, as well as one of its greatest pawns. Her first offer of marriage came when she was three years old, from the Duke of Milan, Ludovico Sforza, on behalf of his son. Although that proposal was rejected, in 1507, at the age of twelve, Mary was betrothed to Archduke Charles of Austria—the son of Joanna the Mad and Philip the Handsome—and the heir to the throne of Spain. A proxy wedding was conducted on December 1, 1508, and from then on, Mary was referred to as the Princess of Castile.

But the wedding plans were scotched when the boy's grand-fathers, Ferdinand of Aragon and the Holy Roman Emperor Maximilian—both of whom had been allied with England against the French—went behind Henry VII's back and signed a truce with France. Years later, on July 30, 1514, Mary was made to renounce her compact with Charles as Henry VIII, now King of England, repudiated the Hapsburg marriage his father had brokered for her. And on August 13, pursuant to a peace treaty negotiated a week earlier by Thomas Wolsey, Mary, "a nymph from heaven," was married instead by proxy to Louis XII, the decrepit, fifty-two-year-old French monarch—thereby allowing England to trump the Spanish ruler and the Holy Roman Emperor after all.

The ceremony was conducted in the Great Hall in Greenwich before the entire court and the wedding festivities proceeded as though the groom himself had been there. Among Louis's wedding gifts to his new bride was a portrait of himself (since Mary had never seen him), and a vast amount of plate and jewels, including "the Mirror of Naples," a diamond as long as a man's finger from which was suspended a pear-shaped pearl "the size of a pigeon's egg." After all the banqueting, the young bride was placed in the huge bed of estate, and Louis's proxy, the duc de Longueville, "consummated" the marriage on his sovereign's behalf by removing his red hose and touching one of Mary's bare legs with his own.

Mary would also bring a sizeable dowry to France, including 400,000 gold crowns—half in plate and jewelry and the balance representing the cost of equipping her for her new role. Aware of Louis's ill health, Henry VIII had insisted on a clause protecting England's investment: if Mary survived her husband and returned to England, then France was to refund the cost of her journey to Abbeville and Mary would retain the personal property she had brought to the marriage. The worth of her personal wardrobe alone was estimated at £43,000—nearly $30 million today.

On Louis's side of the Channel a proxy wedding was held on September 14. The following day he renewed his vow to pay a million crowns to England for Mary's hand, on pain of excommunication if he defaulted. Henry VIII had put a high price tag on his kid sister's womb—500,000 gold coins, in addition to the acquisition of three key port cities in France: St. Quentin, Boulogne, and Thérouanne.

On the Continent, the news of Mary's union with Louis was greeted with disgust. The Dutch were shocked "that a feeble, old, and pocky man should marry so fair a lady." And the Holy Roman Emperor feigned surprise that Mary should be sacrificed to "an impotent, indisposed, and so malicious prune." One reason Louis was so prematurely aged was that he had spent three years in prison during the 1480s after a failed attempt to form a regency on behalf of his imbecilic brother-in-law. An adventurous life and a rich diet hadn't helped.

Vis-à-vis Louis's infirmity, on October 2, as she prepared to embark from Dover, Mary reminded her brother of the promise she had extracted from him: that if she were to become widowed, she would choose her own husband the second time around. Wishing his kid sister *bon voyage*, Henry conveniently pretended he hadn't heard her.

Mary Tudor was Louis's third wife. In 1476 he had entered a dynastic union with his twelve-year-old second cousin, Jeanne of France. Claiming she was lame and hunchbacked and therefore incapable of conceiving, although Jeanne protested that he hadn't really tried, Louis managed to secure an annulment to marry Anne of Brittany, the widow of his predecessor, Charles VIII. Louis and Anne enjoyed a tolerably happy marriage, but their alliance was also strategic, bringing the vast and wealthy duchy of Brittany under French sovereignty. Louis's many reforms, which greatly eased the lives of his poorer subjects, earned him the nickname *Le Père du Peuple*—the father of his people—but he was unable to father any sons with his first two wives. Anne bore him two daughters, Claude and Renée, but because the succession in France was under Salic law, the crown could only pass to a male heir.

After Anne of Brittany died on January 9, 1514, Louis was keen to hop back into the matrimonial saddle as soon as possible. He was riddled with gout and a variety of other ailments, and since Anne's death had harbored presentiments of his own imminent demise. His elder daughter, the fifteen-year-old Claude, was wed that May to François d'Angoulême. That meant if Louis XII and Mary conceived no sons, upon Louis's death his son-in-law would become King of France.

Louis was so eager to catch a glimpse of his beautiful new bride that he flouted the strict court etiquette that prohibited a meeting in advance of their official introduction, staging a chance encounter during a hawking expedition.

Various descriptions of this event survive. The Italian-born chronicler Pietro Mártire d'Anghiera wrote that Louis was "perched elegantly" on a fine Spanish warhorse, "licking his lips and gulping his spittle" at the sight of the beauteous Mary in her jaunty cap of crimson satin. Pietro didn't hold out much hope for the king's health, however. "You may promise yourself five hundred autumns" if Louis lived to greet the spring, he wrote sardonically, adding, "What an old valetudinarian suffering from leprosy, can want with a handsome girl of eighteen." Pietro was kinder to Mary, describing her as beautiful and without artifice, noting that the French couldn't stop gazing at her because she looked "more like an angel than a human creature."

Responding to Louis's chivalrous mood, Mary blew him a kiss. The king returned the gesture and, still on horseback, "boldly threw his arms around her neck, and kissed her as kindly as if he had been five-and-twenty," wrote the Bishop of Asti, the French ambassador to Venice.

Mary and Louis's royal wedding—the third ceremony, but the first at which the bride and the groom were both present—took place in Abbeville, France, at nine a.m. on October 9, the feast day of St. Denis, the patron saint of France. Cardinal René de Prie, Bishop of Bayeux, officiated. The procession was led by pairs of knights, heralds, macers, and musicians, followed by the English lords and ladies. Mary wore a gown of gold brocade cut in the flattering French style. She was weighted down with jewelry, more as a show of wealth and worth than an effort to elegantly accessorize. Accentuated by her jeweled coronet, her abundant copper tresses cascaded down her back.

Louis's cloth of gold wedding ensemble cost 116 crowns per

yard; the fabric had been imported from Italy and the entire outfit, trimmed in sable, was said to be worth about £400 (about $272,000 today).

At the state dinner, Mary presided over the ladies' table in her own chamber. A formal ball followed later in the evening, "the whole court banqueting, dancing, and making good cheer." Louis was so enamored of his bride that he refused to quit her side. At eight p.m., Mary's new daughter-in-law, Claude, conveyed her to the bridal bed, which had already been prepared and blessed.

It was time to beget that son he'd been wanting. Hope sprang eternal in Louis's soul. The following morning the king was giddy as a lark, sporting a goofy expression of satiation and announcing that "he had performed marvels." An unidentified Italian noted that "thrice did he cross the river last night and would have done more had he chosen."

But François d'Angoulême—so close to the throne he could taste it—told his mother, the formidable Louise of Savoy, "I am certain, unless I have been greatly deceived, that it is impossible for the King and Queen to have children."

Still, others gave the impression that Mary might not have been as concerned about that little issue, even though it was her duty to bear an heir. "The queen does not mind that the king is a gouty old man . . . and she herself a young and beautiful damsel . . . so great is her satisfaction at being Queen of France," wrote Marino Sanuto in his *Diarii*, Volume XIX.

But in fact, the union had gotten off to a rocky start.

Mary's vast retinue of English attendants was a huge drain on Louis's Exchequer. And on October 12, just three days after her wedding, Mary fired off a letter of complaint to her brother, informing him that "on the morn after my marriage my chamberlain and all other men servants were discharged," as was "my mother Guildford [her former governess] with my other women and maidens except such as never had experience or knowledge how to advertise or give me counsel in any time of need, which is to be feared more shortly than your Grace thought at the time of my departing." Louis had suffered a severe attack of gout after their wedding night and Mary was convinced that he was already at death's door and she would be left bereft in a foreign land with only a handful of inexperienced teens to aid her. As things transpired, the young queen's timeline was not far off the mark.

But Louis remained adamant regarding the dismissal of Mary's English train. According to Henry VIII's Lord Chamberlain, the 1st Earl of Worcester, ". . . he said he is a sickly body and not at all times that [he would] be merry with his wife to have any strange [foreign] woman there, but one that he is well acquainted with [and before whom he] durst be merry." Worcester reported to Wolsey, "he swore there was never man better loved his wife than he did, but rather than have such a woman about her he had liefer be without her." It certainly would have been disastrous if the king was willing to forswear his wife's company because her old governess was hovering about like a shadow. So Guildford had to go.

Apart from this "bedchamber crisis," the royal couple enjoyed a cordial relationship. They spent many pleasant hours alone, Louis reclining on a couch while Mary entertained him by accompanying herself on the lute. He was a generous husband and a genteel companion. Although she would have preferred a different spouse (and she'd get there within the space of half a year), Mary told Henry, "How lovingly the King my husband dealeth with me," urging her brother to thank the ambassadors who had negotiated her marriage. Whatever she thought after dark, she did relish being queen of the most glamorous and cultivated court in Europe.

By custom an uncrowned Queen of France could not enter Paris, so Mary Rose Tudor, clad in gold and diamonds, was crowned at St. Denis on Sunday, November 5, 1514. To celebrate his wife's coronation, Louis hosted a five-day grand tournament, which included three days of competition between the English delegation, led by Charles Brandon, Duke of Suffolk, and the French team, captained by François d'Angoulême.

After the joust, Suffolk remained in France to fulfill an unspecified diplomatic obligation on Henry's behalf; his mission was such a secret that it was not referred to in any dispatch, for fear of interception. Mary's only role in these talks was to keep her husband receptive to Henry's overtures, which she evidently did with tact and grace, and the council accepted her presence. What none of them knew was that she'd long harbored a *tendre* for Brandon.

In December, Louis became gravely ill. The contemporary historian Robert de la Marck, Seigneur de Fleuranges, was convinced that a dotard's folly to please his nubile wife was the cause of his rapid decline, writing that

> The King . . . desired to be a pleasing companion with his wife; but he deceived himself, as he was not the man for it . . . inasmuch as he had for a long time been very sick, particularly with gout, and for five or six years he had thought that he would die of it . . . and he lived on a very strict diet which he broke when he was with his wife; and the doctors told him that if he continued he would die from his pleasure.

It's a view that historical novelists find too delicious to resist. And it was certainly true that Louis had been keeping late hours since his marriage to Mary, trying to act young and virile by overexerting himself in hunting, riding, and dancing. The Parisians believed their king had been tricked by the "young filly" Henry sent him. But the Earl of Worcester thought the king, though ailing, had never seemed happier. "My lord, I assure you, he hath a marvellous mind to content and please the queen," he wrote to Wolsey.

Mary sat by her husband's bedside every day, fending off sexual innuendo from Louis's son-in-law, François d'Angoulême, who was counting the minutes until he sat on the throne. She had a delicate path to negotiate. Although she had no intentions of entering François's bed, she couldn't afford to alienate or offend him, because she would be at his disposition when Louis died.

On December 28, 1514, Louis wrote to Henry, telling him that the queen "had hitherto conducted herself, and still does every day, towards me, in such manner that I cannot but be delighted with her, and love and honor her more and more each day; and you may be assured that I do, and ever shall, so treat her, as to give both you and her perfect satisfaction."

It was the last letter that Louis XII would ever write. Four days later, on New Year's Day 1515, he died. Mary, his wife of only eighty-two days, fainted at the news. But we can mourn Louis with a hint of gladness. Whatever killed him, he died happy and in love. His funeral was held at Notre Dame and he was laid to rest beside Anne of Brittany in St. Denis.

Louis's son-in-law, the twenty-year-old François d'Angoulême, now François I, was so eager to wear the crown that he shortened the official mourning period. But Mary, now Queen Dowager, got no reprieve from the ritual ascribed to widowed French queens. Clad head to toe in the white gauze mourning gown known as a *deuil blanc*, Mary was confined to an airless chamber in the Hôtel de Cluny for forty days. The walls were draped in black, and no light was permitted to penetrate. There, in the suffocating gloom, Mary was deliberately kept apart from society to ascertain whether she was pregnant—as well as to keep her from seducing another man in the hopes of fobbing off his child as Louis's heir. If Mary *were* carrying her late husband's child, it would take precedence over François because it would be a direct heir of the old king's body. And everyone would have to wait until the baby was born to know whether it (if a male) would be the next king, or (if it was a girl) whether François would inherit the throne after all. Therefore, any question of Mary's possible pregnancy had to be settled before his coronation.

The court chronicler Pierre de Brantôme, who clearly thought very little of Mary, wrote that she had been having such a grand time being Queen of France that she faked a pregnancy by wrapping towels around her waist and fainting in public; but that François's mother, Louise of Savoy, allegedly exposed the charade by demanding that Mary be examined by a physician. Although Mary briefly thought she might be pregnant, no other chronicler or person close to her has mentioned this ruse, and her behavior as Queen Dowager was invariably reported as dignified and discreet.

By February 10, Henry VIII was informed that "there is no truth to the rumor that the French Queen, that now is, is with child." He had dispatched a trio of ministers to sound out François's intentions toward maintaining his predecessor's strong relations with England. Although he was the least experienced diplomat of the three, the senior ranking member of the delegation was Charles Brandon, the Duke of Suffolk, earning that distinction because of his lofty title, in addition to his status as Henry's best friend and sports buddy. The men were also charged with inventorying Mary's valuables and escorting her safely back to England.

Mary was acutely aware that she was a political football, utterly at the mercy of the two kings. François was already scouting for future husbands on her behalf. If she refused his selections, she'd be stuck in France, a fate she hoped to avoid at all costs. Ignoring the fact that he was already married, the French monarch had also been flirting with her himself, urging her not to tell her brother or the ambassadors about it. But one day he began to change his tune, assuring Mary that he "would neither do her wrong, nor suffer her to take wrong of any other person."

François had noticed the undeniable spark between Mary and the Duke of Suffolk. And when she confessed that she had always "been of good mind" toward Brandon, the French king decided to become their advocate. Playing Cupid, he assured Mary he would put in a good word with Henry on their behalf. He was hardly being altruistic; it was good for France if Mary married one of her own, since another foreign marriage might tip the balance of world power in England's favor.

No sooner had Suffolk arrived in France than François accused him of crossing the Channel with the express purpose of wedding the dowager queen. The duke immediately denied it, assuring François,

"I trust your grace would not reckon so great folly in me to come unto a strange realm to marry the Queen of the realm without your knowledge and without authority from my Master, and that I have not nor was it ever intended on my Master's part nor on mine."

So, during the first week in February 1515, Suffolk reported to Henry the details of this delicate conversation with François and made a clean breast of things to Wolsey as well. Henry praised Suffolk's handling of the matter and even granted him a passel of lands as a reward. Wolsey informed Suffolk of the "King's continued friendship in the accomplishment of the said marriage," adding that "his Grace marvelously rejoiced to hear of your good speed in the same, and how substantially and discreetly ye ordered and handled yourself in your words and communication with the said French king, when he first secretly broke with you of the said marriage." Wolsey also urged the duke to make sure that François kept his promise to write to Henry in support of the marriage.

Now, all of this sounds like everything was rosy. But Henry and Wolsey were not men to be taken at face value. For his advocacy of the marriage to Mary, Wolsey wanted a quid pro quo from Suffolk—the duke's intercession with Henry in garnering him the plum appointment as Bishop of Tournai, a lucrative sinecure on the Continent.

And it was important for Henry to get Mary back to England so that François didn't score a diplomatic coup by uniting her to a husband who would benefit France. Henry may have figured that his sanctioning of Mary's marriage to Suffolk would cut François out of the picture, and then, once the couple was back on English soil, he could have the betrothal annulled and bestow his sister's hand on a husband of his choosing.

But Mary reminded her brother that "whereas for the good of peace and for the furtherance of your affairs, ye moved me to marry . . . King Louis of France . . . though I understood that he was very aged and sickly . . . and for the furtherance of your causes I was contented . . . so that if I should . . . survive the said late king I might with good will marry myself at my liberty without your displeasure. . . . Upon . . . your faithful promise, I assented to the said marriage; else I would never have [agreed to it] . . . , as at the same time I showed unto you more at large"—presumably her attraction to Suffolk.

She added a postscript advising Henry that if he refused to honor his promise, then François would surely broker another marriage for her. Several European princes, including the Holy Roman Emperor, had already made their pitch. "I would rather be out of the world than it should so happen," she stated dramatically.

And she assured her brother that she had been the instigator in her relationship with Suffolk. "Now that God hath called my late husband to his mercy and . . . I am at liberty, dearest brother, remembering the great virtues which I have seen . . . in my Lord of Suffolk, to whom I have always been of good mind, as ye well know, I have affixed and clearly determined to marry with him; and the same, I assure you, hath proceeded only of mine own mind, without any request . . . of my said Lord of Suffolk."

When Suffolk arrived in France in early February 1515, Mary was still enduring her mourning quarantine and was lonely and homesick. Desperate and distressed, she poured out her heart to him. Reporting to Henry, Suffolk broke the news as gently as he could manage, opening his letter with the highlights of his mission, his conversations with the French king, and his success at recovering Mary's valuables on behalf of the English crown. Then he tiptoed into the treacherous territory of his marriage to Mary, informing Henry that at their first private meeting a few weeks earlier, Mary had confessed her love for him and her determination not to wed anyone but him. Terrified that she'd be fobbed off on a husband from the Netherlands or France, the queen told Suffolk "that she would rather be torn to pieces" than never see England again. "Sir, I never saw woman so weep," the duke assured his sovereign.

However, Mary suspected Suffolk of being party to a plot to lure her home so that Henry could immediately ship her overseas again into the arms of another unwanted groom. There was only one way he could prove otherwise, the duke explained to Henry VIII in a letter. "She swore she would never have me nor never come to England" if he did not wed her at once—before they were due to sail.

Shortly afterward, Mary and Suffolk were secretly wed by an unknown priest in the Cluny Chapel in Paris. A few of Mary's servants stood as witnesses.

As canny as he was, Henry had not anticipated that the lovers would actually marry in France, presenting him with a fait accompli that would be awkward and embarrassing to undo.

Mary knew she'd taken a rash and potentially dangerous step. But she also knew her brother and counted on his love for her to win his forgiveness—after the requisite displays of the famous Tudor temper. She also reckoned on Wolsey's advocacy because he needed Suffolk's support in the Privy Council.

So who was this man for whom Mary had risked so much?

The Brandon family had an illustrious relationship with the Tudors. Charles's father, Sir William Brandon, had been Henry's father's standard-bearer, and had paid the ultimate price for his service to the crown when he was killed by Richard III during the Battle of Bosworth Field.

Charles Brandon, who was said to resemble Henry so much that some people thought he was the king's "bastard brother," was one of Henry's favorite courtiers. He owed his rapid rise in society to his unique status as Henry's childhood companion. They were cohorts as well as competitors; no two youths were as skilled at jousting, single combat, tennis, riding, dancing, and the other physical activities they enjoyed. Six or seven years Henry's senior, Brandon was bold, enterprising, and ruthlessly ambitious. "A liberal and magnificent lord," wrote a Venetian visitor to the English court. "No one ever bore so vast a rise with so easy a dignity."

Charles Brandon was also a ladies' man. Sometime before 1505, he had made a verbal commitment known as a *de praesenti* marriage (not much more than a handfasting), with a young woman named Anne Browne, who bore him a daughter. He then repudiated the marriage in order to marry Anne's older, wealthy aunt, Margaret Mortimer. Tiring of Margaret, he appealed to Rome for an annulment of their marriage on the grounds of consanguinity, then wed Anne Browne again in a formal ceremony, and they had a second daughter.

But Anne left him a widower in 1512. That December, Brandon purchased the wardship of eight-year-old Elizabeth Grey, the daughter of Sir John Grey, Viscount Lisle, with the intention of wedding her when she came of age in four years; and it was for this reason that in 1513 Henry had created his pal Viscount Lisle, acknowledging little Elizabeth as his wife in the letters patent granting the title. Henry made Brandon a Knight of the Garter and Master of the Horse, and the new viscount distinguished himself in battle during the king's campaigns in France that summer.

Brandon's union with Elizabeth Grey was never consummated, and as part of Suffolk's punishment for marrying Mary without his permission, Henry revoked the wardship. Brandon's other title had been bestowed in anticipation of a wedding as well. Henry had made him Duke of Suffolk in February 1514 to groom him for another match that never went anywhere—with Margaret of Austria, the daughter of the Holy Roman Emperor Maximilian.

Brandon's rise through the ranks of the peerage had many nobles from older and more established families bristling. There were only three dukes in England at the time: Norfolk (the uncle of the Boleyn girls and Kathryn Howard), Suffolk, and the Duke of Buckingham—who wore his disgust on his damasked sleeve, sneeringly commenting that the new duke "was not of a very noble lineage."

At the time he eloped with Mary in early 1515, Suffolk was thirty-two years old, a handsome man in the prime of life. He had risked his sovereign's displeasure—and possibly his head—to wed the eighteen- or nineteen-year-old Mary. It was not so much the *fact* of their marriage that Henry objected to so violently, but that the lovers had wed in secret and without his permission.

By February 20, people were already discussing the scandal. The actual date of the clandestine wedding in the Cluny Chapel remains unknown, but it must have occurred fairly early in February, because by the beginning of March Mary suspected she might be pregnant.

The bridegroom felt guilty after the match had been consummated and confessed as much to Wolsey. "The Queen would never let me rest till I had granted her to be married. And so, to be plain with you, I have married her heartily, and have lain with her insomuch I fear . . . she be with child." To Henry he wrote, "Sir, for the passion of God, let it not be in your heart against me, and rather than you should hold me in mistrust, strike off my head and let me not live."

Although her fears of pregnancy turned out to be a false alarm, Mary and Suffolk had a second wedding ceremony in March. Sanctioned by a bishop, it was public enough to cover the couple's collective derrières.

After receiving Suffolk's admission regarding the consummation of his marriage to Mary, Wolsey went straight to the king. Henry unleashed the royal wrath. There would be no approval of the match and no forgiveness. Writing to Suffolk on the king's behalf, Wolsey delivered the coup de grace. "Ye have failed to him which hath brought you up of low degree to be of this great honour; and that ye were the man in all the world he loved and trusted best. . . . Ye put yourself in the greatest danger that ever man was in."

Although Wolsey had informed Suffolk that there was no chance of clemency, he did mention that there might be a remedy—the only remedy: money. Henry had been hit in the purse by the newlyweds' disobedience. And he demanded restitution. The financial penalty for the Duke and Duchess of Suffolk was enormous. Reimbursement for Mary's dowry, which had been forfeited to France, amounted to £200,000, worth six hundred times that sum in today's dollars. Compensation for the plate and jewels that Louis had bestowed on her was an additional line item. And to repay Henry for the remaining expenses, including the vast sum spent on her wedding to the French king, Suffolk was to tender another thousand pounds per annum for the next twenty-four years.

Suffolk had managed to negotiate the return of Mary's plate and most of her jewels from François, as well as 200,000 gold crowns in restitution of half her marriage portion, 20,000 gold crowns of which were reimbursement for her travel expenses from England to Abbeville. But every bit of it was immediately tendered to Henry upon their return to English soil. Mary retained her jointure from her marriage to Louis, but the revenues from those lands would be passed along to her brother as well. Her final use of her official seal as Queen of France was to make over every shred of her property and possessions to Henry.

On April 16, 1515, the newlyweds left Paris for Calais, then an English stronghold on the Continent. Mary retained the courtesy title of "the French Queen" for the rest of her life, but from then on would be known as the Duchess of Suffolk. They sailed for Dover on May 2, exactly seven months from the date of Mary's departure for France. In that time she'd had more weddings than husbands. Apparently placated by his enormous payoff, Henry welcomed the couple back to England, and on May 13, their nuptials were solemnized for a third time, before the entire court assembled at Greenwich. Although the ceremonies were modest, it was a triumph of true love.

Emotionally, Henry had forgiven them, but the Suffolks were to feel the financial sting of His Majesty's displeasure for the rest of their marriage, frequently unable to make ends meet, which often precluded their appearance at court. Although the duke was cash poor, he was among the kingdom's largest landowners, and Henry had confiscated none of his property. In fact, within a few weeks of Suffolk's return to England, he was granted a stewardship of crown land that brought with it an annuity; and by the end of the year Henry awarded him additional land and possessions worth £500 (more than $337,000 today), and cancelled £5,000 of the duke's £24,000 debt to him.

The official line from the palace was that the kingdom rejoiced at the royal marriage. Certainly, Henry had not remained livid for long.

But foreign ambassadors detected a different mood—which might have been propaganda contrived for the benefit of their respective sovereigns, or simply a misunderstanding of events. The Venetians weren't sure whether to congratulate the bridal couple because the wedding celebration had been so low-key, and no public demonstrations (such as pageants) had followed the ceremony.

Even an English chronicler, Edward Hall, wrote:

> Against this marriage many men grudged and said that it was a great loss to the realm that she was not married to the Prince of Castile [Archduke Charles of Austria, the future King of Spain]; but the wisest sort was content, considering that if she had been married again out of the realm, she should have carried much riches with her; and now she brought every year into the realm nine or ten thousand marks [her dower revenues as Dowager Queen of France]. But whatsoever the rude people said, the Duke behaved himself so that he had both the favour of the king and of the people.

On March 11, 1516, the first of Mary and Suffolk's three children was born—a son named Henry. The king and Wolsey were his godfathers. The Brandons' two daughters, Frances and Eleanor, were born in 1517 and 1519 or '20, respectively.

Mary and Suffolk did not become permanent fixtures at Henry's court, preferring the relative sanity and solitude of the duke's estates, particularly Westhorpe Hall, Suffolk's country seat. Yet the duke's power and influence remained as strong as ever, particularly as he was now the king's brother-in-law. Suffolk was one of the diplomats present at the Field of Cloth of Gold summit between Henry and François I in 1520, where he might have first caught a glimpse of Anne Boleyn, in the train of Queen Claude. He could not have known at the time that the young lady-in-waiting with the dark eyes and sallow complexion would cause a rift with his own wife, and a strained relationship between Mary and her brother.

Mary came to court as infrequently as possible after Anne became Henry's mistress, and she sympathized with Katherine of Aragon during the protracted Great Matter. Because of her rank, Mary could get away with voicing her strong negative opinions of Anne, though Henry didn't have to like them. In 1532, she was heard using "opprobrious language" about Anne that literally sparked violence between her husband's men and those of Anne's uncle, the Duke of Norfolk. Two of Norfolk's men, the Southwell brothers, murdered Suffolk's retainer, Sir William Pennington, as the knight sought sanctuary in Westminster Abbey. Suffolk then "remove[d] the assailants by force" from holy ground.

The court went into an uproar over the incident. Suffolk and Mary retreated to their country estate, but the mood at Whitehall remained so tense that Henry had to smooth things over by riding out to speak with Suffolk directly, and fining one of the Southwells the whopping sum of a thousand pounds (nearly $600,000 today).

At the same time the validity of Henry's marriage to Katherine was being scrutinized in Rome, the Suffolks' union was under papal review. Mary had prodded her husband into securing an airtight acknowledgment of its legitimacy following an incident in which his surviving ex-wife, Margaret Mortimer, had begged for his assistance on a real estate matter. The legality of Suffolk's marriage to Margaret rested on the adequacy of the original authorization for it—a papal dispensation that had been declared invalid by an English court in 1507. Fortunately for Mary, Margaret Mortimer died in early 1528, and Wolsey correctly assumed that the Pope had bigger fish to fry. A May 12, 1528, papal bull issued at Orvieto proclaimed Suffolk's divorce from Margaret to be valid, and ratified his subsequent marriage to Anne Browne. As Anne was also dead, and Suffolk was a widower when he wed Mary Tudor, much to Mary's relief her marriage to the duke was declared to be completely legal.

Whether Rome would proclaim Henry's marriage to Katherine invalid, leaving him free to wed Anne Boleyn, was another matter. Suffolk didn't think much of Anne, either, and as late as May 1530, imperial ambassador Chapuys reported that the duke had been banished from court for warning Henry of Anne's unsuitability to be queen.

Yet, when all was said and done, Suffolk was a loyal courtier, supporting the king in all he sought. He became enough of a proponent of Anne's to remain in Henry's good graces, although he felt awful about some of the unpleasant tasks the king assigned him, such as displacing Katherine of Aragon and dismissing her train. But with one stroke of Henry's pen an Act of Attainder could wipe away all the honors and titles and accumulated wealth and property that the king had bestowed upon him. So he clenched his fists and sucked it up when, upon Anne's coronation in 1533, Henry replaced him in the office of Earl Marshal with his archrival, Anne's uncle, the Duke of Norfolk. From then on, Mary pointedly refused to come to court at all.

She fell dangerously ill that June, and in her dying wishes sought reconciliation with her brother. In her last letter to Henry, she wrote that "the sight of Your Grace is the greatest comfort to me that may be possible." But her illness was a mere footnote amid the weeks of festivity surrounding Anne's coronation. Suffolk hurried back to her sickbed with Henry's reply to her sad little letter, in which the king offered his forgiveness and reconciled her to the royal bosom.

Mary died at Westhorpe Hall on June 25 at the age of thirty-seven. First interred in the abbey at Bury St. Edmunds, in 1784 her corpse was moved to St. Mary's Church.

Suffolk wasted little time in remarrying. On September 7, 1533, the same day as the birth of Anne Boleyn's daughter, the Princess Elizabeth, the forty-eight-year-old duke took a fourth wife—his barely fourteen-year-old ward Katherine Willoughby, the daughter of Katherine of Aragon's trusted friend and lady-in-waiting Maria de Salinas. She had been betrothed to his son, Henry, the 1st Earl of Lincoln, but when the lusty duke became widowed, he broke his son's contract to marry Katherine himself, exercising his *droit du seigneur*, so to speak. The scandal it created was not over the age difference between the groom and his new bride, or even their relative haste to the altar, but over the sordidness of the family dynamic. Henry Brandon, who passed away on March 8, 1534, just three days shy of his eighteenth birthday, was said to have died of a broken heart over his father's betrayal. Although he had been ill for some time, it didn't stop certain tongues from wagging. Anne Boleyn remarked tartly, "My Lord of Suffolk kills one son to beget another."

But the marriage turned out to be a great success, and Katherine grew up to be a passionate Reformer, one of the strongest advocates of the burgeoning Protestant faith.

For his role in supporting Henry VIII in the Great Matter and in the subsequent dissolution of the monasteries, Suffolk was greatly rewarded, receiving a share of the confiscated lands. He also remained a trusted military commander. Back in 1523, Henry had dispatched him to Calais as Marshal of the King's Army. Suffolk's troops invaded France, routing the French at the Battle of the Spurs. In 1544, the sixty-year-old Suffolk was sent back to the Continent to command the forces that besieged Boulogne.

While the court was in Guilford, Suffolk died unexpectedly on August 24, 1545, at the age of sixty-two. The cause of death is unknown; however, since it came quite quickly, it was possibly the result of a heart attack or stroke, rather than an illness.

Henry VIII's last will and testament made in 1546 stipulated that Mary's heirs should take precedence in the line of succession before those of his older sister Margaret, the Dowager Queen of Scotland. Little did he know that his only son, Edward VI, would die young and without issue, and that the boy would declare his half sisters Mary and Elizabeth illegitimate and therefore ineligible to inherit the crown.

In October 1536, the Suffolks' oldest daughter, Frances Brandon, the wife of Henry Grey and Marchioness of Dorset, had given birth to a daughter whom she named for Henry's queen, Jane Seymour. Jane Grey would wear the crown before either of Henry's daughters did so. But on July 19, 1554, this granddaughter of Mary and Suffolk known as "the Nine Days' Queen" would lose her head in the struggle for succession engendered by the death of Edward VI. Poor Jane Grey would be succeeded on the English throne by Mary, the daughter of Henry and Katherine of Aragon.

In the annals of royal marriages, that of Mary and Charles stands out as a monument not only to true love, but to tenacity. We'll never know how things might have transpired had Charles Brandon not been Henry's boon companion; but when all was said and done, a princess of England rejected the role of royal pawn, stuck to her guns, and made one of history's greatest autocrats keep a promise he surely had never intended to honor, thereby choosing her own happiness and charting her own destiny. Sometimes there's much to be said for that Tudor stubborn streak.

Henry VIII

❧ *and* ❧

Anne Boleyn

("The Most Happy")

1500(?)–1536

married 1533–1536

"... Never a prince had a wife more loyal in all duty, and in all true affection, than you have ever found in Anne Boleyn. ..."
—Anne to Henry

*S*HE IS UNDOUBTEDLY THE MOST INFLUENTIAL QUEEN consort in British history, and she would never have been queen at all had her marriage to Henry VIII not been the result of the most famous divorce in the world. As calculating as she was captivating, equal parts sharp and subtle, both virtuous and vindictive, Anne Boleyn was a legend in her own lifetime and her allure remains as evergreen as the *Château Vert*, the fantasy castle of wood and tinfoil whose battlements Henry stormed on the day she bewitched his heart.

Anne Boleyn was the younger daughter of Elizabeth Howard and the ambitious ambassador and diplomat Sir Thomas Boleyn. She was not a conventional beauty like her sister, Mary, who was

buxom, blond, and blue-eyed—the first of the Boleyn girls to capti-
vate the king. Slender, auburn-haired, and sallow-complected, Anne
was of middling stature; her features were angular and fine, though
her mouth was considered wide; and her bosom "was not much
raised"—according to the Venetian ambassador, who evidently got
close enough to evaluate it. Anne's detractors delighted in depicting
her as deformed, with warts all over her body, a huge wen or mole
on her throat (she was described as having a large Adam's apple, but
the wen was a gross exaggeration that seemed to grow with the telling of the tale), and a sixth finger on her left hand. Anne probably
had a vestigial extra nail on her left pinky, but if she had been even
a tenth as malformed as her enemies painted her, the persnickety
Henry, with his discerning eye for beauty, would never have looked
twice at her, let alone moved heaven and earth to wed her.

Anne spent her teenage years first as an attendant to the Archduchess Margaret of Austria at the Burgundian court in the Netherlands, followed by six or seven years at the French court, initially
in the train of Queen Mary, the younger sister of Henry VIII. In
1521, she was recalled to England, possibly because her father
wished to arrange her marriage to a distant cousin, Sir James Butler, Earl of Ormonde, which would have brought Ormonde's wealth
and title into their immediate family.

In the meantime, Anne was placed in Queen Katherine's household. Her ambition was abetted by a canny mind, a lively intellect,
and a quick wit. Some years after Anne's death, a recusant writer
claimed that she'd be remembered as "the model and the mirror of
those who were at court, for she was always well dressed, and every
day made some change in the fashion of her garments." Anne did
indeed have a love of finery, but more important, she was conscious
of projecting an *image*—practicing the politics of ostentation,
which her daughter Elizabeth would eventually raise to an art
form. Anne's cosmopolitan sophistication, her facility with languages, and her skilled repartee made her one of the most popular
young women at court, and she soon had several admirers.

By 1522, she had entranced the handsome courtier Henry Percy, the son and heir of the powerful Earl of Northumberland. Although it was later vehemently denied, the two of them may have entered into a secret precontract of marriage, which in the Tudor era would have been as valid as a marriage itself. To violate a precontract by consorting with—or marrying—another, was tantamount to adultery or bigamy. At the time he met Anne, Percy had already been precontracted to Lady Mary Talbot, the daughter of the vastly wealthy Earl of Shrewsbury. So, Cardinal Wolsey—possibly at the instigation of the king—instructed Anne and Percy to sever their ties and Percy was sent back to marry Mary.

Initially angry and disappointed, by the middle of 1525, Anne, whose "excellent gesture and behavior did excel all other," was in her mid-twenties and had utterly captivated the king with her wit, her grace, and her dark, exotic looks. But not until the Shrovetide merriment in 1526 did people begin to discern the infatuation that Henry had secretly harbored for nearly a year, scarcely daring to confess it to the object herself. Henry was then thirty-five years old, in the seventeenth year of his reign, still vigorous, handsome, and athletically built.

It was not long before Henry asked Anne to be his lover, but her reply took him by surprise. "I would rather lose my life than my honesty," she told the king. "Your wife I cannot be . . . your mistress I will not be."

But Henry would not be deterred, courting her with poetry, love letters, and jewelry. Like an infatuated schoolboy, he designed an emblem with their initials entwined, and the motto *aultre ne cherse*—I seek no other. The pair of them "passed notes" during mass in the royal chapel, defacing a Book of Hours with their scribbles. Below the image of the bloodstained Man of Sorrows, Henry wrote, "If you remember my love in your prayers as strongly as I adore you, I shall hardly be forgotten." He signed it "Henry R forever."

And beneath a detailed miniature of the Annunciation, Anne replied with a rhyming couplet:

By daily proof you shall me find
To be to you both loving and kind.

The royal affair remained a secret for several months, until the foreign ambassadors got wind of it, and soon it was the buzz throughout the court and across the kingdom. On May 15, 1527, Henry and Anne first appeared together as a couple at a reception hosted at Greenwich Palace to honor the French ambassador. Two days later, Cardinal Wolsey opened the secret trial in what came to be known as the King's Great Matter, which Henry fully expected to result in a swift declaration of nullity of his marriage to Katherine of Aragon.

Henry required two separate decisions from Rome: permission to divorce Katherine, and permission to marry Anne—which would include an additional papal dispensation to ignore the issue of the first degree of affinity, because Henry had slept with Anne's sister.

In the early months of 1527, even before Henry had taken any action to secure an annulment or divorce, Anne—one of a group of powerfully placed individuals who championed religious reform— found scholars and theologians to support their theories. She read Henry passages from William Tyndale's *Obedience of a Christian Man*, which argued that a king should be head of the Church in his own country. Anne's encouragement of Henry to break with the Church of Rome eventually led to the British monarch being the Head of the Church of England.

But as time wore on, Anne grew disgusted with the sympathy Katherine was engendering, not merely from the public but from Henry himself, who was growing tired of the fight and anxious about the enemies it was making. Anne feared that he might abandon the Great Matter and return to Katherine after all. By then, she was nearly thirty years old, middle-aged in Tudor terms, and made it very clear to Henry that she might have already sacrificed the best years of her life: "I have been waiting long and might in the meanwhile have contracted some advantageous marriage out of which I might have had issue, which is the greatest consideration in the world, but alas! Farewell to my time and youth spent to no purpose at all."

In December 1530, after Pope Clement VII demanded that Henry dismiss his mistress from court while the matter of the dispensation remained under judicial review, the king pressed Parliament even harder to pass an act that had been under discussion since November 3, 1529, which would grant him supreme leadership of the Church in England. Finally, on February 11, 1531, following a secret meeting between Thomas Cromwell and the Archbishop of Canterbury, William Warham, Henry was acknowledged "Supreme Head of the Church, in so far as the Law of Christ allows."

Anne was ecstatic, "as if she had actually gained Paradise," it was reported.

"Paradise," however, was still a long way off. In the summer of 1532 Anne's old flame Henry Percy, now the Earl of Northumberland, angrily told Mary Talbot during one of their frequent marital squabbles that she was not his wife because he'd previously been legally contracted to Anne Boleyn. This news flash got as far as Anne herself, who immediately shared it with Henry. The king summoned Percy to London, where he was interrogated by a pair of bishops; and in the presence of Anne's father and Henry's two canon lawyers, the earl swore on the Blessed Sacrament that he'd had no precontract with Anne.

By now, Anne's arrogance was testing the patience of her own flesh and blood. According to his wife, who gleefully relayed the information to Katherine of Aragon, the Duke of Norfolk had privately admitted that Anne would be the ruin of the Howards. Henry's support began to hemorrhage, as even his closest advisers feared the potential economic and financial damage to England if Charles V closed off her routes to Spain and the Netherlands as punishment for Henry's casting aside his aunt Katherine.

Mario Savorgnano, a Venetian who visited England soon after Henry's separation from Katherine, observed, "There is now living with him a young woman of noble birth, though many say of bad character, whose will is law to him, and he is expected to marry her, should the divorce take place, which it is supposed will not be effected, as the peers of the realm, both spiritual and temporal, and the people are opposed to it."

One of those people anonymously sent Anne a crude drawing of three figures intended to represent herself, Henry, and Katherine. Summoning her lady-in-waiting Anne Gainsford, she called, "Come hither, Nan, see here a book of prophecy; this he saith is the king, this the queen, and this is myself with my head off."

Mistress Gainsford was said to have replied, "If I thought it true, though he were an emperor, I would not myself marry him with that condition."

"Yes, Nan," sighed Anne, "I think the book a bauble, yet for the hope I have that the realm may be happy by my issue, I am resolved to have him whatsoever might become of me."

For some time Anne had harbored a sense of foreboding. But instead of resigning herself to it, she had all but enthusiastically embraced it. Back in 1530, when Henry had reminded her how many enemies she had made him and how much she therefore owed him for his resoluteness, Anne had retorted, "That matters not, for it is foretold in ancient prophesies that at this time a queen shall be burnt. But even if I were to suffer a thousand deaths, my love for you will not abate one jot."

In 1532, plans were under way for a continental summit meeting between Henry and François I, but for Anne to be able to accompany Henry she would have to be a person of rank. Her appearance itself would need to be delicately negotiated, as she was not yet his wife.

So on September 1, in a pomp-filled ceremony at Windsor Castle, Henry created Anne Marquess of Pembroke, using the male form of address for the title, a common custom in Tudor times, although making a woman a peer in her own right was anything but common then. Equally unusual was the clause assigning the remainder to Anne's offspring, whether or not they were legitimate. But even with her new title, Lady Pembroke would have to meet the king in Calais after the official diplomatic mission had been concluded. Still, Anne made the best of it, and at François's court (where she had spent her teenage years as a lady-in-waiting to Mary Tudor and then to Mary's successor, Queen Claude), she was treated like the prodigal daughter, fawned over and admired, with a retinue of English noblewomen at her beck and call that included her sister, Mary—and a mild-mannered blonde named Jane Seymour.

Following the festivities, while most of their attendants returned to England, Anne and Henry spent a fortnight in Calais enjoying a romantic idyll that resembled a honeymoon. Rumors circulated that the couple exchanged vows. Anne finally surrendered her body to Henry and they made love for the first time since the king's infatuation with her had sparked nearly seven years earlier. As a point of law their intercourse validated their "marriage," on the assumption that Henry's union with Katherine would eventually be nullified. Regardless of whether their coupling was enjoyable, it was certainly fruitful, for by the end of the first week of December 1532, Anne was pregnant.

Like all brides, particularly those who feel as though they've waited a lifetime for the Big Day, Anne Boleyn wanted a big showy wedding—at Westminster Abbey. It didn't quite happen the way she'd dreamed, but at least, after so many years of judicial wrangling, it *happened*. In Whitehall Palace on St. Paul's Day, January 25, 1533, Anne and Henry were secretly wed at dawn in the upper chamber over the Holbein Gate. The king lied outright to Dr. Rowland Lee, the cleric traditionally believed to have been their officiant, claiming that he had a document from the Pope giving him permission to marry again. But Henry refused to produce the paper, testily insisting, "If I should now that it waxeth towards day, fetch it, and be seen so early abroad, there would rise a rumor and talk thereof other than were convenient." He commanded the celebrant to "Go forth in God's name and do that which appertaineth to you." Henry was *not* legally divorced according to the Church of Rome, but in the king's mind he had never been legally married to Katherine, and therefore, he was a bachelor, free to wed whomsoever he chose.

Anne was now Henry's "most dear and well-beloved wife." But in wedding her he destroyed the delicate foreign policy he had so recently forged with François the previous autumn. Regardless of his appreciation of Anne's numerous charms, the French king had been adamantly against Henry's marriage to her.

By mid-February, Anne felt the urge to flaunt her delicate condition, announcing in company that she had "a fearsome and unquenchable longing to eat apples." Henry remarked that it was a sure sign she was pregnant, to which Anne responded she "was sure [she] was not," with a silvery peal of laughter. She exited the room without another word; eyewitnesses were shocked by her lack of discretion.

Anne appeared for the first time as Queen of England on Easter Sunday, April 12. "All the world is astonished at it, and even those who take her part do not know whether to laugh or to cry," wrote Eustache Chapuys, the imperial ambassador.

On May 23, Archbishop Cranmer reached his decision on the Great Matter, with the assent of the learned divines of the court. Henry's marriage to Katherine of Aragon was "null and absolutely void," and "contrary to divine law." Five days later, from a gallery in Lambeth Palace, the archbishop declared Henry's marriage to Anne "good and valid." Anne was now Henry's legal bride and the child she carried in her womb would be legitimate.

Cranmer was about to crown the king's pregnant new wife, but despite the fact that he and Anne were England's keenest supporters of reform, he wasn't altogether comfortable about it. As archbishop, he was technically the Pope's legate and not the king's servant. Therefore, Cranmer felt obligated to threaten Henry with excommunication if the monarch didn't "put away" Katherine—who still considered herself Henry's wife and queen.

So Henry shoved a history-making law through Parliament called the Act of Restraint of Appeals, which proclaimed England "an empire governed by one supreme head and king," who answered to no one but God for his actions. It was also made an act of treason to write or speak against his marriage to Anne, and all adult males were forced to uphold it.

Anne's household now numbered two hundred retainers and attendants, liveried in her chosen colors of purple and blue, embroidered with the motto *La plus heureuse*—"the most happy."

Preparations then began in earnest for the four-day coronation celebration. Cloth of gold adorned Anne's burgeoning figure as she sailed in state up the Thames from Greenwich on May 29, 1533, in a richly appointed barge accompanied by a flotilla of fifty other vessels sponsored by the kingdom's various mercantile and crafts guilds. At the Tower of London, Henry greeted her with great pomp and the royal couple spent the next two nights celebrating under its battlements. The next time Anne would be conveyed to the Tower, it would be under distinctly less glamorous and celebratory circumstances.

Unfortunately, Anne's official progress through London was somewhat marred by the banners that lined the streets, emblazoning the entwined initials of the monarch and his new queen consort. *HA HA* they read, and the public loved the unintentional joke on Anne.

On June 1, Whitsuntide, the six-months-pregnant Anne was crowned queen at Westminster Abbey. She wore an ermine-trimmed mantle of violet-colored velvet with a high starched ruff. The folds of her gown cleverly concealed her condition. According to tradition, the king did not attend the coronation. Greeting Anne afterward at Westminster, Henry asked her, "How liked you the City, sweetheart?"

The new queen replied, "Sir, the City itself was well enow, but I saw so many caps on heads and heard few tongues."

Henry had pulled out all the stops to give his new wife a spectacular celebration. But very few people would have been described as enthusiastic about Anne's coronation. According to a contemporary witness to events, "The initiatives of the gentlemen and lords were notable as the English sought, unceasingly, to honour their new princess. Not, I believe, because they wanted to, but in order to comply with the wishes of their king. The lords and ladies set to dances, sports of various kinds, hunting expeditions, and pleasures without parallel."

As spring turned to summer, the royal couple was in high spirits as they awaited the birth of the son they had so long desired. Anne had endured a difficult pregnancy, particularly in her final months. The king was so anxious about her health that it was said he'd welcome a miscarriage if it would save Anne's life.

Henry had confided to François I that he had to have a son "for the quiet repose and tranquility of our realm." He'd already chosen the baby names, expressing a preference for Edward or, of course, Henry. However, at three p.m. on September 7, 1533, Anne gave birth to a flame-haired daughter, whom the monarchs named Elizabeth after both of their mothers.

Because of Anne's rough pregnancy, Henry's initial reaction was relief that both mother and child were healthy, followed briefly by delight that his daughter's coloring was identical to his own. But he could not conceal his overall disappointment at the birth of a girl.

Nor, at the outset, could Anne. Her fortune had risen as far as it ever would, reaching its zenith on September 6, 1533, the day before Elizabeth's birth. Within the space of a year, Anne had become a marquess, the king's wife, the Queen of England, and the mother of the heir to the throne—but when that heir turned out to be a girl, her star plummeted. For all Anne's education, culture, and wit, she was already failing in the one job requirement of a royal consort: she could not bear Henry VIII a son.

Henry cancelled the joust and the other grand celebrations that had been set to take place upon the birth of his son. He had been so sure Anne would give him a boy—she had practically guaranteed it—that the formal documents had been drawn up with the word "Prince" on them. All that was lacking was the insertion of the heir's name and date of birth. Henry seethed as "ss" was added to every announcement.

By September 1534, Anne was several months pregnant again, her "goodly belly" a subject of discussion since April 27. As a precautionary measure to protect the well-being of both mother and child, it was common custom for a king to refrain from bedding his pregnant wife, and rarely did a sovereign remain celibate during those long months of prescribed absence from his spouse.

Although Henry had sacrificed much to wed Anne, he was no exception, and she was unable to contain her jealousy over his little infatuations and dalliances with her ladies-in-waiting. "Coldness and grumbling" characterized their arguments. Chapuys reported that the king had renewed his interest in one of Anne's maids of honor. Naturally, Anne wanted the girl dismissed. But Henry testily informed his wife that "she had good reason to be content with what he had done for her, which he would not do again, if he were starting afresh. . . ." During one of their frequent lovers' quarrels, when Anne complained about Henry's infidelities using "certain words" that he disliked, according to Chapuys, he advised her to "shut her eyes and endure, just like others who were worthier than she, and that she ought to know that he could humiliate her in only a moment longer than it had taken to exalt her!"

Henry might have lashed out in anger at Anne, but at the same time he was instructing Thomas Cromwell to draft the statute that would make their children his heirs. In November 1534, Parliament passed the Act Respecting the Oath to the Succession, which required all adult males to take an oath recognizing Anne as Henry's lawful wife and their children as the legitimate heirs to the throne. Anyone refusing to take the oath was guilty of treason.

Anne was in her mid-thirties during her second pregnancy in 1534, and Henry was forty-three. To their mutual consternation, she miscarried the fetus, and both of them were desperate for her to become pregnant again as soon as possible.

Yet Anne had not utterly forgotten her daughter, Elizabeth, in her rage to give birth to a son. She doted on her little girl, and breast-fed the baby herself, scandalizing the court. Anne even forced Elizabeth's half sister to dance attendance on her as a servant, banishing Mary to a tiny, dark room and demanding that the eighteen-year-old girl's ears be boxed by her governess "for the cursed bastard she is," if Mary dared refer to herself as "Princess." Henry's elder daughter was now styled the Lady Mary, stripped of her title and birthright when Henry's marriage to her mother was annulled.

Anne was pregnant again in October 1535, though her condition did not deter Henry from paying a visit early in the month to the Seymour family at their home of Wulfhall. There, Sir John Seymour made certain that his demure and modest daughter Jane fell under the royal gaze as much as possible. It was not long before Henry gave Jane a miniature portrait of himself, which she ostentatiously wore about her throat at court. Anne was so infuriated by Jane's impudence that she ripped the chain from her neck.

Anne's predicament was unusual. Most royal unions were political and dynastic alliances. Her marriage had been a love match—and yet she had no security in it. Consequently, she was prepared to protect it at all costs. More than her crown and marriage were at risk: her *love* for Henry and his for her—the very raison d'être for their union—were at stake, so she couldn't afford to take the high road traveled by a traditional queen and ignore her husband's infatuation with Jane Seymour. The ironic result of Anne's making a big deal out of Jane was that Jane became a bigger deal than she might otherwise have been.

On the day of Katherine of Aragon's funeral, Anne lost a male fetus said to be fifteen weeks old, blaming the miscarriage on two incidents that had caused her great anxiety. Sparked by Henry's latest flirtation, they'd had a violent quarrel, during which Anne angrily exclaimed, "I saw this harlot Jane sitting on your lap while my belly was doing its duty!" And on January 24, 1536, five days before Anne's miscarriage, Henry's horse had fallen heavily in the tiltyard at Greenwich, and after the king in his hundred pounds or so of armor was thrown from the saddle, the mount may have rolled on top of him. Henry had lain unconscious for two hours, and naturally his queen despaired for his life and feared for her own future, should the king die of his injuries.

But Henry wasn't buying either reason. Utterly insensitive to Anne's grief at losing another baby, he bewailed the death of his son. "I see God will not give me male children," he lamented, leaving his wife devastated, and terrified of losing his love.

Yet Anne may have conceived again soon after this miscarriage, because in April, Henry was very indiscreetly boasting to his ambassador in France that God might yet see fit to "send us heirs male," averring, "You do not know all my secrets." However, there is no mention of this pregnancy in any surviving records. As Henry would never have executed his pregnant queen, it's likely that if Anne had been with child in the spring of 1536, she lost that fetus as well, unless Henry's "secret" was his plan to marry Jane Seymour.

There were also international matters that were nearly as pressing as Henry's need for a son. Charles V was willing to enter an alliance with England, and even accept the legitimacy of Henry's marriage to Anne, if his cousin Mary were to be recognized as Henry's heir presumptive. But Henry refused to countenance the validity of his first marriage, which meant that Mary remained illegitimate and therefore unable to succeed him. The way Henry's Chief Minister Thomas Cromwell saw it, Henry's allegiance to Anne was jeopardizing, if not obstructing, England's safest and most effective foreign policy.

Therefore, Anne had to be eliminated from the picture. So Cromwell, who had once been Anne's staunchest ally for religious reform, switched horses and allied himself with the court's pro-Seymour faction. It took the crafty Cromwell just a month and a day to transform Anne from Henry's beloved wife and queen to the executioner's victim.

On April 24, 1536, at Cromwell's prompting, the king signed a document appointing a committee to investigate Anne's possibly treasonous activities. Yet historian Eric Ives believes that Cromwell may have been acting of his own volition, presenting Henry with a fait accompli—a committee that he'd already covertly appointed—because the commission wasn't set up according to the customary procedure. Its aim was to make Anne appear unfaithful and disloyal so that Henry would have an airtight reason to be rid of her.

Cromwell worked swiftly. On Tuesday, April 24, Anne had been

Henry's "entirely beloved wife"; yet by Thursday, April 27, she was the devil incarnate. According to Ives, Cromwell may not have told Henry why he called the commission; his intention to use it as an engine of Anne's destruction was his own little secret; therefore, by the time the legal machinery was already grinding away it was too late to halt it.

It was politically expedient for the minister to destroy Anne's supporters as well, and within a brief space of time, Cromwell had all his scapegoats in the pen, awaiting slaughter.

On the weekend of April 29 and 30, Anne had an enormous spat with Henry Norris, the king's groom of the stool, in which she accused him of being attracted to her. Norris stammered that if he ever had such a thought, "he were his head were off," whereupon Anne threatened to undo him if she chose. Witnesses to their altercation interpreted the quarrel as a come-on from Anne to Norris. To succeed in toppling Anne from the throne, Cromwell's commission needed to compile a dossier of Anne's purported lovers; the contretemps between the queen and Norris (because it included a hypothetical exchange about the king's death), allowed them to put a treasonous construct on it, thereby ensnaring Norris in their lethal net.

Anne's argument with Norris led to another, even more volatile one with Henry. A letter sent twenty years later to Queen Elizabeth from an eyewitness to the aftermath of the royal squabble, a Scottish Lutheran clergyman named Alexander Ales, describes the mood:

Never shall I forget the sorrow which I felt when I saw the most serene queen, your most religious mother, carrying you, still a little baby, in her arms and entreating the most serene king your father, in Greenwich Palace, from the open window of which he was looking into the courtyard, when she brought you to him. I did not perfectly understand what had been going on, but the faces and gestures of the speakers plainly showed that the king was angry, although he could conceal his anger wonderfully well. Yet from the protracted conference of the council (for whom the crowd was waiting until it was quite dark, expecting that they would return to London), it was most obvious to everyone that some deep and difficult question was being discussed.

On April 30, a court musician and dancer named Mark Smeaton was arrested on the grounds that he had committed adultery with the queen. After being put to the rack the hapless and innocent Smeaton confessed to the blatant lie. The following day, three men of Henry's Privy Chamber—Sir Francis Weston, Sir Henry Norris, and Sir William Brereton—were arrested, also charged with having bedded Anne. Weston was tagged because the previous year he had been overheard boldly telling Anne that Norris came to her chamber to see *her*, and not his intended bride, Madge Shelton. Brereton allegedly owed Cromwell money. The witch hunt was under way.

The indictment against the queen stated that "she, following daily her frail and carnal lust, did falsely and traitorously procure by base conversations and kisses, touchings, gifts, and other infamous incitations, divers of the king's daily and familiar servants to be her adulterers and concubines." She also stood accused of promising to marry one of her lovers after Henry's death, and for swearing "that she would never love the king in her heart."

Anne was arrested on May 2, 1536, on the charges of adultery, incest with her brother George, and conspiracy to kill the king. As her barge was rowed to the Traitors' Gate, Anne was on the verge of collapse. "I was treated with greater ceremony last time I was here," she exclaimed woefully, referring to her coronation procession. During her imprisonment Anne's every word and movement were jotted down by the wardresses who had been entrusted with watching her, in the hope that the queen might say something to implicate herself and give Henry legitimate proof of her infidelity or other treasonous act.

Anne's trial began on May 15 in the Great Hall of the Tower of London. Her brother George, Viscount Rochford, was to be tried by the same council of peers, on the charge of committing incest with his sister. Their uncle, the Duke of Norfolk, presided over the proceedings as High Steward. Two thousand spectators watched the circus from purpose-built stands. Among the bogus charges against the queen was an allegation of statutory treason pursuant to the 1534 Succession Act: "slander, danger, detriment and derogation of the heirs" of Henry and Anne. In other words, Anne was charged with being a traitor to her own daughter, Elizabeth.

She was also accused of a bizarre form of adultery. According to Chapuys, the most Protestant of the bishops claimed that "according to their sect, it was allowable for a woman to ask for aid in other quarters even among her own relatives" when her husband failed to satisfy her sexually. It beggars belief that anyone could have testified to such an absurdity. But rumors like these served to galvanize and maintain public opinion against the queen. Other stories that gained traction years later were the reports by Nicholas Sander, an exiled Catholic propagandist, of the "shapeless mass of flesh" or deformed fetus that Anne miscarried in 1535 as proof that the queen had indulged in unnatural sexual acts (such as incest with her brother) or dabbled in the dark arts, so desperate was she to conceive a son. Sander was also the author of the treatise alleging that Henry was Anne's father, so nothing he wrote should be credited by historians.

Yet in an age when "witches" were routinely rooted out and brutally executed, there are no mentions of witchcraft or the dark arts within the annals of the investigation and trial. The notion of witchcraft took root in yet another dispatch of Chapuys's, which reads more like a Tudor game of "Telephone." The imperial ambassador wrote that according to the Exeters, Henry told a courtier (in total secrecy, of course) that he had "made this marriage seduced and constrained by sortileges and for this reason he held the said marriage void and that God had demonstrated this in not allowing them to have male heirs and that he considered that he could take another" [wife]. Chapuys wrote his dispatches in French and the word "sortileges" as used at the time translated to "divinations" or witches' spells.

Also among the more ludicrous allegations was the accusation that Anne had slept with her own brother. The charge was made by George's jealous wife, Lady Rochford—a lady of Anne's bedchamber. She thought her husband spent far too much time in his sister's company in preference to her own, and therefore accused the Boleyn siblings of "undue familiarity." As the prime architect of Anne's downfall and her bitterest enemy during her final days, Cromwell hoped that the charge of incest would suitably shock and appall the council, with its titillating allegations of Anne's "alluring [George] with her tongue in [his] mouth and his tongue in hers."

According to the herald, Charles Wriothesley, Anne gave "wise and discreet answers" to her examiners, concealing her terror beneath a calm and regal demeanor. Chapuys wrote that when Anne addressed the court, she stated that she was ready to die, but regretted that loyal and innocent men should be executed as well. Of her own conduct, she allegedly admitted, "I do not say that I have always borne towards the king the humility which I owed him, considering his kindness and the great honor he showed me and the great respect he always paid me; I admit, too, that often I have taken it into my head to be jealous of him. . . . But may God be my witness if I have done him any other wrong."

All four men accused of adultery with the queen were found guilty and sentenced to a traitor's death—beheading, followed by castration, disembowelment, and quartering. However, in a fit of generosity, Henry commuted the sentence to a simple beheading. At the trials of the two peers, Anne and George, their uncle Norfolk read the sentence: the queen and her brother were either to be burned at the stake or executed, according to the king's pleasure.

Two days after the verdict, George Boleyn, Mark Smeaton, and the men of the Privy Chamber were beheaded on Tower Hill. The throng that had amassed to witness this judicial murder placed bets on the possibility of a last-minute reprieve, particularly for the viscount, but none came.

"They will not let me live," Anne acknowledged. "I am too great a threat to their religion." In fact, many years later her daughter, Elizabeth, was told, "True religion in England had its commencement and its end with your mother."

As a final gesture of kindness to the woman he once called his "fresh young damsel," Henry, moved by pity to spare her from the flames, had spent £24 (roughly the equivalent of $12,600 today) to hire the executioner from St Omer in Calais. This agent of death wielded a sword rather than an axe, ensuring a swifter and less painful demise.

In a letter to Thomas Cromwell on the day of Anne's execution, Sir William Kingston, Constable of the Tower, recorded his conversation with Anne when she heard the news:

> This morning she sent for me, that I might be with her at such time as she received the good Lord, to the intent I should hear her speak as touching her innocency. . . . And . . . at my coming she said, "Mr. Kingston, I hear I shall not die afore noon, and I am very sorry therefore, for I thought to be dead by this time and past my pain." I told her it should be no pain, it was so little. And then she said, "I heard say the executioner was very good, and I have a little neck," and then put her hands about it, laughing heartily. I have seen many men and also women executed, and that they have been in great sorrow, and to my knowledge this lady has much joy in death.

But before she was executed, Anne suffered another ignominy. She was stripped of her title as queen, and her marriage—after all the struggles to achieve it—was declared invalid. It fell to Archbishop Cranmer to divorce them. He had been one of Anne's closest confidants during the King's Great Matter, and even as the hour of her death loomed large, Cranmer admitted, "I never had better opinion in woman than I had in her."

The Decree of Nullity was dated May 17, though it was not

signed until June 10, and it would be another two weeks before both houses of Parliament subscribed to it. Henry had gotten his marriage to Anne annulled on the grounds that his affair with her sister, Mary, had placed him and Anne within the first degree of affinity, even though, in 1528—*at Henry's urging*—the Pope had issued a special dispensation that *set aside* the subject of Henry's affinity to Anne based on his romantic history with Mary Boleyn.

But Henry had cleverly inserted a clause into the 1534 Act of Supremacy to the effect that any existing papal dispensations would no longer be considered valid if they were contrary to Holy Scripture and the law of God. This phraseology was relied upon to justify the invalidity of Henry's marriage to Anne as incestuous. Their daughter, Elizabeth, not yet three years old, was made a bastard by it. Elizabeth, in fact, was the real target of the May 17 decree. The absurdity of it all was that if Henry's marriage to Anne had never been valid, then how could she have committed adultery? Yet her guilt was accepted with the straightest of faces.

On May 18, Anne made a full confession to Cranmer, swearing on the sacrament that she had never been unfaithful to Henry. She went to the block maintaining her love for him and her innocence of the crimes for which she had been convicted.

Though she was to die as the Marquess of Pembroke, Anne looked every inch a queen as she mounted the scaffold on Tower Hill on May 19, 1536. Her red petticoat resembled a swath of blood beneath her dark gray gown of damask trimmed in fur. An ermine mantle enveloped her slender shoulders. Her long auburn hair was bound up under a simple white linen coif over which she wore a gabled headdress in the English style. Witnesses described Anne's steps as light, almost blithe. Perhaps she was relieved to be released from her mental torment, knowing there was nothing left for her in the temporal world.

According to custom, she handed the headsman his fee, for which he thanked her, begging her forgiveness. After a brief exhortation to the crowd to pray for her, Anne knelt upon the platform and removed her headdress. "O, Jesu, have mercy on my soul . . . O, Jesu have mercy on my soul," she repeated as she awaited the fatal blow.

Historian Antonia Fraser claims that the headsman, taking pity on Anne's terror, deliberately and generously distracted her by turning toward a staircase, as if to call for his weapon. Anne instinctively followed the sound, giving the executioner just enough time to retrieve the Sword of Calais from the straw and remove her head with one swift, smooth stroke.

Although Anne had been Queen of England for only a thousand days, her legacy is enormous. Profoundly influential on the development of the Christian religion, Anne's convictions were genuine. Eric Ives in his exemplary biography makes the point that she truly wanted to see the religion reformed, corrupt practices ended, and the Bible and Church services printed and performed in the vernacular so that the people could become more personally connected to their own religion.

The venerated English chronicler Raphael Holinshed praised Anne's "singular wit . . . zeal of religion and liberality in distributing alms for relief of the poor." She annually gave away £1,500 to the less fortunate—nearly $800,000 in today's economy. She and Henry enjoyed a meeting of the minds as well as a shared physical passion, and a mutual interest in the arts, culture, and building—taking particular pleasure in renovating the properties that had once belonged to Cardinal Wolsey. Anne's political influence on her husband and his kingdom remains undeniable; during their marriage English policy took directions that continue to shape and impact the kingdom's constitution.

By dint of her own intellect and abilities, Anne achieved what others could merely dream of. Although her ambitious father and uncle were seasoned courtiers whose success afforded her an entrée into the highest echelons of Tudor society, once she arrived, she was there to stay—*despite* her family—until an equally self-made individual, Thomas Cromwell, destroyed her. Few question the fact

that Anne Boleyn was innocent of the charges for which she forfeited her head. But neither her bloodline nor her spirit perished on
Tower Hill, for she left behind a daughter who would become England's most venerated queen, and perhaps the greatest female
monarch the world has ever known: Queen Elizabeth I.

HENRI II
1519–1559
RULED FRANCE: 1547–1559

❧ *and* ❧

CATHERINE DE MEDICI
1519–1589

married 1533–1559

". . . never did a woman who loved her husband succeed in loving his whore."
—Catherine de Medici

$\mathcal{O}$N A BRISK OCTOBER DAY IN 1533, IT WAS LUST AT FIRST sight when Catherine de Medici first beheld her fiancé, Henri d'Orleans, the second son of King François I of France. Unfortunately, the feeling wasn't mutual.

The royal wedding was the result of a round-robin of international negotiations. Henry VIII of England needed a favor from Pope Clement: the annulment of his marriage to Katherine of Aragon so that he could replace her with Anne Boleyn. François agreed to intercede with the pontiff as long as Henry didn't object to France's regaining Milan. And since the marriage would create a Franco-Italian alliance that might displease Spain, His Holiness decided to bring the Spanish king into the loop, asking Charles V (who was also the Holy Roman Emperor) if he had any objections to a match between his niece and François's second son. Charles's army had sacked Rome just a few years earlier and temporarily taken Clement hostage, so the Pope had every reason to tread carefully with him.

Because Pope Clement's family, the powerful Medicis, had been in the textile and spice trade before they became bankers, Charles readily assented, never for a moment believing that the fastidious French ruler would allow his boy to espouse a "grocer's daughter." But he guessed wrong: François chose to accept Clement's offer, and Catherine de Medici began her journey from merchant princess to real one.

It cost Clement a fortune to fund the colorful pageant that marked Catherine's entry into the city of Marseille, where the wedding was to take place, but it was important for him to make an excellent impression on the French. His Holiness had to take out a loan to afford Catherine's trousseau. Three pounds of gold, two pounds of silver, and two pounds of silk were purchased just for the embroidery on her garments. Her gold brocade wedding gown was trimmed in ermine; the purple velvet bodice was richly embroidered with pure gold thread, edged in ermine, and studded with glittering precious gems.

François greeted his future daughter-in-law with grace and dignity, but she only had eyes for Henri—who looked as though he'd rather be anywhere else. Fair-skinned and clear-complected, the prince was tall with an athletic physique, brown hair, dark, almond-shaped eyes, and a straight nose. Most likely, Catherine couldn't believe her good luck. Henri, however, saw a short, stumpy girl with long dark hair and thick eyebrows, a protruding lower lip, and a receding chin.

The marriage contract was signed on October 27, 1533, and the following day the two fourteen-year-olds were wed in a religious ceremony.

The masked ball held after the wedding banquet on October 28 quickly assumed orgiastic proportions when a Marseille courtesan disrobed and dipped her breasts into wine goblets and invited the male guests to lick them off. She also lay utterly nude on a table with her naughty bits strategically covered with nibblies and urged people to partake of the evening's bounty. Not to be outdone, some of the female guests undid their bodices and vied for attention with the professional.

Catherine herself missed all the fun, having been decorously led to the bridal chamber. But she, too, was expected to put on a show. According to the custom of the day, the couple's embarrassing consummation was witnessed by several spectators.

It could have been the beginning of a beautiful marriage, as the hapless bride and groom had more in common than one might think. Both Henri and Catherine had spent a significant amount of their childhoods in captivity and deprivation, pawns in their respective families' political squabbles. King François had been taken prisoner by Charles of Spain after the Battle of Pavia in 1525, but had managed to secure his release upon the agreement to a treaty that was highly unfavorable to France. However, as a surety that he would uphold his end of the bargain after gaining his freedom, François's two oldest sons were sent to Spain to be imprisoned in his stead. Henri had been six years old at the time; he and the dauphin, his older brother, François, were incarcerated in increasingly sordid conditions for nearly five years while their father blithely reneged on the terms of the treaty. The poor boys were not even welcomed home with open arms. From our perspective, it's clear they had been psychologically damaged during their captivity and had difficulty readjusting, but the king declared he had no time for "dreamy, sullen, sleepy children."

Orphaned within a month after she was born, Catherine's childhood had been no picnic, either. Her mother, Madeline de la Tour d'Auvergne, a French countess, died on April 28, 1519, of puerperal fever when Catherine was just fifteen days old. On May 4, Catherine's father, Lorenzo II de Medici, Duke of Urbino, succumbed to syphilis, hastened to his grave by consumption. Catherine was raised by relatives and given a humanist education in Greek, Latin, French, and mathematics—a subject in which she excelled. But in 1527, Florence suffered a series of uprisings and was subsequently placed under siege, resulting in severe famine. The ruling Medici family was blamed for all the strife. During that time Catherine was shuttled from one convent to another, always in fear for her young life. After the siege was lifted in August 1530, the Medici heiress became a political pawn, the primary bargaining chip of her uncle, the Pope.

In order to bring the royal marriage to fruition, Clement had promised a great deal to François. Not only would the French king achieve considerable material and financial gain from the match, but the pontiff had secretly agreed to join forces eighteen months from the wedding date to help François reclaim the two Italian duchies of Milan and Urbino. However, within a year of the "I dos," Clement was dead and his guarantees died with him. The new Pope, who was not a Medici, had neither motive nor inclination to make good on his predecessor's agreements, and the French were stuck with their lopsided royal *mésalliance*. Catherine was neither pretty nor pregnant, nor prosperous, nor politically useful. "*J'ai eu la fille toute nue,*" François griped, as her dowry remained largely unpaid. "She came to me utterly naked."

Speaking of utterly naked bodies, young Henri did his duty on their wedding night, but thereafter did everything in his power to ignore Catherine. Henri didn't find her sexually alluring, nor was he even interested in talking to her. She had not been warmly welcomed at court, nor was the atmosphere conducive to conception. Because Henri's older brother was still unwed, protocol dictated that the newlyweds had to share the boys' "bachelor" apartments, affording precious little privacy, a perfect excuse for Henri not to sleep with his wife.

In order to ease Catherine's assimilation, King François had assigned one of his wife's ladies-in-waiting to be her guide, schooling her in the manners and protocol of the French court. This woman was Catherine's second cousin, Diane de Poitiers, the thirty-three-year-old widow of the Sénéchal of Normandie, Louis de Brézé. Although she was nineteen years Henri's senior, Diane was also his secret crush, and held him completely in her thrall. Within a few years, she would be his lover in every way, destroying Catherine's pathetic hopes that her handsome husband would ever reciprocate the love she bore him.

On August 2, 1536, the eighteen-year-old dauphin felt ill during a game of tennis and grew sicker after drinking a glass of cool water. Eight days later, he was dead.

Henri was now the dauphin and Catherine the dauphine—the first lady in France after the queen—but after three years of marriage, she and her husband remained childless. Catherine's apparent barrenness was a continual source of anxiety to everyone, but no one felt the stigma more than she did and she greatly feared repudiation. Consequently, she resolved to cultivate the goodwill of everyone at court.

Catherine easily earned the sympathy of the Venetian ambassador Matteo Dandolo, who reported that "The most serene dauphine is of a fine disposition, except for her inability to become a mother. Not only has she not yet had any children, but I doubt that she will ever have them, although she swallows all possible medicines that might aid conception. . . . She is, *as far as we can see*, loved and cherished by the dauphin her husband. His Majesty is also fond of her, as are the court and the people, and I don't think there is anyone who would not give their blood for her to have a son."

As Dandolo suggested, Catherine had tried every quack remedy available in an effort to become fertile. She cheerfully gulped down Dr. Fernel's myrrh pills, which were probably among the more benign cures. And after she gamely drank great quantities of mule's urine, and applied foul-smelling poultices made from ground stag antlers and cow dung, it's no wonder the ambassador diplomatically asserted that "From this I would deduce she is more at risk of increasing her difficulty than finding the solution." Henri might not have been able to get anywhere near her, let alone become aroused in her presence.

And Catherine certainly wasn't going to conceive if her husband was elsewhere. In 1537 the eighteen-year-old Henri urged his father to allow him to fight on his behalf against Charles V of Spain. François reluctantly agreed, and Henri distinguished himself on the field in Provence.

He also cheated on his wife.

Depending on the source, Filippa Duci was either a Piedmontese courtesan, the sister of a local squire Henri met during the military campaign in the Piedmont and Savoy, or the sister of one of Henri's Piedmontese grooms. Whatever her origin, Filippa became the mother of Henri's first child. He named the baby Diane de France, after the goddess of his heart, Diane de Poitiers, who raised his illegitimate daughter alongside her own two girls, while Signorina Duci more than likely got to spend the rest of her days in a convent.

Having developed a taste for adultery, or at least good sex, soon after he returned from northern Italy, Henri consummated his passion for Diane de Poitiers. To Catherine's humiliation, her husband copied Diane's habit of dressing and accoutering herself only in black and white. He adopted Diane's symbol, the crescent moon, as his own, and designed a device formed from their interlocking initials, which was embroidered or embossed on his clothing, his servants' livery, his horses' caparisons, and was eventually carved, sculpted, and otherwise emblazoned all over his residences. Everywhere his poor wife looked, there were Hs and Ds, as entwined as the illicit lovers' limbs were in bed.

Little Diane de France was all the proof the French required to claim that the fault lay entirely with Catherine for her failure to conceive. A secret campaign to repudiate her was being orchestrated by François's paramour, Anne de Pisseleu d'Heilly, whose real target was the rival mistress at court, Diane de Poitiers. If Henri were to get a new wife who was both alluring and fecund, Diane's star would plummet.

One day, Catherine took a huge risk, throwing herself at the king's feet like a penitent and submissively offering to step aside to make way for a fertile bride, as long as she could remain in France as her replacement's humble servant. Touched to the core, François assured her, "My child, it is God's will that you should be my daughter and the wife of the dauphin." With those words all plans to repudiate Catherine were jettisoned. Once the king had spoken, the sycophants, regardless of their opinions, had no choice but to follow suit.

Diane de Poitiers also proved a most unexpected ally to Catherine. After all, it inured to Diane's benefit that her lover's wife was homely. But both women acknowledged that Catherine's fate in France could only be secured if she gave birth. So Diane became the royal couple's sex therapist. After she made love with Henri, she would send him directly upstairs to do the same thing with his wife, urging him "to that couch which no desire draws him." If it cost her emotionally, she kept it to herself. Instead, Diane counseled Catherine as to which sexual positions would be the most beneficial in facilitating conception.

According to the court physicians, Henri and Catherine each suffered from problems with their reproductive organs. Catherine had an inverted uterus. Henri had been diagnosed with a mild deformity of the positioning of the urethra called hypospadias. According to a number of diplomatic dispatches he also suffered from a common side effect of this condition known as "chordee," the downward curve of the penis. This trajectory did not preclude the ability to father children, but in order to do so he had to learn the most effective techniques. Two renowned medical experts of the day recommended acrobatic sexual positions, but it seems that for the longest time Henri had no interest in practicing them with his wife.

He was far more athletic and inventive with his mistress, as Catherine found out. All this time she'd considered herself inept in bed and thought that perhaps she hadn't been doing things right. Horribly jealous of her husband's passion for Diane and curious to know what it was he saw in her and what they did together, she hired an Italian carpenter to drill two small spy holes in her floor, through which she watched Henri and his mistress making love all over Diane's room, including her velvet rug, until it was time for her to send him upstairs to do his conjugal duty. According to the court chronicler Pierre de Brantôme, after witnessing the lovers in action, Catherine, who was tragically in love with her husband, tearfully told her friend the duchesse de Montpensier that Henri had "never used her so well."

Both Diane and the court physician Jean Fernel separately advised Catherine that the royal couple's peculiar anatomies would be best served if they enjoyed sex *à levrette,* a *levrette* being a greyhound bitch. Essentially, he was recommending that they practice what we call the doggie style. One historian has acerbically hypothesized that Henri could only do what was required of him with such frequency if he did not have to look at his wife's face. And when he was finished, Henri would rejoin Diane downstairs and spend the rest of the night in her arms.

Finally—in the spring of 1543, after a decade of marriage—Catherine became pregnant. On January 19, 1544, she went into labor, and late that afternoon she gave birth to a son, whom the royal couple named François, in honor of the king. After ten agonizing years, Catherine had finally achieved her goal and secured her place at court.

But the dauphine's postpartum relief was short-lived. During the next dozen years Henri visited her bed regularly enough to keep her almost perpetually pregnant, for which she was no doubt grateful, but his passion for Diane remained as strong as ever.

Realizing that her husband shunned their bed entirely after she announced a new pregnancy, Catherine began to delay the news for as long as possible so that she could continue to enjoy her husband's body, even if the feeling was not mutual. She bore ten children between 1543 and 1555. Seven of them survived to adulthood, although all but their youngest child, Margot, were sickly runts with weak lungs, perpetually runny noses, and delicate constitutions. Three of the four boys would end up suffering dementia as young adults; two of those crackpots became King of France. Catherine's final pregnancy ended on June 26, 1556, with the birth of twin girls. It nearly killed her. One of the twins, Jeanne, died during the birthing process and her leg had to be broken in order to remove her from the womb. The other twin, Victoire, only survived a few weeks.

With three people in their marriage, Catherine was certainly the odd one out. So one might think that after her children were born she would refocus her energy and devote herself to them. But even in this realm, Diane de Poitiers seemed to reign. Her cousin Jean d'Humières was awarded the governorship of the royal nursery and, at her lover's insistence, Diane was a de facto third parent, as involved in decision making as Henri and Catherine when it came to the raising and education of their children. To retain her husband's affection and respect, Catherine had no choice but to suffer it all with the utmost dignity. It was her modus operandi when it came to everything at court, and had allowed her to remain on good terms with everyone.

François I became ill in March 1547, and it was clear that the fifty-two-year-old king would never recover. On the thirtieth of the month a tearful Henri asked for his father's blessing and the two men held each other tightly until the dauphin "fell into a swoon." The following day, Henri received the twenty-eighth birthday present of a lifetime: the crown of France. François died that afternoon—his myriad illnesses (including cancer) possibly exacerbated by his advanced gonorrhea.

After thirteen years in France Catherine still spoke the language with a heavy Italian accent, but now, at the age of twenty-eight, this daughter of Florentine "merchants" was their queen. Sadly, her marital situation didn't magically change when she acquired her crown. Henri created his mistress duchesse de Valentinois and treated Diane as his queen, while Catherine was more or less a "legal concubine," in the words of the Venetian envoy Lorenzo Contarini.

As the years progressed Henri came to appreciate and ultimately rely on his wife's judgment and loyalty. But at the outset of his reign, he created an intimate circle comprised of fiercely loyal nobles—and Diane—excluding Catherine from his confidences. Contarini confirmed as much. Catherine was "not beautiful but possesses extraordinary wisdom and prudence—*there is no doubt that she would be capable of governing*. However, she is not consulted or considered as she merits, for she is not of royal blood, but she is liked by everyone including the king for her character and her kindliness."

In the grand scheme of things, apart from the number of Protestant heretics he consigned to the flames, Henri was a relatively progressive ruler. He instituted a sort of Renaissance socialism, where each district in Paris was required to pool its wealth for the needs of the poorer citizens of the quarter. On certain days convents dispensed money and free food. A "workfare" program employed able-bodied mendicants to repair the city's infrastructure, while the crippled or otherwise disabled beggars were placed in hospitals.

After observing the traditional ninety days of mourning for his father, Henri was crowned at the Cathedral of Rheims on July 26, 1547. The very pregnant Catherine was just an honored spectator, resplendently attired in white satin and crimson velvet, her garments edged in gold and dripping with gems. But Diane was dressed just as ornately and, as an added insult, atop her flaxen hair was a diamond crescent, resembling a crown. Catherine did not even get to enjoy her husband's coronation night with him. According to the Italian ambassador, after the banquet Henri "went to find the Sénéchale."

The Venetian ambassador summed up Catherine's reaction to her husband's grand dalliance: "Since the beginning of the new reign, the Queen could no longer bear to see such love and favor being bestowed by the duchess, but upon the King's urgent entreaties she resigned herself to endure the situation with patience. The Queen even frequents the duchess, who, for her part, serves the Queen well, and often it is she who exhorts him to sleep with his wife."

Many years later, Catherine wrote to an envoy who was trying to help her daughter Margot out of a bad marriage to Henri of Navarre. Referring to her own difficult ménage, Catherine confided, "If I made good cheer for Madame de Valentinois, it was the king that I was really entertaining, and besides, I always let him know that I was acting sorely against the grain; for never did a woman who loved her husband succeed in loving his whore. For one cannot call her otherwise, although the word is a horrid one to us."

In August 1548, the five-year-old Mary, Queen of Scots arrived in France at Henri's invitation. That year he had sent forces to Scotland to aid in their ongoing skirmishes with the English. In return, he had asked for the child's hand in marriage for François, the dauphin, who was a few months younger than Mary. Mary would be raised at the French court and the children would wed when they came of age. Accompanying Mary to France was her governess, the gorgeous, redheaded Janet Fleming, a bastard daughter of James IV of Scotland. When Diane de Poitiers broke her leg in 1550 and left court to recuperate, Henri indulged in a highland fling with Lady Fleming, resulting in a bastard son. Little Henri, duc d'Angoulême, was raised in the royal nursery alongside his legitimate children and Mary, Queen of Scots. That year Henri fathered another royal bastard by a married woman named Nicole de Savigny. Although the child was named Henri, the king did not legitimize him and he was given the surname of Nicole's cuckolded spouse, Saint-Rémy.

Catherine played the role of the outraged wife to the hilt, even as she enjoyed her longtime rival's public humiliation.

Henri may have felt guilty about his flurry of infidelities, because by 1551 he was evidently paying marked attention to his wife. A court insider observed, "The King visits the Queen and serves her with so much affection and attention that it is astounding." Their relationship must have turned a corner because Henri finally began to rely on Catherine's political counsel, particularly as he embarked for Germany in 1552 to defend its Lutheran princes against Charles V's religious and political aggression. However, he didn't trust his wife to run things entirely on her own in his absence, appointing one of Diane's cronies to share the duties of regent.

When it came to politics and power, Catherine was a quick study. Eager to please her husband, she would do whatever it took.

In August of 1557, Henri's army suffered its worst defeat ever at Saint-Quentin in Picardy, trounced by the allies of King Philip of Spain, who had succeeded his father, Charles V.

Back in Paris, Catherine helped calm the populace, who feared that the enemy no longer had any barrier to marching on the capital. Alone, but for two remaining advisers—and Diane—Henri sent word to Catherine to raise money from the Parisians with which to fund more troops. Finally, after twenty-four years of marriage, the thirty-eight-year-old queen got the call she had been waiting for: her husband needed her and had given her a task that no one else could accomplish. For nearly a quarter century their subjects had regarded her as little more than a broodmare and a merchant's daughter unworthy of the French throne. Catherine was keenly aware of their unfavorable opinion; at this juncture it was crucial that she not only change their minds and demonstrate her ability to lead and inspire, but also to raise the desperately needed revenue.

Accompanied by her sister-in-law and wearing black mourning, Catherine stood on the steps of Paris's town hall and gave her first major public address. She appealed to the hostile citizenry with grace and humility, seasoned with more than a soupçon of flattery. Speaking of the peril facing all of them, she humbly asked for their aid, and after only a few moments of deliberation, she received a unanimous vote of confidence—and the impressive sum of 300,000 livres.

Catherine's success with the people of Paris marked a turning point on two levels. First, she'd won the respect and admiration of her subjects. Moreover, she had tasted power and authority—and found them to her liking.

According to the Venetian ambassador Michele Sorzano, in a dispatch written in 1558, Catherine "is loved by all and more than anyone else she loves the king, for whom she overcomes all fatigue to follow. The king honors her and confides in her . . . the fact that she has borne him ten children counts very much for this attachment to her."

But even the fruits of Catherine's womb could never be entirely hers without some intrusion from her husband's mistress, who insisted on employing the queen's private pet names for the royal offspring.

By the middle of 1559, Catherine had grown anxious about Henri's health. Ever since the military debacle at Saint-Quentin he had been exhausted, overstressed, and had begun to suffer from episodes of vertigo.

On June 29, the night before Henri was scheduled to participate in the joust to celebrate the marriage of their daughter Princess Elisabeth to Philip of Spain, Catherine had a prophetic dream in which she saw her husband lying wounded on the field, his face covered in blood. Over the years, four different forecasters, including Nostradamus, had predicted the identical outcome: Henri's death in his forty-first year during a duel in an enclosed arena. Echoing Caesar's wife, Calpurnia, Catherine urged Henri not to enter the tournament. But Henri pooh-poohed the prognostications.

The following day, June 30, 1559, Henri took the field. After triumphing over his first two opponents, he faced the comte de Lorge, Gabriel de Montgomery. But just before their third pass the king's Master of the Horse warned Henri that his helmet was not properly fastened. And de Montgomery had not realized that the metal tip of his lance was missing.

The combatants spurred their horses and charged at each other. One eyewitness, the Bishop of Troyes, Antoine de Caraccioli, wrote to Corneille Musse, the Bishop of Bonito, "The king was struck on the gorget [the armorial element that protects the wearer's throat], the lance broke, but the visor was not strapped down and several splinters wounded the king above the right eye. He swayed from the force of the blow and the pain, dropping his horse's bridle, and the horse galloped off to be caught and held by the grooms. Helped from his horse, his armor [was] taken off, and a splinter of a good bigness was removed."

For the next ten days Catherine maintained a vigil by Henri's bedside while the physicians did everything they could to save him. Throughout their twenty-six years of marriage, Catherine had been robbed of her husband "by Diane de Poitiers in the sight and knowledge of everyone." Now, in the king's final hours, his wife would claim her due, preventing Diane from coming anywhere near her dying lover. She even demanded the jewels Henri had given to Diane, but while there was breath and life in him, his *maîtresse en titre* refused to relinquish them. And as soon as Henri expired, Catherine also exercised her authority as the widowed queen and stripped Diane of all but one of the properties Henri had bestowed upon her, including the breathtakingly glorious Château de Chenonceau, which Catherine had long coveted and Henri had always denied her.

The king's funeral was held between August 11 and 13, 1559, and he was buried in the Valois crypt at Saint-Denis. The fifteen-year-old dauphin became King François II and Mary, Queen of Scots, only sixteen, was now the Queen of France. Henri's death left Catherine distracted with grief, but their children were his legacy and she vowed to do everything in her power to fiercely protect them. As two of their sons, François and Charles, inherited the crown when they were minors, Catherine, styled as the Queen Mother, played an enormous and powerful role in their respective regencies.

Over the next thirty years Catherine became a consummate intriguer and a canny politician. One Englishman observed that "she hath too much wit for a woman and too much honesty for a queen." Everything she did as a regent and later as an adviser—no matter whether it was popular—was intended to preserve the throne of France for her sons.

History has painted her as an evil schemer who dabbled in the occult, earning her various unpleasant nicknames, including "Madame la Serpente," "the Black Queen," and the lurid "Maggot from Italy's tomb." Part of that portrait is accurate. It is true that Catherine maintained a chamber in the Château de Chaumont that contained alchemical paraphernalia, including the "philosopher's egg," an incense burner, a death's-head, a purification fountain "with its pentacles and avocatory spells," an astrolabe, and a divining rod. On one wall hung the infamous "magic mirror" in which her astrologer Cosimo Ruggieri foretold the number of years that each of her sons would rule France. The shocking surprise at the end of his mystical prophecy was that Henri of Navarre would succeed her own blood on the French throne, signifying the end of the Valois dynasty and the birth of the Bourbons. It's been said that Catherine insisted on marrying her daughter Margot to the King of Navarre in a last-ditch hope of continuing her bloodline.

During the reign of François II, the kingdom was plagued by violent uprisings from French Protestants, known as the Huguenots—the name derived from a meeting of rebel dissenters held near the port city of Hugues on February 1, 1560. That March, some fifty-two rebels—members of the nobility—were publicly beheaded. But the antagonism between the Catholics and Protestants was just heating up. Over the next several years there would be three civil wars between Catholic and Huguenot factions, as the Huguenots would see their religious freedom alternately tolerated and restricted numerous times.

Shortly after sixteen-year-old François's death from an ear infection in December 1560, Catherine wrote a letter to her eldest daughter, Queen Elisabeth of Spain, confiding, ". . . I was not loved as much as I wished to be by the King your father, who honored me more than I deserved, but I loved him so much that I was always in fear, as you know; and God has taken him from me and, not content with that, has deprived me of your brother whom you know how I loved, and has left me with three little children and a divided kingdom, where there is not one man whom I can trust. . . ." At the end of 1560, Catherine's surviving boys were ages five, nine, and ten; but in her letter to Elisabeth she must have conveniently forgotten to count seven-year-old Marguerite (Margot), whom she never had much use for anyway.

Her grief remained palpable, but at the age of forty-one, Catherine was at the pinnacle of her power, the *de jure* as well as the de facto ruler of France, as the new king, Charles IX, was all of ten years old. Faced with massive debt, she drastically cut expenditures while enacting reforms to protect the peasants from abuses by the nobility. A system of unified weights and measures was adopted. In a pragmatic step to preserve her young son's reign, she concluded that violence was an ineffective tool for bringing the Huguenots into the Catholic fold. Not above using sex as a weapon—or at least as an effective form of espionage—the woman who as queen had expelled her ladies from court if they became pregnant now employed between eighty and three hundred of the most beautiful and alluring females in France as a "flying squadron." Dressed according to Catherine's dictate "like goddesses in silk and gold cloth," their brief was to behave most decorously in public, but in private were encouraged to act as they liked, using sex and seduction as a method of obtaining information, "provided they had the wisdom, ability, and knowledge to prevent a swelling stomach." Catherine always wore black mourning, a raven presiding over a bevy of swans.

On August 18, 1572, Catherine and Henri's youngest child, Margot, was wed to Henri of Navarre, an on-again, off-again Protestant. While we can't be certain she was influenced by the prophecy of Cosimo Ruggieri in arranging this marriage, we do know that Catherine had hoped that the union would ease religious tensions by bringing a Catholic and a Huguenot together. Unfortunately, the royal wedding had the opposite effect. When Catherine discovered that prominent Protestants at court had formed armed factions that endangered the life of the royal family and the stability of the crown, she retaliated quickly. The result was an unmitigated slaughter and an even deeper rift between the Protestants and Catholics that no mixed marriage could repair. On August 24, the eve of Saint Bartholomew's Day, a hit list of Huguenot leaders compiled by Catherine were assassinated, but the violence escalated when the Parisian mob turned butchers, viciously murdering every black-clad Huguenot they could find.

On May 30, 1574, the twenty-three-year-old Charles IX died of tuberculosis and his younger brother, the twenty-two-year-old duc d'Anjou, who had recently been elected King of Poland, returned to France to claim the throne as Henri III. As it would be weeks before he arrived in Paris, Catherine's regency was officially published on June 3. Henri would remain on the throne until his death in 1589.

Toward the end of 1588, the sixty-nine-year-old Catherine took to her bed with a lung infection. On January 5, 1589, she dictated her will to King Henri III. At one thirty that afternoon, the eve of Epiphany, or as the French call it, *le Jour des Rois*—the Day of the Kings—Catherine de Medici, the mother of three kings and the widow of a fourth, succumbed to pleurisy and breathed her last.

Her body was dressed in garments belonging to Henri II's maternal grandmother, Anne of Brittany. Political unrest in Paris made it too dangerous to transport her lead-lined coffin to Saint-Denis, so her ineptly embalmed and steadily reeking body remained at Blois, where the funeral was conducted on February 4. Henri III ordered her corpse to be temporarily dumped into an unmarked grave in the churchyard of Saint-Sauveur, but it remained there for twenty-one years, until Henri II's illegitimate daughter Diane de France had Catherine's coffin moved to Saint-Denis to repose in the Valois rotunda beside that of the husband she had adored nearly to distraction.

Born a commoner of mercantile stock, Catherine had been determined to prove herself worthy of her royal title as Queen of France. But not until she was a widow did she come into her own as a woman, as a ruler, and as a force of nature. She adored her husband, but their relationship was an entirely lopsided one; compared to his lover Diane de Poitiers, she always came up short. Much has been written about the power, sway, and allure of Henri's far more attractive paramour. The royal mistress, the star-crossed desired one who could never fully possess him—the sexually confident and magnetic personality—is far more intriguing to the pages of posterity than a drab, dumpy, and desperate wife. And so the enduring love story of Henri II and Diane de Poitiers is the stuff of high romance, with Catherine de Medici invariably cast as the jealous villainess. Yet the circumstances of Catherine and Henri's royal marriage were not of their making. The homely but highly intelligent heiress was lucky enough to have wed a man she loved on sight, but fate played a cruel joke on both of them. Catherine's handsome spouse was hers for life, yet never entirely hers, unable to reciprocate her passion because Diane de Poitiers was the guardian of his heart. Henri, too, had been tripped up by duty, destiny, and dynasty; yoked to a woman he hadn't chosen, he was never able to fully possess the one he so feverishly desired.

HENRY VIII

❧ *and* ❧

JANE SEYMOUR

("BOUND TO OBEY AND SERVE")

1509–1537

married 1536–1537

"[She will] not in any wise to give in to the king's fancy
unless he makes her his queen."
—excerpt from April 1, 1536, report of imperial ambassador Eustache Chapuys to Charles V of Spain regarding the courtship of Henry VIII and Jane Seymour

So, AFTER MARRYING AND RIDDING HIMSELF OF TWO
fiery and temperamental auburn-haired forces of nature—Katherine
of Aragon and Anne Boleyn—what did Henry want with Jane Seymour, a whey-faced woman with washed-out blond locks and a
pointy little chin? The answer is obvious, actually. Peace and tranquility. He craved harmony, not just in his marriage, but throughout his realm. Following his failed union with a dragon, Henry
wanted a doormat, and the modest and docile twenty-five-year-old
Jane was the perfect antidote to Anne Boleyn. So, okay, Jane was
a drip and a pill, but that was the medicine the self-diagnosing
Henry required. She was also likely as anyone else to produce sons.

Her mother had given birth to ten children, so her fecundity pedigree was high.

Although Henry was taunted about his new in-laws' comparatively low connections, the Seymours were a respected family within the Tudor court, even if their associations were nowhere near as powerful, nor their lineage as illustrious, as the Boleyns or the Howards. Sir John Seymour, Jane's father, had served with Henry in France in 1513. Her mother, Margery Wentworth, was descended from Edward III. Jane's brother had recently been in service to the Spanish king and Holy Roman Emperor Charles V. And Jane herself had been a lady-in-waiting to Katherine of Aragon, so it stands to reason that Eustache Chapuys, the imperial ambassador to Henry's court, would have something nice to say about her. However, the diplomat described Jane as being "of middling height and nobody thinks she has much beauty. Her complexion is so whitish that she may be called rather pale."

Yet this young woman whom the ambassador also characterized as "not very intelligent, and . . . said to be rather haughty," knew how to play the hand that was dealt her. Until the autumn of 1535, when Anne Boleyn was enduring a difficult pregnancy (that would result in yet another miscarriage the following winter), Jane was just a speck on the walnut-paneled walls; yet she had spent a lifetime at court, observing and absorbing what to do and, more to the point, how *not* to behave around the king. Most important, she'd proven clever enough to remain chaste in a court renowned for its flirtatious, if not outright licentious, behavior.

Enough people knew Jane well and could confirm her pretensions to purity, although a doubting Chapuys tartly remarked that "You may imagine whether being an Englishwoman and having been long at court, she would not hold it a sin to be a maid." However, the ambassador's view of Henry was equally jaded, suggesting that the king "may marry her on condition she is a maid, and when he wants a divorce there will be plenty of witnesses to testify that she was not."

Carefully coached by her family and by others who wished to

see the dousing of the Boleyn-Howard dynasty's star and the end of the English Reformation, Jane was taught how to massage the king-sized ego once Henry's infatuation with her had begun. However, she kept her ambition to be queen well concealed. She told the king what he wanted to hear and appeared to be everything he now sought in a consort. Her handlers also taught her how to disparage Anne in the king's presence and insidiously poison Henry's mind regarding the validity of their marriage. However, great care was taken to ensure that Jane always tarnished her royal rival in the company of other Seymour team members so that her clique would appear to be the instigators while the insipid Jane simply parroted her agreement.

Behind the scenes Jane had two patrons who were eager to advance their own agendas and saw in her the best means to achieve them. Gertrude, Marchioness of Exeter, and Sir Nicholas Carew, Master of the Horse, were convinced that Jane, who had always been passively sympathetic to the disinherited Mary, would repair the relationship between Henry and his daughter. Carew and the marchioness were Catholics who hoped that Jane's intervention would result in the Lady Mary regaining her rights of succession, with the bonus that perhaps Henry's Reformation would come to a grinding halt.

It's unfair to cite Henry's passion and priapic urges as the only reason he so rapidly went from Anne to Jane. Once Anne was clearly destined for the history books, the king's Privy Council began pressuring him to find another bride and beget a male heir ASAP to ensure the smooth succession of the realm. Jane was the council's first choice, but she was proving not such an easy mark. Though she openly flirted with Henry, even to the point of sitting on his lap and accepting his presents of jewelry, it's ironic that she had learned how to play hard-to-get from the best of them—Anne Boleyn herself.

According to Ambassador Chapuys's report of February 10, 1536, Henry gave "great presents" to Jane after Anne Boleyn's miscarriage. And when Henry subsequently sent Jane a bag of gold sovereigns accompanied by what was presumably a passionate love letter, her reaction was swift and decisive. Jane acted as appalled as if Henry had left the money on the nightstand. On April 1, the ambassador wrote that she kissed the love letter, but pointedly left it unopened and fell to her knees before the king's messenger, "begging him to tell the king that she was a well-born damsel, the daughter of good and honorable parents, without blame or reproach of any kind; there was no treasure in this world that she valued as much as her honor, and on no account would she lose it even if she were to die a thousand deaths. That if the king wished to make her a present of money, she requested him to reserve it for such a time as God would be pleased to send her some advantageous marriage."

Taking a leaf from Anne Boleyn's courtship playbook, Jane had clearly decided "not in any wise to give in to the king's fancy unless he makes her his queen." Henry got the point. In fact, it increased his respect for the bland blonde. And he relied upon his ever-faithful Archbishop of Canterbury Thomas Cranmer to secure him a dispensation to marry Jane; because her grandmother was a cousin of Henry's great-grandmother, they were related within the forbidden degree of affinity. Cranmer signed the dispensation on May 19, the same day as Anne Boleyn's execution. That afternoon, Jane and Henry recommenced the public displays of affection they'd discreetly refrained from during Anne's trial and enjoyed a sumptuous meal amid much unrestricted canoodling. They were secretly betrothed the following day.

Henry and the Catholic factions adored her, but Jane was not particularly admired by the average Briton. A love letter from Henry describes not only his feelings for her but those of lesser mortals:

My dear friend and mistress,
The bearer of these few lines from thy entirely devoted servant will deliver into thy fair hands a token of my true affection for thee, hoping you will keep it for ever in your sincere love

for me. There is a ballad made lately of great derision against us; I pray you pay no manner of regard to it. I am not at present informed who is the setter forth of this malignant writing, but if he is found out, he shall straitly be punished for it. Hoping shortly to receive you into these arms, I end for the present

Your own loving servant and sovereign

H.R.

On May 30, 1536, just eleven days after Anne's death, Jane and Henry wed quickly and quietly at Whitehall in the Queen's Closet. Jane immediately became known at court as "the Peacemaker," a role she was ambitious to embrace and maintain, going to her grave with that legacy.

The Seymour family did well for itself once Jane was anointed Henry's chosen one. Jane's dower properties included 104 manors, five castles, and a number of forests, chases, and woodlands. And a week after the royal wedding, Jane's brother, Sir Edward Seymour, was created Viscount Beauchamp. More blatantly ambitious than his sister, the new viscount harbored dreams of one day becoming regent if Jane should bear the increasingly ailing Henry a son.

On June 4, Jane was proclaimed queen, and three days later the royal couple entered London by barge from Greenwich to Whitehall. The new queen was pasty-faced and lusterless, but her husband was a piggy-eyed, forty-five-year-old with a head "as bald as Caesar's," according to one contemporary report. Henry had taken to disguising his follicle issue by wearing hats. A beard hid his nonexistent chin.

Despite the lack of a formal coronation, Jane was still Henry's queen consort. And she set to work making the role her own. For starters, the conservative new queen had some definite ideas about how the court ladies should dress. Jane banned the opulently sexy "French style" wardrobe and accessories that were favored by her predecessor, Anne Boleyn. Instead, women were to wear dowdy gabled caps and a somber palette of drab-hued gowns, filling in their plunging necklines with "chests"—dickie-like inserts—that served as modesty panels.

In the political arena, Jane usually kept her mouth shut, but for a religious woman who did not embrace the new reform, Henry's dissolution and destruction of the monasteries was too much. On bended knee, she pleaded with the king to restore the abbeys; but according to an English correspondent of the era Henry growled at her to get up, unleashing his temper full bore as he advised her to "attend to other things, reminding her that the last Queen had died in consequence of meddling too much in state affairs." The issue was particularly sensitive for Henry because he had just crushed a rebellion that had begun in the north, demanding the restoration of Christ's Church.

Immediately chastened, if not entirely cowed, Jane never again interfered in matters of policy or state—except in one instance, but it was one where she knew she would eventually have more success. Jane was very aware that, issues of politics and religion aside, Henry really did love his children. So she pressured Henry to reconcile with Mary, and even with little Elizabeth, but the new Act of Succession continued to shut out both of Henry's daughters in favor of any sons Jane might bear.

In early January 1537, Jane got pregnant. Yet it was pointedly noted that she had not become *enceinte* during the first six months of her marriage—which says more about the forty-six-year-old king's potency issues than Jane's fecundity. To support this conjecture, on August 12, 1536, less than three months after the royal wedding, Henry had confided to Chapuys that he was feeling old and doubted he should sire any children with the queen.

Jane gave birth to Henry's miracle child—the much desired son, whom he nicknamed "God's imp"—on October 12, 1537, in the wee hours of the morning at Hampton Court. After twenty-eight years of rule, the monarch finally had his heir. The boy was named Edward after his great-great-grandfather and because he was born on the eve of the saint's feast day. Henry's infant son was placed in his arms, and witnesses reported that the king wept to see him.

Just three days later, wrapped in velvet and fur, a game but hopelessly fatigued Jane forced herself to attend her son's lavish christening in Hampton Court Chapel. She remained on her feet for nearly the entire day, receiving the compliments of the hundreds of guests who were permitted to witness the ceremony and take part in the celebrations afterward, which dragged on into the wee hours of the next morning. The following week Jane's family was granted additional honors. On October 18, the tiny Edward was proclaimed Prince of Wales, Duke of Cornwall, and Earl of Carnarvon.

But the exertion of childbirth and the exigencies of playing hostess when her body was utterly exhausted contributed to Jane's swift demise. She fell ill within a day or two of giving birth, possibly due to a tear in her perineum that became infected, owing to the general ignorance of and inattention to hygiene. Jane developed puerperal, or childbed, fever, which turned into septicemia and eventually led to delirium. An alternative medical opinion hypothesizes that Jane had retained parts of the placenta within her uterus, which led to a catastrophic hemorrhage, septicemia, and death. Proponents of this theory cite the fact that Edward's birth was attended by a team of male physicians who, according to decorum and custom, never examined Jane physically; the men may have paid more attention to the fact that Henry finally had an heir than to ministering to the boy's mother—whereas an experienced midwife, had she been in the room, would have made sure the afterbirth was expelled and seen to it that Jane was immediately cleaned up and good to go.

The king placed the blame for Jane's illness "through the fault of those that were about her, who suffered her to take great cold and to eat things that her fantasy in sickness called for." Twelve days after giving birth, on October 24, at eight a.m., Jane's confessor was summoned. After receiving extreme unction, she died shortly before midnight, at all of twenty-eight years old.

The inconsolable king ordered the churches to be draped in black and wore full black mourning for three months. On November 8, 1537, Jane's body was taken in great pomp and solemnity to Windsor and interred four days later in St. George's Chapel, the only one of Henry's six queens to be buried there. A decade later the dying Henry requested that he be entombed beside her. Jane's chief mourner was Princess Mary, restored to her father's affections, thanks to the queen's assiduous campaigning.

Jane Seymour's epitaph, inscribed in Latin, translates roughly to:

Here lies Jane, a phoenix
Who died in giving another phoenix birth.
Let her be mourned, for birds like these
Are rare indeed.

Their son, Edward, Prince of Wales ascended the throne on his father's death in 1547 to become Edward VI. However, his reign was brief; in 1553 Edward died at the age of fifteen. Although he was consumptive, some scholars believe that he may have suffered other illnesses, such as measles and smallpox, which hastened his demise.

Edward's premature death sparked civil strife between Catholics and Protestants. As his two half sisters had been delegitimized and Henry VIII's will had stipulated that the succession pass to the heirs of his younger sister, Mary, it was Jane Grey, Mary Tudor's granddaughter, who became England's next monarch, queen for all of nine days.

Henry VIII

❧ *and* ❧

Anne of Cleves

("God Send Me Well to Keep")

1515–1557

married 1540

> "When he comes to bed he kisses me and taketh me by the hand and biddeth me 'Goodnight sweetheart'; and in the morning kisses me and biddeth me 'Farewell, darling.' Is this not enough?"
>
> —Anne of Cleves, on her sex life with Henry VIII

*H*ENRY VIII'S THIRD WIFE, THE TWENTY-EIGHT-YEAR-old Jane Seymour, had died of puerperal fever at midnight on October 24, 1537, twelve days after giving birth to Henry's coveted male heir, Prince Edward.

Although he grieved for Jane immensely, practically martyring her memory, the king acknowledged that he still needed to propagate the proverbial "spare"; barely a month after Jane's death his ambassadors drew up a list of eligible continental beauties and went about the business of making inquiries.

Fully aware of Henry's penchant for violently ridding himself of unwanted spouses, his first few choices for Wife Number Four wriggled out of consideration by claiming precontracts of marriage elsewhere, or by reminding the king's emissaries that they were related to his first wife, Katherine of Aragon. Gorgeous sixteen-year-old Christina, the Danish-descended Duchess of Milan, wittily insisted that if God had given her two heads she would willingly risk one to marry the King of England, but as she only had *one* . . .

The search finally came down to Anne and Amelia, the two younger sisters of Wilhelm, Duke of Cleves, an independent duchy in the western region of Germany known as Westphalia, bordering the Netherlands. Ever since Henry's 1534 Act of Supremacy had proclaimed him Supreme Head of the Church in England, his kingdom stood dangerously isolated as Europe's lone Protestant superpower. Evangelical reformers, particularly Henry's chancellor, Thomas Cromwell, viewed an alliance with one of the German duchies as a way to strengthen England's commitment to the reformed religion. The Duke of Cleves was a Lutheran; his affiliation with England might counterbalance the amity between the powerful Catholic kingdoms of France and Spain by providing a Protestant partnership on the Continent. Cleves would benefit by the match by securing England's martial might, should the forces of the Holy Roman Empire consider an invasion.

But Henry, being Henry and always in love with Love, insisted that he would wed no woman who was not to his physical liking.

So, early in 1539, the English ambassador Christopher Mont was dispatched to Cleves with two sets of instructions: the official ones from Henry that were more of a formal sounding-out of the viability of a Cleves marriage, and the secret ones from Cromwell, which specifically ordered Mont to get the lowdown on Anne, the elder of the two available Cleves girls, instructing him to report back on "her shape, stature, and complexion." If Mont determined that "she might be likened unto His Majesty," then he was authorized to suggest a royal marriage to the Saxon ministry.

His mission was a success. Mont reported back to Cromwell that "Everyman praiseth the beauty of the said lady, as well as for the face, as for the whole body, above all other ladies excellent" and "she excelleth as far as the Duchess [of Milan, Christina of Denmark] as the golden sun excelleth the moon."

By March, England was involved in direct negotiations with Cleves for a marriage between Henry and *either* Anne or her younger sister, Amelia. Henry's delegation—the Ambassador to Cleves, Nicholas Wotton, known as "Little Dr. Wotton," and his companion Mr. Beard, a Gentleman of the Privy Chamber—were much annoyed that they were unable to return immediate eyewitness descriptions of the two young women, having only barely glimpsed them in their elaborate German court dress. "We had not seen them, for to see but a part of their faces, and that under such monstrous habit and apparel was no sight, neither of the faces nor of their persons," complained Beard and Wotton. But the Germans were unapologetic. Olisleger, the Cleves minister, retorted, "Would you see them naked?"

The months dragged on.

After Beard was able to return to England with a favorable report, in July he was dispatched to Germany once more, this time in the company of the King's Painter, Hans Holbein. The following month, Holbein began his portraits of Anne and Amelia.

Although Henry had yet to receive a comprehensive physical description of the women, by this time it was considered a fait accompli that he would espouse one of them. Henry did have a preference, however. The king's forty-eight-year-old rather immense gut told him that the older of the two sisters, the twenty-three-year-old Anne, would make a more appropriate wife and companion.

Meanwhile, Wotton was befriending the girls' mother, Maria, the better to learn about their upbringing. Anne had spent her life in the ducal court at Düsseldorf, "brought up with the Lady Duchess her mother and . . . never from her elbow." In other words, she was sheltered. And her accomplishments extended primarily to the domestic arts, such as needlework. She read and wrote in her own language, but lacked French and Latin, and evidently was devoid of such intellectual pursuits as avid reading and musical talent, which were so prized in Henry's sophisticated court. "They take it here in Germany for a rebuke and an occasion of lightness that great ladies should be learned or have any knowledge of music," Wotton reported. By those standards, Anne Boleyn would have been an überslut for her intellect alone.

However, Anne of Cleves was not without her merits. "Her wit is so good that no doubt she will in a short space learn the English tongue, whenever she putteth her mind to it," concluded Wotton.

Another positive, "which appeareth plainly in the gravity of her face," according to ambassador Christopher Mont, was that Anne was also free of the perceived German exuberance or "the good cheer" that accompanied her countrymen and -women's passion for food and drink. She was judged to be loyal and gentle, quiet, and despite her extremely modest education, not at all a dullard.

In early September 1539, shortly after Holbein had returned with his two portraits, an embassy from Cleves set off for England to conclude the necessary nuptial negotiations. The German embassy arrived in England on September 18, and on October 4, the marriage treaty was signed.

The bride and groom had yet to meet.

A week later, having traveled overland from Düsseldorf in a horse-drawn cart covered with cloth of gold, Anne arrived in Calais, which was then an English continental stronghold. But heavy winds prevented her party from crossing the Channel, so she spent the next two weeks learning popular English card games, which she evidently played with some skill, despite the language barrier. Anne won many plaudits from Henry's courtiers, and her goodness, gentleness, and willingness "to serve and please" were also applauded by Anne Bassett, who became one of the new queen's ladies-in-waiting. Surely from these descriptions of her character, Henry must have expected the second coming of Jane Seymour.

Anne arrived in Rochester on New Year's Eve 1539, as excited to meet Henry as he was to see her. The king was supposed to have waited until she came to Blackheath on January 3; instead, he decided to surprise his intended with an impetuous gesture straight out of the Legends of Chivalry playbook: a disguise game that any avid reader of Arthurian romances would instantly recognize. But as Anne had no familiarity with the literature of love, it was a stunt that was destined to backfire loudly, greatly embarrassing both the bride and groom.

Here's what happened next, according to Eustache Chapuys, ambassador to the court of the Holy Roman Emperor and King of Spain, Charles V:

And on New Years Day in the afternoon the king's grace with five of his privy chamber, being disguised with mottled cloaks with hoods so that they should not be recognized, came secretly to Rochester, and so went up into the chamber where the said Lady Anne was looking out of a window to see the bull-baiting which was going on in the courtyard, and suddenly he embraced and kissed her, and showed her a token which the king had sent her for a New Year's gift, and she being abashed and not knowing who it was thanked him, and so he spoke with her. But she regarded him little, but always looked out the window . . . and when the king saw that she took so little notice of his coming he went into another chamber and took off his cloak and came in again in a coat of purple velvet. And when the lords and knights saw his grace they did him reverence . . . and then her grace humbled herself lowly to the king's majesty, and his grace saluted her again, and they talked together lovingly, and afterwards he took her by the hand and led her to another chamber where their graces amused themselves that night and on Friday until the afternoon.

Well—that's one account. Other eyewitnesses reported that Anne, who had never seen an image of the king, gently rebuffed the inordinately tall, stout, red-bearded man who kept trying to embrace and flirt with her. To anyone other than Henry, Anne's maidenly modesty would have served her well. After all, what sort of noblewoman flirts back with the first lusty stranger to cross her path? Besides, she was supposed to be saving herself for the king! The only problem was, the lusty swain *was* the king.

Although the mortified Anne realized her mistake once she saw Henry in full regalia, by then the damage had been done.

According to Henry's herald Charles Wriothesley, whose impressions of the event were similar to those of Eustache Chapuys, the king behaved with the utmost chivalry and courtesy. But Sir Anthony Browne, a Gentleman of the Privy Chamber, came away with an entirely different sense of the circumstances. He drew the portrait of a curt and insulted sovereign who scarcely spoke another word to Anne and rushed from the room without bestowing upon her the bejeweled sables that were to be her New Year's gift. Because of the intimate nature of Browne's office, he was privy to Henry's innermost thoughts and moods, and was able to get a better read on the king's emotions. Having observed Henry's face, Browne's impression was that the first encounter between bride and groom had come off very poorly indeed.

Henry's king-sized ego had been humiliated. Not only that, in his opinion, the flesh-and-blood female fell far short of the painted image. "I see nothing in this woman as men report of her," the king lamented to Anthony Browne, "and I marvel that wise men would make such report as they have done."

He sought a second opinion, asking Lord Russell, "How like you this woman? Do you think her so fair and of such beauty as report hath been made unto me of her? I pray you tell me the truth."

Russell confessed that he found Anne ". . . to be of a brown complexion," which certainly contradicts the porcelain skin that Holbein had depicted.

"Alas, whom should men trust?" Henry bemoaned—and went in search of a way out of the marriage treaty.

When he returned to Greenwich Palace he tracked down his chancellor, Thomas Cromwell, who had so vociferously promoted the match with Anne of Cleves, tersely informing the minister that he found the Lady Anne "nothing so well as she was spoken of." If he had known before what he had just of late discovered, "she should not have come within this realm."

"What remedy?" the king demanded of Cromwell. He wasn't looking for a shoulder to cry on; he wanted hard and fast answers that were legally airtight.

The wedding was scheduled to take place on Sunday, January 4, 1540, but at the last minute, Henry was still searching for loopholes. At the eleventh hour he grasped at a proverbial straw: in 1527, when Anne was only twelve years old, she had been betrothed to François, the heir to the duchy of Lorraine. Several times since then, it had been broken off and reaffirmed, although the emissaries from Cleves had assured the English that the precontract with Lorraine was a dead deal. Anne was immediately questioned on the subject, and willingly signed a document averring that she had no binding precontract of marriage with François of Lorraine, or with anyone else.

If Henry were to worm out of the marriage now, it would have disastrous consequences for his relations with Cleves. The duke might even be tempted to ally himself with England's long-standing Catholic enemies, France and Spain.

"Is there none other remedy but that I must needs against my will put my neck in the yoke?" Henry demanded of Cromwell.

The short answer was "no." On the face of it, everything seemed perfectly valid.

"My Lord, if it were not to satisfy the world and My Realm, I would not do that I must do this day for none earthly thing," the unhappy bridegroom confided to his chancellor on the morning of his wedding, Tuesday, January 6, 1540.

At eight a.m., Henry, attired in cloth of gold embroidered with flowers of silver thread, waited for his bride in the Queen's Closet at Greenwich Palace, the same room in which he had married Jane Seymour. Anne wore a cloth of gold gown richly embroidered with flowers fashioned from hundreds of pearls and a bejeweled gold coronet decorated with sprigs of rosemary, an emblem of remembrance. Her hair, "fair, yellow and long," cascaded down her back in the manner of virgin brides.

She curtsied low to Henry three times and he placed a ring on her finger inscribed with the words *God send me well to keep*, which became Anne's queenly motto. Then Thomas Cranmer, the Archbishop of Canterbury, married them.

The ceremony must have been the highlight of the day, because the wedding night was a disaster.

On the following morning, in reply to Cromwell's inquiry as to how he liked the queen, Henry soberly confided, "Surely as ye know, I liked her before not well, but now I like her much worse. For I have felt her belly and her breasts and thereby as I can judge, she should be no maid . . . when I felt them . . . I had neither will nor courage to proceed any further in other matters."

What was Henry really saying? "Belly" was at the time an accepted euphemism for "vagina." Did he poke around a bit and conclude that the twenty-four-year-old Anne wasn't a virgin? Or did "belly" simply mean "belly," and because Anne didn't have a taut midsection Henry decided that she was damaged goods?

Anne had been raised in such a cloistered manner that it was extremely probable she was still *intacta*. So, was Henry making a lame excuse for his own physical failures?

To this day, it is believed that Anne's body so disgusted the morbidly obese Henry that he could not get an erection in her presence, which gave rise to the accepted wisdom that she was undesirably hideous. For this, the poor woman earned the nickname "the Flanders Mare," bestowed on her nearly 150 years later by a Stuart factor, Bishop Gilbert Burnet, who for some reason insisted that Holbein's miniature had unduly flattered Anne. Yet Holbein's portraits, including the one he painted of his royal patron, are considered to be impeccably accurate. It's highly unlikely that he would jeopardize his place at court and any future commissions—to say nothing of compromising his artist's ego—by painting a likeness that *so* little resembled the original. To bolster this theory, it should be noted that the king never castigated or blamed *Holbein* for deceiving him. There must have been more than met the eye, popular conceptions of beauty aside, in the person of Anne of Cleves that caused Henry to be so repulsed by her.

Cromwell encouraged Henry to keep trying for the sake of the realm. So he visited Anne night after night, but could not become aroused enough to consummate the marriage, although he insisted to one of his doctors, William Butts, that he was not impotent because he'd recently had two wet dreams. Additionally, the king told Butts that he thought himself "able to do the act with other, but not with her."

Henry was sure there was nothing wrong with his plumbing: it was simply—according to his physicians—that "he found her body in such sort disordered and indisposed to excite and provoke any lust in him." He "could not in any wise overcome that loathsomeness nor in her company be provoked or stirred to that act."

Meanwhile, what was Anne thinking? Historians have traditionally depicted her as utterly clueless in matters of human biology, averring to her ladies in the Oesterse dialect—an early form of Dutch, and the only language Anne could speak well at that point— "When he comes to bed he kisses me and taketh me by the hand and biddeth me 'Goodnight sweetheart'; and in the morning kisses me and biddeth me 'Farewell, darling.' Is this not enough?"

To this, the Countess of Rutland, the wife of Anne's Lord Chamberlain Thomas Manners, exclaimed, "Madam, there must be more than this, or it will be long ere we have a Duke of York [the title given to a king's second son]."

"Nay, I am content with this, for I know no more," Anne averred.

That's what she said to her ladies. But soon after the wedding night, she had sought a private conversation with Cromwell. Having an inkling about the subject matter, Henry had, surprisingly, given his chancellor permission to speak to Anne, but Cromwell kept weaseling out of it. Instead he passed the baton to the Count of Rutland, who in turn drafted his wife to handle the situation.

The countess encouraged Anne to go out of her way to act more pleasantly to the king when he visited her bedchamber.

Everyone may have been trying to tiptoe around the matter of the forty-eight-year-old Henry's possible impotence. So, Anne of Cleves *might* in fact have been utterly unschooled in sexual matters and been far too shy to talk about it with anyone, even among her ladies. *Or*, she may have cleverly and diplomatically put the focus on her supposed ignorance of the birds and bees in order to deflect attention from her husband's little problem.

Beyond the royal couple's most intimate circle of acquaintances, everything appeared normal. The king and queen enjoyed considerable time together and seemed quite companionable. And the romantic May Day festivities in 1540 fueled speculation that Anne's coronation would be imminent.

But as things turned out, May Day was Anne's last official appearance as Queen of England.

By mid-June it was obvious to all, including Anne, that Henry's head had been turned by another woman. He was spotted being rowed across the Thames to the two residences of the Dowager Duchess of Norfolk, whose vivacious redheaded teenage niece, Kathryn Howard, was one of Anne's ladies-in-waiting. The king knew all too well that he was running out of time to beget that Duke of York and had convinced himself that the diminutive and curvaceous Kathryn was the woman of his dreams. Moreover, Kathryn's physical charms proved that there was nothing wrong with the royal libido.

The conclusion was obvious: Anne must be put aside.

Henry's revulsion over Anne's body and the consummation of his infatuation with Kathryn Howard were only two reasons to seek the annulment of his fourth marriage. France and Spain had resumed their customary enmity, so the chance of their forming an alliance against England was now moot, and Henry no longer needed a Protestant ally on the Continent. He was also facing a considerable backlash of resentment from his courtiers and Catholic nobles, who felt that the common-born Cromwell had far exceeded the purview of his offices. They would be delighted to see the arrogant reformer—the architect of the Cleves marriage—out of the picture. All it took was for the king to give the nod and the chancellor's descent was both swift and vertiginous.

Henry had created Thomas Cromwell Earl of Essex and Lord Great Chamberlain of England on April 18, 1540. But on June 10, he was arrested on charges of heresy and treason, stripped of his accoutrements of rank and office, and taken to the Tower. A week later, a Bill of Attainder was introduced in the House of Lords to dispossess the former chancellor of his properties and appurtenant titles. The bill passed on June 29.

Meanwhile, the loopholes regarding Henry's marriage to Anne were pried open once more. When the ambassadors from Cleves could not produce concrete evidence that Anne's precontract to François of Lorraine had ever been officially nullified, Henry believed he'd struck gold. In Tudor times, a precontract had all the validity of a marriage; therefore, Anne was technically still betrothed to François and could not have lawfully entered into a marriage contract with another.

On June 24, Anne was packed off to Richmond Palace, ostensibly for her health, as there had been an outbreak of plague. But she knew that Henry had treated Katherine of Aragon in a similar manner when he decided to cast her aside, and astutely guessed that she was being sent away from court for the same reason.

Not long after her ostracism a delegation was dispatched to inform Anne that Henry intended to submit their marriage to the judgment of an ecclesiastical inquiry called a convocation. At first Anne was hysterical; some accounts state that she fainted on the spot when she was given the bad news. According to Karl Harst, a Cleves agent based in London, "She knew nothing other than she had been granted the king as her husband, and thus she took him to be her true lord and husband." He added, "She made such tears and bitter cries, it would break a heart of stone."

And no wonder. For it seems that Anne was certain her death warrant had just been signed. Understandably, she feared the worst—a sham trial on some trumped-up charges, imprisonment, and execution. Best case scenario, she'd be shoved into a convent somewhere. She also feared repercussions from Cleves. If Henry didn't execute her, but sent her packing back to her homeland instead, she was convinced that her brother would do the deed himself for all the shame she had brought upon her family.

Sources differ as to Anne's reaction once she recovered from her swoons and tears. But over the next few days, with her emotional outburst behind her, Anne began to reconsider her situation, particularly because Henry was ready to offer a deal: Anne could remain in England as the king's "good sister," outranking all other women in the realm except Henry's daughters and any (future) queen. She would receive a generous annual allowance of £4,000 (over $3.25 million today) as well as two residences near the court, Bletchingley and Richmond, and an allotment of eight thousand nobles to staff her new households. The terms were excellent, but Anne was anxious to clarify that Henry would visit her there, and that she would remain welcome at court—proof to those who always wondered how Anne felt about Henry that she was indeed fond of him and enjoyed his company.

Most important, Anne had dodged an axe, and she knew it. Her consent to convocation was delivered to Henry and on Wednesday, July 7, 1540, the ecclesiastical tribunal convened. For the next three days, the convocation took the depositions of several witnesses regarding the legitimacy of a precontract with Lorraine, as well as the failure of Anne and Henry's marriage. They read two confessions written by Cromwell containing intimate details about the problems in the royal bedchamber. There was a concordance among all parties that the marriage had never been consummated, and to further underscore that point, some of Anne's ladies-in-waiting testified as to the queen's complete innocence of sexual matters. On Friday, July 9, the royal marriage was deemed invalid.

Two days later, Anne sent a very cordial letter to the king, submitting to the judgment of the convocation and accepting the invalidity of their union. She had been Queen of England for less than seven months.

Anne returned to Henry "the ring delivered unto her at their pretenced marriage, desiring that it might be broken in pieces as a thing which she knew of no force or value." And on July 17, she resolved to "receive no letters nor messages from her brother, her mother, nor none of her kin or friends, but she would send them to [the king]." Four days later, she wrote to the Duke of Cleves, informing him that "the king's highness whom I cannot have as a husband is nevertheless a most kind, loving and friendly father and brother." She added that she was being treated well, writing, "God willing, I purpose to lead my life in this realm."

Unbeknownst to her, the king did not seem to have considered Anne's execution an option. His chief desire was to extricate himself from their disastrous marriage as quickly and painlessly as possible, and he was delighted that she proved amiable, amicable, and amenable to his terms of settlement.

However, their matchmaker Thomas Cromwell was beheaded on July 28, 1540, the day Henry married his fifth wife, Kathryn Howard.

Years later, Sir Walter Raleigh would describe Henry as "the merciless prince," adding, "for how many servants did he advance in haste and with the change of his fancy ruined again, no man knowing for what offence?"

In the space of five years Thomas Cromwell, acting on Henry's behalf, had transformed England. The break with Rome accomplished much: it launched the tiny island nation as an independent world power, financed the treasury through the dissolution of the monasteries, and created a new class of gentry that resembled a meritocracy, as well as a more centralized government that resulted in a stronger, even tyrannical, monarchy. But the Reformation had become bigger than both Henry and Cromwell and soon grew beyond their control. In the end, its divisiveness, like Cromwell himself, became more of a liability than an asset.

Anne of Cleves remained a great favorite at court—admired by Henry's elder daughter, Princess Mary, and respected by her immediate successor, Kathryn Howard. She grew to love English ale, and developed a taste for gambling. And she seems to have genuinely loved the man who had cast her aside, even hoping to remarry Henry after Kathryn's ignominious execution for adultery. But, for all his own deficiencies of appearance, Henry remained physically unattracted to Anne. As a consolation prize, perhaps, in his last years he gave her three manors in Kent, including the Boleyns' former demesne, Hever Castle. Anne remained something of an anomaly at court: an unmarried woman of independent means and wealth, answerable to no man for her conduct.

After Henry's death in 1547, Anne evidently expressed the desire to return to Cleves, telling her brother that she remained a foreigner in England; but she never did depart for her homeland. Anne made her last public appearance at Mary I's coronation and banquet on September 29, 1553, riding beside the Princess Elizabeth, a place of honor. She died of "a declining illness" at Chelsea Manor on July 16, 1557, at the age of forty-one. In her will, Anne left jewelry to her two stepdaughters, Mary and Elizabeth, and bequeathed gifts to nearly everyone who had served her during her lifetime. Her funeral was held at Westminster Abbey on August 4.

Anne's peers always treated her with tremendous respect, complimenting her "accustomed gentleness" and her religious devotion. It might not have seemed so at first glance, but Henry's high honor of considering her his "good sister" was, in his own way, a mark of the genuine esteem in which he held her character, if not, alas, her face and figure.

HENRY VIII

and

KATHRYN HOWARD

("NO OTHER WILL THAN HIS")

1521(?)–1542

married 1540–1542

> "What a gracious and loving prince I had . . . the fear of
> death grieved me not so much before, as doth now the
> remembrance of the king's goodness."
> —Kathryn Howard's last confession to Thomas
> Cranmer, Archbishop of Canterbury

*B*Y THE BEGINNING OF 1540, HENRY HAD GROWN SO
massive that three large men could fit inside one of his doublets.
The corsets he wore, which made him creak when he walked, little
constricted his girth. But he still considered himself quite the stud
and desperately wanted another son.

The king had married Anne of Cleves on January 6, 1540. But
by April, tongues were wagging about his new infatuation with the
curvaceous redheaded girl the French ambassador had marked for
her exceptional grace.

The previous December, Kathryn Howard, another dark-eyed
auburn-haired niece of the powerful Duke of Norfolk, had come to

court to serve the new queen as a lady-in-waiting. Kathryn's father and Anne Boleyn's mother were siblings, making the young women first cousins. But Kathryn, who was raised as a traditional Catholic rather than as an evangelical, lacked Anne's intelligence, canniness, and political acumen. She also had no qualms about bestowing before marriage what Anne so assiduously withheld. Kathryn was still a teenager when she arrived at court, as much as thirty years Henry's junior, but the king was utterly thunderstruck by her, behaving like an adolescent boy in love, positively giddy with desire.

Many things about Kathryn Howard's early life remain a mystery because they are not well documented, if they are recorded at all. The spelling of her name has been variously Catherine, Katherine, and Kathryn—the last of which, though a contemporary spelling, comes closest to the way she spelled it herself: Katheryn. Her date of birth is also a subject for conjecture, variously given as anywhere from 1518 to 1527. But if she was born at the latter end of the spectrum, she would have been just thirteen years old in 1540, when she married Henry, yet had already been sexually active for years. In Kathryn's case, pinning down a birth date is crucial since it makes all the difference between a lusty teenager capable of making more informed decisions about her body and a sexually precocious child. The latter possibility is the opinion of historical biographer Joanna Denny, who believes that Kathryn was "sexually abused" when she was as young as ten years old.

Denny surmises that Kathryn had to have been born between 1524 and 1527, simply because she is named in a will written in 1527 by Kathryn's step-grandmother Isabel Legh, whereas she is not referred to in a 1524 will written by Isabel's husband, John. Denny speculates that Isabel wanted to wait until Kathryn survived infancy to name her as a beneficiary, which is why Kathryn could have been a toddler at the time of the 1527 will. While Kathryn's inclusion in Isabel Legh's last will and testament offers a plausible argument for a birth date later than 1520 or so, it is equally possible that any previous omission from a will was an oversight; or that more closely related beneficiaries had already died off; or merely that Legh would not have been under any obligation to include a step-grandchild in her will. Too much is open to conjecture to rely on the will of Isabel Legh as an accurate anchor for pinpointing Kathryn's date of birth.

Another factor to consider in arriving at a relatively accurate birth date for Kathryn is Henry's sexual proclivity—which, even in his own youth, had never been for prepubescent girls. Both Anne Boleyn and Jane Seymour were in their mid-twenties when he became infatuated with them. Even his earliest mistresses, like Bessie Blount and Mary Boleyn, were in their late teens. And in 1539 he had deliberately chosen the elder of the two Cleves sisters because he thought that a narrower age gap would increase their chances of marital compatibility.

Kathryn's father, Lord Edmund Howard, was the third son of the 2nd Duke of Norfolk. He had acquitted himself bravely as a soldier and was knighted in 1515, but the world beat him down, and his lifetime was hampered by poverty as he endeavored to provide for an enormous family while keeping one step ahead of the bailiffs. The best that he and Kathryn's mother, Jocasta Culpeper, could do was to place some of their large brood with more affluent relatives who could afford to give them a better upbringing.

Jocasta had already passed away when Kathryn was sent to live with her other step-grandmother, Agnes Howard, the Dowager Duchess of Norfolk. Most historians agree that Kathryn was around twelve years old at the time, one of a number of poorer female Howard relations who served the duchess as junior ladies-in-waiting; they were also schooled and boarded in the duchess's homes—Chesworth, her estate in Horsham, Sussex, or her London home at Lambeth.

Kathryn was housed with the other girls of her ilk in a large room known as the Maidens' Chamber. And it was during her years in the duchess's household that Kathryn received her sexual initiation, flirting and petting with her music tutor, Henry Manox. When the dowager duchess caught them, Kathryn spurned Manox for one of her clerks, a distant relation named Francis Dereham.

Although the duchess locked the Maidens' Chamber every evening and pocketed the key, Kathryn bribed Lady Agnes's maid, Mary Lascelles, into stealing it night after night. For several months, if not for close to five years, depending on the source, Francis Dereham became Kathryn's nightly visitor.

The duchess's solution, now that her charge had been compromised? Send Dereham back to Ireland, and find a position for the spirited Kathryn at court. But when Dereham departed, he left a hundred pounds—a vast sum, especially for a clerk—in Kathryn's safekeeping, which suggests that they might have entered into some form of a precontract of marriage.

Kathryn had not been at court for long when she took notice of one of Henry's higher-ranking courtiers, Thomas Culpeper. Thomas was her distant relation on her mother's side, and one of the king's Privy Chamber. When rumors of marriage plans between them began to spread, Kathryn hotly contradicted the gossip, stating, "If you heard such a report, you heard more than I do know." It was only a matter of weeks before Kathryn would make a far bigger conquest.

By this time, the king was already head over heels in lust with her. Although he was married to Anne of Cleves, Henry courted Kathryn in a big way. On April 24, 1540, Henry made her a gift of lands that had been confiscated from a felon. A month later, Kathryn received several bolts of silk. The French ambassador reported that Henry could not "treat her well enough." She was showered with jewels, and given such authority and power as she had never known—all heady stuff to a teenager who had been raised in genteel poverty.

On the twentieth of June, Queen Anne complained of Henry's attraction to Kathryn to Karl Harst, the Duke of Cleves's ambassador. Harst reported to the duke that the royal affair had been going on for months.

Within days of Anne's complaint the king had their marriage annulled. And on July 28, in the middle of a particularly hot and dry summer, he and Kathryn wed at Oatlands Palace in Surrey in a secret ceremony conducted by Bishop Bonner. Kathryn vowed to be "bonair and buxom in bed," and to cherish her husband "in sickness and health, till death us depart."

The king's ambassadors to foreign lands were informed of his nuptials in a statement issued on August 8, 1540, that "upon a notable appearance of honor, cleanness and maidenly behavior . . . [and that] His Highness was finally contented to honor that lady with his marriage, thinking in his old days—after sundry troubles of mind which had happened to him by marriage—to have obtained such a perfect jewel of womanhood and very perfect love towards him as should have been not only to his quietness but also to have brought forth the desired fruits of marriage."

For her queenly motto, Kathryn had chosen the submissive phrase *non aultre volonté que le sienne*—no other will than his—an unfortunately ironic selection, as things turned out.

Henry's king-sized ego blinded him to the flaws of his diminutive new bride. "The king's affection was so marvelously set upon that gentlewoman, as it was never known that he had the like to any woman," wrote Ralph Morice, secretary to Archbishop Cranmer. He spent more on Kathryn's gowns, jewels, and household expenses than he had for any of his other wives. It cost Henry £46,000 a year—over $26 million in today's economy—to maintain Kathryn's personal establishment.

Kathryn found places in her household for most of the young ladies from her Maidens' Chamber days. And when her former lover Francis Dereham turned up at her doorstep, she made him one of her clerks, a move that was ill-advised at best; but her step-grandmother, the dowager duchess, had pressed her for the favor. There may also have been another motive for the plum appointment: blackmail.

But if Kathryn had expected to purchase Dereham's silence regarding their former love affair, her plan backfired ostentatiously. Dereham abused his position, behaving like one of his betters. When he was caught lingering over his dinner, a perquisite reserved for members of the Queen's Council, he retorted somewhat cryptically,

"I was of the Queen's Council before [his accuser] knew her, and shall be when she hath forgotten him."

In October 1540, the Queen Consort Act was passed by Parliament, giving Kathryn the right to "act as a woman sole, without the consent of the King's Highness." Unfortunately, the teen queen would end up taking her privileges of autonomy too literally.

The following February, Kathryn ended up presiding over the court entertainments on her own, because Henry's mobility was sorely restricted due to his painful ulcerated leg wound. Preferring solitude to the company of others, he lapsed into severe melancholia, described by the French ambassador Marillac as a *mal d'esprit*. By this time, Henry was positively Leviathan; although he was extremely self-conscious about his girth, he continued to eat and drink like a glutton. His irascibility and mood swings were noticed by the court, and remarked upon, with Marillac reporting to his sovereign that "people say he is often of a different opinion in the morning than after dinner."

In July 1541, Henry deemed it the right time to finally make a Royal Progress, an official tour of his kingdom that had been postponed several times because of various northern uprisings.

During this journey, a change in Kathryn's behavior began to be noted. At their stop in Lincoln, Henry retired early, but the queen's apartments were lit until the wee hours of the morning. The night watchman observed that the door to her back stairs was ajar, so he locked it, but not too much later, he saw two figures approach the door. After fumbling with the lock, they slipped wordlessly into the queen's rooms.

A few days later, Henry took the court on a hunting break at Hartfield Chase. Kathryn's ladies spied her glancing out the window of her bedchamber at Thomas Culpeper, fixing him with a look of purest lust. It was a gaze her minions would long remember.

So—did they become lovers? As history has made all too clear, Kathryn's position depended on giving the king another son. Henry's numerous infirmities, his enormity, and his advancing age might have already rendered conception improbable, if not impossible. Nonetheless, for the good of the realm (and of the Howard family), the Duke of Norfolk was impatient for his niece to become pregnant. Time was of the essence; already a year of marriage had come and gone. It was not beneath the duke's morals to suggest that Kathryn hasten the process. If she could not conceive with the king, then Kathryn could pass off Culpeper's bastard as Henry's, on the assumption that the egotistical monarch would cheerfully claim paternity because it would confirm his virility.

Kathryn later insisted that she and Culpeper had a platonic relationship and were simply conversing all night, but a locked door never looks good.

On November 1, with the Progress over and the court back in London, Henry declared his happiness in a solemn thanksgiving service, ironically enumerating among his blessings the virtuousness of his wife.

With theatrical timing, the following day Thomas Cranmer, Archbishop of Canterbury, approached Henry with the document that would destroy the king's fantasies and bring down the fragile house of cards of his fifth marriage. Early in October, Cranmer had received a letter from John Lascelles informing him of Kathryn's infidelity. John was the brother of the Dowager Duchess of Norfolk's maid, Mary Lascelles—the same Mary Lascelles who used to procure the keys to the Maidens' Chamber so that Francis Dereham could sneak into the room to have orgiastic sex with Kathryn. And Kathryn had managed to find a place in her establishment for all of her former acquaintances—except Mary Lascelles.

So Mary had a motive for destroying Kathryn.

But there was more to the picture. The Lascelles family were staunch Reformers, as was Cranmer; and the Reformers wanted nothing more than to bring down the powerful (and Catholic) Howards before they gained so much influence at court that Henry would become dissuaded from reforming the religion. Cranmer didn't really have anything against Kathryn *per se*, but he weighed the consequences and concluded that it would be all right with his conscience to sacrifice the queen if it meant saving his infant church.

When Henry read the accusations against Kathryn, his first reaction was disbelief. He insisted that an investigation into these allegations be conducted in secret. Meanwhile, Kathryn was kept at Hampton Court while Henry developed excuses for not visiting her. In fact, he would never see his wife again.

The investigative hearings began on November 5, 1541. Kathryn stood accused of fornicating before marriage with both Henry Manox and Francis Dereham. The transcripts of the hearings include testimony so graphic that a twenty-first-century tabloid couldn't print it without running afoul of the pornography laws.

Mary Lascelles, the first to testify, claimed that she had reproved Manox for his presumption in thinking that Kathryn would ever be his, adding that on hearing this, Manox had laughed in Mary's face and boastfully replied, "I know her well enough, for I have had her by the cunt, and I know it among a hundred. . . . And she loves me and I love her, and she had said to me that I shall have her maidenhead, though it be painful to her. . . ."

According to Manox's version of events, although Kathryn had withheld her virginity from him, she had promised that he would not go entirely unsatisfied. "Yet let me feel your secret place," the music teacher cajoled. According to Manox, Kathryn assented, "and I felt more than was convenient," he admitted. However, Manox swore "upon [his] damnation and the most extreme punishment of [his] body" that he never did more with Kathryn than that act of groping, and had never known her carnally.

Throughout the hearings, Manox would not be budged from this testimony. It would ultimately free him, as there was nothing for which he could be convicted. Manox would be the only one implicated in the scandal to walk away with his head on his shoulders.

But Dereham was another story. Referring to their sexual hijinks in the Maidens' Chamber, long before Kathryn came to court, under oath he confessed "carnal knowledge with the Queen . . . lying in bed by her in [his] doublet and hosen divers times and six or seven times naked in bed with her." He further admitted that on two separate occasions, after the commencement of his employment in her household, Kathryn had bribed him to keep quiet about their shared past.

Mary Lascelles, who averred that Kathryn was "light in both living and conditions," offered a lurid description of the lovers' canoodling, "for they would kiss and hang by their bills together as if they were two sparrows."

"There was such puffing and blowing between them that [she] was weary of the same," testified Alice Restwood, Kathryn's former bedfellow in the Maidens' Chamber.

Another eyewitness was just as much of a voyeur. Margaret Benet, also a former resident of the Maidens' Chamber, told the council she peered through the hole in a door, "and there saw Dereham pluck up Kathryn's clothes above her navel so that [Margaret] might well discern her body." Margaret overheard Dereham say "that although he used the company of a woman . . . yet he would get no child except he listed [desired to have one]." The voluble Miss Benet had heard Kathryn reply that "a woman might meddle with a man and yet conceive no child unless she would herself."

Dereham's friend Robert Davenport confessed that he had heard Francis Dereham call Kathryn "his own wife" before witnesses, which would certainly imply a precontract of marriage between them. Even more damaging was his testimony regarding Dereham's recent boast that if Henry "were dead I am sure I might marry her." According to the 1534 treason act, maliciously desiring the death of the king was a treasonable offense—enough to condemn Dereham to death regardless of whatever else he might have done with Kathryn.

Henry was moved to tears. His virtuous wife had turned out to be nothing but a harlot. And yet he had never inquired about her past sexual experience, nor sent someone to ascertain the details for him before he chose to marry her.

Even as the council heard witness after witness shred Kathryn's virtue, the queen herself, holed up at Hampton Court, remained unaware of the investigation. When the king's men came to place her under house arrest and found her making merry with her maids, they informed the queen that it was "no more the time to dance."

Kathryn was first informed about the proceedings on November 7, two days after they had commenced. But the evidence against her had been so well rehearsed that a refutation of the charges was impossible. She could only counter them with resignation and abject humility.

The authorities gave Kathryn every chance to admit a precontract with Dereham, which would have saved her life, since the precontract was itself tantamount to a marriage. If she *had* been contracted to Dereham, then her marriage to Henry would have been null and void—and she could not possibly have committed adultery if she was not Henry's wife.

But Kathryn was unschooled in canon law, and too hysterical to comprehend the nuances of the situation. She insisted that Dereham had forced himself upon her in the Maidens' Chamber, averring that she had never welcomed his advances. But no one believed her version of events because of the duration of their relationship and the numerous love tokens exchanged.

On November 11, the Privy Council ordered the queen's household to be broken up. Most of Kathryn's ladies were dismissed, leaving her with a minimum of attendants. Kathryn's jewels and sumptuous gowns were confiscated. The council issued a public statement intended for dissemination abroad: "The king . . . being solicited by his Council to marry again took to wife Katherine . . . but this joy is turned to extreme sorrow . . . having heard that she was not a woman of such purity as was esteemed. . . . Now you may see what was done before marriage. God knoweth what hath been done since."

Kathryn was arrested on November 12, 1541. When Henry refused to see her, she wrote him a desperate request for clemency, admitting that she was now unworthy of being his wife, let alone his subject. She confessed that she had

> been so blinded by desire of worldly glory that I could not . . . consider how great a fault it was to conceal my former faults from Your Majesty, considering that I intended ever during my life to be faithful and true unto Your Majesty ever after.
>
> . . . First, at the flattering and fair persuasions of Manox, being but a young girl, I suffered him at sundry times to handle and touch the secret parts of my body. . . .
>
> Also, Francis Dereham, by many persuasions procured me to his vicious purpose and obtained first to lie upon my bed with his doublet and hose and after within the bed and finally he lay with me naked, and used me in such sort as a man doth his wife many and sundry times, but how often I know not.
>
> Our company ended almost a year before the King's Majesty was married to my Lady Anne of Cleves and continued not past one quarter of a year or a little above.

In her defense, Kathryn urged Henry "to consider the subtle persuasions of young men and the ignorance and frailness of young women."

Kathryn had been guilty of being young and lusty, something Henry understood firsthand. For that, he could consign her to a convent forever, but at least her life would be spared. Surprisingly— maybe because he was older, or perhaps because part of him remained infatuated with Kathryn—Henry was inclined to consider clemency. On November 14, he sent Kathryn to Syon, a former convent, while the whole sordid business could be sorted out.

The Privy Council had described Henry's profound sorrow and distress in a November 12 letter to Sir William Paget, the resident ambassador in France, informing him that the king had been so overcome with emotion over Kathryn's betrayal that he wept "plenty of tears." But then Jane Rochford, Kathryn's Lady of the

Bedchamber and the sister-in-law of the late Anne Boleyn, stepped forward. After she unburdened her conscience, any consideration of royal mercy was mooted. Lady Rochford informed the king that she had acted as go-between and gatekeeper when Kathryn admitted Thomas Culpeper to her bedchamber on numerous occasions after Kathryn had married Henry.

If Kathryn had slept with Culpeper during the Royal Progress, she had indeed committed adultery—as well as high treason, because she had cuckolded a king. And the penalty was death.

On November 12, 1541, Culpeper was arrested and taken to the Tower. His rank prohibited him from being subjected to torture or undue duress, but even without those encouragements he did have more to say on the matter. Culpeper delineated in chapter and verse the extent of his affair with the queen, stating that on Maundy Thursday (April 14, 1541), he was summoned by one of Kathryn's servants to the queen's presence, where Kathryn gave him "by her own hand a fair cap of velvet garnished with a brooch, along with three dozen pairs of aglets [decorative pins] and a chain, [advising him to] 'Put this under your cloak [and let] nobody see it.'"

Culpeper explained that their subsequent meetings consisted of considerable flirtatious banter, during which he received additional gifts and marks of favor from Kathryn; and he admitted to having been the one who picked the lock with his servant in order to gain access to her chamber when the Royal Progress stopped in Lincoln. But what would consign the young queen to the block was the letter she subsequently wrote to him after learning that he was ill:

Master Culpepper,
I heartily recommend me unto you, praying you to send me word how that you do. . . . For I never longed so much for a thing as I do to see you and to speak with you. . . .
. . . and when I think again that you shall depart from me . . . it makes my heart to die to think what fortune I have that I cannot be always in your company.

. . . I would you were with me now, that you might see what pain I take in writing you.

> Yours as long as life endures,
> Katheryn

Though this missive provides no proof of *sexual* intercourse, to write it and send it was spectacularly ill-advised. And perhaps Kathryn was telling the truth when she insisted that she and Culpeper were not making love all those nights they spent together during the Progress. Historian Retha Warnicke hypothesizes that the subject of their furtive clandestine meetings might have been blackmail instead—Culpeper's threats to spill the beans about Kathryn's relationship with Francis Dereham and her efforts to forestall him. Knowing that he wanted to bed her, did Kathryn intend to string Culpeper along just enough to keep him hopeful, aware that he'd stay mum as long as he expected her to yield her body to him as a reward for his silence?

On the other hand, Kathryn had left her door ajar for Culpeper on purpose, and there was that night that he had broken the lock to Kathryn's bedchamber so that they could enjoy their preplanned rendezvous. Culpeper had admitted he "meant to do ill with the Queen, and that likewise the Queen so minded with him."

His testimony would be enough to convict them both.

The royal ego was crushed. Not only had the Howards sold Henry damaged goods, but he had been cuckolded in the bargain. And the entire court knew it. So would the rest of the world, once the foreign ambassadors sent their dispatches.

It's hard not to feel somewhat sorry for Henry, so self-deluded was he about his virility. Or was he? To condemn Kathryn was to air his own fragile insecurities about his age, his health, and his sexual prowess. His mortality mocked him, and with each passing day it became more important to insure the succession of his crown and the propagation of the Tudor dynasty. Yet court insiders claimed that Henry seemed to age overnight when he learned that his beloved "rose without a thorn" might have played him for a fool. Chapuys reported that "the king has wonderfully felt the case of his wife. He has certainly shown greater sorrow and regret at her loss, than at the faults, loss or divorce of his preceding wives," and he had never seen Henry "so sad, pensive and sighing." Henry openly "regretted his ill luck in meeting with such horribly ill-conditioned wives." Enraged and horribly disappointed by Kathryn's conduct, he called for his sword that he might kill her "that he loved so much." All the pleasure "that wicked woman" had derived from her "incontinency" should not equal the pain she should receive from torture.

Anne of Cleves also weighed in on the subject of Kathryn's downfall, remarking that "she was too much a child to deny herself any sweet thing she wanted." On November 19, Chapuys reported, "I hear also that the Lady Anne of Cleves has greatly rejoiced . . . and that in order to be nearer the King she is come to, if she is not already at, Richmond."

As eager as Anne had been to extricate herself from her royal marriage with all limbs intact and as large a settlement as possible, she remained extremely fond of Henry—even sexually attracted to him—and wasn't about to miss the opportunity to become his consort again.

But Henry remained staunchly uninterested in such a reunion. On December 15 the Privy Council issued a formal statement: "The separation had been made for such just cause that [the King] prayed to the Duke [Anne's brother] never to make such a request."

By official proclamation Kathryn had been demoted from queen on November 22, 1541, to be called simply Kathryn Howard from then on. That day she was indicted for having led "an abominable, base, carnal, voluptuous, and vicious life before her royal marriage," behaving "like a common harlot with divers persons, maintaining however the outward appearance of chastity and honesty." She was accused of leading the king "by word and gesture to love her," and "arrogantly coupled herself with him in marriage," concealing her precontract with Francis Dereham "to the peril of the king and his children to be begotten by her," as well as seducing Culpeper and telling him that she preferred him to the king.

On December 1, 1541, although both men refused to confess to carnal knowledge with Kathryn after she had become queen, Culpeper and Dereham were tried for treason and found guilty. They were executed on December 10.

In mid-January 1542, at the urging of Parliament, a Bill of Attainder in the form of a petition was drawn up, permitting Henry to execute Kathryn and her lady-in-waiting Lady Rochford for high treason, the penalty for which was "death and the confiscation of goods." Although Kathryn had never confessed to adultery, it was Henry's will that she be put to death under the "violent assumption" that she had been unfaithful to him. It was also considered misprision of treason for anyone to conceal knowledge of such an offense—and that's what convicted Lady Rochford.

There was some hesitation about using an Act of Attainder against the former queen without her being afforded the opportunity to speak for herself, so a delegation was dispatched to Syon House to hear her side of the story. But Kathryn refused to defend herself, openly acknowledging her guilt instead. However, she did request that Henry spare her relations from being punished, that he "would not impute [her] crime to [her] whole kindred and family." She also asked that Henry give some of her fine attire to her household, "since she had nothing now to recompense them as they deserved."

On February 10, Kathryn, clad in black velvet, was taken by barge from Syon to the Tower, amid a bout of perfectly understandable last-minute hysterics. She spent her final days in the Queen's Apartments at the Tower, amid the same honors and ceremonies that had been accorded to her when she was Queen of England, despite the fact that she had been stripped of her title.

The Act of Attainder received Henry's assent in absentia on February 11. Although the words *le roi le veut* (the king wills it) had been printed at the top of the document, Henry never actually signed it and both women would meet their gruesome ends without the king's formal imprimatur.

Kathryn was brought before Cranmer to make her confession. It was a pitiful sight. Cranmer said, "I found her in such lamentation and heaviness as I never saw no creature, so that it would have pitied any man's heart in the world to have looked upon her." Endeavoring to calm her troubled soul, the archbishop gave her some false hope for the king's mercy, which did have the intended effect.

"What a gracious and loving prince I had," she wept. "Alas, my lord that I am still alive; the fear of death grieved me not so much before, as doth now the remembrance of the king's goodness."

But there was to be no clemency.

On Sunday, February 12, Kathryn was told that she would die the next day. In an oft-repeated anecdote, the utterly terrified young woman asked for the block to be brought to her, so she could "make trial of it, that she might know how to place herself." She tearfully confessed that she deserved a thousand deaths for so offending a king who had treated her so graciously.

Kathryn Howard was executed on Tower Hill, where Anne Boleyn had met her end six years earlier. She was probably only twenty years old, and had been queen for just over eighteen months.

The weeping ladies-in-waiting wrapped her bleeding body parts in blankets and Kathryn's remains were placed in a coffin that was buried alongside Anne Boleyn's in the little Tower church of St. Peter ad Vincula.

Lady Rochford was then beheaded on the block still red with Kathryn's blood.

Though Henry enjoyed a court banquet and feasted his eye upon numerous attractive young ladies just two weeks later, it would take nearly eighteen months before his heart and his ego recovered sufficiently from the queen's alleged infidelity to consider remarrying. In April 1542, imperial ambassador Chapuys reported to Charles V that "since he has heard of his late wife's conduct he has not been the same man."

The Act of Attainder against Kathryn and Lady Rochford stood until 1553, when Queen Mary reversed it because it lacked the sovereign's signature. Although it was obviously too late for the queen and her lady-in-waiting to materially benefit from Mary's action, it restored a measure of their dignity.

Within Hampton Court Palace is a corridor known as the Haunted Gallery. Legend has it that while Henry was attending services in the chapel, Kathryn managed to escape from her guarded chamber and ran down the corridor hoping to speak with her husband and beg his mercy. Over the centuries there have been several sightings of a ghost dressed in a white Tudor-era gown shouting Henry's name as it races desperately down the length of the hallway toward the chapel, knocking unsuspecting tourists to their feet in its effort to reach the door.

Henry VIII

❧ *and* ❧

Catherine Parr

("To Be Useful in All That I Do")

1512–1548

married 1543–1547

"... And thus love maketh me ... set apart mine own ...
pleasure and to embrace most joyfully his will and pleasure whom I love. ..."

> —Catherine Parr, in a letter to Henry written in
> July 1544

$\mathscr{H}$ENRY VIII'S WIVES ARE SIX OF THE MOST FAMOUS
women in history, in part because their husband had a singular
view of marriage. He was determined to wed for *love* as well as
dynasty, which he managed to do five out of six times; but when he
became disappointed in both, he coldly moved on, saddled up, and
sought a woman who could bring him his heart's desire. Even his
passions were larger than life and anomalous in his own era.

After Kathryn Howard's execution in 1542, Henry dipped his
gouty toes in the marital waters one more time, wedding the childless, twice-widowed, wealthy, "middle-aged" (at thirty) Catherine
Parr. At the time, the massively corpulent king suffered from high

blood pressure, chronic indigestion, and debilitating headaches in addition to a festering, ulcerated leg wound. Unbeknownst to Catherine, she'd successfully auditioned for the role of wife and queen by assiduously nursing her dying second husband, Lord Latimer, a man of the king's vintage some two decades Catherine's senior. But Catherine possessed other redeeming qualities as well. Prudent, dignified, and virtuous, she was also well bred, exceptionally well educated for a gentlewoman of the day, and extremely lovely—a slender, gray-eyed redhead of medium height (four of Henry's six wives were auburn-haired) with an exquisite fashion sense and a passion for diamonds. Her only drawback was that during four years of marriage to her first husband and nine years to her second, she had not borne any children, leading to the presumption of barrenness. But Henry was ever-hopeful that Catherine would give him a Duke of York.

Derided by her detractors as a mere Yorkshire housewife, Catherine was a commoner, but she came from a family with generations of royal service. Her father, Sir Thomas Parr, had been a respected career courtier, well born and well connected. Maud Green, her mother, was a lady-in-waiting to Katherine of Aragon. Catherine, the eldest of the three Parr children, had been named in the queen's honor; in all likelihood (and ironically, if true), Henry VIII's first wife was the godmother to his sixth.

Although Sir Thomas died when Catherine was only five years old, she grew up in an atmosphere of comfort and privilege. Widowed at the age of twenty-two, Maud never remarried. Instead, she founded and ran a highly respected academy that taught "courtesy"— the skills necessary for one to become a crackerjack courtier—to young boys and girls. Catherine was among the pupils who learned languages, the art of conversation, dancing, musicianship, manners, deportment, and court etiquette, although legend has it that when Maud ordered her to attend to her instructions in needlework, the girl pertly replied that according to a fortune-teller, her "hands were ordained for scepters" instead.

During the winter of 1542–43, while Catherine's second husband, Lord Latimer, was on his last legs in London, Catherine re-kindled her connection with the Lady Mary and was granted a position of responsibility in the princess's household. It was there that Catherine caught the king's eye. Soon, observers were commenting that Henry "was calling at [Mary's] apartment two or three times a day."

Lord Latimer was buried on March 2, 1543, leaving Catherine at liberty to wed the man who had utterly captured her heart—but he wasn't the king. Her inamorata was Sir Thomas Seymour, the darkly handsome, ambitious, and reckless older brother of the late queen Jane. Charismatic and cosmopolitan, Seymour cut a romantic dash at court. Being widely traveled and battle-hardened on both land and sea made him even more of a chick magnet.

Unfortunately, he didn't make his move in time; by the late spring of 1543, Henry had exercised his *droit du seigneur* and proposed to Catherine. However, she had no hunger to be Queen of England. The king's attentions terrified her. "Better to be his mistress than his wife," she purportedly exclaimed, having seen or heard enough about the way Henry treated his spouses to not want the job. Although an offer of marriage from the king was one she couldn't refuse, Catherine still suffered a crisis of conscience, asking God to impart His plan for her. An "evangelical," or proponent of the reformed religion, Catherine ultimately had an epiphany: It was the will of the Almighty that she accept Henry's hand, becoming his wife and queen, in order to have a profound effect on completing England's conversion to the new religion.

So she laid aside her attraction to Thomas Seymour and accepted her destiny.

Catherine rejoined the court at Greenwich on June 19, which is probably when she gave the king her consent. On July 11 the Archbishop of Canterbury, Thomas Cranmer, issued his license permitting the couple to wed "in any church, chapel, or oratory without the issue of banns."

Catherine and Henry were married in the Queen's Privy Closet in Greenwich on July 12, 1543, in a quiet ceremony conducted by

Stephen Gardiner, the Bishop of Winchester. The two most honored of the twenty or so guests were Henry's daughters, Mary—
just four years younger than her new stepmother—and nine-year-old
Elizabeth.

Omitted from the guest list was Henry's "good sister," Anne
of Cleves, who was still angling for a second shot at being Mrs.
Tudor, and was rather miffed that she had been passed over for a
commoner who was "by no means so handsome as she herself is."
Perhaps the pill would have been less bitter for Anne to swallow if
Henry had wed a womb again, a young and fertile teen, rather than
someone who was three years Anne's senior, a woman who "gives
no hope of posterity to the king, for she had no children by her first
two husbands." Even so, Catherine was twenty-one years younger
than her third bridegroom.

Henry recited his vows "with a joyous look" as he held Catherine's hands. When asked by the bishop if he took Catherine to be
his wife, he replied with a resounding "yea." No record has been
made of what might have been going through the bride's head at
the time. Perhaps she was hoping she'd get to keep it. That day,
Catherine was proclaimed Queen of England. But there was no
grand procession into London or lavish coronation ceremony.

A few days later the newlyweds embarked on a Royal Progress—a
tour of the kingdom that kept them together for the next six
months. For much of the time during the early part of the marriage
Catherine, Henry, and all three of his children lived in one household. Although the king himself suffered from myriad ailments, his
domestic situation was the healthiest it had ever been.

Catherine may have thought of Thomas Seymour every time she
gave herself to Henry, but she did her best to keep the king enticed
in the boudoir. Among her first purchases as a newlywed were
"eleven yards of black damask for a nightgown" and "for the making of a nightgown of black satin with two burgundian garde[s]
[sleeve trimmings] embroidered and edged with velvet." As fastidious as Henry about personal hygiene, Catherine routinely soaked
in a leaden tub, indulging in milk baths scented with aromatic oils,

such as cinnamon, clove, and olive. She purchased rosewater and other fragrances; groomed her eyebrows with silver tweezers; and was never without her breath mints flavored with clove, licorice, or cinnamon.

Catherine's relations benefited enormously from her new status. Over the Christmas holidays in 1543–44 her brother was created Earl of Essex and her uncle, Lord Parr, was made a baron. It was during that same holiday season that Henry met with the Viceroy of Sicily, an envoy of Charles V of Spain, to discuss plans for a joint invasion of France.

On July 7, 1544, the Privy Council convened at Whitehall to hear and endorse Henry's plans for Catherine's regency in his absence. She would be responsible for "His Highness's Process," which included all governmental, financial, and legal business, and which "shall pass in her name." A five-man council was appointed to assist her.

Henry departed for France on July 11 and Catherine rode with him as far as Greenwich. Soon after they said farewell, Catherine wrote to her husband, to tell him,

> Although the . . . time . . . of days neither is long nor many of your Majesty's absence, yet the want of your presence [is] so much . . . desired of me . . . that I cannot quietly pleasure in anything until I hear from your Majesty . . . and thus love maketh me in all things to set apart mine own commodity and pleasure to embrace most joyfully his will and pleasure whom I love. God, the knower of secrets, can judge these words not only to be written with ink, but most truly impressed in the heart.

Her words show how adept Catherine had become at managing her often difficult husband, playing to his vanity, assuring him of his supremacy in their relationship, and being artfully female while remaining heartfelt. If nothing else, they were intellectually compatible, and Catherine had entered the marriage with her eyes wide open. Although she hadn't been in love with Henry at the time she accepted his hand, time and proximity had metamorphosed her feelings into an affectionate and respectful, if not wholly ardent, love.

But Catherine's personality was not as placid as her champions would lead us to believe. She shared the king's passion for such lively recreational pursuits as hunting and dancing, and no doubt her quick wit and her outspokenness helped divert Henry from his troubles. She was indeed loyal and affectionate to a fault—but she also had a fiery temper.

During Catherine's regency she was the de facto head of the royal family. Aware of the precariousness of her husband's health and the possibility that he might not return from the war, she went on Progress with the three royal children in order to present to the country a show of unity and continuity. She considered it vital to familiarize herself with the needs of her subjects throughout the kingdom in addition to proving that she could handle the regent's responsibilities, should the job become a permanent one. Catherine also managed the council and oversaw the supplies of troops, materiel, and money for Henry's multifronted military campaigns, as well as rendering decisions on issues that affected northern England, signing five royal proclamations during her regency. Her formal signature, "Catherine the Queen KP," radically included the initials of her maiden name.

Catherine had adopted as her royal motto *To Be Useful in All I Do*, and indeed she was. Before her patience was required to help nurse Henry during his final illnesses, she reconciled him to his two daughters, leading to the 1544 Act of Succession that permitted Mary and Elizabeth to accede to the throne—although the act did not relegitimize them. Despite their widely divergent religious views, Catherine and Mary got along very well, as they were both among the increasing number of noblewomen described by the scholar Nicholas Udall as "given to the study of devotion and of strange [that is, foreign] tongues."

Catherine also had a profound influence on her younger stepdaughter. While Henry was in France, the eleven-year-old Elizabeth wrote Catherine a warm and articulate letter in her newly learned language of Italian, reminding the queen that it had been "a whole year" since they'd seen each other. She missed Catherine, hoped to see her again soon, but also eagerly anticipated a reunion with her father on his return from the Continent.

So Catherine brought Elizabeth to court for the summer, where the young princess received an up-close-and-personal object lesson in her stepmother's evangelical convictions as well as in Catherine's prodigious competence, efficiency, capability, and the respect she commanded in a man's world. During those few months Elizabeth also established relationships with members of Catherine's household. Fourteen years later, as Queen of England, she would tap some of the same talent.

Catherine was the epicenter of a literary circle focused on evangelical tracts written or published in the vernacular. At a time when most women of the gentry were barely educated, Catherine was the author of at least one devotional work. One of only seven early-Tudor-era females to be a published writer, her intellectual accomplishments were rare for her day. Catherine's first book, *The Prayers Stirring the Mind unto Heavenly Meditations*, was published by the royal printer in June of 1545 and became an immediate bestseller. It was reprinted that November, and went through nineteen editions during the sixteenth century. Another of Catherine's books, *Lamentation of a Sinner*, was published nine months after Henry's death; the queen had kept her manuscript hidden from her husband because of its subversive ideology, which included the concept that worldly princes were impotent in comparison to the heavenly prince, Jesus Christ. Catherine also commissioned translations of works that required more scholarship than she possessed; the Princess Mary, with her superior knowledge of Latin, was persuaded to be one of the translators.

But Catherine became overconfident in Henry's affections. Evincing a surprising insensitivity to the right time and place for evangelizing in his presence, she was not attuned to Henry's sudden and volatile mood swings and his capacity for unrepentant cruelty, which intensified in his final years. Not having been at court when other royal favorites, including Thomas More, Cardinal Wolsey, Anne Boleyn, and Thomas Cromwell, had fallen from the king's grace and met their grisly ends, Catherine overestimated Henry's tolerance.

Therefore, her spirited sparring with Henry over the hot-button theological issues of the day nearly cost *her* her head. She didn't merely debate with her husband; she contradicted him and presumed to correct and instruct him. According to a contemporary, John Foxe, Catherine's regular prayer meetings and religious discussions in her Privy Chamber "were not secretly done, so neither were their preachings unknown to the King . . . whereof at first, and for a great time, he seemed very well to like." But Foxe felt that Catherine pushed the envelope just a smidge too much and this hubris presaged her downfall.

The winter of 1545–46 marked a sea change in the royal marriage. By January 1546, a full year before Henry's death, he and Catherine no longer enjoyed lighthearted pleasures together. Henry's immense girth and numerous ailments rendered him practically immobile, and rather than wait for him to visit her, Catherine spent long hours in his apartments in order to share quality time with him. Their conversations invariably turned to the subject of religion, but one day, plagued by pain from the ulcerated wound on his leg, Henry nearly lost his temper in her presence. He bid her a hearty "Farewell sweetheart," but no sooner had her footsteps become a distant echo than the king exclaimed, "A good hearing it is when women become such clerks; and a thing much to my comfort, to come in mine old days to be taught by my wife." Testy and cranky, Henry had no desire to hear Catherine's moralizing and sermonizing. The tenets of the new religion—which he had enthusiastically embraced in order to justify his divorce from Katherine of Aragon and his marriage to Anne Boleyn—now got on his very last nerve. All too aware that the meeting with his Maker was on the horizon, Henry flirted with reverting toward his former, more traditional convictions, although he thoroughly enjoyed his religious autonomy and would never have considered reconciling with Rome.

Eager to bring Catherine down, Stephen Gardiner, Bishop of Winchester—who had officiated at her wedding to Henry—in concert with the Lord Chancellor Sir Thomas Wriothesley, conspired to turn the king against her. It was forbidden for most of Henry's subjects, especially women of all social strata, to possess religious tracts—including the Bible—that were written in the vernacular (English), because it gave them a measure of power that made both crown and clergy uncomfortable. Wriothesley and Gardiner aimed to convince Henry that his wife's ambitious religious goals should be viewed as treacherous. Their plans for a coup included arresting the queen's three leading ladies-in-waiting, seizing the contraband books in their possession, and sending Catherine to the Tower.

On the surface, Henry appears to have been a key player in this scheme, confiding to one of his physicians—both of whom were closely tied to Catherine—how he intended to rid himself of such a "doctress" as his wife. But if he had *really* been on board with the plan, wouldn't it have been an odd thing to discuss it with his doctor? The king swore the medical man to secrecy "on peril of his life," which he must have done with a nudge and a wink, knowing that the doctor would probably go straight to the queen with the news.

So maybe Henry was not quite as keen to be rid of Catherine as it seems. Perhaps he had not been entirely convinced that her actions were treasonous and was appearing to appease his councilors by permitting them to go ahead with their scheme, all the while knowing that he would personally abort it. What seems to have taken place is that Henry outgamed the gamers, as he had done once before on a similar occasion. The king had rescued Archbishop Cranmer from imminent arrest by his conservative enemies, by giving him his ring to show to the Privy Council as a mark of royal protection. Therefore, by informing the doctor of Gardiner and Wriothesley's plans Henry may have deliberately intended for the plot to be leaked to Catherine or her supporters.

Catherine discovered the warrant when it accidentally fell from the pocket of a councilor's robe—literally hours away from being arrested on charges of treason for her political and religious opinions. Her hysterics brought Henry's doctor to her chamber; he told her about the plot and persuaded the queen to muster every shred of dignity and immediately appeal to the king, begging his forgiveness. "If she would do so, and show her humble submission into him . . . she should find him gracious and favorable unto her."

A terrified Catherine took to her bed and pled mortal illness. Henry usually avoided his wives after taking the decision to dump them, but fearing that she was at death's door, he rushed to Catherine's chamber, where she confided her terror at having unintentionally displeased him, assuring Henry that she was eager to atone for her errors. She was heartened by his invitation to talk things over in his room; it was an indication that the door was open to reconciliation, something that had not been the case when Henry had wished to terminate his previous marriages.

That evening, Catherine visited Henry alone. She began to mollify him with endearments, protesting that she had no opinion worth having since "must I, and will I, refer my judgment in this, and all other cases, to your Majesty's wisdom, as my only anchor, Supreme Head and Governor here on earth, next under God."

"No so by St. Mary," Henry demurred, not so easily appeased. "You are become a doctor, Kate, to instruct us (as we take it) and not to be instructed or directed by us."

The queen saved herself only by putting a quick and clever spin on her words, playing the weak and feeble-brained female who needed schooling by her worldly husband—explaining that she took an opposite view to Henry's in order to reinvigorate the ailing king's mind, giving him the chance to exercise his mental faculties by rebutting her.

"Is that even so, sweetheart?" Henry asked her. "And tended your arguments to no worse end?"

No doubt, Catherine's head nodded vigorously.

"Then we are perfect friends again," he added.

Their quarrel repaired, a reconciliation was sealed with several grateful kisses.

The following day, when Catherine's arrest was to have taken place, she and Henry were enjoying a constitutional in the garden when Wriothesley crossed their path with a detachment of the Guard, undoubtedly the very men who were conscripted to convey her to the Tower. As Wriothesley fell to his penitent knees, Henry royally chewed out his chancellor with a few choice words—most notably "Knave! Arrant knave, beast, and fool!"—at which point Catherine sweetly interceded on Wriothesley's behalf for Henry's clemency.

Henry would continue to make it up to Catherine by showering her with "all manner of pearls and precious stones . . . of skins and sable furs . . . clothes and new gentlenesses of fashion . . . for the pleasure of us [and] our dearest wife the queen." As a mark of his trust and favor Henry also gave little Edward into Catherine's care from midsummer until the onset of winter.

Yet that year brought another scare for Catherine. Henry's long-time friend Charles Brandon, Duke of Suffolk and former husband to the king's younger sister Mary, died. He was survived by his much younger widow, and rumors swirled that the king was showing the dowager duchess—another Katherine, and another evangelical intellect—"great favor" during her grief and that he was considering making her wife number seven.

But Henry was in no shape—literally—to even think about putting aside Catherine for another woman. His bulk was so immense that he had to be wheeled about or carried from place to place in purpose-built chairs that resembled iron baskets, winched up by chains when he needed to move from one floor of the palace to another. By the middle of January 1547, his various ailments and illnesses had finally caught up with him. After languishing for several days, on January 26, according to some sources, he summoned Catherine to his side for a tearful farewell, telling her, "It is God's will that we should part."

The fifty-five-year-old Henry died at Whitehall in the wee hours of January 28, 1547. His death was kept secret for three days so that matters regarding a smooth succession could be put in order. On February 14, Henry VIII was buried at Windsor beside his beloved third wife, Jane Seymour. Their nine-year-old son succeeded him, to become Edward VI.

By the terms of Henry's will Catherine was excluded from the regency, to be known henceforth as Queen Dowager and not Queen Regent. During the days between Henry's demise and the announcement of his passing Edward Seymour, the brother of Catherine's former inamorata Thomas, made a power grab and created himself Duke of Somerset and Lord Protector of the realm, claiming the regent's mantle on behalf of his little nephew.

Within weeks of Henry's death, although she was technically still in mourning, Catherine secretly became the mistress of her old flame. Although she had put aside her feelings for Thomas Seymour when she wed Henry, she had never forgotten her attraction to the dashing hero. She wrote to inform him that "I would not have you think that this . . . honest good will toward you [a] sudden . . . passion, for as truly as God is god, my mind was fully bent [inclined to be yours] the other time I was at liberty to marry you before any man I know."

Tongues wagged like mad over their clandestine affair even though they attempted discretion. The lovers soon became the target of court gossip and ribald tavern jokes. Accused of wantonness and the libidinousness of a barren woman, Catherine's honor was so maligned and the jests so bawdy that Seymour tried to get an Act of Parliament passed forbidding public slander of the former queen.

Then, having surreptitiously tied the knot toward the middle of the spring, Seymour and Catherine campaigned for royal permission for their fait accompli. Finally, on June 25, 1547, nine-year-old King Edward wrote to his stepmother in support of the marriage. But when he learned that he had been tricked into sanctioning a done deal, the boy king felt utterly betrayed by the woman he had believed so sage and virtuous. Mary, too, whose trust and friendship Catherine had nurtured for years, was insulted that her step-mother had not observed a proper mourning period for her father before remarrying.

And Thomas Seymour, Lord Admiral of England as of February 1547, turned out not to be such a terrific catch. He vastly abused his office, permitting pirates to roam the high seas as long as he got a percentage of their bounty. His marriage to Catherine was often marked by tension, especially when the nubile Princess Elizabeth was placed under their care. Much to his wife's humiliation, Sey-mour openly flirted with and fondled the girl. According to Eliza-beth's governess and confidante, Kat Ashley: "He wold . . . strike hir upon the bak, or on the buttocks familiarly . . . And one morn-yng he strove to have kissed hir in hir Bed." Once, Catherine even caught her husband holding the princess in his arms.

After three childless marriages, on August 30, 1548, at the age of thirty-six, Catherine gave birth to a daughter, whom they named for the Princess Mary. But thanks to her doctor's dirty hands she developed puerperal fever, just as Jane Seymour had, and died on September 5. Catherine was buried in the manor chapel at Sudeley, her husband's country seat. Her chief mourner was ten-year-old Lady Jane Grey, whose wardship Thomas Seymour had pur-chased. Lady Jane was being raised in their home as a surrogate daughter so that the ambitious Thomas would be responsible for arranging her eventual marriage, which of course he did—to his own nephew, Edward Seymour's son, Lord Guilford Dudley.

Catherine's death was followed by her husband's swift descent. By the fall of 1548, having embezzled funds from a Bristol mint to finance the raising of his own private army, Thomas Seymour had become the most dangerous man in England. And it's just as well that Catherine didn't live to see him break into Edward VI's bed-chamber on January 16, 1549, with a retinue in tow and mischief on his mind, having first obtained a stamp of the young king's sig-nature and keys to several of the royal apartments. Moreover, Thomas shot his nephew's lapdog when it tried to bite him.

He received his just deserts on Tower Hill on March 20, 1549, having been charged by the Privy Council with thirty-three counts of treason.

Although their daughter did not survive childhood, Catherine Parr's legacy lived on through her stepdaughter Elizabeth. Her capability as well as her religious convictions left an indelible stamp on Elizabeth's reign, and by extension, had a lasting effect on the kingdom and the history of England.

MARY, QUEEN OF SCOTS

1542–1587

RULED SCOTLAND: 1542–1567

QUEEN CONSORT OF FRANCE: 1559–1560

and

FRANÇOIS,

DAUPHIN OF FRANCE, LATER FRANÇOIS II

1544–1560

married 1558–1560

and

HENRY STUART,

LORD DARNLEY

1545–1567

married 1565–1567

and

JAMES HEPBURN,

4TH EARL OF BOTHWELL

c. 1534–1578

married 1567–1578

"For all the offense that is done to me, my lord, you have
the weight thereof, for . . . which I shall be your wife no
longer nor sleep with you any more, and shall never be
well until I have caused you to have as sorrowful a heart
as I have at this present."

—Mary, Queen of Scots to Lord Darnley, March 9,
1566

MARY, QUEEN OF SCOTS WAS BORN ON DECEMBER 8,
1542, to Marie of Guise, the French-born wife of Scotland's dying
king, James V. The English had just routed James's army at Solway
Moss, and upon the birth of little Mary, the sonless king foretold
that a daughter would spell the end of the family line. Alluding to
the Stuarts' history (which began with the son of Marjory, daughter
of Robert the Bruce), James lamented, "Woe is me. My dynasty cam
wi' a lass and it'll gang [go] wi' a lass."

The granddaughter of Henry VIII's older sister Margaret, Mary
was only nine months old when she was crowned Queen of Scotland on September 9, 1543. And she was still an infant when her
great-uncle brokered her marriage with his five-year-old son, Prince
Edward. But in 1548, with Henry dead, Marie of Guise, as the
little queen's regent, decided not to honor her daughter's betrothal
to Edward. Instead, Marie sent Mary across the North Sea to be
raised in the court of Henri II, not merely as a playfellow for the
royal children, but as the intended wife of François, the frail and
sickly four-year-old dauphin.

The little Scots queen was not quite six years old when she left
her mother and made the journey to France. But Mary was cosseted
and loved by her foster family, who treated her with deference and
respect. Henri II called Mary his "reinette" or "little queen," declaring her to be "the most perfect child I have ever seen," and
preferring her to his own offspring. She was tall for her age, tower-

ing above the runty, stuttering dauphin, who followed her about like a spaniel. Mary, it seems, returned his affection, but in the way that seemed more appropriate for a younger brother rather than an intended spouse. François was a weak little boy with a delicate constitution, an adenoidal voice due to a chronic respiratory infection, and a perpetual runny nose that made him into something of a sniveler. Henri's mistress, Diane de Poitiers, coached Mary on how to ensure the dauphin's fondness for her: the little queen was to indulge him, never permitting him to be overly ambitious about anything, lest he unregally fail in the attempt.

On April 24, 1558, at the age of fifteen, Mary, Queen of Scots married the dauphin at Notre Dame. François was given the "crown matrimonial" of Scotland by the Scottish Parliament, so the teens were henceforth known as the Queen-Dauphine and the King-Dauphin. They made an odd couple at the altar. The fourteen-year-old dauphin, puffy-faced, pale, and sickly, was significantly shorter than his statuesque, redheaded bride. Nearly six feet tall, Mary was clearly the main attraction, dazzling spectators in her shimmering gown, "white unto a lily, fashioned so richly and beautifully that none could imagine it," according to the French court chronicler Pierre de Brantôme. "The train thereof six ells in length was borne by two maids. About her neck hung a circlet of untold value." Mary's white wedding gown was a daring choice, as it was the traditional color of mourning for French queens. Adorned by a golden crown studded with pearls and precious gemstones, her auburn hair cascaded down her back. That morning Mary had written to her mother, declaring "all I can tell you is that I account myself one of the happiest women in the world."

After the ceremony, conducted by the Archbishop of Rouen, a herald standing outside the cathedral cried "Largesse!" and gold and silver coins were tossed into the crowd. The mad scramble to retrieve them resulted in several bodily injuries. A Scottish student standing amid the throng recalled, "The gentlemen took their cloaks, gentlewomen their farthingales, merchantmen their gowns, masters in art their hoods, students their peaked caps, and religious men had their scapulars violently riven from their shoulders to gather the showers of money."

No expense was spared at the lavish wedding banquet and the intriguing entertainments that followed. Twelve man-made horses covered in gold and silver carried the young princes and the Guise children—Mary's cousins from her mother's side of the family. Later in the day they pulled carriages transporting the singers for the banquet, which rivaled any Long Island bar mitzvah. Six silver ships glided onto the dance floor. On board each of them was a man who selected a lady to join him. Henri chose the bride, while the groom extended his invitation to his mother.

Because Mary's marriage to François was a political one, there were numerous agreements that had been executed before the "I dos" could be uttered. Nine days before the marriage, Mary affixed her signature to a document confirming Scottish autonomy. But two days earlier, at Fontainebleau, she had signed three secret premarital treaties, cleverly devised by her powerful Guise uncles (the brothers of her mother, Marie), that were not only highly beneficial to France but were extremely prejudicial to Scotland. Naturally, no one told the fifteen-year-old Mary that the agreements were illegal according to Scots law.

A little more than a year later, the forty-year-old Henri II died after a freak jousting accident on July 10, 1559, and Mary and her young husband became the King and Queen of France. François II was crowned at Rheims on September 18, although the royal family and the court were still in mourning. Because Mary was already the crowned Queen of Scotland, she could not be crowned twice.

Her joy at becoming Queen of France was tempered with sorrow, as Mary was not able to cast off her mourning clothes for long. In June 1560, her mother died of dropsy. When the news reached Mary in France, the devastated young queen suffered a nervous collapse. Throughout her life, this was Mary's reaction to undue stress. Death, bloodshed, strife—all would send her into nearly paralytic hysteria. She began having fainting spells, which she misinterpreted as signs of pregnancy, and took to wearing a tunic—the maternity fashion of the day.

But the ambitious Guise family wasn't counting their chickens. Their hopes for a healthy baby were doubtful in the extreme, given the problems with François's "secret parts." It appears that no one had given Mary that little talk about the birds and the bees before her wedding night. She couldn't have become pregnant because their marriage had never been consummated. Even if it had, they might never have conceived a child, as François had an undescended testicle that probably rendered him infertile.

To compensate, perhaps, for his lack of masculinity, he dressed like a popinjay and became obsessed with riding. Although he'd grown taller during the autumn of 1559, François's health remained poor. His dizzy spells had worsened. When he felt himself losing consciousness, he'd flail his limbs about in an effort to avoid passing out. His skin was blotchy and his face had become extremely swollen and was covered with pimples and boils.

Just as Mary was beginning to cope with the death of her mother, in November the fifteen-year-old king developed an agonizing abscess in his left ear, which oozed with a foul-smelling pus. He also began experiencing seizures accompanied by a stabbing pain in his head, and soon he became incapable of speech. The doctors bled the young king, administered enemas, and considered drilling a hole into his skull to release the fluid. Regardless of (or perhaps hastened by) these ministrations, on December 5, 1560, he died. Although he and Mary had been wed for a little more than two years, they had been companions for a full decade before their nuptials took place—almost the entirety of their youth.

Mary, who had loved her husband as a childhood friend, if not as a childhood sweetheart, "was as dolorous a wife as she had good cause to be," reported Sir Nicholas Throckmorton, the English ambassador. She had been a good nurse to François, though she had exhausted herself "by long watching with him during his sickness."

Almost as soon as her forty-day formal mourning period had

ended, the eighteen-year-old Mary was urged by the royal family to remarry. But as the uncrowned widow of the king, she was merely an extraneous cipher in France, so she sailed back to Scotland in 1561.

The young queen found her country in turmoil, governed by a body of regents that included the evangelical Protestant vicar and theologian John Knox and Mary's bastard half brother, James Stewart, who chose to spell his name the Scots way, rather than the Francofied "Stuart."

In addition to the crippling poverty facing her wild and rugged nation, Mary had a lot of institutionalized hostility to handle. And because the core of the Scots queen's foreign policy was for her cousin, Elizabeth of England, to acknowledge her as heiress presumptive, owing to her status as Margaret Tudor's granddaughter, Mary had to manage Elizabeth's increasing wariness that she might want to claim the throne of England sooner rather than later.

Mary had many strikes against her on her return: she was a female, a foreigner (having been raised in France), and she was a devout Catholic in a Protestant country that had embraced the Reformation with a vengeance. But unlike her royal counterparts in other countries, Mary drew a distinction between private faith and public policy, and religious tolerance became a hallmark of her reign. "She wishes all men to live as they please," wrote the resident English ambassador, Thomas Randolph.

Additionally, Mary's eagerness to give positions of power and influence to baseborn men because they lacked the personal agenda and the clannish ties of the nobility worked to her detriment. Such rare egalitarianism won the people's hearts, but Scotland was a land where kinship was more important than government. Mary's efforts to strip the nobles of their power and instead consolidate it within the purview of the crown angered many of the lairds whose backing she needed most—misogynists who were already malcontented at being ruled by a lassie. And Mary, Queen of Scots reveled in her femininity. She was a striking, though fragile, beauty—slender and unusually tall for the era, with high cheekbones, hazel eyes, and the Tudor red-gold hair. Her speaking voice was praised as *très douce et très bonne*—"very sweet and very pretty," and she excelled at artistic as well as athletic pursuits, such as archery, hawking, and hunting.

John Knox denounced Mary for her womanhood and "the monstrous rule of women" in general. To allow these "weak, frail, impatient, feeble, and foolish creatures" to rule a realm was "the subversion of good order, of all equity and justice." Knox equated Mary's Catholicism with unbridled female lust and uncontrollable passion. And he arrogantly and most emphatically believed that Mary should secure *his* approval before choosing a husband.

An enraged Mary, all of twenty-one years old at the time, summoned the fifty-year-old Knox to Holyrood on June 24, 1563. In "vehement fume," she claimed that even though she had done everything in her power to extend the olive branch to him, no prince had been so "ill treated by a subject in all your rigorous manner of speaking both against myself and my uncles [the Guises of France]; yea, I have sought your favors by all possible means. I offered unto you presence and audience whensoever it pleased you to admonish me; and yet I cannot be quit of you." Choked with tears, Mary demanded, "What have you to do with my marriage? What are you within this commonwealth?"

"A subject born within the same," Knox replied tersely. He went on to say that he had never been much moved by tears, even from his own boys after he beat them.

Enraged by his temerity, Mary ordered him to quit her sight.

Queen Elizabeth weighed in on the subject of Mary's marriage as well. She would never conscience her cousin's union with a Frenchman, nor to anyone from Spain or the Holy Roman Empire. If her new husband were otherwise foreign-born, that would be satisfactory as long as he was prepared to live in Scotland after the wedding, although Elizabeth's preference was for a man who would support amity between her kingdom and Scotland, and who was "naturally born to live this isle." That said, Mary would be expected to seek her permission to marry an English subject.

Mary was justifiably insulted by Elizabeth's conditions—to demand that an anointed sovereign of an independent realm submit to the approval of a sister monarch. The stress and the pressure, particularly from Knox and Elizabeth, made her physically ill.

Elizabeth took it into her head to fob off her own sometime paramour, Robert Dudley, Earl of Leicester, onto Mary, which would insure that Scotland would be governed according to Elizabeth's wishes. But Leicester was damaged goods. His wife, Amy Robsart, had died under suspicious circumstances, and his father, the 1st Duke of Northumberland, had been executed for treason. However, Mary conceded that she would be willing to marry Leicester if Elizabeth named her as her heir.

In 1563 Elizabeth wrote to Mary asking her to grant a passport for the Earl of Lennox to return to his native Scotland after a lengthy exile in England. Elizabeth did not expect the earl to be accompanied by his handsome son and heir, Henry Stewart, Lord Darnley. Darnley, who had been living at the English court, had the second-best hereditary claim to the English throne after Mary's. Both were grandchildren of Margaret Tudor, the elder sister of Henry VIII. And like Mary, Darnley's veins ran thick with both Scottish and English (Stuart and Tudor) royal blood. He, too, was Catholic, though he wore his religion lightly. Were Mary and Darnley to marry, her rights of succession to the English crown would be strengthened significantly.

When Sir James Melville, Mary's Scottish envoy, first saw the six-foot-one-inch-tall Darnley, his impression was that "No woman would make choice of such a man that was liker a woman than a man, for he is very lusty, beardless, and lady-faced." He was wrong.

Mary first met Darnley on February 17, 1565, at Wemyss, a tiny coastal village near Fife, before he went to greet his returning father at Dunkeld. She declared the nineteen-year-old urbane fop to be "the best proportioned lang [tall] man [she] had ever seen." Darnley remained at Mary's court in Edinburgh while bad weather kept everyone snowed in. While she awaited Elizabeth's reply regarding her agreement to wed the Earl of Leicester as long as she was named Elizabeth's heir, Mary made no outward show of any interest in Lord Darnley. But her attempt at subterfuge didn't fool the gossips. It was widely thought that "if she take fantasy to this new guest, then they shall be sure of mischief," because a marriage to Darnley would give the Lennox branch of the Stewarts additional status, potentially reigniting the rivalry between his family and some of Scotland's other powerful clans.

After Elizabeth informed Mary that "nothing shall be done until Her Majesty [Elizabeth] shall be married, or shall notify her determination never to marry," Mary realized she had been checkmated. Since Elizabeth declined to name a successor, Mary refused to marry Leicester and stubbornly proceeded with her plans to wed Darnley. By the first week of April 1565, the pair were clearly courting. They spent most of their time together, and Mary nursed Darnley back to health when he became ill with a cold that developed into a "marvelous thick" skin rash—which was probably the onset of syphilis, contracted in England.

Fearing that Mary's marriage to Darnley could result in a civil war between Protestants and Catholics if he chose to raise an army in support of the latter's cause, Elizabeth instructed her Privy Council to find a way to thwart it. They reminded her that Darnley was an English subject, and therefore she could conceivably step in and refuse her consent to Mary's marriage. It would have been disastrous for Elizabeth if the Scots Catholics invaded England, asserting Mary's claim to the English throne, galvanizing their English coreligionists, and rallying them to the cause. The Privy Council ultimately demanded that Mary renounce Darnley to marry Robert Dudley or some other English noble instead.

Although Darnley was English, he was not a noble. So in the space of one afternoon Mary knighted him, made him a Scottish baron, and then created him Earl of Ross. But in ennobling her intended groom, Mary had created a monster. Eager to be made Duke of Albany, as Mary had promised, he drew his knife on the lord who brought news of a delay in the ceremony. Meanwhile, Elizabeth was so angry at Mary's elevation of Darnley, which was tantamount to a betrothal, that she confiscated his English estates.

During the three brief months that Mary and Darnley had known each other, he had been on his best behavior, but the prospect of marriage to the queen had broadened his arrogant streak and his true colors were beginning to emerge; he was roundly described at court as being "proud, disdainful, and suspicious."

It's remarkable that Mary refused to be put off by his behavior, which included frequent drunkenness and rumors of dubious sexual proclivities. Darnley's flamboyant bisexuality at Elizabeth's court had earned him the reputation as a "great cock chick." And according to a dispatch from Thomas Randolph, Queen Elizabeth's ambassador to Scotland, Darnley was on an intimate footing with Mary's personal secretary David Rizzio (also spelled Riccio by some scholars). Rizzio had come to the Scottish court as a musician in the train of the ambassador from Savoy and stayed on in Edinburgh initially to sing bass in Mary's choir. But he soon became a particular favorite of Darnley's as well. According to Randolph, "They would lie sometime in one bed together."

Despite her awareness of Darnley's conduct, by the third week in May, Mary had convinced herself that she was in love with him. Yet just a few weeks later, by the third of June, the bloom was off the rose and the scales had fallen from her eyes. Unfortunately, by then she was stuck. To renounce her intention to wed Darnley, even if the decision was predicated on his arrogance and unpleasant personality, would have been to play into Elizabeth's hands. Mary had to stand firm. She would marry Darnley—but it would not be a love match; it would be a marriage of convenience that would place her in a better political position. Not only would she be Elizabeth's plausible heir in her own right, laying claim to the English throne should Elizabeth remain childless, but unlike the "Virgin Queen," Mary stood to produce heirs through her marriage to Darnley—thereby securing the continuation of the Stuart dynasty.

Although she embraced the fate she'd so stubbornly chosen for herself, according to Ambassador Randolph's dispatches, Mary remained so disturbed by Darnley's "intolerable" behavior that she plummeted into depression. "Her Majesty is laid aside," Randolph wrote to Dudley, the Earl of Leicester, "her wits not what they were, her beauty another than it was, her cheer and countenance changed into I wot not what." The alteration in Mary's appearance was so dramatic that in Randolph's opinion, she was "a woman more to be pitied than any that I ever saw."

Despite her melancholy, Mary vigorously defended her right to choose her own husband, angrier than ever at Elizabeth's continual interference. And when Randolph had the nerve to suggest that if Mary converted to Protestantism Elizabeth might have a more favorable reaction to her proposed marriage, Mary exploded. "Would you that I should make merchandise of my religion, or frame myself to your ministers' wills?" she demanded of Randolph. "It cannot be so," she announced with finality and left the room.

According to Mary's twenty-first-century biographer Roderick Graham, the queen and Darnley were secretly wed before about seven witnesses on July 9, 1565, in an informal ceremony—probably a handfasting—conducted most likely in David Rizzio's apartments at Stirling Castle. Afterward, the newlyweds consummated their clandestine union at Lord Seton's house.

Outwardly, however, the official wedding plans continued apace. On Sunday morning, July 22, the banns were read in St. Giles Kirk. That afternoon, Mary created Darnley Duke of Albany. The following Saturday it was proclaimed at the Market Cross in Edinburgh that the queen would marry Darnley the following day, after which he would be made King of Scotland. Unfortunately, she should have allowed her Parliament to do their duty and vote on the subject, since they were usually consulted before such titles were bestowed. In acting by royal fiat, Mary began to annoy some of the lords who had finally agreed to make Darnley king.

The sun was not yet up on the morning of July 29, 1565, when Mary was led down the aisle of the Chapel Royal at Holyrood by Darnley's father, Lord Lennox, and the Earl of Argyll. Over her wedding gown she wore her *deuil blanc*, a white gauze sack that covered her from head to toe—the traditional mourning garment for French queens—emblematic of her status as a widow, and by extension, the Dowager Queen of France.

Darnley entered the chapel and the bridal couple exchanged vows. Since they were first cousins, a papal dispensation was necessary in order for them to marry. It had not arrived in Edinburgh by July 29, but Mary blithely assumed the document was en route, and therefore, she married Darnley without it. Although the dispensation finally made it to Scotland, the July 29 marriage was technically not legal because it had been performed while the bride and groom remained within a proscribed degree of affinity.

After the rings were exchanged, despite the fact that he, too, was a Catholic, Darnley quit the chapel to avoid being charged with "idolatry," leaving his bride at the altar to continue the mass. As soon as the ceremony was over, Mary invited her guests to help her cast aside her mourning garments by each removing one of the pins that affixed the *deuil blanc* to her wedding gown.

Thomas Randolph noted that the newlyweds headed for the ballroom, rather than the bedroom; they "went not to bed, to signify unto the world that it was no lust [that] moved them to marry, but only the necessity of her country, not long to leave it destitute of an heir." Little did the ambassador know that the reason the royal couple didn't dash off to the boudoir to have their first sexual encounter with each other was that they had secretly consummated their nuptials twenty days earlier.

On the day after the wedding the heralds proclaimed Darnley King of Scotland. From then on, power would be "conjointly" exercised. All state papers would bear the words "Henry and Marie, King and Queen of Scotland."

The news was greeted with sullen silence. A cluster of dissident nobles, led by Mary's bastard half brother, James Stewart, the Earl of Moray, was already raising an army. Mary's marriage to the objectionable Darnley, followed by his proclamation as their king, had provided the perfect excuse to rebel. But Mary reacted swiftly to their uprising. She raised an army of eight to ten thousand men, and, leading the charge in her steel cap, put the fractious nobles on the run in what would come to be known as the Chase-About Raid.

Unbeknownst to Mary, in a behind-the-scenes effort to become a player alongside the Catholic big boys—the monarchs of France and Spain—her husband had begun plotting to restore Catholicism as Scotland's institutional religion, cutting deals with Moray and the other exiled nobles. The ultimate goal was to effect a coup and seize power from Mary. If the next Parliament would vote to award him the "crown matrimonial," which would grant him full governmental rights as king, then Darnley would overturn the Scottish Reformation. But that was only the first part of his treacherous plot. As soon as he accomplished his initial goal, he would then perform an about-face, recall the exiles, and return the kingdom's official religion to Protestantism—as long as he still got to remain the sovereign. Darnley had no interest in either faith, nor in the impact his scheming would have on the delicate religious compromise it had taken his wife four painstaking years to craft. Immature and vain, all he sought was power and prestige. His ultimate aims were to be king in his own right, preferably with his wife out of the picture, and to earn the respect of the Catholic sovereigns on the Continent. Darnley didn't care what religion his coconspirators practiced as long as they helped him achieve the crown, and he had no qualms about promising something to one faction, only to rescind his pledge as soon as their usefulness was over, and supporting the interests of their enemies if it achieved his ends.

Mary's half brother, Moray, accepted Darnley's terms; but to make the scheme work the lairds needed a plausible scapegoat—someone who could be accused of feeding Mary the disastrous political advice that diminished the nobles' clout and therefore jeopardized the health of the realm, *and* who could conceivably have persuaded Darnley to embrace Catholicism. His sometime bedfellow, David Rizzio—long (but incorrectly) rumored to be a papal spy—made the perfect foil.

One of the conspirators, William Maitland, already had Darnley in his confidence and handily managed to convince the vain and gullible king consort that Rizzio was Mary's lover, easily piquing Darnley's sense of vengeance. It was a masterful stroke of propaganda, and one that Queen Elizabeth's closest advisers were well aware of. On February 13, 1566, Elizabeth's ambassador, Thomas Randolph, wrote to the Earl of Leicester:

> I know for certain that this Queen repenteth her marriage, that she hateth Darnley and all his kin. I know there are practices in hand contrived between father and son to come by the crown against her will. I know that if that take effect which is intended, David [Rizzio], with the consent of the king shall have his throat cut within these ten days. Many things . . . worse than these are brought to my ears, yea, of things intended against her own person.

During the Christmas season in 1565 the royal couple had quarreled loudly and frequently in the privacy of their apartments, but soon everyone at court knew that the marriage was on the rocks. According to Randolph, Mary had demoted her husband. Whereas, for "a while there was nothing but 'King and Queen, His Majesty and Hers,' now 'the Queen's husband' is the most common word." A new silver coin called a "ryl" worth about thirty shillings Scots had been issued to commemorate the royal wedding. It depicted Darnley and Mary facing each other with their names engraved in Latin around the perimeter: "Henricus et Maria (D)ei Gra(tia) R(ex) et R(egina) Scotorum," clearly giving preference to Darnley by listing his name first. That coin was taken out of circulation and a new ryl was minted with the order of the names reversed.

What had changed? Well, apart from her disgust at Darnley's dissolution, drunkenness, and infidelity, she was pregnant. He'd done his marital duty and Mary no longer needed to humor him. It's also likely that she regretted her decision to have him styled as king; but he had insisted on it and Mary had to keep him happy, at least for a while, because like all monarchs, she needed an heir for the security of her realm. But now he'd done his job, and had out-lived his usefulness.

At Holyrood Palace on the night of March 9, 1566, Rizzio and Mary were in her supper room enjoying a game of cards amid ser-vants, guards, and other companions, when a group of men, led by Patrick Lord Ruthven, sneaked up the privy stairs from Darnley's apartment below. Around 150 armed men had secretly been admit-ted to the palace. Darnley entered alone, surprising Mary, but he acted affectionately to her, his arm encircling her waist. This was Ruthven's cue to batter at the door, demanding, "Let it please Your Majesty that yonder man David [Rizzio] come forth of your Privy Chamber where he hath been overlong."

Mary turned to her husband and asked Darnley if he had any-thing to do with the unwanted intrusion. He muttered an incoher-ent and sheepish demurral. She refused to open the door, insisting that Rizzio was there by her invitation. A quintet of assassins then barged into the room, knocking over a table. Mary's card-playing companion Lady Argyll caught a candle as it was about to fall and snuffed it out, leaving the room illuminated only by the fire in the hearth. Mary accused the men of treason and ordered them to leave, but Ruthven told Darnley to "take the queen your sovereign and wife to you." Darnley restrained Mary while Rizzio hid behind her skirts. Ruthven and another conspirator then stabbed Rizzio in the back with their daggers. Mary later admitted that the blows had come so close to her own person that "she felt the coldness of the iron."

"All that is done, is the king's own deed and action," Ruthven told the queen.

As Ker of Fawdonside leveled his pistol at Mary's swollen belly, Rizzio was dragged into the next room, pleading for his life. Ac-cording to Mary, "at the entry of our chamber [the assassins] gave him fifty-six strokes with whiniards [daggers] and swords." Rizzio's bloody, battered body was tossed down a staircase.

Turning to Darnley, Mary demanded, "Why have you caused to do this wicked deed to me, considering I took you from a low estate and made you my husband? What offense have I made you that you should have done me such shame?"

Utterly convinced that Rizzio had been her lover, Darnley's weak defense (since he couldn't very well admit that he was plotting a coup) was that Mary hadn't had sex with him in ages, and on the occasions when he came to visit her for that purpose, she "either would not or made herself sick." Ever since the previous Christmas she had been cold to him and he wanted to know why.

A tearful Mary reminded him that "it is not a gentlewoman's duty to come to her husband's chamber, but rather the husband to come to the wife's." According to royal protocol, it was incumbent upon the husband to initiate all sexual advances.

But Darnley countered, "How came ye to my chamber at the beginning and ever, until within these few months that Davie fell into familiarity with you? Or am I failed in any sort with my body? Or what disdain have you at me? Or what offense had I made you that you should not use me at all times alike? What offenses have I done you, seeing that I am willing to do all things that becometh a good husband? Suppose I be of the baser degree, yet I am your husband and your head, and you promised me obedience on the day of our marriage and that I should be participant and equal with you in all things. I suppose you have used me otherwise at the persuasions of Davie."

Enraged at his collusion in the murder of her secretary and by his refusal to defend her life when one of Rizzio's assassins held her at knifepoint, the twenty-three-year-old Mary then dropped a marital bombshell: "For all the offense that is done to me, my lord, you have the weight thereof, for the which I shall be your wife no longer nor sleep with you any more, and shall never be well until I have caused you to have as sorrowful a heart as I have at this present." It was a decision she should have made months earlier, but she needed to conceive an heir. For good measure Mary warned, "If I or my child die, you will have the blame thereof."

The assassination of David Rizzio was only step one of the plotters' coup. On Sunday morning, March 10, although Mary was essentially under house arrest for ruling contrary to the advice of her Privy Council (which included at least one of Rizzio's killers), she affected a placid and composed demeanor. She pardoned the conspirators, and when the rebels from the Chase-About Raid showed up, she made a grand show of affection with her bastard half brother, Moray, after which she suddenly cried out hysterically that she was going into early labor. Embarrassed and freaked out by the subject of gynecology, the men beat a hasty retreat.

But Mary had faked the miscarriage, which bought her some time to plot and threw the assassins off guard. Then, over the course of the next several hours, by pointing out his own expedience to Rizzio's murderers, she convinced Darnley that his life was as endangered as hers. As an assurance that her affection for him had not altered, she pretended to appeal to her husband's vanity by inviting him to spend the entire night in her chamber—counting on the fact that by the time he showed up for sex he'd be piss drunk and ready to pass out. But when Darnley boasted to some of his coconspirators about how easily *he* had swayed his wife, they derided him for having grown "effeminate again" by giving in to Mary's desires, even as he was supposed to be opposing her. So he never made it to her boudoir—although he *did* pass out drunk.

Mary's midwife showed up the following morning to warn that if she didn't take some fresh air soon, she might miscarry for real. By now, Darnley, eager to save his own hide, had become his wife's ally. Only fifty-two hours after Rizzio's murder, Mary and Darnley escaped the rebels by tiptoeing down the privy stairs that led from her apartment to his, through the servants' quarters, and out of the palace. All through the night, they rode to Dunbar Castle and safety, managing at breakneck speed a twenty-five-mile journey in five hours. Mary, riding pillion, urged Darnley to have more care for her condition, to which he angrily replied that if she lost the baby, they could just as easily make another.

The courage Mary displayed during these dark and dangerous days rallied her subjects. By March 18, she had amassed eight thousand men behind her, and rode victoriously back into Edinburgh, taking up residence in the castle.

Despite their escaping the rebels together, relations between the royal couple were now at an all-time low, and there was a rumored split in April 1566. Mary punished some of Rizzio's assassins, executing two of them. Meanwhile her husband denied any role in the plot—an ill-advised move because the convicted killers produced incontrovertible detailed evidence of his involvement. Hoping it would reconcile them to the queen's good graces, the rebel lords sent her the bond that Darnley had signed pledging his support for Rizzio's murder in return for the crown matrimonial. Upon reading this treasonous document, Mary evidently heaved "so many great sighs that it was a pity to hear." By now, Darnley had become a pariah at court. Even his own father blamed him for destroying the Lennox clan's grand plans.

On June 19, 1566, after a painful and difficult labor, Mary gave birth to a son, the future James VI. She intended to eliminate her husband's participation in the governing of the kingdom as soon as it was clear that their heir was healthy.

"Is this your answer to forgive and forget all?" Darnley demanded of Mary.

"I have forgiven, but will never forget!" Mary raged, vowing to have as little to do with him as possible from then on.

She kept her word. On August 3, the Earl of Bedford wrote to Queen Elizabeth's Secretary of State, William Cecil, informing him that Mary and Darnley rarely supped together and she never slept "nor keepeth company with him," a euphemism for sex. In any case, Darnley was out "vagabondising" every night and insisting that the castle gates remain open in anticipation of his return, which posed a security risk to his wife and infant son.

Mary had been in ill health ever since her son's birth, collapsing in October 1566 with vomiting and convulsions, briefly losing consciousness as well as the power of sight and speech. Darnley did not even visit her sickbed. "She has done him so great honor . . . and he . . . has recompensed her with such ingratitude, and misuses himself so far towards her that it is an heartbreak for her to think that he should be her husband, and how to be free of him she sees no way out," Mary's adviser William Maitland informed the Scottish ambassador in Paris.

Toward the end of the year, Mary became gravely ill again. Her attendants heard her repeatedly lament, "I could wish to be dead." The queen's depression was as severe as her physical complaints—and the cause of her misery was Darnley. He visited only once during her recuperation and the couple had a dreadful argument. "Things are going from bad to worse," wrote the French ambassador, Philibert du Croc. "I do not expect upon several accounts any good understanding between them." Darnley had threatened to depart permanently for the Netherlands, where it would be even harder for the Scots queen and her advisers to control him, admitting to Mary in the presence of du Croc that he had a ship at the ready. When Mary asked why, her husband sullenly muttered something about not being given the crown matrimonial. He then strode out of the queen's presence without first requesting her permission to withdraw.

By then, Mary realized that the best way to protect her infant son's life, as well as his dynastic rights, was to put James into Elizabeth's care and protection if anything should happen to her. The English sovereign was delighted and the two women, queen to queen, began drafting a new treaty that would grant Mary and her heirs the rights of succession to the English throne, as long as there were no heirs of Elizabeth's body. Things were going very well—until an explosive event would destroy everything Mary had strived to achieve.

Mary was toying with the idea of divorcing Darnley, but the nobles would only consent to it if the queen would pardon the conspirators who had scattered to the four winds after Rizzio's murder. Mary agreed—if it was formally stipulated that her son, James, was legitimate. The nobles thought this compromise would be feasible if Darnley could be arraigned on some trumped-up charges of treason, but Mary refused to do anything underhanded. At Stirling Castle on December 17, 1566, Mary and Darnley's son was christened. Though she did not attend in person, Elizabeth I was his godmother. Darnley was conspicuous by his absence. At the end of the month he departed for Glasgow, a center of Lennox Stewart power, to spend some time in the bosom of his family. Sometime toward the New Year, he was diagnosed with secondary, if not tertiary, syphilis.

Late in the year the Earl of Bothwell and a handful of other disgruntled nobles met with Mary to discuss the Darnley problem. According to the laird of Ormiston, "it was thought expedient and most profitable for the commonwealth . . . that such a young fool and proud tyrant should not reign or bear rule over them . . . and that he should be put off by one way or another." Historians continue to argue whether Mary was aware of the plot to assassinate Darnley that was hatched by these lords, and if so, how much she knew and when she knew it.

Mary visited Darnley on January 22, 1567—not out of love, but to checkmate his ability to stage a coup and kidnap their son. Her formerly handsome husband was covered with odiferous pustules and was being treated with mercury, which caused him to salivate uncontrollably. He had lost most of his hair and teeth.

Darnley disingenuously pleaded with her, "I am but young and you will say you have forgiven me sundry times. May not a man my age for lack of counsel, of which I am destitute, fall twice or thrice, and yet repent himself and be chastised for experience? . . . I desire no other thing but we may be together as husband and wife."

It must have been hard for Mary to take his words seriously as he vouchsafed his eternal fidelity with his nose rotting off from venereal disease. During several visits she endeavored to convince him to return with her to Craigmillar Castle, where her advisers could keep an eye on him. But Darnley was reluctant to trust his wife, so Mary brought out the big guns and promised to sleep with him—at Craigmillar—as soon as his pustules healed. Convinced, as always, that Mary couldn't live without his body, he agreed—but only if they returned to Edinburgh instead, because he didn't trust the owner of Craigmillar to guarantee his safety.

Rather than take up residence in the damp and drafty Holyrood, on February 1, 1567, Darnley chose to move to a modest house just inside the city wall, known colloquially as Kirk o' Field. Mary stayed there with her husband, in a bedroom upstairs from his. In Darnley's words she "hath all this while and yet doth use herself like a natural and loving wife." So congenial did Darnley feel toward the queen that he unburdened his conscience, informing Mary of certain plots against her, adding that even *he* had been approached by malfeasors who had suggested that he murder Mary himself! You can just hear the nervous laughter.

There were three separate intrigues afoot by this point: Darnley was indeed conspiring with the Lennoxes to imprison Mary and rule Scotland for the next several years as regent for their infant son; Mary (correctly surmising that he was plotting against her and her throne) was scheming to convey Darnley to a convenient location where she might be able to keep tabs on him; and the Douglas clan, in tandem with the Earl of Bothwell—who hoped to step into Darnley's shoes—were plotting to assassinate Darnley.

On the night of February 9, Darnley was celebrating because his pustules had subsided, and was looking forward to hot sex with his compliant wife. Even in the privacy of his own room the vain Darnley wore a taffeta mask over his face to conceal the effects of his syphilitic pockmarks and decomposing features. Mary spent the early part of the evening with her husband, then departed to attend the masque in celebration of the marriage of a favorite valet. While she was out, Kirk o' Field was filled with gunpowder. At two a.m. on February 10, the house was blown sky-high.

Around the time when the long fuse was lit, Darnley had heard someone fumbling with keys in his locks—not trying to get inside, but to lock Darnley *into* the house. He peered out the window and saw the conspirators outside. Fearing that they were about to set the house afire with him in it, Darnley and one of his servants, William Taylor, tried to escape. They managed to scale the city wall adjacent to the property, but ran straight into another knot of conspirators.

No one knows exactly what happened next but Darnley's body, naked beneath his nightgown, was found in a little garden beyond the city wall. There were no burn marks on his body. He had been strangled to death, most probably with the sleeves of his nightshirt. He was only twenty-one years old.

At Holyrood, where she had gone after remaining at the wedding masque past midnight, Mary was awakened with the news of Darnley's death. Her gut reaction was relief at so narrow an escape, for she might just as well have slept at Kirk o' Field that night. A few hours later she wrote to her ambassador in Paris, vowing to punish those who "have taken this wicked enterprise in hand," since "we assure ourself it was dressed always for us as for the king; for we lay the most part all of the last week in that same lodging." She ordered an immediate investigation into Darnley's murder, offering a magnanimous £2,000 reward (nearly $640,000 today) to anyone willing to inform against the assassins.

Whispers had begun almost immediately that James Hepburn, the Earl of Bothwell, was at the head of the conspiracy, and after being tortured, the captured plotters all implicated him as the ringleader.

Dashing, stocky, and sporting a mustache in the fashion of French courtiers, Bothwell had received a comprehensive education in France, but was a man of action, preferring the sword to the pen. And he was no saint. John Leslie, Bishop of Ross, thought the earl "of great bodily strength and beauty, although vicious and dissolute in his habits."

Mary had recalled Bothwell from France ten days before she married Darnley, in order to check any rebellion on the part of her illegitimate half brother, James Stewart, the Earl of Moray. In the days after Darnley's death, instead of arresting Bothwell, Mary showered him with political offices and other examples of preferment, believing him to be the only man she could trust. Bothwell's power seemed to grow daily as her ill health and depression brought on by stress and grief increased her dependence on the Protestant earl.

Seven years Mary's senior and brimming with bravado, Bothwell was already Lord High Admiral, and one of Mary's key advisers on matters relating to the border territories; now he began to act as her policy director as well. Mary even gave him her late husband's best horses. Such favoritism caused tongues to wag even faster. Word on the Edinburgh High Street—probably encouraged by Bothwell himself, as Mary was not so inclined—was that they would soon marry.

It boggles the mind that Mary heaped so many favors on Bothwell, and is all the more incredible that she eventually agreed to wed him, because he had always been a ruthless opportunist with a recognizable vicious streak. True, he had commendably led her armed forces into battle on more than one occasion, and had helped her escape Holyrood House after Rizzio's murder, but his motives were never altruistic. Early in Mary's reign he had been arrested for plotting against her, but managed to escape, fleeing to his own castle. And around the time she was considering the marriage to Darnley, Bothwell had openly called her "the Cardinal's whore," a reference to her being politically in bed with her uncle the Cardinal of Lorraine. He vowed never to receive favor at her hands.

How times had changed.

Her increasingly close relationship to Bothwell cost the queen any good PR she had won after Darnley's demise. At first, people had been willing to give her the benefit of the doubt when it came to any connivance in her husband's murder. But her preferential treatment of the earl, who was largely surmised to be the ringleader of the regicides (particularly when his trial for complicity in the king's death was impending), caused suspicion to fall on the queen herself. Continental monarchs, Queen Elizabeth, Mary's subjects, and even her own family in France grew quick to presume her guilt. Goodwill continued to plummet when Mary attended the wedding of her favorite bedchamber woman on the day after Darnley's murder. Although the ceremony had been planned for some time, it didn't look good for the newly widowed queen to be seen at a celebration. And on the night of February 14, when Darnley was buried without fanfare in the tomb of the kings in the old Abbey-Kirk at Holyrood, the modesty of his funeral did not go unremarked.

On April 21, the twenty-four-year-old queen went to visit her son at Stirling Castle, unaware that on April 23 she would be kissing the ten-month-old boy good-bye for the last time. The following day, as Mary was en route from her birthplace of Linlithgow to Edinburgh, her party was intercepted by Bothwell and eight hundred of his men. He told Mary that her safety was in jeopardy, urging her to place her trust in him by permitting him to escort her, and several of her key attendants, including some of her male advisers, to Dunbar Castle. In order to avoid bloodshed, Mary assented. The incident was so odd and Mary's conciliation so easily won that many people surmised (and still do) that she had been complicit in the "abduction."

At Dunbar, Mary may have been raped by Bothwell. Several historians believe so, yet others have a hard time accepting that a woman of Mary's substantial mettle would ever agree to wed her rapist, an opinion that overlooks the mores of the era. If Mary had indeed been violated by Bothwell, it placed her in an untenable position. According to Sir James Melville, "the Queen could not but marry him, seeing he had ravished [seized] her and lain with her against her will." It had been a cultural axiom for centuries that when a man raped a woman, he had ruined her, and whether or not she became pregnant, he was honor-bound to make her reputation whole again by wedding her—which is exactly what Bothwell intended.

Mary allowed Bothwell to win her over in a matter of a couple of days, even as she admitted, "Albeit we found his doings rude, yet were his answer and words both gentle." On April 26, Bothwell galloped for Edinburgh, where he achieved a hasty divorce from his wife, Lady Jean Gordon, on the grounds of consanguinity as well as adultery, seeing as he had publicly fornicated in Haddinton Abbey with Lady Jean's maid, the "bonny little black-haired"

Bessie Crawford. The judges delivered their decree on May 3, effective immediately. As an example of Mary's participation in the scheme to wed Bothwell, on April 27, while his divorce decree was pending, she was busy requesting the Archbishop of St. Andrews to grant the earl an annulment of his marriage to Lady Jean.

The poor, vulnerable queen had three reasons (two of which were political) for resigning herself to marrying Bothwell: he had convinced her that he was the skilled and masterful consort she needed to rule Scotland; he showed her a document, known as the Ainslie Tavern Bond, signed by several powerful nobles pledging their support to him as their overlord; and the rape (if there was one) had "consummated" their union, so that Mary could not go back on her word to marry him once they reached Edinburgh. Ironically, it served Mary better if Bothwell had raped her, because if the consummation had been consensual, then Mary had knowingly slept with a married man at Dunbar and was therefore an adulteress.

In addition, Mary's domestic policy had always been the pursuit of peace. She had a horror of violence, insisting that she would "rather pray with Esther than take the sword of Judith." She had angered the nobles by marrying Darnley, against their advice. If they supported Bothwell, and her marriage to him, perhaps the civil strife would cease.

On May 6, Mary and Bothwell entered Edinburgh. He was leading her horse by the bridle as though she were his captive or a spoil of war. However, John Knox's assistant John Craig refused to proclaim the banns without a royal writ signed by Mary, stating she had not been raped by Bothwell.

Craig received his writ and read the banns, but only after publicly proclaiming that he deplored the impending royal marriage. On May 9, Bothwell called Craig to account for his remarks, but the cleric stood firm: "I laid to his charge the law of adultery, the ordinance of the Kirk, the law of ravishing, the suspicion of collusion between him and his wife, the sudden divorcement, and proclaiming within the space of four days, and last, the suspicion of the king's death, which her marriage would confirm."

Two days later, Craig repeated his misgivings from the pulpit; Bothwell threatened to hang him. The following day, Mary pardoned Bothwell for abducting her, then elevated him to the peerage so that he would be a fitting king consort, creating him Duke of Orkney and Lord of Shetland.

The marriage contract was signed on May 14, justifying the queen's nuptials on the grounds that she was a young widow "apt and able to procreate and to bring forth more children." On Thursday, May 15, 1567, in a Protestant ceremony conducted by one of his relatives, the Bishop of Orkney, Mary and Bothwell were married in the Great Hall at Holyrood Palace. Mary's wedding gown, though covered by the white gauze mourning *deuil*, was cut from a sumptuous black-patterned velvet, lavishly embroidered with gold and silver thread. After the ceremony she changed into a gown of yellow silk, but few people saw her in it, as there was no wedding banquet, no dancing, and no masque to mark her third marriage. Instead of being in a celebratory mood, she remarked to the French ambassador that she "wanted only death."

In the ensuing days, when others were present, Bothwell treated Mary with deference and respect, but privately, "not one day passed" that the new bride was not in tears. Bothwell prohibited her from participating in the leisurely pursuits she had once enjoyed—hawking, hunting, and music—accusing her in the crudest language of frivolity and wantonness. He allowed her no contact with other males and replaced her female servants with his own retainers. He issued proclamations as though he were the king, while Mary meekly acquiesced. And he continued to regularly visit Jean Gordon, who still resided at his seat, Crichton Castle.

According to Sir William Drury, an English statesman and an eyewitness to events, "There hath been already some jars [quarrels] between the queen and the duke and more looked for. He is jealous and suspicious and thinks to be obeyed. . . . The opinion of many is that the queen is the most changed woman of face that in so little time without extremity of sickness they have seen." Only twenty-four years old, Mary seemed to have aged overnight.

It was not long before the rebels turned on their leader. Bothwell had become even more of a tyrant than the man they'd assassinated, and now he was cutting them out and making a power grab on his own, with no intention of sharing it. The lords didn't think twice about eliminating him. They arrived at Borthwick Castle on the night of June 10, 1567, looking for blood. Bothwell managed to flee, unchivalrously leaving Mary to fend for herself. She was able to break free the following night, disguised as a man. Astride a servant's horse she met up with Bothwell at three a.m., taking refuge in Dunbar Castle while he mustered an armed defense.

Meanwhile, Mary's Privy Council declared that as she was now a prisoner, all steps must be taken to liberate her. They accused Bothwell of "ravishing and invading the Princess's body," and of having "put violent hands on [Mary] and that he seduced [her] into an unhonest marriage and murdered Darnley."

Mary and Bothwell both rode into battle against his former co-conspirators. By then, he had admitted to a certain degree of complicity in Darnley's assassination. But Mary had wed him for better or worse and he was her only protector; therefore, she was determined to make his cause her own.

Mary's Privy Council urged her to abandon Bothwell to save herself, leaving him to fight on his own, but she refused—for two reasons. She did not trust the conspirators to see her safely restored to her throne (she was right; they were already hastily forging documents to implicate her in Darnley's murder), and by now she realized she was pregnant by Bothwell.

On June 15, 1567, at Carberry Hill, Bothwell was deserted by his supporters, leaving him to face the rebels alone. Mary negotiated a deal with the lords permitting him to escape, with the knowledge that she would then become their captive. The weeping queen passionately kissed her husband and bid him farewell. He had enjoyed the perquisites of power for only five weeks. Bothwell galloped north toward Dunbar Castle to amass more troops. Mary never saw him again.

In Edinburgh, Mary was briefly detained at a modest home owned by a brother-in-law of one of the conspirators. From there, she was taken to Lochleven Castle. Cast as Darnley's assassin and Bothwell's mistress, the story was spun that Mary was a murderous adulteress who was unfit to reign.

But Mary had her own side of the story: she sent envoys to the courts of England and France defending her conduct after Darnley's murder and explaining her hasty marriage to Bothwell on the grounds that her fractured kingdom needed healing, and that the lords who had been most irksome had demonstrated by their signatures on the Ainslie Tavern Bond that they wanted her to wed a native Scot—specifically Bothwell. She also admitted she had been hoodwinked by him, and became the victim of his brutality and duplicity.

On June 16, 1567, the warrant for Mary's imprisonment was signed by a number of the rebels. The initial charges included the murder of Darnley—for which the conspirators themselves were guilty—and governing her realm under Bothwell's undue influence. But it was hard to make the latter allegation stick with Bothwell out of the picture.

Her captors pressured Mary to divorce him, but she resisted, fearing that if she agreed to do so, the child she was carrying would be denounced as a bastard.

Mary miscarried on July 24 with some accounts referring to twin fetuses. That day, she was compelled to abdicate her throne in favor of her infant son, James, who was immediately crowned at Stirling. Mary's bastard half brother, James Stewart, whom she had created the Earl of Moray in 1562, was made regent. She would subsequently renounce her abdication, claiming it had been made under duress, and she continued to consider herself the true ruler of Scotland until James reached his majority.

Mary finally escaped Lochleven on May 2, 1568, with the aid of some of her more sympathetic captors. Within days she amassed an army, and faced Moray's men at Langside on May 13, where her troops were soundly routed. But rather than sail for her foster country of France, she fled south, making the fatal decision to escape into England, in the romantic hope that Elizabeth would receive her.

However, Elizabeth would not see her until she had been purged of the taint of Darnley's murder—and only she could decide whether Mary was sufficiently innocent.

For the next nineteen years, Mary remained in Elizabeth's custody, moved from castle to castle, her deprivation increasing, her treasures and possessions looted and destroyed, and each jailer crueler than his predecessor. As the years wore on, Mary, who had always made religious tolerance a hallmark of her reign, recast herself as a Catholic martyr incarcerated for her convictions. Eager to do anything to secure her release, she began corresponding with another Catholic monarch, Philip II of Spain, England's greatest enemy during the 1580s.

In October 1584, when Mary was forty-one years old, and had already been in prison for sixteen years, the English Parliament enacted a law called the Bond of Association that rendered Mary guilty of any plot instigated in her name, whether or not she knew of it. The groundwork thus in place, Francis Walsingham, Queen Elizabeth's brilliant spymaster, began to spin the web that would ensnare the Scottish queen. Anthony Babington, a young Catholic zealot, sent Mary a letter in which he outlined the details of a plot to dispatch "the usurping competitor," Elizabeth. A desperate Mary approved his plans and the drums began to rumble with her death march.

On August 14, 1586, Babington was captured and taken to the Tower, where four days later he confessed everything.

Mary was arrested and brought to Fotheringhay Castle, seventy miles from London. On October 11, the commissioners began to arrive for her trial, and the following day Mary spoke to a delegation of lords deputized to convince her to testify in person. With great dignity, she told the nobles, "I am myself a Queen, the daughter of a King, a stranger [foreigner], and the true kinswoman of the Queen of England. I came to England on my cousin's promise of assistance against my enemies and rebel subjects and was at once imprisoned. . . . As an absolute Queen, I cannot submit to orders, nor can I submit to the laws of the land without injury to myself, the King my son and all other sovereign princes. . . . I do not recognize the laws of England nor do I know or understand them. . . . I am alone, without counsel, or anyone to speak on my behalf. My papers and notes have been taken from me, so that I am destitute of all aid, taken at a disadvantage."

The five-month trial was utterly illegal, for all the reasons Mary enumerated. It was no surprise that she was convicted and sentenced to death. On the morning of February 8, 1587, Mary Stuart, the forty-four-year-old Dowager Queen of Scotland and France, was executed in the Great Hall at Fotheringhay Castle.

An eyewitness, Robert Wynkfielde, wrote a famous account of Mary's final minutes, describing her forgiveness of the executioner, her devotions on the block, and the ritual she and her maids performed before the witnesses, removing her black garments to reveal a crimson underskirt and sleeves, the symbolic color of Catholic martyrs.

But the executioner's blow missed, striking the back of Mary's skull through the knot of her blindfold, after which she was allegedly heard to have whispered, "Sweet Jesus." It took a few more tries to hack off her head, and when the headsman triumphantly displayed the severed appendage, Mary's white cap and red wig came off in his hand and the queen's head, with its scraggly gray locks, tumbled to the floor. Then, according to Wynkfielde:

. . . one of the executioners, pulling off her garters, espied her little dog which was crept under her clothes, which could not be gotten forth but by force, yet afterward would not depart from the dead corpse, but came and lay between her head and her shoulders . . .

Mary's body was wrapped in the green fabric that had covered her billiard table during her lengthy incarcerations. Several months later, her coffin was entombed within Peterborough Cathedral across the aisle from the final resting place of another queen who was betrayed, then disgraced by her husband—Katherine of Aragon.

After Bothwell had departed from Mary on Carberry Hill, he traveled north to Scandinavia, where he intended to raise another army. In Norway, a former paramour, Anna Throndsen, accused him of pledging to wed her and never returning her dowry. Bothwell was about to face imprisonment for breach of promise, when the Danish king, Frederick II, learned that he was wanted for Darnley's murder. Frederick brought Bothwell back to Denmark. At first he was treated as a prisoner of state, but after a few years, Frederick sent him to the dank and remote fortress of Dragsholm Castle, where he remained for a decade, drinking copiously and dying—allegedly of madness—on April 14, 1578, at the age of forty-three.

On the death of Elizabeth I in 1603, the son of Mary, Queen of Scots and Lord Darnley became James VI of Scotland and James I of England, ruling both realms. Only then did James decide that a proper monument should be erected for his mother. Mary's body now reposes in Westminster Abbey beneath a white marble tomb.

One of Mary's greatest problems as a sovereign and as a woman was that she wanted things both ways, simultaneously pursuing incompatible policies with equal sincerity. As a teenage queen in France she signed away her kingdom to the French while also supporting Scottish autonomy. Once she returned to Scotland she was as adamant about Catholic tolerance as she was about maintaining the realm's religious status quo by respecting the Protestant Reformation. During her imprisonment in the 1580s she kept several international plates spinning at once as she tried to broker deals with Spain, France, and England; each set of plans, had they ever materialized, would have been detrimental to the other nations. And Mary genuinely desired to be Elizabeth's friend; yet she did plot against her.

Mary's personal tragedy is that she was every inch a queen—

noble, glamorous, charismatic, fair-minded—with a traditional mind-set when it came to the roles of the sexes. She wanted a consort to rule beside her, but none of her three husbands was worthy of her, not even François, who was born to rule. She also wanted to love and be loved, and in marriage those aims eluded her as well. For personal as well as political reasons she desired to be mated. As she told the English ambassador Sir Thomas Randolph at St. Andrews, shortly before she wed Lord Darnley, "Not to marry—you know it cannot be for me."

GEORGE I
1660–1727
ELECTOR OF HANOVER: 1698–1727
RULED ENGLAND: 1714–1727

≈ *and* ≈

SOPHIA DOROTHEA OF CELLE
1666–1726

married 1682–1694

"I will not marry the pig snout!"
—Sophia Dorothea to her parents, 1682

YOU KNOW THERE'S TROUBLE AHEAD WHEN THE IN-LAWS hate each other long before the betrothal even takes place.

Sophia Dorothea of Celle was a love child, the daughter of George William, the Duke of Brunswick Lüneburg, who ruled the postage-stamp-sized Celle portion of the duchy, and his mistress Eleanore Desmier d'Olbreuse, an exiled French Protestant aristocrat.

George William had been all set to inherit the far more prestigious duchy of Hanover, but it came with strings attached: he had to marry the mannish-looking bluestocking his father had selected for him, Princess Sophia, daughter of the Palatine King of Bohemia.

Evidently Sophia was so repugnant to George William that he ceded part of his inheritance, offering his Hanoverian claim to his younger brother, Ernst Augustus, if he would take the homely Sophia off his hands. The ambitious Ernst Augustus agreed, as long as George William promised never to marry and sire heirs, because they would end up rivaling their own first cousins for the Hanoverian throne.

There was only one major problem with this fraternal bride swap: Sophia had been in love with George William and didn't much appreciate his foisting her on his kid brother.

Seven years later, in 1665, George William fell head over heels for the dark bouncing curls, enchanting smile, and sparkling eyes of Eleanore d'Olbreuse. He had to have her, but there was that pesky promise to his brother. He got around it by arranging a sort of unofficial morganatic marriage to Eleanore, meaning that she derived no title, nor would their offspring have any claims to their father's property.

But when Sophia Dorothea was born out of formal wedlock in 1666, Eleanore worried about the difficulties of securing a husband for a bastard daughter and began campaigning for the girl's legitimization and for a proper marriage to George William. The process took years. By 1676, because Ernst Augustus and Duchess Sophia already had plenty of sons as potential successors to the duchy of Hanover, they no longer perceived the daughter of George William and Eleanore as a threat. Their original objections to the marriage mooted, little Sophia Dorothea was legitimized, and her parents were legally wed.

Sophia Dorothea grew up to resemble Snow White, with thick dark hair, doelike eyes, an ivory complexion, and tiny hands and feet. With her stunning figure, she was grace personified. Flirtatious and vivacious, she excelled in all the womanly arts and talents of music, dance, singing, and needlework. To most suitors for her hand, her birthright mattered little. Besides, she had been declared retroactively legitimate.

Although Duchess Sophia despised her sister-in-law Eleanore, she recognized that the best way to get control of Celle was to keep it in the family. So she saddled up her horse and rode over to visit her in-laws, proposing that they wed Sophia Dorothea to her eldest son, George Ludwig, six years the girl's senior. A perfect match! the elder Sophia urged. No other could be considered! Not only that, Sophia Dorothea would eventually be duchess of a far vaster domain than she would if she wed any of her other prospects.

George Ludwig had already distinguished himself as a soldier. His two talents revolved around killing things, as his greatest extracurricular passion was hunting, if you don't count his ardor for his invariably hideous mistresses. His union with Sophia Dorothea would certainly not be the love match her parents enjoyed. It was closer to Beauty and the Beast, minus the transformation and the happy ending. Nicknamed "the pig snout," George Ludwig lacked looks, culture, intellect, and regal bearing. Where Sophia Dorothea was lively, charming, and musical, George Ludwig was slow and sullen with a chilly disposition that masked a vindictive core.

Even his mother didn't like him. As she cheerfully looked forward to receiving the annual installments of Sophia Dorothea's substantial dowry, the Duchess Sophia wrote to one of her other nieces:

One hundred thousand thalers a year is a goodly sum to pocket . . . without speaking of a pretty wife, who will find a match in my son George Ludwig, the most pigheaded, stubborn boy who ever lived, and who has round his brains such a thick crust that I defy any man or woman ever to discover what is in them. He does not care much for the match itself, but one hundred thousand thalers a year have tempted him as they would have tempted anybody else.

When young Sophia Dorothea learned she would have to wed her twenty-two-year-old first cousin, she rebelled, declaring "I will not marry the pig snout!" as she hurled his miniature portrait, encrusted with diamonds, across the room. But it was a fait accompli; the Hanovers were waiting downstairs. Sophia Dorothea's father was adamant about the match and Eleanore was powerless to stop him, even as she anticipated clashes between Sophia Dorothea and the mother-in-law from hell. When the sixteen-year-old sacrificial bride-to-be was escorted down to meet Duchess Sophia and kiss her jeweled hand, she fainted. She had the same reaction a few days later when she was presented to her betrothed.

George Ludwig was just as insulted by the match. In his eyes, his luscious cousin's looks were nothing compared to her initial bastardy.

Nonetheless, the young couple's wishes were ignored in favor of dynastic and political goals. So on November 22, 1682, each looking like a prisoner en route to the scaffold, the pale and trembling Sophia Dorothea was wed to the chilly and distant George Ludwig in the chapel of Celle Castle. The bride's mother sobbed loudly during the entire ceremony. The groom's mother, having sacrificed her ego to politics, looked grim. Only the fathers were smiling at the thought of the sizeable double duchy that would be created by the uniting of their adjoining realms. Ernst Augustus in particular couldn't wait to have Celle added to his Hanoverian holdings. The more land his family acquired, the more power they would have, and the better his chances of convincing the Holy Roman Emperor to make him an Elector, one of the German rulers with the prestigious privilege of selecting the emperor.

The newlyweds formally resided at the Leine Palace in Hanover. Sophia Dorothea was immediately made miserable not only by her husband's remoteness but also by her mother-in-law's perpetual scolding regarding her ignorance of court etiquette. Luckily for Sophia Dorothea, George Ludwig became literally distant when he embarked on various military campaigns for significant stretches of time. But he kept *au courant* with his wife's activities through the reports of spies he had placed among her servants, who chronicled everything she did or said, particularly when she turned her wit on him, shredding his personality in public.

In between arguments, they did manage to have two children. In 1683, after Sophia Dorothea gave birth to a son and heir, George Augustus, things became more cordial. Sophia Dorothea endeavored to ingratiate herself with her in-laws and George Ludwig promised to swear off adultery. His paramour was Sophia Charlotte von Kielmannsegg, the married daughter of his father's mistress, the blowsy Countess Platen. Although the countess had numerous lovers, it was widely assumed by all but the related parties that the woman Platen had placed in the prince's bed was her daughter by Duke Ernst Augustus, making the happy couple half siblings.

In 1685, Sophia Dorothea took off on an Italian holiday with her father-in-law. While she was away, George found a new lover among his mother's maids of honor—Ehrengard Melusine von der Schulenberg—as freakishly tall and anorexically thin as Frau von Kielmannsegg was short and portly.

When the princess returned from her vacation to find that her husband had taken up with a *second* hideous mistress, she was livid; but the royal couple must have kissed and made up just long enough for Sophia Dorothea to become pregnant again. Their daughter—also named Sophia Dorothea—was born on March 16, 1687. But during the particularly acrimonious celebration of the little girl's birth, after George nearly strangled his wife in public, the battling Hanovers wanted nothing more to do with each other.

Sophia Dorothea's complaints about her husband's infidelities were ignored, even by her own father, whose prime minister had for some strange reason filled his head with stories about his daughter's less sympathetic wifely qualities, including her arrogance and her sharp tongue.

Sophia was indeed far from the perfect wife. As heedless and selfish as she was lovely, in 1689 she commenced a torrid epistolary affair with a tall, handsome, and rakish Swedish mercenary in her father-in-law's army. By the time he fell shako over spurs for the princess, Count Philipp Christoph von Königsmark had left his curly black wig and shiny boots on the floor of many a European lady's boudoir. Sophisticated and cultured, and as flirtatious as his inamorata, he enjoyed literature and dancing and all the refined and elegant trappings of polite and elegant society. His previous paramours even included the scheming and jealous Countess Platen, Ernst Augustus's mistress. However, his liaison with the Hanoverian hereditary princess, his soul mate and fellow sensualist, was True Love, and by 1690 he had dropped the countess like a contaminated object and become Sophia Dorothea's paramour in every way. Their romance was filled with clandestine trysts, coded correspondence, secret signals, and a trusted confidante to act as a go-between.

The couple spent as much time in each other's arms as possible and exchanged lurid love letters. The count wrote to his beloved, "I embrace your knees" and expressed a longing to "kiss that little place which has given me so much pleasure." But around 1692 the latter letter, and many others, found its way into the hands of Sophia Dorothea's father-in-law, most probably through the machinations of the spurned Countess Platen.

That year, Ernst Augustus had finally been granted his dearest wish, the honor of becoming an Elector. With his newfound status, he began to care more about keeping up appearances and therefore had to do something about the von Königsmark affair, which had become too indiscreet to ignore. Countess Platen convinced him to exile the count, but no sooner was he banished than the handsome Swedish mercenary got himself a new post with the Elector of Saxony. However, at an officers' party one night in Dresden, von Königsmark became a bit too voluble under the influence and dished the dirt on the Hanoverian royal family. Naturally, the trash talking got back to his former employer.

The one most injured by von Königsmark's mockery around the punch bowl was the tall and skeletal Ehrengard Melusine von der Schulenberg. She ran to her lover, tearfully complaining that his wife's banished paramour had mortally insulted her. George Ludwig confronted Sophia Dorothea, who promptly let him have it, insisting that the real sex scandal was *his* affair with Melusine! A pitched battle ensued between the royal spouses and George Ludwig tried to choke his wife to death. Shoving her to the floor, he vowed never to see her again. Unlike his earlier promise to quit committing adultery, *this* pledge he kept.

With nothing left of her marriage, Sophia Dorothea and von Königsmark elected to throw caution to the winds and scheduled an elopement. Arriving at the Leine Palace, von Königsmark made straight for his lover's boudoir; after enjoying a passionate reunion, the count planned to come back for her the following day.

But Countess Platen discovered the plan and reported it to Ernst Augustus, who had his guards waylay von Königsmark as he left Sophia Dorothea's bedroom. The stories about the count's subsequent murder are as colorful as they are varied. What is certain is that he was ambushed—either on the open road or in the Leine Palace—and that he fought back valiantly, wounding one of his assailants. The count was slain; his body disappeared entirely. Most historians believe it was buried right under the bloodstained floorboards of the corridor where he may have been summarily dispatched, his corpse covered in quicklime to eradicate the stench of decay and hasten decomposition.

A hysterical Sophia Dorothea was detained in her rooms, under house arrest. Adultery could not be mentioned since it cast doubt on the legitimacy of her children (and therefore, their inheritance), although they had been born long before Sophia Dorothea first met von Königsmark.

George Ludwig had ignored his wife's infidelity for years because von Königsmark was such a crack soldier and one of the best swordsmen in Europe. And it's possible that if neither spouse had flaunted their respective extramarital liaisons, the royal marriage might have clattered along tolerably well, or at least as well as most other arranged unions between two first cousins.

But enough was enough. A kangaroo court found Sophia Dorothea guilty of "malicious desertion"—a far greater crime than adultery, since desertion would create problems with the collection of her annual dowry installments. And on December 28, 1694, her marriage to George Ludwig was legally dissolved—a relief to the princess, who was now officially rid of a husband she found revolting. "We still adhere to our oft-repeated resolution never to cohabit matrimonially with our husband, and that we desire nothing so much as that separation of marriage requested by our husband may take place," she had averred during the divorce proceedings.

All traces of Sophia Dorothea's existence in Hanover were expunged. Her name was obliterated from government documents and was no longer uttered in the clergy's recitation of prayers for the royal family. Her former in-laws did, however, continue to pocket her annual dowry installments.

On February 28, 1695, Sophia Dorothea was "banished" to a lovely moated country home in Ahlden, where, after the first, exceptionally restrictive year of her incarceration, she lived out the rest of her days in what most of us would consider luxury, attended by a modest retinue. She was given the new title duchess, or princess, of Ahlden. Although her children were taken away and raised by their paternal grandmother, Sophia Dorothea would not have been the recipient of any mother-of-the-year trophies, so this sacrifice was probably for the best.

Meanwhile, George Ludwig continued to enjoy the charms of his two lovers. By then, Melusine—acknowledged since 1691 as his *maîtresse en titre*—had given him two daughters, who were immediately reborn as the prince's "nieces." She would bear a third daughter in 1701. Although he never acknowledged paternity of any of the girls, he did make sure they were very well provided for as they were growing up and they were included in his intimate family circle.

George Ludwig became the Elector of Hanover on the death of his father in 1698. He promptly dismissed Countess Platen from court. On her deathbed she confessed to her complicity in the murder of Count Philipp Christoph von Königsmark, and the details of his brutal, bloody demise came to light, exonerating George Ludwig, who in any case had always been assumed to have been ignorant of the plot. Nonetheless, his wife's adulterous affair and the strange case of von Königsmark's disappearance, as well as Sophia Dorothea's subsequent imprisonment, had been the talk of European courts for years.

Yet even as she remained under lock and key, Sophia Dorothea's existence remained a problem. George Ludwig was actively campaigning to be placed on the short list for succession to the English throne. According to the 1701 Act of Succession, all future rulers of England had to be Protestants descended from the Stuart line. George Ludwig's accession was a long shot at the time because Queen Anne, who ascended the throne in 1702, seemed exceptionally fertile. Anne ultimately endured seventeen pregnancies but none of her children survived into adulthood. George Ludwig's mother, the Dowager Electress Sophia, was a granddaughter of the Stuart king James I, and a Protestant to boot, so her claim—as well as George Ludwig's if his mother predeceased him—was genuine. However, his divorce from Sophia Dorothea was both a political and a religious embarrassment, especially in England. She could very well manage to attack George Ludwig's character, adding fuel to the cause of the Jacobites, who wanted to see the Catholic descendants of James II and his second wife, Mary of Modena, on the British throne.

But on April 12, 1714, the House of Lords resolved that a request be sent to Queen Anne to issue a proclamation offering a reward to anyone who apprehended and brought to justice the Jacobite "Pretender" James Francis Edward Stuart, the son of James II and Mary of Modena. Anne signed the proclamation on June 21, paving the way for a Protestant successor—which meant that George Ludwig, Elector of Hanover, was next in line for the throne; his mother had died just weeks earlier, on June 8.

Less than two months after the issuance of the proclamation, on August 1, 1714, Queen Anne died.

If Sophia Dorothea had remained married to George Ludwig, she would have been Queen of England. Some historians believe that her divorce papers might not have been ironclad; this would explain why, after George Ludwig's accession as George I of England, she was watched even more closely for fear that she might escape Ahlden and demand to share his throne. Their daughter, Sophia Dorothea the younger, had become Queen of Prussia, but her own husband was such a tyrant that he forbade her to help her mother in any way.

On November 13, 1726, lonely and all but forgotten, Sophia Dorothea died at the age of sixty, some say of a possible stroke or heart attack, while others claim she suffered a fever. She had been a prisoner for thirty-one years with the exception of a few months in 1700, when Ahlden lay in the path of a French invasion. After the danger had passed, her father sent her back to the castle.

Evidently, as she lay dying in agony, Sophia Dorothea scrawled a letter to her ex-husband, cursing him from the grave. On her death the court of Hanover went into mourning, but George sent word from London that no one was to wear black. Sophia Dorothea had inherited her mother's property in 1722 upon Eleanore's death and willed it to her children, but George destroyed the will and appropriated her property for himself. Then he ordered all her personal effects at Ahlden to be burned. He insisted on her ignominious burial at Ahlden, but the ground was too waterlogged, so her coffin sat around in a dreary chamber for two months until his superstitious mistress Melusine claimed to see Sophia Dorothea's unfettered spirit flying about in the guise of a bird.

In May 1727, Sophia Dorothea was finally interred within the family crypt in the Old Church at Celle, where visitors honoring her martyrdom to true love still place flowers on her unprepossessing lead coffin.

That June, the sixty-seven-year-old monarch embarked on his

fifth excursion to Hanover since the beginning of his reign as King of England. On June 20, his little entourage stopped en route in Delden, Holland, at the home of a friend, Count de Twillet, where George enjoyed an enormous supper, overindulging in a dessert of oranges and strawberries. Despite a dreadful bellyache the following day, the king was eager to get back on the road. When he reached Ibbenburen, he suffered an attack of apoplexy.

A contemporary described the incident. "He was quite lethargic, his hand fell down as if lifeless, and his tongue hung out of his mouth. He gave, however, signs of life by continually crying out as well as he could articulate, 'Osnabrück! Osnabrück!' [the name of his birthplace]." According to the Historical Register, his last words were in French—"*c'est fait de moi*"—I am done for. He died in the early hours of the morning on June 22, 1727, and was buried near his mother's monument at the Leineschloss Church in Hanover.

Some believe the catalyst for George's sudden fatal illness was not a surfeit of fruit but an incident that occurred on June 19, 1727, when he received a mail delivery as he traveled to Hanover. It was his wife's ghostly epistle. George suddenly remembered that decades earlier a fortune-teller had prophesied that if he were in any way responsible for his wife's death he would die within a year of her demise.

With the exception of Ehrengard Melusine von der Schulenberg, very few people mourned the passing of George I. As King of England, his political agenda often favored his Hanoverian interests; in 1720 he had been personally involved in England's worst financial disaster, the South Sea Bubble; he had never bothered to learn more than the rudiments of the English language; and he had masterminded an attempt on his own son's life.

George and Sophia Dorothea's son succeeded his father on the British throne, ruling as George II. He ordered Hanover's records unsealed and discovered 1,399 pages of love letters—only a fraction of those exchanged—between his mother and Count von Königsmark. His idyll was shattered: his mother was no saint and had indeed been an adulteress. But George also recognized that his father had behaved dreadfully to her. Had Sophia Dorothea lived, George II would have liberated her from Ahlden and installed her as the Dowager Queen of England.

In any event, the lesson was not fully learned. George II took mistresses as well, although for a while he did his best to be discreet about it—which, in his view at least, was his way of respecting the feelings of his purportedly beloved wife, Caroline of Anspach.

EMPEROR PETER III
1728–1762
RULED RUSSIA: 1762

❊ and ❊

SOPHIE FRIEDERIKE AUGUSTE
OF ANHALT-ZERBST,
A.K.A. CATHERINE II [CATHERINE THE GREAT]
1729–1796
RULED RUSSIA: 1762–1796

married 1745–1762

"... In the very first days of our marriage I came to a sad conclusion about him. I said to myself, 'If you allow yourself to love that man, you will be the unhappiest creature on this earth.'"
—Grand Duchess Catherine Alexeyevna, later Catherine the Great

*L*ET'S DISPENSE WITH THE PRELIMINARIES: *THERE WAS NO horse.* Yes, when she was a little girl and couldn't fall asleep at night, boisterous young Sophie Friederike Auguste of Anhalt-Zerbst would stick her pillow between her legs and ride it like a stallion. But, contrary to the royal equivalent of urban mythology, she did not *die* in the process of making love to one.

In 1739, ten-year-old Sophie, a blue-eyed, fair-skinned blonde, met her future husband (and second cousin), eleven-year-old Karl Peter Ulrich, Duke of Holstein-Gottorp. At the time, Karl Peter, a good-looking, well-mannered boy, had just become an orphan, and more than anything was a kid starved for affection.

The children's relatives—one of whom was Karl Peter's aunt Elizabeth, the childless Empress of Russia—already assumed they would eventually marry. Three years later, in November 1742, Elizabeth summoned the fourteen-year-old Karl Peter to Russia and named him her heir. Part of the deal was that the youth convert to Russian Orthodoxy. He did so, more as a matter of expediency than from any religious conviction, and took a new name: His Imperial Highness the Grand Duke Peter Fyodorovich.

Aware that Peter was now an even more excellent catch, Sophie's ambitious mother, Johanna, kept in touch with the Russian empress. And on New Year's Day 1744, Johanna received a letter from Elizabeth inviting her to bring Sophie to Moscow. Although the lengthy journey was billed as a casual visit from distant relations, no one was fooled: it was an audition for the role of future Empress of Russia.

On her arrival, deliberately timed to coincide with Peter's sixteenth birthday, the fourteen-year-old Sophie was much impressed with the majesty and bearing of Empress Elizabeth, though less so with her future spouse. Rather small for his age and brimming with nervous energy, Peter was all gangly angles, with a long, pale face, straight nose, and firm chin.

Although she quickly proved herself to be ambitious, determined, confident, and a quick study in all that would be expected of her from deportment to religious conversion, including full mastery of the Russian language, Sophie soon realized that the royal marriage was not in fact a foregone conclusion. Given little guidance on how to survive and thrive at the Russian court, So-phie's trial lasted for months, during which her every word and gesture was watched, appraised, and reported to the empress.

Eventually, the poor teenager broke under the stress of perform-ing to perfection and late nights spent cramming Russian vocabu-lary. She came down with pleurisy and was confined to bed for weeks. However, she had passed the test. On May 3, 1744, a few weeks after her fifteenth birthday, Sophie wrote to her father, Chris-tian August of Anhalt-Zerbst, to request his consent to her be-trothal, although she may have neglected to tell her papa that her new fiancé only had two topics of conversation: soldiers and his toys (which happened to be toy soldiers). She would later write that she was only marrying Peter because her mother told her to do it. In truth, it was not daughterly devotion but the crown of Russia that was so devilishly attractive.

For Peter's part, he acknowledged that he would have to marry *someone*, so it might as well be his pretty second cousin.

On June 28, in a lavish service during which Sophie flawlessly recited copious amounts of Russian liturgy, she was formally ad-mitted into the Orthodox Church and took a new name: Grand Duchess Ekaterina (Catherine) Alexeyevna. An opulent engage-ment ceremony followed Catherine's conversion. All summer Rus-sia celebrated with fêtes and balls—including Empress Elizabeth's famous Tuesday evening cross-dressing "Metamorphoses" mas-querades, secretly detested by all but the empress and Catherine, because each looked splendid in knee breeches and hose.

During the engagement Catherine devised a three-point checklist for her future. In order of importance, her chief aims for her new life would be: to please the grand duke; to please the empress; and to please the nation. But her status grew a bit wobbly when, in No-vember 1744, Peter contracted measles and along with his entire entourage was quarantined from the rest of the court. He emerged from his sickbed taller and physically stronger, but Catherine no-ticed no other improvement. "His mind was still very immature. He spent his time in his room playing soldiers with his valets, flunkeys, his dwarfs, and his gentlemen-in-waiting," she observed in her memoirs.

Yet no sooner did Peter rebound from the measles than he contracted smallpox. He recovered by January 1745, but according to Catherine, his entire appearance had been altered by the disease. "He had grown a great deal, but his face was unrecognizable. All his features were coarsened, his face was still all swollen, and one could see that he would no doubt remain badly scarred. As his hair had been cut off, he had an enormous wig which made him look even worse."

As their wedding day loomed, Peter's court endeavored to school him in how to manage a wife, filling his head with advice that would surely lead to Catherine's unhappiness if he heeded it. A clever girl, she decided to adopt a diplomatic tack with him: she would listen to Peter and give him every impression that she was in sync with his views. Her aim was to win him over as a friend, a system she applied to the entire court. "I tried to be as charming as possible to everyone and studied every opportunity to win the affection of those whom I suspected of being in the slightest degree ill-disposed towards me; I showed no preference for any side, never interfered in anything, always looked serene and displayed much attentiveness, affability, and politeness all around."

Although she was still in her mid-teens, already Catherine had the makings of an empress.

She was not remotely attracted to Peter, yet during the months before the wedding she wept bitterly over his lack of affection toward her. The infrequent time they spent together consisted mainly of Peter putting his future bride through military drills and teaching her how to handle a rifle. Nevertheless, Catherine maintained her spirits by keeping her eye on the prize, and endeavoring to overlook her fiancé's oddity.

Meanwhile, clueless about the facts of life, she tried to find out from the ladies in her entourage about what went on between the bedsheets, but they were equally naïve. Yet it was not only Catherine who felt unprepared for a conjugal relationship. Court physicians unsuccessfully tried to convince the empress that Peter was physically too immature for marital relations. However, Elizabeth refused to postpone the royal wedding on those grounds.

Finally, the big day came. At five a.m. on August 21, 1745, booming cannons awakened the court. Catherine, wearing a formal dishabille of white and gold, was escorted by her ladies to the empress, who was similarly dressed. A turf war ensued over Catherine's bridal hairstyle—the coiffeur favored fashionable curls; the empress insisted on a smooth do that would enable the jewels to be properly secured in her hair. Elizabeth "blinked" first and Catherine's shiny dark tresses were curled and left unpowdered.

The young archduchess then donned her heavy wedding dress, made of cloth of silver and embroidered with silver at the hem and seams. Over it went a cloak of silver lace; two spots of rouge stained her cheeks. Peter's wedding garments were the masculine equivalent of Catherine's, accessorized with diamonds and a ceremonial sword.

A resplendent procession made its way to Our Lady of Kazan, where the two teenagers were wed in a lavish ritual. Hundreds of people partook of the wedding feast that ended at eleven p.m., just in time for the ball to commence. By the time the bride and groom were led to their marriage bed and dressed in identical nightclothes, it was well after one in the morning, and Catherine was exhausted.

The marital chamber, lined with red velvet, resembled a cross between a jewel box and a bordello. Ensconced in the double bed, Catherine sat and waited. Her groom had disappeared. She described her wedding night in her memoirs:

> Everybody left me and I remained alone for more than two hours, not knowing what was expected of me. Should I get up? Should I remain in bed? . . . At last Mme. Krause, my new maid, came in and told me very cheerfully that the Grand Duke was waiting for his supper which would be served shortly. His Imperial Highness came to bed after supper and began to say how amused the servant would be to find us in bed together.

As things transpired (or didn't), Catherine needn't have spent so many anxious hours fretting over what might happen on her wedding night. Peter was as naïve about sex as she was, and so uninterested in it that he didn't even make a clumsy attempt to consummate their marriage. Realizing that nothing was going to occur, Catherine rolled over and went to sleep.

Years later, Catherine observed of her days as a newlywed, "I would have been ready to like my new husband had he been capable of affection or willing to show any. But in the very first days of our marriage I came to a sad conclusion. I said to myself 'If you allow yourself to love that man, you will be the unhappiest creature on this earth.' "

The court, surprisingly, seemed to regard their marriage as a success. Of course, they were unaware that Peter and Catherine remained virgins, and every time he became ill, her existence at court hung in the balance. If Catherine failed to produce an heir and Peter died, the empress could send her packing back to Germany or shove her into a convent. Elizabeth could still disinherit Peter if he showed signs of not fulfilling her expectations, and he was certainly not shaping up to be an emperor. Recovering from yet another illness in 1746, the eighteen-year-old grand duke set up a puppet theater in his rooms, inviting members of the court to attend performances.

An exasperated Elizabeth hired a pair of minders for the newlyweds, whose chief assignment was to get the teens to have sex. And she drew up a set of instructions on what constituted acceptable behavior at court, addressing certain examples of Peter's puerile conduct. Among the guidelines: "The person selected to keep the Grand Duke company will endeavor to reprimand certain unseemly habits of his Imperial Highness. He must not, for instance, when at table pour the contents of his glass over the servants' heads, nor must he address coarse expressions or improper jokes to those who have the honor to come near him, including foreigners of distinction received at Court; or publicly make grimaces and continually jerk his limbs."

Catherine was given rules to abide by as well. She was supposed to strictly adhere to Russian Orthodoxy, not to meddle in affairs of state, and not to treat her husband coldly. The fact that she was there solely to produce an heir was baldly restated. After a year had passed during which the young archduchess had still not conceived, Empress Elizabeth unleashed her fury on the hapless Catherine, accusing her of being in love with another man, or else willfully conspiring with her archenemy Frederick of Prussia by deliberately failing to get pregnant. This upbraiding so upset Catherine that she attempted suicide by stabbing herself through her stays with a blunt knife.

Naturally, the longer it took Peter and Catherine to consummate their marriage, the greater the embarrassment for all concerned. It's possible that Peter suffered from phimosis, the same painful condition shared by Louis XVI of France—an inability to fully retract the foreskin, making an erection excruciatingly painful. But Catherine became convinced that part of the problem was political—that various factions at court were trying to keep them apart by telling her that Peter was infatuated with other women.

Even their official babysitters were at odds with each other. Madame Krause, the German woman in charge of Catherine's maids, disliked the Choglokovs, the Russian couple assigned to mind the young royals. In 1747, the results of this churlishness turned the marriage bed into a playground. According to Catherine, Madame Krause "procured for the Grand Duke toys, dolls and other childish playthings which he adored. During the day they were hidden inside and underneath my bed; the Grand Duke would be the first to go to bed after supper, and as soon as we were both in bed, Mme. Krause would lock the door and then the Grand Duke would play until one or two o'clock in the morning. I was obliged willynilly to join in with this delightful entertainment, as was Mme. Krause."

As Peter's emotional maturity stagnated, Catherine was becoming a beauty. She wrote, "I was tall and had a magnificent figure but I could have allowed myself a little more weight as I was rather thin. I did not like using powder and my hair was soft brown, very thick and well planted on the forehead. The fashion for leaving one's hair unpowdered was beginning to wane and that winter I used it now and then." When the court moved to Moscow that December, Catherine and Peter were lodged near each other, to facilitate connubial relations. But Peter still wasn't up for it. Instead, Catherine—who had busied herself reading Voltaire and the letters of Mme. de Sevigné—wrote, "At that time the Grand Duke had only two occupations. One was to scrape the violin, the other to train spaniels for hunting. So, from seven o'clock in the morning until late into the night, either the discordant sounds which he drew very forcefully from his violin or the horrible barking and howling of the five or six dogs which he thrashed throughout the rest of the day, continually grated on my ears. I admit that I was driven half-mad and suffered terribly as both these musical performances tore at my ear-drums. . . . After the dogs I was the most miserable creature in the world."

By 1752, the young royals had been married for seven years, and the exasperated Maria Choglokova finally admitted to Her Imperial Highness that Peter and Catherine were still virginal. Empress Elizabeth was shocked. She instructed Maria to get her nephew tutored in the facts of life, and to see to it that Catherine got pregnant—by anyone. After several days of lobbying, the widow of Elizabeth's court painter Georg Christian Grooth was persuaded to initiate Peter into the mysteries of sex.

And despite the fact that he had been lucky enough to marry for love not two years earlier, it didn't take too much encouragement to nudge Peter's twenty-six-year-old chamberlain Sergei Saltykov in Catherine's direction. She tried to resist him but "unfortunately I could not help listening to him. He was as handsome as the dawn. There was no one to compete with him in that, not at the Imperial Court, and still less at ours. Nor was he lacking in intelligence or the accomplishments, manners, and graces which are a prerogative of the *grand monde*, but especially at the Court."

By this time, the twenty-three-year-old Catherine was also

sleeping with her husband, and it's not clear which man took her virginity. But practically as soon as he made his conquest, Saltykov began to tire of his royal mistress. The empress and Maria Choglokova remained impatient. If Peter couldn't deliver the goods, and Saltykov was beginning to balk, Maria privately suggested another gentleman of the bedchamber who might make a suitable stud.

Saltykov would be the first of a dozen (known) lovers Catherine would take over the course of her lifetime. Between the winter of 1752–53 and May 1753, the archduchess twice became pregnant and twice miscarried, each time losing the fetus after a couple of months, if not within a few weeks of conceiving. While Catherine recovered, her husband passed the time getting drunk with his servants, his maturity level in his mid-twenties no higher than it had been when he and Catherine first met. For instance, it was at this time that he made an example of a rat that had eaten two of his toy sentinels by submitting it to a public hanging. When Catherine scoffed, Peter grew incensed at her "womanly ignorance of military law."

Finally, on September 20, 1754, after an exceptionally difficult labor on the birthing couch, Catherine was delivered of a son. The poor archduchess was left all alone in the hot and airless chamber, lying in her amniotic fluids, entirely forgotten and neglected, while the empress removed the infant, saw that he was swaddled, and then summoned her confessor, conferring on the boy the name of Paul without consulting either of his parents. If there was any question as to the boy's paternity, it would soon become apparent, or at least widely accepted, that Paul Petrovich was most certainly Peter's son. The child had none of Saltykov's handsome looks and resembled Peter both physically and temperamentally.

On February 20, 1755, to honor her husband's twenty-seventh birthday, Catherine made her first public appearance since Paul's birth. Now that she had borne an heir for Mother Russia—and was not even permitted to raise him herself—the archduchess was forced to recognize that she was otherwise disposable. As a measure of how little she mattered, her husband had begun to pay court to one of her maids of honor, Elizaveta Vorontsova. From that point on, Catherine knew she would have to take her destiny into her own hands.

She was acquiring a reputation as a shrewd, intelligent woman who was a good listener. By 1756 she had quietly amassed a network of spies and informers at court.

Catherine's status there had never been entirely secure. Nor was her husband's situation any safer. Although Peter was Elizabeth's heir, a Russian ruler had the power to "fire" his or her eventual successor and choose a different one for any reason. The empress had always been concerned that Peter might not live up to his potential; legally, she could rescind his inheritance at any time, which would therefore make Catherine a royal nobody. Additionally, there were many at court who thought Peter would be a disastrous emperor and might plan a coup after Elizabeth's demise. Consequently, acknowledging that she needed to cover all her bases, Catherine intended to insure that she and Peter would take the throne together with the backing and support of the elite Guards officers.

"I shall either perish or reign," the archduchess declared. However, she knew that Peter's rule might be a dicey sell: Russia and Prussia were archenemies and the German-born archduke was "Prussian to the death." It was "engrained in his disposition," according to Catherine. Her husband, who so desired to emulate his hero, Frederick the Great, refused to accept the fact that the man was Russia's greatest threat.

In March of 1757, Catherine confirmed that she was pregnant again, but this time her husband most vociferously doubted that he was the father. In the presence of several members of his household Peter exclaimed, "Heaven alone knows how it is that my wife becomes pregnant. I have no idea whether this child is mine and whether I ought to recognize it as such."

Catherine learned about this remark from a gentleman of the bedchamber. So, she instructed him to return to Peter and ask him to swear upon his honor that he had *not* slept with her—and if

Peter was prepared to so swear, Catherine would take that oath straight to the empress's Head of the Secret Chancery.

She had called his bluff. Naturally, Peter wasn't about to do any such thing. For him to baldly confess to Elizabeth's ministers that he was no longer having relations with his wife would have been an enormous embarrassment, tantamount to hanging the royal couple's dirty linen in the public square.

Catherine gave birth to a daughter, Anna Petrovna, on November 29, 1757, but the girl never lived to see her second birthday, dying on March 9, 1759. By 1758, if not considerably earlier, both spouses had resumed their extramarital affairs—Peter with Elizaveta Vorontsova, and Catherine with her man of the moment. Often the royals would socialize as a foursome, playing cards and talking late into the night. And when it was bedtime, the royal spouses retired with their respective lovers rather than with each other.

After several years of declining health, the fifty-two-year-old empress finally died at three p.m. on December 25, 1761. Peter instructed his wife to remain by Elizabeth's body until he sent for her. When Catherine was summoned to the palace chapel, her husband took the oath as Emperor Peter II. There was no mention in the liturgy of Catherine, or of their son, Paul.

Catherine had managed to conceal thus far that she was five months pregnant. Her marriage had eroded to the extent that it would have been all but impossible for the child to be Peter's. It was a near certainty that paternity could be claimed by Catherine's lover, who at that time was the burly and formidable Lieutenant Grigory Orlov of the elite Izmailovsky Guards, the handsomest of five strapping Orlov brothers.

At the burial ceremony of Empress Elizabeth on January 25, 1762, the new emperor, nearly thirty-four years old, gave his subjects a sharp taste of his unsuitability to rule. Rather than walk somberly and respectfully behind his aunt's coffin, Peter made a game out of continually letting the funeral cortege pull ahead of him some thirty feet, then dashing madly to catch up with it.

As emperor, Peter had a tendency to spring things on people without taking the time for study and reflection. Consequently, many of his reforms were ill conceived. For example, on February 18, 1762, barely two months into his reign, Peter issued a manifesto absolving nobles from service to the state during peacetime. But the decree precariously tipped the balance of Russia's class system. Serfs served the nobles who served the state. If the upper crust's public service commitment was eliminated to a large degree, the serfs would be the only ones working.

Peter also abolished the secret police—a nice idea, but the dissolution prevented him from discovering the coup that would topple him in just a few months' time. And he alienated many of his subjects by westernizing the Russian Orthodox Church, compelling the clergy to shave their beards and ridding the churches of their icons, except for those representing Jesus Christ. Additionally, Peter angered the members of his armed forces by calling a halt to the war with Prussia just as his army was about to crush that of his idol, Frederick the Great.

Eleven days before her thirty-third birthday, on April 10, 1762, Catherine gave birth to Grigory Orlov's son. As it would have been politically imprudent to bring up her obvious bastard in the palace beside her legitimate son, she immediately placed the infant with her valet and his wife, who would raise the boy as their own.

By now, Catherine had realized that although she was Empress Consort, her husband had no intention of permitting her to be a coruler of Russia. Moreover, it was becoming apparent that if he could, he would find a way to get rid of her and replace her with his mistress, Elizaveta Vorontsova. He had taken to referring to Catherine as "she," and humiliated her before the entire court at a gala dinner on June 9 when he called her the equivalent of a moron for refusing to stand for a toast to the royal family.

What her husband didn't know was that by this time her plans to effect a coup were fully in place. On June 28 the elite guards swore allegiance to Catherine as empress as she stood on a balcony of the Winter Palace in St. Petersburg, dressed like one of them in a borrowed uniform of red and green. Beside her stood the seven-year-old Archduke Paul. A young petty officer noticed that Catherine had neglected to affix a sword knot to her weapon and gave her his own. The gallant young man was Grigory Potemkin, who years later would become Catherine's most notorious lover and adviser.

As manifestos were read proclaiming Catherine's assumption of the imperial throne and justifying the coup by highlighting Peter's erosion of Russia's grand institutions, the emperor spent the day getting drunk. When he sent a few loyal men to counteract Catherine's army of followers, they deserted as soon as they saw the magnitude of their enemy. The man who played at soldiers all his life proved utterly inept at actual troop maneuvers.

At midnight Peter tried to escape the city by boat, but his flight was checked by an armed vessel blocking his way to the open sea.

On June 29, Peter's name day and the eighteenth anniversary of his betrothal to Catherine, he sent his wife a letter of conciliation but received no reply. At Peterhof, she received his signed letter of abdication, confirming that the handwriting was his. She withdrew into the upper castle so as not to witness Peter's humiliation as a security detail of three hundred men escorted him into the palace, where he was asked to hand over his sword and divest himself of his elite guard uniform. Peter fainted from the shock. Later that afternoon the deposed emperor was taken by guarded coach to Ropsha, an estate some twenty miles inland, where he was imprisoned in a cramped chamber.

On June 30, Catherine reentered St. Petersburg in triumph, believing that she had fulfilled God's plan and her destiny by becoming empress. But then the hard work began. Catherine had inherited a mess. The treasury was in disarray, prisons overflowed, and political corruption was rampant.

From Ropsha Peter wrote to his wife, assuring her that he would not "undertake anything against her person or her reign," and humbly requesting that she remove the guards from his room because he was compelled to attend to calls of nature in their presence.

With little else to do all day, Peter and his guards (at least one of whom, Alexei, was a brother of Catherine's lover Grigory Orlov) drank and played cards together. On July 2, Alexei Orlov wrote to Catherine informing her that Peter was "gravely ill with an unexpected colic. The first fear is caused by the fact that he talks nonsense the whole time which amuses us, and the second is that he is really a danger to us all and behaves as though nothing had happened."

The following evening, after suffering diarrhea for a day, Peter was attended by his physician. Over the next two days his condition alternated between worsening and showing signs of recovery. But on July 6, Alexei Orlov wrote a stunning letter to Catherine:

> . . . I swear that I cannot understand how this has happened. We are finished if you do not pardon us, our little mother, he is no more! No one wanted it to come to that, how we would dare to raise our hand against our sovereign! Nevertheless, Your Majesty, the misfortune has happened. At table he got into an argument with Prince Fyodor [Baryatinsky], and before we could have time to separate them, he was no more. . . . I have admitted everything to you, it would be useless to have an investigation . . .

Catherine placed this letter in a cabinet in her study and locked it away. There it remained throughout her reign, discovered after her death by the new emperor, her son, Paul. By that point, he had long surmised that his mother, Grigory Orlov, and Orlov's brothers had had a hand in his father's judicial murder.

In fact, even at the time of Peter's death no one believed that the tsar had died of a violent stomachache and hemorrhoidal colic, as stated in the formal declaration of his demise. Catherine had told a former lover that her husband drank excessively on the date of his death, adding "that the illness affected his brain. . . . I had him opened up—but his stomach showed no traces of ill-health. The cause of death was established as inflammation of the bowels and apoplexy." Indeed, the autopsy of Peter's body confirmed that he had died of natural causes.

However, according to one witness, Peter's "face was extraordinarily black . . . he was oozing through the skin an extravasated blood which could be seen even on the gloves which covered the hands. . . . Finally, people claim to have noticed on the corpse all the symptoms which may indicate poisoning."

Peter's body was dressed in the light blue uniform of his beloved Holstein guards. A large hat was tugged down over his face, obscuring the discoloration, and an ample cravat disguised evident marks of strangulation. On July 10, he was buried in the Nevsky monastery. Catherine was not present.

Two days after Archduke Paul's eighth birthday, on September 22, 1762, Catherine was crowned empress. Her subjects didn't seem to care that Grigory Orlov was her lover, and he remained so for another decade. Catherine had immediately recognized that if she was to remain an absolute ruler, she could never remarry because the Russian people would want (and expect) power to be concentrated in her husband's hands.

As empress, Catherine saw herself as an "enlightened autocrat" and began her reign as an innovator and a pragmatist, convinced that the best way to discover whether a proposed law would be effective was to discuss it fully and solicit opinions from the people it would affect before implementing it. And she believed in the importance of respecting religion, but not in allowing it to influence matters of state.

Catherine supported the radical new vaccination against smallpox, founded a medical college, built hospitals, and, entirely from her own purse, funded the creation and maintenance of a foundling home that offered free care to the indigent. Her massive art collection became the basis for the renowned Hermitage. And in 1785 she took up playwriting; her works were produced, albeit under a pseudonym, at the palace.

Then there were the more mundane, but charming and deeply

personal, innovations. Catherine invented an eighteenth-century "onesie" for her six-month-old first grandson. "His whole outfit is sewn together, is put on in one go and is fastened behind with four or five little hooks; around the costume there is a fringe, and in that he is perfectly well dressed. . . . There is no tying to be done in any of it, and the child is hardly aware that he is being dressed; one stuffs his arms and feet into his costume at the same time, and it's done; this costume is a stroke of genius on my part. . . ."

A verbal portrait of Catherine survives from visiting Briton William Richardson. He found the thirty-nine-year-old empress ". . . taller than the middle size, very comely, gracefully formed but inclined to grow corpulent and of a fair complexion, which like every other female in this country, she endeavors to improve by the addition of rouge. She has a fine mouth and teeth; and blue eyes, expressive of scrutiny, something not so good as observation and not so bad as suspicion. . . . Indeed, with regard to her appearance altogether, it would be doing her injustice to say it was masculine, yet it would not be doing her justice to say it was entirely feminine."

Catherine was Empress of all the Russias until her death in 1796. On June 8, 1774, she and her longtime lover and political adviser Grigory Potemkin had a secret ceremony at the Church of St. Samson, not far from the Summer Palace in Petersburg. It may have been a sort of "commitment ceremony," although over the centuries assertions have been made referencing the existence of actual marriage certificates. Such documents, if they ever existed, have never surfaced.

And even so, her relationship with Potemkin eventually cooled and he was replaced in the empress's bed with a number of handsome studs several years her junior—some of whom were handpicked by Potemkin to gratify Catherine's libido, while never presenting a political threat to his own power and authority, as granted to him by the empress. As Catherine's favorite, Potemkin held several key governmental and military positions and reaped substantial material rewards, becoming the most powerful man in Russia. Long after their love affair had ended, he remained her primary, and most trusted, counselor.

As the years went by, Catherine grew even more estranged from her son, Paul, and continued to insist that he was utterly unsuited to succeed her, refusing to cede him the merest scintilla of power or responsibility. He had married twice, his first wife dying while giving birth to a stillborn girl in 1776. Later in the year his mother arranged a marriage with Sophia Dorothea of Württemburg, who took the Russian name of Maria Feodorovna. Luckily for the young royals, it turned out to be a love match and the couple had ten children.

The final year of Catherine's life was devoted to the dismemberment of Poland, which was divided between Russia, Prussia, and Austria, and to making brilliant marriages for her numerous grandchildren.

On Wednesday, November 5, 1796, Catherine suffered a stroke while in her water closet. When she was found by her valet Zakhar Zotov, the empress's eyes were closed, her face was purple, and her breathing was labored. A number of servants were summoned but could not budge the rotund autocrat—partially because she had collapsed in such a position that her leg was wedged against the lavatory door. Finally, with the aid of additional manpower, Catherine was conveyed to her bedroom.

After diagnosing a stroke, her doctor bled her and applied plasters of Spanish fly to her feet. At five p.m., the empress was still unconscious, a dark liquid seeping from her mouth.

Last rites were administered on November 6. That afternoon Paul combed through all of his mother's personal papers, discovering Alexei Orlov's pseudo-confession to the murder of his father. He allegedly found another document that removed him from the imperial succession, which he immediately burned.

At nine forty-five p.m., Catherine died, having never regained consciousness. An autopsy revealed a cerebral stroke. After a four-week period of national mourning, on December 5 she was buried in the Cathedral of Sts. Peter and Paul, the traditional resting place of the Romanov dynasty, Russia's royal family.

On February 22, 1788, seven and a half years before her death, with tongue firmly planted in cheek, Catherine had drafted her own epitaph. After referring to her arrival in Russia at the age of fourteen, she added, "Eighteen years of boredom and solitude made her read plenty of books. Arrived on the throne of Russia she desired its good and sought to procure for her subjects happiness, liberty, and prosperity. She forgave easily and hated no one; indulgent, easy to live with, naturally cheerful, with a republican soul and a good heart, she had friends: she found work easy, she liked good society and the arts."

There was nothing about horses.

As part of the burial rite, Catherine's son, now Emperor Paul I, had his father's body exhumed and the imperial crown brought from Moscow and placed on Peter's resealed coffin in a gesture of posthumous coronation. At their son's insistence, the spouses, who had abhorred each other since their betrothal, were united in death, despite the fact that Catherine had deposed—and possibly conspired to murder—her husband.

LOUIS XVI
1754–1793
RULED FRANCE: 1774–1792

and

MARIE ANTOINETTE
1755–1793

married 1770–1793

"The King is not fond of sleeping in the same bed with me."
　　　—Marie Antoinette, in a letter to her family

*I*N MAY OF 1770, A GERMAN UNIVERSITY STUDENT AND his buddies managed to sneak into the lavish pavilion under construction on the Ile des Epis in the center of the Rhine, a "no-man's-land" near Strasbourg that straddled the borders of the Austrian empire and France. The walls of the five-room pavilion were hung with elaborate Gobelin tapestries and furnished as sumptuously as any room at Schönbrunn, the Viennese palace where the fourteen-year-old bride-to-be, Archduchess Maria Antonia of Austria, was to be handed off to the representatives of her fifteen-year-old groom, Louis-Auguste, Dauphin of France.

As they roamed about the pavilion, one of the German youths—

Johann Wolfgang von Goethe—immediately recognized that among the classical subjects depicted in the tapestries was the wedding of Jason and Medea, a mythological love story in which a foreign princess journeys to Greece and marries the hometown sovereign. Things don't end prettily, to put it mildly. Aghast, Goethe exclaimed aloud, "What? Is it permissible thus unreflectingly to display before the eyes of a young queen entering upon married life this example of the most horrible wedding that perhaps ever took place?"

Goethe saw the writing on the wall, but no one else appeared to be concerned. Not enough to remove the offensive tapestry and certainly not enough to reconsider an alliance that had been four years in the making.

Maria Antonia Josepha Johanna von Hapsburg-Lothringen (Antonia to her family) was the youngest of the numerous daughters born to the Hapsburg empress Maria Teresa of Austria and Francis of Lorraine, the Holy Roman Emperor by virtue of his marriage.

The Bourbons, who sat on the thrones of France, Spain, and Naples, had been a rival dynasty for centuries. Part of the empress's life's work was to make brilliant political matches for her thirteen surviving children, but during the mid-1760s, both Catherine of Russia and Frederick the Great of Prussia were becoming territorial threats to her realm. She desperately needed to cement a powerful alliance and the French Bourbons filled the bill to perfection.

Antonia was a pretty little blue-eyed blonde with a high forehead, and a long neck—a Sèvres porcelain figurine, in the flesh, although she had yet to reach puberty. "The little one," as her mother called her, was graceful and vivacious, but a spoiled, temperamental little hoyden. So perhaps it was a good thing that by the time Antonia turned thirteen in 1768, her marriage negotiations were still pending. Her mother was both frustrated and disgusted that the future Queen of France still couldn't read and write French and German correctly and remained clueless as to the barest rudiments of history.

It was time for a major makeover. A French dentist was brought in to straighten Antonia's teeth with an eighteenth-century form of braces. A Parisian hairdresser came to Vienna to do something about the girl's unfashionable forehead and uneven hairline. But just as important, her brain needed to be kick-started.

It was an uphill battle for Abbé Vermond, the tutor hired to turn Antonia into an intellectual. "She is more intelligent than has been generally supposed," he acknowledged. But "she is rather lazy and extremely frivolous, she is hard to teach. . . . I came in the end to recognize that she would only learn so long as she was being amused." Physically, however, Vermond noted that "she has a most graceful figure; holds herself well; and if (as may be hoped) she grows a little taller, she will have all the good qualities one could wish for in a great princess. Her character, her heart, are excellent."

The venerable abbé neglected to mention another international concern, but perhaps it wasn't foremost in his mind: Antonia's bosom was still as flat as a flapjack.

Finally, in 1769, Louis XV made the official request for Archduchess Maria Antonia's hand on behalf of his young grandson, and Easter 1770 was the proposed date for the marriage. Empress Maria Teresa was both relieved and delighted, but made sure to give the monarch a heads-up about her flighty and high-spirited daughter: "Her age craves indulgence," she warned.

On April 17, 1770, Antonia renounced her rights to succeed her mother, an act of protocol, as she was going to become French by virtue of her marriage. Two days later, she was married by proxy in the Augustinian Church. The Dauphin of France was represented by Antonia's brother, Archduke Ferdinand. To complete the transformation, she had to change her name. No longer Austrian, but French, the little girl called Maria Antonia would henceforth be known as Marie Antoinette.

Thus rechristened and remade, on April 21, her face wet with tears, Marie Antoinette paid her formal farewell to her family and was driven away from Vienna in an elaborate coach owned by the King of France. She would never see her formidable mother again.

When the carriage reached the temporary pavilion on the Ile des

Epis that Goethe had sneaked into when it was under construction, Marie Antoinette entered one of the two antechambers that were located in Austria. There, she was to dispense with *all* things Austrian, from her gown to her shoes and hose to her underwear to her hair ribbon. Historians disagree as to whether Marie Antoinette was literally stripped down to her birthday suit in the presence of prying eyes, effecting the erotic and voyeuristic transition from archduchess to dauphine as her fourteen-year-old body, more childlike than womanly, was dressed in garments constructed entirely in France.

The marriage contract was signed in the central chamber of the five-room pavilion, literally neutral territory. Marie Antoinette then swallowed her tears, ginned up her courage, and walked into the next room—into France—led in an elaborately choreographed routine by the duc de Choiseul, who handed her over to the French delegation as the Austrian delegation slowly retreated, walking backward into their homeland.

After grand celebrations in the streets of Strasbourg, the lavish procession then conveyed Marie Antoinette to the forest of Compiègne, where she would meet her bridegroom for the first time.

Her new "grandfather," the sixty-year-old rakish King Louis XV, who was still considered the handsomest man at court, was immediately captivated by the dauphine's charm, her looks, and her grace. But Marie Antoinette received not a word from the five-foot-ten-inch fifteen-year-old dauphin—a podgy, lumbering youth with heavy-lidded eyes. A novelist would be hard pressed to invent a pair of spouses who were so opposite in every way as Marie Antoinette and Louis XVI. She was vivacious where he was dull, mercurial where he was plodding and indecisive, graceful where he was awkward, frivolous where he was studious, devoted to gaiety where he was antisocial, extravagant where he was economical, and as physically lovely and lithe as he was obese and coarse-looking. It also didn't help that the youth's tutors had inculcated him with the belief that women were the cause of all evil, public and private, and that most of all to be feared were Austrian women, who were controlling creatures with dangerous minds, only interested in annexing his kingdom to their homeland.

Just about the only thing the teens had in common was nearsightedness. The dauphin could barely see a thing without a lorgnette, which might have accounted for his clumsiness and his dread of graceful activities, such as dancing. His nasal voice and guttural laugh only added to his physical deficits. But in many ways, Louis is more to be pitied than censured. His parents—Louis, Dauphin of France and Marie-Josèphe of Saxony—had died of tuberculosis a few years earlier, as had his elder brother. Louis was always made to feel guilty that he had survived and would one day wear the crown instead of his adorable, smarter sibling.

Only the highest-ranking nobles were permitted to attend the official wedding ceremony on May 16, 1770, conducted by the Archbishop of Rheims in the chapel of Louis XIV at Versailles. Later in the day six thousand lucky spectators, chosen by lottery, were allowed to watch the wedding feast.

After the banquet the newlyweds were led to the bridal chamber. The king himself handed his grandson his nightgown, while Marie Antoinette received her chemise from the most recently married lady of semi-royal rank, the duchesse de ChâRtres, and each of the teens retired to a separate, private closet, where they changed clothes. The archbishop sprinkled the mattress on the enormous four-poster with holy water, and everyone retreated so that the young couple could consummate their royal marriage.

But they didn't. What happened was exactly nothing, confirmed by the dauphin in his diary the following morning—*Rien*—although Louis would also write the same single word on July 14, 1789, the day the Bastille was stormed. Of course, most historians now believe the diary was more of a hunting journal, in which Louis meticulously recorded the details of his daily haul, and that *rien* simply indicates that he didn't hunt that day, and therefore had killed nothing. In any event, the wedding night was a bust.

And in May 1771, when the young dauphin and dauphine should have joyously celebrated their first anniversary, if not the recent birth of a royal infant, or even a pregnancy—still *rien*. Although Louis had confided to Marie Antoinette that he was not ignorant of the mechanics involved, she remained puzzled and frustrated by her husband's complete disinterest in sex, conveying this dismay in several detailed letters to her mother.

In reply, Maria Teresa cautioned her daughter not to become peevish about it. She counseled "*caresses, cajoleries*"—tenderness and cajoling caresses—but warned Marie Antoinette, "if you show yourself impatient, you may spoil the whole thing."

By the royal couple's second anniversary in 1772, the empress had grown very concerned regarding *la conduite si étrange*—"the rather odd conduct"—of Marie's *mari*. It was perfectly legitimate for a barren royal bride to be returned to her homeland for failing to provide an heir, and Austria could not afford that fate.

Evidently, Louis was doing his level best to be a good husband, making regular conjugal visits to his wife's boudoir, but in the final analysis, he could never get beyond a certain state of arousal and had so far been unable to close the deal. The still virginal Marie Antoinette attributed this failure to her husband's *maladresse et jeunesse*—his clumsiness and youth. But there was more to the story. Something was medically amiss.

Empress Maria Teresa was finally able to convince Louis XV to summon the royal physician, Monsieur Lassone. He determined that the dauphin's romantic troubles were due to phimosis, a condition where the foreskin is so tight that it cannot be retracted from the penis, rendering copulation extremely painful. But Lassone also counseled that the operation to remedy the problem—circumcision—might do as much harm as good, and advised against it.

The years stretched on. After reigning for six decades, Louis XV died of smallpox in the spring of 1774 and the young dauphin assumed the throne of France as Louis XVI.

According to the memoirs of Madame Campan, a loyal member of Marie Antoinette's entourage, at the death of Louis XV Louis and Marie Antoinette fell on their knees, embraced each other, and appealed to God to guide them: "Bless us, for we are too young to rule." Although some twentieth-century historians dismiss Campan's version of events as sentimental hogwash that was completely out of character for both Marie Antoinette and her husband, others give it credence, because the fact in and of itself is patently true. Empress Maria Teresa knew too well that the nineteen-year-old king, and more particularly her daughter (who was a year younger), were absolutely out of their depth. "There is nothing to calm my apprehensions in the situation of the King, the ministers, or the state. She herself is so young, has never had any power of application, nor ever will have—unless with great difficulty."

With great prescience about the future of France, the empress advised the new monarchs to "change nothing; let matters go on as they are, otherwise chaos and intrigue will become insurmountable, and my dear children, you will find yourselves in such a tangle that you will be unable to extricate yourselves." Maria Teresa specifically warned her daughter, "You must learn to interest yourself in serious matters, for this may be most useful if the King should ask your counsel. . . . Be careful to avoid misleading him into any great or unusual expenditure."

By now, all of France seemed to know about the king's impotence. Scurrilous pamphlets and nasty little ditties made the rounds of coffeehouses. Back in 1773, the Spanish ambassador, Count d'Aranda, had felt compelled to share every juicy detail in dispatches to his sovereign, informing him that there were stains, which proved emissions were taking place outside the proper place because of the pain of introducing the member. Foreign courts were indeed affected by these events because they impacted the future of the powerful Bourbon dynasty.

The public awareness of Louis's private shame soon affected other aspects of his life, including his inability to make firm decisions about anything. Destiny and birthright had made him a king. But all the comparisons of Louis XVI to a peasant, including his rather oxlike appearance, more accurately reflected where his true interests lay. He adored outdoor sports; he skillfully worked a lathe, and wielded the hammer in his own forge, where he was a talented locksmith under the tutelage of France's master craftsman. Yet he never seemed happy and rarely laughed, taking out his frustrations in these pursuits while remaining tacitly disgusted by the way his vivacious wife expressed her own dissatisfaction and discontent—her noisy frivolity, financial extravagances, and relentless pursuit of distraction and pleasure. Blazing her own social trails, she rebelled at the French court's rigid and scripted behavior, wounding the pride of legions of influential nobles accustomed to centuries of perquisites. It would eventually cost her dearly.

Still *intacta*, Marie Antoinette poured her passions into outrageously costly fashion, garish makeup, outlandish coiffures, and high-stakes gambling, hosting lavish parties and sneaking into Paris late at night to attend masked balls while her husband snored away in his bedchamber. "I am terrified of being bored," she admitted. Her sexuality was by now fully awakened and she could only tremble, blush, and stammer in the presence of courtiers who stirred her heart, aware that she could not get too close to them. She couldn't even consider taking a lover, a perfectly acceptable custom within France's aristocratic circles, until she produced an heir.

Maria Teresa routinely scolded her daughter for wasting her time on nocturnal exploits and disdained the French custom of separate bedrooms that regulated marital intimacy and stifled one's natural biological inclinations. She also reminded her daughter to maintain the impression of a completely submissive wife and not to meddle in politics or governmental affairs—yet at the same time, instructed Marie Antoinette to dominate her husband *beyond* the marriage bed, never forgetting that she was an agent of Austrian interests. These mixed signals completely confused the bubbleheaded queen, who had already demonstrated her naiveté by falling under the influence of Louis's three maiden aunts, a fat and sour-dispositioned trio who had clear political agendas of their own, schooling the young queen in palace intrigues, gossip, and *médisance*—the art of backbiting.

After nearly seven years of marriage with nothing to show for it, very few people in France believed that Marie Antoinette was not satisfying her sexual urges elsewhere. Speculation took on a life of its own; stories abounded of orgies and lovers of both genders. Provocative poems and songs soon burst the locked confines of nobles' *secretaires* and made their way onto the streets and into the burgeoning hotbeds of reform.

Her frivolity, arrogance, and heedless extravagance prompted a flurry of scalding scoldings from her mother.

. . . Your good luck will not last forever and by your own fault you will be plunged into the depths of misfortune. The trouble arises because you lead so terribly dissipated a life and never apply your mind to anything. What books do you read? Yet you venture to thrust your finger into every pie to meddle with affairs of State, with the choice of ministers!

. . . I have news from Paris to the effect that you have been buying bracelets at the cost of two hundred and fifty thousand livres, with the result that you have thrown your finances into disorder and have heaped up a burden of debt. . . . A queen only degrades herself by decking herself out in this preposterous way; and she degrades herself still more by unthrifty expendi-ture, especially in such difficult times. . . . Everyone knows that the king is very modest in his expenditure, so the whole blame will rest on your shoulders. I hope I shall not live to see the disaster that is likely to ensue.

It was fruitless for Marie Antoinette to convince her pious and prudish mother that *everyone* at court was spending extravagantly on jewels, gowns, and modish coiffures, and that as queen she was expected to set the tone—and that her levity was characteristic of her generation. In the artificial Rococo era, filled with women who were highly cultivated, delicate hothouse blooms with idle hands and coddled minds, she was the most contrived. In a coterie of

spendthrifts, she was the biggest; and among a generation of co-
quettes, she was the most flirtatious and charming.

Where Louis could not satisfy his wife sexually, he tried to make
up for it by lavishing material treasures upon her, among them le
Petit Trianon, the little summer villa on the grounds of Versailles,
about a mile from the palace. But her exorbitant expenditures on
furnishings and refurbishment for this little pleasure idyll would
eventually come back to haunt her. As would le Petit Trianon's
exclusivity. It was the queen's domain alone and she chose to sur-
round herself with a clique of intimates and family members, insulting high-ranking nobles by shutting them out. Marie Antoinette
saw no reason to host at her safe haven those who detested her,
who spoke ill of her behind her back, and who after all those years
still thought of her as the outsider—*L'Autrichienne*—a pun that
reflected her heritage as well as the French word for a female dog,
or bitch.

When Louis would visit his wife at le Petit Trianon—which, very
graciously, he only did by invitation—he would complain about the
numerous violations of court etiquette and she would laugh him off
as dull and pedantic. He cast a pall on the lively discussions because
in a world where wit was prized, he lacked the gift for it. When
Marie Antoinette tired of his company and wished to be rid of him
so that she and her coterie could rattle off to Paris and avail themselves of the nightlife, she would deliberately set the clock at the
Petit Trianon ahead by an hour and the too-trusting monarch,
thinking it was his bedtime, would slouch off to the palace.

Yet there were occasions when the king showed himself to be a
true romantic—even in public. One day when he was riding through
the Bois de Boulogne he saw the queen sitting on the grass with
his aunts, enjoying a repast of strawberries and cream, an image
straight out of the pastoral canvases of Fragonard. He alit from the
saddle, clasped his wife by her waist, and kissed her. All who witnessed this charming display of domestic bliss and marital harmony
applauded.

Louis was as much in awe of his beautiful, graceful wife as her behavior irritated him. And despite the best efforts of his courtiers and ministers to find him a paramour to teach him the arts of love, the pious and moral Louis only had eyes for his spouse.

But in 1777, Marie Antoinette was twenty-two years old and still a virgin. Among the married friends and female relatives her own age, she was the only one without a child. Immensely frustrated sexually, she was running out of self-control. To prevent disaster, such as an extramarital dalliance, Marie Antoinette's brother Joseph, the Emperor of Austria (who now coruled the empire with Maria Teresa), decided to pay his little sister a visit.

Like their mother, Joseph proved to be a prophet when it came to predicting Marie Antoinette's future, able to read the writing on a wall that the French queen refused to recognize even existed. "In very truth, I tremble for your happiness, seeing that in the long run things cannot go on like this . . . the revolution will be a cruel one, and perhaps of your own making," Joseph scolded.

After three weeks at Versailles, he began to understand the gravity of the situation and what seemed to be keeping Marie Antoinette and Louis apart, physically and emotionally. The king had confided in him frankly, devoid of all prudery, which gave Joseph the opportunity to reassure Louis that contrary to his assumptions, he was *not* "endangering his health by fulfilling his conjugal duties."

In a letter to his younger brother Leopold, Joseph violated the king's confidence by sharing the lurid details of Louis's sexual problems:

In his conjugal bed he has normal erections; he introduces his member, stays there without moving for about two minutes, then withdraws without ejaculating, and still erect, bids good night. This is incomprehensible because he sometimes has nocturnal emissions, but while inside and in the process, never; and he is content, and says quite frankly that he was doing it purely from a sense of duty and that he did not like it. . . . My sister, moreover, has very little temperament [hot blood] and together they are two complete fumblers.

Having realized that Marie Antoinette "had no affection for her husband" and was indifferent to the point of disdain, when he was about to return to Vienna, Joseph left his "giddy-pate" little sister a thirty-page letter, containing some astute marital advice:

Do you try to make yourself necessary to him; do you endeavor to convince him that no one loves him more sincerely than you, and that no one has his glory or his happiness more at heart? . . . Do you ever suppress any of your own wishes for his sake? . . . Do you occupy yourself with matters which he has neglected in order to produce the impression that you are meritorious where he has failed? . . . Do you sacrifice yourself to him in any way? . . . Do you maintain an inviolable silence as concerns his errors and infirmities?

Not only that, it rankled Joseph that "the king is left alone at night while you defile yourself by mixing with the *canaille* [riff-raff] of Paris!" Then the widowed emperor spoke of more intimate matters:

Do you really seek opportunities [to spend quality time with the king]? Do you honestly respond to the affection he manifests for you? Are you not cold or absentminded when he caresses you or when he speaks to you? Do you not show yourself bored, or even repelled by him? If so, how can you expect that a man of cold temperament who has never experienced carnal pleasures should make advances to you, become aroused, love you and successfully complete his great act, or at least taste the possible pleasures with you? This point requires all your attention, and whatever you do to reach this great goal will be your strongest link to happiness

in life. Never get discouraged and always give him the hope
that he will still be able to have children; don't ever let him
give up or despair of it. You must avoid this idea and any
separation of beds with all your powers, which consist only
of your charms and friendship.

The Emperor Joseph's multiple admonitions—or Marie Antoinette's "charms and friendship"—evidently yielded results. In a letter to Vienna dated August 30, 1777—seven and a quarter years
after her wedding—Marie Antoinette trumpeted the good news:

I have attained the happiness which is of the utmost importance
to my whole life. More than a week ago my marriage was
thoroughly consummated. Yesterday the attempt was repeated,
with results even more successful than the first time. . . . I don't
think I am with child yet, but at any rate I have hopes of
becoming so from moment to moment.

This happy event soon became the topic of international buzz,
as the various ambassadors reported the news of the queen's deflo-
ration to their respective sovereigns. According to the Spanish
envoy to the French court, "His Majesty has become more cheerful
than he used to be, and no one can fail to note that the Queen has
blue circles around her eyes far more often than of yore."

Louis finally had something to smile about. He confided to one
of his maiden aunts, "I find the pleasure very great, and I regret
that so long a time has passed without my being able to enjoy it."

Unfortunately, ten days later, the new toy was already cast aside.
Marie Antoinette lamented, "The King is not fond of sleeping in
the same bed with me. I do my best to ensure that there shall not
be a total separation between us in this matter. Sometimes he comes
to spend the night with me, and I think it would be a mistake for
me to urge him to do so more often."

But even too little, too late turned out to be just enough. Marie
Antoinette's pregnancy was officially made known to the court on

August 4, 1778. The queen derived the greatest joy from announcing the blessed event to her husband. Affecting a glum countenance, she entered his presence and declared, "I have come, Sire, to complain of one of your subjects who has been so audacious as to kick me in the belly." Louis could not have been more proud or delighted, enveloping Marie Antoinette in a spontaneous hug. Now, his succession would be secure.

On December 18, Marie Antoinette went into labor. It was the custom in France for the queen to give birth in the presence of several royal witnesses, with the room shut tight so that no harmful drafts could penetrate. Marie Antoinette lost consciousness immediately after the delivery, perhaps due to the claustrophobic atmosphere, combined with the pain of childbirth and the stress of endeavoring to suppress her cries and act queenly in the most unregal of circumstances. She was bled, and when she recovered, she was told she had a daughter. The queen named the baby Marie-Thérèse, after her mother, and throughout her life the girl was formally known as "Madame Royale."

Despite the honor of her grandchild's name, Maria Teresa was still unsatisfied; Marie Antoinette had not given Louis an heir.

The queen had told Louis that the immediate aftermath of their daughter's birth had left her with a frightening and painful memory and that she didn't wish to become pregnant again for several months; so the French royal couple didn't sleep together for a year after Marie-Thérèse was born. But after courtiers launched plots to find the king a mistress, Marie Antoinette, fearing she might lose her influence over Louis, changed her mind. She went to her husband and did a bit of coaxing, after which, according to the Austrian ambassador, Count Mercy, "he told her that he loved her with all his heart and that he could swear to her that he never had sensations or feelings for any other woman besides her."

Marie Antoinette told her mother, "I am too aware of the necessity of having children to neglect anything on that score," adding, "If I was wrong in the past, it was due to childishness and irresponsibility, but now I am much more levelheaded." After suffering a miscarriage in 1780, on October 22, 1781, Marie Antoinette gave birth to a boy, Louis-Joseph. The king himself broke the news to her, announcing proudly, "Madame, you have fulfilled our wishes and those of France, you are the mother of a dauphin." Marie Antoinette described the birth as "The happiest and most important event to me," and Louis wept profusely during his son's baptism.

After another miscarriage in 1783, the queen bore a second son, Louis-Charles, on March 27, 1785. "He has in strength and health everything that his brother is lacking. He is a real peasant's child, big, fresh-faced, and fat," Marie Antoinette wrote to her brother. And the following year, on July 9, several weeks premature, she bore another daughter, Sophie Hélène Béatrix, the child of an unwanted pregnancy. But the infant died on June 14, 1787, before reaching her first birthday.

Motherhood had been metamorphosing Marie Antoinette into a more grounded and responsible woman. Her pregnancies had necessitated several months' absence from her usual round of gay amusements and she discovered that it was more fun to spend time with her children than it had been to play faro deep into the wee hours of the morning.

But her reputation as a frivolous, extravagant ninny and the marital issues in the royal bed had already demonized her in the eyes of the people at all levels of society. Harvests had been bad, and bread was scarce. The royals and their favorites had indeed been profligate spendthrifts, but France's foreign policy during the reign of Louis XV had also eaten up an enormous chunk of cash. The country had never quite recouped its expenditures on the costly Seven Years' War (1756–1763) fought on the European continent as well as on American soil (where the conflict is known as the French and Indian War). Then Louis XVI had been persuaded by the leaders of the American colonists to aid them financially and materially in their revolution against France's age-old enemy, England. The French stock market had dropped precipitously as well, further tanking the economy.

Yet even as Louis was funding the American Revolutionary War, he and his wife were utterly unaware of the changing mood in their own kingdom. A burgeoning middle class, inspired by the philosopher Jean-Jacques Rousseau, averred that they, too, had rights. From the earliest intellectual voices of reform within the nobility to the Parisian fishwives, the French subjects knew their sovereign was an indecisive man and blamed all failed policies and bad decisions on the malevolent influence of his foreign-born wife.

The Swedish military man Count Axel von Fersen, who would become Marie Antoinette's lover, observed that "the queen is universally detested. Every evil is attributed to her and she is given no credit for anything good," including her generosity to the poor and her philanthropy. "The King is weak and suspicious; the only person he trusts is the Queen and they say she does everything." Even the paternity of her younger son was up for public lampoon and debate, although Louis never raised any doubts about it. To make sure that the monarchs knew what the people thought of them, unseen hands slipped mean-spirited pornographic cartoons, leaflets, and pamphlets, such as the popular "List of all the Persons with Whom the Queen Has Had Debauched Relations," into the folds of their dinner napkins, among a sheaf of Louis's state documents, or affixed to the inside of their box at the opera. Louis was portrayed as a hapless cuckold, an impotent lout who was the utter puppet of his wife, the monstrously dissipated Austrian whore. By the time they were brought before the revolutionary tribunals they were already as good as executed, the "proof" of their "guilt," of Marie Antoinette's obscene excesses and heinous crimes (adultery, lesbianism, nymphomania) having previously been supplied not by a hungry, angry, and illiterate mob, but by the bejeweled hands of a disgruntled aristocracy who had found an avenue for revenge following their ostracism from the queen's inner circle.

After the people nicknamed Marie Antoinette "Madame Deficit," she finally began to economize. But it was too little, too late.

In early June 1789, the representatives from the three Estates General—the clergy, the nobility, and the bourgeoisie—met to demand more self-determination in government, and to limit the powers of the sovereign. But at the time, the monarchs were faced with a sorrow of a more domestic nature. The frail, seven-year-old dauphin died of tuberculosis of the spine on June 4. The king and queen took the luxury of grieving for an entire day in seclusion. But any extended mourning was cut short when, on June 17, the representatives from the third estate—the bourgeoisie—declared themselves to be a National Assembly.

The dichotomy between the national mood and the royal one was not lost on Marie Antoinette. While the French were in "a delirium" of anti-monarchical, power-to-the-people fervor, she could not control her tears. "At the death of my poor little Dauphin, the nation hardly seemed to notice," she wrote to her brother Leopold in Austria.

On July 14, 1789, falsely believing that the king was sending a foreign army to crush them, a mob of Parisians stormed the Bastille in search of weapons with which to defend themselves. A horrid scene ensued during which the prison's governor was beheaded with a knife. But in Louis's diary (which as previously indicated was primarily a hunting journal, with scant references to other quotidian events), he wrote *rien*—and some historians have interpreted the comment as a cynical assessment that nothing of moment happened that day. Nevertheless, the king did believe that the fall of the Bastille was merely another petty insurrection. It fell to the duc de La Rochefoucauld-Liancourt, who brought the ugly news to Versailles, to correct the royal misconception: "No, Sire. It is a *revolution*."

Husband and wife did not see eye to eye when it came to dealing with the rebellious mob. Louis had studied England's Charles I and believed the way to avoid his fate was to negotiate with the revolutionaries. But Marie Antoinette insisted *mon métier est d'être royaliste*—"royalty is my career," and harbored nothing but hatred for the great unwashed masses that had traduced her for years.

On October 5, 1789, an angry army of women marched from Paris to the palace of Versailles demanding bread, and although Louis acceded to their request, the instigators amid the rabble spread the propaganda that he was lying. The following day, the mob stormed the palace. When they failed to locate the queen—whom they intended to murder—they destroyed her rooms and assassinated several of the royal guards, whose heads they stuck on pikes. The following day the rabble insisted on conveying the royal family back to Paris, where the new National Assembly could keep an eye on them. Marie Antoinette bravely insisted that as long as she was not separated from her husband, she could endure anything.

In Paris, they were placed under what can best be characterized as a dignified house arrest in the Tuileries, a palace that had fallen into disuse and disrepair since it had been forsaken more than a century earlier for Versailles. The monarchs behaved more like a close-knit, "normal" couple when they were most in adversity, taking meals together, playing with and educating their children, and enjoying games of billiards, although the queen lamented, "We have seen too much horror and too much bloodshed ever to be happy again."

Marie Antoinette, now thirty-four years old, finally began to realize her potential—and rose to meet it. In effect, she became the king. Everyone shunted aside her ineffectual husband. So she grabbed hold of the royal defense. It was Marie Antoinette who held council with the ambassadors and ministers, who learned to read and write in cipher, and who developed the secret diplomatic channels necessary to maintain the reins of government. She had no assistance, no clerks or secretaries. Spies abounded, even in the Tuileries.

Meanwhile, anti-royal fever continued to mount, but the monarchs held out hope that either the winds of revolution would blow over or that some sort of compromise with the rebels could be reached. Mirabeau, one of the original revolutionary leaders, asserted, "The King has but one man to support him—his wife . . . the only safeguard for her lies in the reestablishment of the royal authority . . . of this much I am certain, that she will not be able to save her life unless she saves her crown."

Behind the scenes, Marie Antoinette and her lover Axel Fersen, along with a few trusted confidants, worked to plan the family's escape. But the June 20, 1791, flight to safety in eastern France ended in disaster at Varennes when the royal party was unmasked, and unceremoniously escorted back to Paris. From then on, they were kept under heavier guard and enjoyed fewer privileges.

The political climate in France had shifted once again, which was very bad news for Marie Antoinette and Louis. "There exists within this realm no power to restrain the armed populace. . . . The very chiefs of the Revolution are no longer listened to when they try to talk to each other about order," the queen told Count Mercy, the Austrian ambassador to France. Her husband was useless. "You know the person with whom I have to deal. When one believes him persuaded into accepting any course, a single word, a trifling argument, may make him change his mind and his purpose without warning. That is why a thousand things I should like to do can never be undertaken." But, for all their distress, she had found her spine, even as Louis had lost his. "Tribulation first makes one realize what one is," she told Mercy.

On August 10, 1792, the Tuileries palace was stormed for the second time that summer—a day that was referred to as "the Second French Revolution." The king's Swiss Guard were brutally massacred and the royal family was taken to the Temple, the former Parisian castle of the Knights Templar. There they were placed "under the safeguard of the nation." That night, the guillotine was erected in the Place du Carrousel.

As of that day, Louis XVI was no longer in charge of France. The bloody period known as the Terror had begun. Louis was accused of being a "tyrant" and an "oppressor" and separated from his family. After more than twenty-two years of marriage, when he and Marie Antoinette finally came to realize that they might actually love and respect each other, all contact was forbidden.

But on January 20, 1793, Marie Antoinette was told by an official of the Commune, the new government, that by an exceptional indulgence, she and the children would be allowed to visit the king. She knew that it meant his execution was imminent. They spent a few final, tearful hours together and then, at about ten p.m., Louis said farewell with dignity, assuring his wife that he would visit her again in the morning. They both knew he was lying. Hours before his death, Louis lamented to Cléry, his valet, "Unfortunate Princess! My marriage promised her a throne; now what prospect does it offer her?" He handed Cléry his wedding ring and asked him to give it to Marie Antoinette. "Please tell her that I leave her with sorrow."

The following morning, Marie Antoinette was forbidden to go downstairs. But she heard the distant drumbeats and the rumble of carriage wheels and—at 10:22—the cheerful shouts that meant she was now a widow.

She was taken away from her children, confined as "prisoner 280" within the walls of La Conciergerie, the Paris prison where only the most dangerous of criminals were housed and from which very few people were freed. On October 16, 1793, after a mockery of a trial, frail, white-haired from grief and stress, and suffering from severe gynecological hemorrhaging, Marie Antoinette followed her husband to Madame la Guillotine. She had left the Conciergerie with her hands bound behind her, the cord held by the executioner Henri Sanson, as if she were on a leash. Forbidden to mount the scaffold in traditional black mourning, she was attired instead in white (the color of mourning worn by France's medieval and Renaissance-era queens), with black satin shoes. At 12:15 p.m., the blade fell. Marie Antoinette was only thirty-eight years old, the same age as Louis had been upon his execution. Her remains were taken to the Cimitière Madeleine, but the cost of digging a single grave was considered too high, so not until sixty corpses— all victims of the revolution—were accumulated, was her coffin smothered with quicklime and buried amid the others. After Napoleon's exile to Elba and the restoration of the Bourbon monarchy, an effort was made to accord a proper burial to the executed monarchs. On January 15, 1815, Marie Antoinette's bones were located, identified by scraps of her black filoselle stockings and the garters she customarily wore. Louis's XVI's remains were found the following day. On January 21 (which was not-so-ironically the twenty-second anniversary of Louis's execution), the royals' remains were placed in the crypt at Saint-Denis, the traditional final resting place of France's monarchs.

Marie-Thérèse, the daughter of Louis and Marie Antoinette, remained incarcerated for another three years, after which she was released by officials within the new government (the Directoire, or Directory), in exchange for imprisoned commissaries of the revolution, and permitted to join her mother's family in Vienna. She eventually married her first cousin the duc d'Angoulême, the eldest son of Louis's youngest brother, the comte d'Artois, and died in 1851.

The dauphin, Louis-Charles, died in the Temple on June 8, 1795, at the age of ten. For many years, it was suggested that he had been replaced with a hapless changeling and smuggled out of the Temple. Several young men came forth during the beginning of the nineteenth century to claim that they were the Dauphin of France. Marie-Thérèse refused to meet any of them.

However, the boy's heart was taken away by the doctor who performed the autopsy on his body, and it ended up in a crystal urn in the Cathedral Saint-Denis. Mitochondrial DNA testing on the organ in the year 2000 proved conclusively that the DNA sequences were "identical with those of Marie Antoinette, two of her sisters, and two living relatives on the maternal side."

The more one comes to know and understand Louis XVI and Marie Antoinette as human beings, however flawed, the easier it becomes to summon up sympathy for them. From his youth, Louis was controlled by forces more powerful than his own lethargy—his grandfather, his ministers and ambassadors, his wife, and finally, by the radical elements of the government that deposed him. History has been no less unkind to Marie Antoinette. And yet her demonization by the forces of revolution in some respects made her a heroine, if not perhaps a martyr, more admired today than despised. Although theirs was a dynastic match from day one, both Marie Antoinette and Louis came of age within the context of their royal marriage. Beginning as frightened and indifferent teens who got in their own way as much as they got in each other's, time and adversity turned them into a loving, if still dysfunctional, unit. Goethe's fears that day on the Ile des Epis were only partially requited. Intrinsic differences of character aside, during the final days of their marriage Louis and Marie Antoinette were finally able to appreciate each other's worth and how deeply their bonds of affection held—which is significantly more than one can say for Jason and Medea.

GEORGE IV
1762–1830
REGENT: 1811–1820
RULED ENGLAND: 1820–1830

and

MARIA FITZHERBERT
1756–1837

married 1785–1830

"... All I can say is that since it is to be I shall make it the Study of my life to make him happy."
— Mrs. Fitzherbert, writing to Lady Anne Barnard, November 1785

O**N JULY 27, 1784, THE DAY AFTER MARIA FITZHERBERT'S** twenty-eighth birthday, the *Morning Herald* proclaimed: "A new Constellation has lately made an appearance in the fashionable hemisphere that engages the attention of those whose hearts are susceptible to the power of beauty. The widow of the late Mr. Fitzherbert has in her train half our young nobility. As the Lady has not, as yet, discovered a partiality for any of her admirers, they are all animated with hopes of success."

Mrs. Fitzherbert is often depicted as the patient, saintly, and long-suffering romantic victim of the Prince of Wales. In truth, she was a woman of spirit and spunk who liked an off-color joke, spoke frankly, and, although her income had derived from her marriage settlements, was remarkably self-reliant. Like her royal admirer, she was vain, proud, and had a sizeable ego.

She was born Mary Anne Smythe at Tong in Shropshire to an affluent Catholic royalist family and was educated at an English convent school in France. By the time she met the Prince of Wales in March 1784, she was a twenty-eight-year-old childless widow with eighteen hundred pounds a year to live on—over half a million dollars today.

After attending the opera one evening, the prince became transfixed by Maria as she waited for her carriage. That night her fate would change dramatically.

Described by his friend Georgiana, Duchess of Devonshire as "inclined to be too fat and looks much like a woman in men's cloaths [sic]," the prince was six years younger than Maria. Throughout his life, he exhibited a penchant for older women, especially those who combined sexuality with a certain maternal quality; in other words, he was a sucker for an ample bosom.

Although the heir apparent found her irresistible, Maria was not a classic beauty. Indeed, she mocked her own aquiline "Roman Catholic" nose. Her chin was considered too "determined" and there was rather a vast amount of cheek along the sides of her oval face, described by contemporaries as "a very mild benignant countenance without much animation." And even in her twenties, she had ill-fitting false teeth. But she made up for it with her hazel eyes, silky blond hair, and flawless complexion, not to mention the requisite *poitrine*.

By March 10, 1784, just days after George demanded an introduction to the mysteriously veiled beauty, rumors abounded that the Prince of Wales was making "fierce love to the widow Fitzherbert." He sent her gifts of jewelry, peppered her with invitations to Carlton House, and commissioned Gainsborough to paint her portrait. But Maria failed to be dazzled. "My mother always recommended . . . to throw cold water on my lovers if I did not like them," she told Lady Anne Lindsay—which might account for the Duchess of Devonshire's observation during the early stages of the prince's pursuit that "Mrs. Fitzherbert is at present his favorite, but she seems, I think, rather to cut him than otherwise." Maria made it quite clear to the prince that she had no interest in becoming his mistress.

So he proposed marriage.

Mrs. Fitzherbert countered with every pragmatic reply. First of all, she was a devout Catholic with no intentions of renouncing her faith. Should she marry him, it would cost him his crown, contravening the Royal Marriages Act, which prohibited a royal under the age of twenty-five from marrying without the king's permission; the 1701 Act of Settlement, which settled the succession on the Protestant heirs of the Electress Sophia of Hanover, as long as they did not marry a Catholic, as well as—to some degree—the 1707 Act of Union, which also barred any Catholics, or anyone married to a Catholic, from inheriting the throne. Even a secret marriage would violate those laws.

But the prince was uninterested in a rational argument for rejection. Maria thought it was one of his practical jokes when late in the evening of July 8, 1784, four men from his household showed up at her doorstep, informing her that George had stabbed himself, and demanding that she return to Carlton House with them immediately.

To preserve her honor from malicious gossip, she insisted that their mutual friend Georgiana accompany her as a chaperone. At Carlton House, they found the prince in a bloodstained shirt tearing at his bandages, foaming at the mouth, and banging his head against the wall. The only thing that could "induce him to live," George insisted, was Maria's consent to marry him. So she relented, signing a hastily written promissory note, and the duchess pulled a ring from her own finger, as the prince had none of his own to bestow upon his bullied bride.

Back at Devonshire House, Georgiana wrote up a deposition stating that Maria was aware that a written promise extracted under such threats was invalid, thus protecting themselves against the illegality of the bedside agreement.

Maria packed her trunks as soon as she arrived home, and the following day she went abroad (soon followed by her friend Lady Anne Lindsay) in the hope that the whole messy business with the prince would blow over. Lady Anne intimated in her journal that "Fitz" was too proud to take the "common packet" boat with the rest of the riffraff—"her who was running away from being Queen of England!"

After learning that Maria had fled, the twenty-two-year-old heir to the English throne wept uncontrollably, tore at his hair, banged his head against hard objects, and vowed to relinquish his rights to the crown, sell his plate and jewels, and elope to America with Maria. The prince wrote to his "wife" regularly (and copiously), pledging his eternal fidelity. He even had the chutzpah to assure Maria (in a whopper of a lie) that his father was aware of their plans to wed and approved wholeheartedly. And in an eighteen-page love note, George told Maria that he now looked upon himself as married. "You know I never presumed to make you any offer with a view of purchasing your virtue. I know you too well," he insisted. Imploring her to return to him, the prince signed this letter, "Not only the most affectionate of lovers but the tenderest of husbands."

According to Lady Anne, by this time Maria was of two minds when it came to the prince. His pestering barrage of correspondence drove her crazy, but she complained when she didn't hear from him. By the end of October 1785, having spent more than fifteen months in France, Maria resolved to come back to England and commit herself to the prince, accepting that the marriage would not be valid "according to law in England," but that it certainly was such "according to every other law, both human and divine." To Lady Anne, who had departed before her, Maria wrote:

. . . I have told him I will be his. I know I injure him and perhaps destroy forever my own tranquility. . . . Could I banish from my idea the fatal consequences that may attend such a connexion I then might be happy in attaching myself for life to the man that has gone thro' so much for my sake & to whom I feel myself very sincerely attach'd to, but alas whenever I look upon it in a favourable light, that Idea vanishes. . . . All I can say is that since it is to be I shall make it the Study of my life to make him happy.

The prince wanted to wed almost as soon as Maria landed in England. But because George had to keep their marriage a secret, she insisted on certain terms before she would tie the knot: she would always be known as "Mrs. Fitzherbert," would maintain her own separate address and establishment, would have the place of honor at George's table, and an annual allowance of £10,000 (over $1.5 million today). Furthermore, she would not spend a single night under the prince's roof until their marriage was made public.

It was not easy to find a clergyman willing to risk the wrath of heaven and earth to perform a wedding ceremony that violated at least five statutory acts. Finally, a young curate, the Rev. John Burt, was located—in the Fleet, where he was incarcerated for debt. Most historians believe that Burt struck a hard bargain: he would marry the prince to Mrs. Fitzherbert for £500, payment of all his debts, an appointment as one of the prince's chaplains, and a future bishopric.

The ceremony was performed on the frosty afternoon of December 15, 1785, behind the curtained windows and locked doors of Maria's Park Street parlor. The twenty-nine-year-old bride wore a simple suit of traveling clothes. Maria's uncle, Henry Errington, and one of her brothers, John Smythe, stood as witnesses, endangering themselves if their complicit participation was ever discovered. The prince's friend Orlando Bridgeman stood guard outside the door. After the groom and the two witnesses signed the marriage certificate, George gave it to Maria to keep. It is currently in the Royal Archives.

Although the marriage was illegal in the eyes of the state, it was valid in church law; therefore, any issue would be considered illegitimate according to English civil law, but legitimate by canon law. Nevertheless, the royal wedding was almost immediately followed by the systematic public denials of the event, particularly by George's pals in Parliament.

The few people who knew the truth were sworn to secrecy, yet everyone seemed to know about it immediately and caricatures of the prince and Mrs. Fitzherbert appeared in every shop window. The *Daily Universal Register* bawdily punned, "The Prince's musical talents are of the first rate. . . . He is *attached* to, and peculiarly happy in *humming* old *pieces*. His Highness has lately *set 'The Dainty Widow'* much *higher* in order to suit his *pipe*." A clandestine royal marriage, true or not, was the talk of the town. Maria herself later referred to her union as "the *One Truth which all the world knows*." The rumors increased after Maria let one of the thirty-six boxes at the opera house—real estate that was the purview of the tippy top of the haute ton.

Without officially admitting to anything George endeavored to make things right for her. Although Maria remained adamant about maintaining separate residences, his carriage was seen every morning at her door, and he footed the bills for her establishment. Maria had precedence at every function. The prince let it be known that Mrs. Fitzherbert was to receive the courtesy of any social invitations extended to him, and if precedence could not be waived in her favor by other hosts, then His Royal Highness would refuse to attend their affairs. And he was as solicitous and attentive to her in public as if she were his legal wife.

But the idyll couldn't last forever. By the summer of 1786, the sum total of George's debts was a whisper below £270,000—a shade over $4.1 million today. Parliament, and his father, refused to give him a bailout. So, with no financial relief in sight, the prince closed up Carlton House and decamped to Brighton with Maria. A frequent tourist to the burgeoning seaside resort commented on Mrs. Fitzherbert's popularity there: "Though nobody ventured to call her 'Princess,' everyone of her innumerable admirers of both sexes enthroned her as a queen. She was recognised as the 'Queen of Hearts' throughout the length and breadth of fast-expanding Brighton. . . . They honoured her, they almost worshipped her."

That July, those who glimpsed Mrs. Fitzherbert with the prince in Brighton were certain she was visibly pregnant. Most people believe that she and George had at least one child, and Maria never denied having any. On the death of George IV in 1830, Lord Stourton, a distant cousin of Maria's and one of her executors, as well as her eventual biographer, asked her to sign a declaration written on the back of her marriage certificate that read, "I, Mary Fitzherbert, testify that my Union with George P. of Wales was without issue."

"She smilingly objected on the score of delicacy," said Stourton. Surely she would have signed the endorsement without hesitation if she had never given George any children. Considering their relationship lasted several years, and contraception was still in its infancy, so to speak, it is certainly likely that she became pregnant by him and carried to term.

Her first child may have been born in the early autumn of 1786. There was a baby boy given the name of his foster father, James Ord, who was taken first to Bilbao, Spain, and then to Norfolk, Virginia, raised by prominent Catholic families and afforded the best education available. The boy's key connections were all distantly related to Mrs. Fitzherbert through her previous marriages. When he reached adulthood, Ord—who was given a plum job at the Spanish court, also courtesy of one of Maria's well-placed relatives—was told by his "uncle" (James Ord) that he was the son of *one* of the sons of King George III. Although the elder Ord had assumed that the boy was the Duke of York's child because the duke had handled the negotiations with the Ord family for his care, Ord himself believed ". . . the probabilities were that I was the child of Mrs. Fitzherbert and the Prince of Wales, to which he [Father William Matthews, an intimate friend of his "uncle"] replied that he *had heard this stated by others*, but he declined to say by whom."

Maria and the prince may have had another child in addition to "James Ord"—if Ord indeed was their son. A little girl named Maryanne Smythe (a version of Maria's birth name) was born around 1800, although she did not enter Mrs. Fitzherbert's household until 1817. Maryanne was passed off as Maria's niece, the daughter of her younger brother John—although official records reflect that John and his wife had no children. The page that spans the years 1799 to 1801 is missing from the baptismal register of St. John the Baptist Church in Brighton, where Maria worshipped, so we'll never know if it contained anything incriminating. It was purportedly removed by George in 1811 when he became the regent.

Despite the pledges he'd made in his correspondence, the prince's eternal fidelity to Maria was short-lived. George continued to dally with other women, while she was expected to play the traditional role assigned to wives of her class and suffer in quiet dignity. But Maria had a "fierce temper," according to the prince, and that, combined with her jealousy of his frequent conquests and rather publicly conducted affairs, put a tremendous strain on their marriage.

In September 1788, while the semi-royal couple remained in Brighton, the press continued to speculate on the reasons for their absence from London. The *World* published an "epitaph" of Maria that was probably ghostwritten by the renowned playwright and Whig MP Richard Brinsley Sheridan:

MRS. F-TZHE-B-T
To the Remembrance of one
Who was, Wife, and no Wife, Princess
and no Princess, sought, yet shunned,
courted, yet disclaimed: the Queen of all
parties, yet the Grace of none: the
Theme of Wonder, Curiosity, and

Submissive respect: yet
The Constant Subject of Doubt, reserve, and
Apprehension.
Mrs. F—
Was fond of Sovereignty, and obtained it: fond
of the World's Friendship, and secured it:
fond of that best Courage, the Courage of being
unabash'd and contrived
To exercise it safely.

A sum paid by Carlton House to the editor of the *World* silenced that particular anonymous pen.

But there were others. In 1792, as the health and sanity of George III continued to remain uncertain, a pamphlet was circulated proclaiming that the prince's relationship with Mrs. Fitzherbert would "one day become a matter of most serious national discussion," and that "his behavior to her . . . has not been of the most grateful, delicate, or honorable nature."

But by the winter of 1793, Maria's marriage to the prince was floundering. Their diverging tastes became an increasing problem. The diarist Thomas Raikes averred that the Prince of Wales was "young and impetuous and boisterous in his character and very much addicted to the pleasures of the table." Maria preferred intimate, quiet evenings at home and her husband's rowdy, often childish, excesses were wearing very thin. Additionally, by the following summer, his debts had swelled to upwards of £500,000 (well over $66 million today), and Maria was lending *him* money out of her £3,000 royal annuity!

George had commenced a relationship with the forty-one-year-old former Frances Twysden, now the beautiful but diamond-hard Lady Jersey, cleverly introduced to him by his mother the queen in the hopes of detaching him from his Catholic inamorata. Married to the 4th Earl of Jersey, who was thirty-five years her senior, her ladyship was one of the Devonshire set, the fast crowd of Whigs who orbited around the glamorous Duchess of Devonshire, Georgiana. Lady Jersey convinced George that the reason he was so unpopular was because Maria was a Roman Catholic and that he might redeem his reputation if he married a Protestant princess.

By the autumn of 1793, George's affair with Lady Jersey had caused what was left of his marriage to Maria to deteriorate even further. But according to some sources, their union had really hit the skids in the early part of 1793, after Maria had an affair—or was widely rumored to have done so—with a twenty-two-year-old Frenchman named Charles de Noailles, who was said to be "as handsome as the day." The liaison, which many believed to have been little more than a mild flirtation, ended that summer when Maria went to Brighton.

In any event her conduct was a public humiliation that threw George back into full-bore victim mode. During the summer of 1794 he continued to rave at anyone who would listen that Maria "has dishonor'd me in my own eyes and in the eyes of the world," melodramatically adding that he felt as though someone "had first open'd my breast and then poured boiling lead into it." Although he had no tangible proof of Maria's affair with Charles de Noailles, "the strongest probability" that it had taken place was enough for him to convict her.

On June 23, 1794, Maria received a note of apology from the prince just as she was about to depart for Bushy Park, the residence shared by the Duke of Clarence and his mistress Dorothy Jordan. The note expressed the prince's regrets at being unable to join her, as he had just been called to Windsor. That evening, Captain Jack Willet-Payne, the head of the prince's household, arrived at Bushy Park with a subsequent letter from his employer, tersely telling Mrs. Fitzherbert that their relationship was over.

A livid Maria rallied support from her friends as well as from within the royal family, several of whom were fond of her. Lady Clermont advised her to "rise above her own feelings and to open her house to the town of London." Lady Anne Lindsay, assuming that her old friend's temper had a lot to do with the break, urged, "Dearest Fitz, be not too violent for your own sake," and to remain calm in Pall Mall. As for her rival, Lady Jersey, Anne reminded Maria that "it is not in her power, a married woman as she is, with other dutys to fulfill, to supply your place to him."

Although George still seethed a bit over what he assumed was Maria's betrayal of their vows, he had admitted to Jack Willet-Payne, "to tell you what it has cost me to write, and to rip up every and the most distressing feelings of my heart . . . which have so long lodged there, is impossible to express." He ended the letter with the words "whichever way this unpleasant affair ends, I have nothing to reproach myself with."

All through the summer, the rumors spread that the twelve-year connection had ended. After George informed his next youngest brother, Frederick, Duke of York, that he and Maria were "*parted, but parted amicably*," the soldier-duke replied, "I am rejoiced to hear that you are now out of her shackles." The Duke of York was pleased to hear of his older brother's intention to marry their first cousin, Princess Caroline of Brunswick.

Marriage was the only way out of the hole, according to their father, George III. And to underscore his point, he promised the prince that his debts—which in 1794 had topped £600,000 (nearly $80 million in today's economy)—would be paid the day he wed.

It had been some time since Maria received her allowance from George and her funds were dwindling rapidly. She wrote to him requesting payment, "thinking it would be proper to settle this matter before the Princess of Brunswick came to England, as after that period it might have appeared indelicate" for her to contact him. The situation was an emotional one for both of them. Still angry about the vast amounts of money she had spent to entertain the prince and his friends for the previous dozen years, she pointedly ignored George when, two days before the royal wedding, he rode back and forth in front of her house, desperate to get her attention, so he could show how much he missed her.

The prince married Caroline on April 8, 1795; but before the year was out, he began to resent his enforced separation from Maria. George confessed to Lord Moira, "It's no use. I shall never love any woman but Fitzherbert," repeating the same sentiment to the Duke of Clarence. Evincing a modicum of sensitivity to her feelings, he urged his friends to show her the same attention as they had done before the split.

On January 10, 1796, three days after Caroline gave birth to their daughter Charlotte, the Prince of Wales wrote his last will and testament, a document of some three thousand words, bequeathing all his "worldly property . . . to *my Maria Fitzherbert, my wife, the wife of my heart and soul.* Although by the laws of this country she *could not avail herself publicly of that name, still such she is in the eyes of Heaven, was, is, and ever will be such in mine* . . ." He also desired to be buried with "the *picture of my beloved wife, my Maria Fitzherbert* . . . suspended round my neck by a ribbon as I used to wear it when I lived *and placed right upon my heart.*"

But this outpouring of self-pity did not lead to a reunion. After several months elapsed, the prince actively sought a reconciliation with his "second self" during the summer of 1798. By then he had separated from Caroline for good and was bored with Lady Jersey. Maria, however, was not so easily won and did not return to his arms.

In February 1799, the prince read a newspaper report of Maria's death in Bath. He was utterly devastated. "To describe my feelings, to talk even of the subject is totally impossible, for I could neither feel, think, speak; in short, there was almost an end to my existence."

The account turned out to be false, but it exponentially increased the prince's desire to rekindle their romance. Once again, he assumed his desperate stance. In a letter sent to Maria in June 1799, which reportedly took him two days to compose, he melodramatically begged her, "Save me, save me on my knees I conjure you from myself. IF YOU WILL NOT ADHERE TO YOUR PROMISE I WILL *CLAIM YOU AS SUCH, PROVE MY MARRIAGE,* RELINQUISH EVERYTHING FOR YOU, RANK, SITUATION, BIRTH, AND IF THAT IS NOT SUFFICIENT, MY LIFE SHALL GO ALSO."

By mid-July, Maria advised the prince that a *rapprochement* would be possible only if the Pope deemed their marriage legitimate. The prince was on tenterhooks while they awaited a decision from Rome. Finally, the pontiff ruled that Maria Fitzherbert was the true wife of the Prince of Wales in the eyes of the Catholic Church, as long as His Royal Highness was penitent for his sins.

But if George was considered legitimately wed to Mrs. Fitzherbert, then his marriage to Caroline was bigamous, and Charlotte was a bastard. Yet, he didn't seem to care that his reunion with Maria jeopardized Princess Charlotte's chances of succession.

Maria claimed that the next eight years of her life were her happiest, telling Lady Anne, "He is so much improved . . . all that was boyish and troublesome before is now become respectful and considerate. . . . He is not so jealous of me with every foolish fellow that I speak to. . . . We live like brother and sister. I find no resentment tho' plenty of regret that I will have it on this footing and no other, but he must conform to my stipulations. I did not consent to make it up with the Prince to live [with] him either as his wife or his mistress."

On July 4, 1799, the *Times* reported that "A gentleman of high rank and MRS. FITZHERBERT are once more *Inseperables*. Where one is invited, a card to the other is a matter of course." By the early spring of 1800, the couple was frequently seen out together in public. Unaware of the Pope's sanction of their union, or of the fact that it was no longer sexual, people were shocked. What made this new incarnation of their relationship such a scandal was that the prince was now a married man. Ironically, Maria found herself snubbed by the very members of the haute ton who had previously welcomed her most warmly.

Between 1801 and 1804, the Prince of Wales used his influence to secure Maria's adoption of Minney Seymour, the youngest child of their friends Lord Hugh and Lady Horatia Seymour, who had died within a couple of months of each other in 1799, shortly after asking Mrs. Fitzherbert to look after their baby girl. After the Court of Chancery ruled against Maria in 1804, George brought the case to the House of Lords, the highest appeals court in the land, where Maria was granted permanent custody of little Minney. At his spectacular Marine Pavilion in Brighton, George and Maria "played house" with the child. It was the closest they would ever come to any semblance of "family" and the only one they could safely get away with.

Maria never lived at the Pavilion, but she often dined there, as one of a party of twelve or fourteen. The Hon. Mrs. Calvert, a recognized beauty of the day, was one such dinner guest on an evening in 1804. She described Mrs. Fitzherbert as ". . . about fifty . . . but with a charming countenance, her features are beautiful, except her mouth which is ugly, having a set of not good false teeth, but her person is too fat, and she makes a great display of a very white but not prettily formed bosom, which I often long to throw a handkerchief over."

Although by 1806 Maria and the prince may have thought of each other as "brother and sister," in her mind they would always be married; so she panicked during the so-called Delicate Investigation into the possible sexual misconduct of the Princess of Wales—specifically whether Caroline of Brunswick had given birth to an illegitimate son in 1802, six years after her formal separation from the prince. Caroline's lawyer was the anti-Catholic Spencer Perceval, who had represented Minney Seymour's uncle during the lengthy and contentious custody battle, and Maria worried about what Perceval might dredge up during the investigation. Caroline would certainly want to shred her husband's reputation in retaliation for dragging her through an inquest, and Maria would undoubtedly be cross-examined about her relationship with the Prince of Wales. So she snipped out the names of the witnesses to her royal wedding from her marriage lines, to "save them from the peril of the law," in case she was called to testify, as their presence at the illegal ceremony rendered them complicit in the violation of the various acts and statutes.

Ironically, in gaining Minney Seymour, Mrs. Fitzherbert lost the prince—again. The custody suit had bonded them, but once it was settled there was nothing much beyond long-standing respect and affection, along with a dollop of nostalgia, to keep them together. Maria and George had tried to make things work between them, but they were fundamentally unsuited to each other temperamentally. Not only did George continue to behave like a frat boy, drinking and gaming deep into the night, but he was also not remotely monogamous.

The prince still financially supported Mrs. Fitzherbert, although he remained unable to meet the promise he had made upon their marriage to give her £10,000 a year. He had raised her annuity incrementally, but now she was in an embarrassing financial situation. Her house had burned down and the prince had hired an architect to build her a new one. However, the building costs had run woefully over-budget, and now she was in dire need of funds. In 1809, Maria wrote to the prince:

It is with the greatest reluctance I take up my pen to address you upon a subject very painful to my feelings. . . . For though we have now been married three-and-twenty years I have never at any period solicited you for assistance.

The fifty-three-year-old Mrs. Fitzherbert explained that she had twice been threatened with arrest and debtors' prison. Although she assured George that she "would feel no degradation going to a jail, I thought it my duty to inform you of these circumstances, for which I hope I shall not incur your displeasure, for as your wife, I feel I still have a claim upon your protection which I trust is not entirely alienated from me."

The prince must have paid the debts because no more was said about them and Maria was never arrested or incarcerated. But her influence was waning in direct proportion to the ascendance of George's new mistress, Lady Hertford.

By December 1809, Maria had endured enough of her husband's flagrant fickleness. She wrote him a letter on the eighteenth of the month, explaining why she could not accept his most recent invitation to the Pavilion:

> The very great incivilities I have received these past two years just because I obeyed your orders in going there was too visible to everyone present and too poignantly felt by me to admit of my putting myself in a situation of again being treated with such indignity . . . I feel I owe it to myself not to be insulted under your roof with impunity.

On February 5, 1811, the prince was sworn in as regent, initially for a period of one year. By this time George III was nearly blind as a result of cataracts, and was riddled with rheumatism. Additionally, he had been suffering from bouts of "madness" since the 1780s (believed nowadays to be a symptom of porphyria, a rare metabolic disorder). When it became apparent that the king would never recover his wits, the Regency was made permanent. The prince hosted a fête for himself at Carlton House on June 19, where two thousand guests—except for Princess Caroline and their daughter, Charlotte, who weren't invited—celebrated the inauguration of the Regency. Although the regent had sent Maria a gown, she refused to attend because she would not be seated at his table, where the two hundred highest-ranking guests would be placed, according to the strictest court etiquette. George's insult was keenly felt. For decades Maria had received the honors of his consort and wife at his own table as well as that of every other host and hostess who had invited the prince to attend their events.

That contretemps spelled the end of their romance. Maria demanded—and received—a formal separation. The regent agreed to provide her with an income of £6,000 a year (over $481,000 today), paid from a mortgage on the Brighton Pavilion.

The regent became king at the age of fifty-seven upon the death of his father on January 29, 1820. Now George IV, he and Maria rarely crossed paths, but evidently she was never terribly far from his thoughts. Their relationship was certainly uppermost in *her* mind during the 1820 hearing on the Bill of Pains and Penalties, through which George sought a divorce from Caroline. The sixty-four-year-old Maria decamped to Paris, where she endured a few uneasy months, anxious that she'd be called by the defense to testify before the House of Lords and be compelled to produce the documents pertaining to their wedding. Mercifully, her name was never placed on the witness list.

During the first few years of his reign George turned against Maria as he did, Prince Hal–like, to several of his former associates. Sir William Knighton, his physician (and private secretary after 1822), insisted that whenever the king mentioned her name it was "with feelings of disgust and horror," claiming that their union "was an artificial marriage . . . just to satisfy her; that it was no marriage—for there could be none without a license or some written document." Of course we know that there *were* documents, which were in Maria's possession. From time to time after their final break, Maria's demands for her annuity payments were accompanied by veiled threats to go public with her papers if she did not receive the funds.

The king's revisionist reminiscences of the good old days with Maria were far from rosy. He confided in Knighton that her temper "was violent in the extreme and there was no end to her jealousies," recalling that during "one fit of fury" she lobbed a slipper at him.

In June 1830, when the king was dying, he refused to have her visit his bedside, because he was ashamed of his appearance, but eagerly seized her "get well soon" letter and, after reading it, placed it under his pillow. George had grown so obese that he had to sleep in a chair. On June 26 at 3:15 a.m., Maria Fitzherbert—who had no idea just how ill he was and was deeply hurt that he had never replied to her final letter—was made a widow for the third time. The king was buried wearing the Maria Cosway miniature of Mrs. Fitzherbert about his neck, carrying "with him to the grave the image of her, who was perhaps the only woman he had respected as well as loved," according to George Keppel.

George's successor, William IV, offered to make Maria a duchess, but she declined a title. And he unhesitatingly settled her £6,000 charge on the Royal Pavilion at Brighton. Maria signed a release on any claim to George IV's property, but she would continue to receive the same annual pension (now £10,000—nearly $1.1 million today—although George had changed his 1796 will that had initially left her everything). She often had to fight for her royal annuity payments, which were not always paid in a timely fashion, or in full, but her relationship with the new king was an amicable one. When William first called on the widowed Maria at her Brighton residence, Steyne House, she proudly showed him her marriage certificate, and his eyes filled with tears.

Maria now spoke openly of her marriage to George, and William's court happily accepted her as a respected in-law. A wealthy woman, at the time of her death she possessed £28,726—over $3.1 million today. But much of her history as a royal wife cannot be fully pieced together because almost all of her correspondence with George and his family was burned pursuant to his instructions. From 1833 to 1836 the Duke of Wellington, as one of George IV's executors, consigned numerous packets of letters to the flames. Maria herself had agreed to destroy most of her own papers pertaining to her royal relationship, leaving her emotionally drained and complaining of the lingering odor of "burnt paper and sealing-wax" in her Tilney Street drawing room. She did retain certain "essential documents"—her marriage certificate, George's will made in January 1796, a letter from Reverend Burt attesting that he had performed their wedding ceremony, and George's passionate forty-two-page letter to her written in November 1785. Those papers she deposited in Coutts Bank. They remained there until the early twentieth century, when Edward VII permitted a biographer to peruse them, after which they were placed in the Royal Archives.

The remainder of Maria's life was gracious and genteel. She was a devoted mother and grandmother to Minney and Maryanne and their children, hostessing parties, traveling throughout England and abroad. When she was in Brighton, she attended the Church of St. John the Baptist every week for confession. Only a young char-woman was permitted to remain in the building on these occasions, and she was told by the priest to curtsy deeply to the mysteriously veiled old lady, "for maybe it was the queen of England and maybe not."

One day in March 1837, Maria collapsed. For years she had suffered from lumbago, rheumatism, and gout. She died at her Brighton home on Easter Monday, March 27, at the age of eighty. On April 6 she was buried in St. John the Baptist church. The ring finger of her stone effigy is carved with three wedding bands.

In March 2009, the *Wall Street Journal* reported that England's prime minister Gordon Brown was looking into changing Britain's rules of succession, effectively overturning the seventeenth- and eighteenth-century laws prohibiting the heirs to the throne from marrying a "papist." Even if England's Parliament approved such a measure, the proposed new law would have to be presented, de-bated, and voted upon by the parliaments in each of Britain's commonwealth realms—a lengthy process that may close more doors than it opens, because in some dominions, including Australia, there is widespread sentiment in favor of breaking with the monar-chy altogether.

One can't help but wonder what might have been had George and Maria Fitzherbert been permitted to live openly and legally as a married couple. For one thing, she would have genuinely been Queen of England.

For another, there would have been no Caroline of Brunswick.

George IV

❦ *and* ❧

Caroline of Brunswick

1768–1821

married 1795–1821

"Judge what it was to have a drunken husband on one's wedding day, and one who passed the greatest part of his bridal night under the grate, where he fell, and where I left him."

—Caroline of Brunswick to Lady Charlotte Campbell

"*H*ARRIS, I AM NOT WELL, GET ME A GLASS OF brandy," the Prince of Wales said curtly.

James Harris, the Earl of Malmesbury, embarrassed for both Caroline and the prince, diplomatically endeavored to smooth things over. "Sir, had you not better have a glass of water?"

"No," the prince replied, adding an oath presumably too crude for Malmesbury to record in his diary. "I will go directly to the queen." George then turned on his heels and strode out of the room without another word.

The astonished Caroline of Brunswick inquired of Malmesbury (in French), "My God! Is the prince always like that? I find him very fat and nothing as handsome as his picture."

The royal match, made first in haste and then in Hanover, might just as well have begun in hell.

First cousin to the Prince of Wales, Caroline was the second daughter of the unhappy marriage between Karl II, the Duke of Brunswick-Wolfenbüttel and George III's favorite sister, Augusta. Her education had been minimal, and her knowledge of English merely rudimentary, owing to her mother's understanding that King George disapproved of marriages between first cousins. She was also brought up without any religion, as her parents figured she'd end up adopting whichever one her future husband practiced.

More crucially, Caroline seemed, even by her parents' admission, to be lacking the most basic elements of tact and discretion. She frequently lied, because she thought it made her conversation more entertaining. Her easygoing, lighthearted banter would have seemed impertinent in a dairy maid. She also had the unfortunate habit of blurting out whatever popped into her head and an indelicate curiosity to know everyone's business, especially as it concerned the particulars of their love lives.

Was it any wonder then that by the age of twenty-six she was still unmarried? Given Caroline's lusty streak and the inability of her parents to control her behavior, it was likely, however, that she had premarital affairs. It was assumed that her trips to the countryside to distribute food and alms to the poor provided a convenient cover for romantic assignations.

George Augustus Frederick, the Prince of Wales had not planned to take a wife—beyond Maria Fitzherbert. It was only the sheer magnitude of his debts—which by 1794 had topped £600,000 (nearly $80 million today)—and his father's promise to pay them on his wedding day that spurred his decision to find a suitable bride. That August, George told his father that he had "broken all connections with Mrs. Fitzherbert" and was ready to begin "a more creditable line of life" by marrying the Princess of Brunswick. His choice of words is telling.

However, Queen Charlotte had heard enough anecdotes about Caroline's indiscreet conduct to have formed the opinion that the young lady was a bona fide nymphomaniac, and British diplomats were also convinced that the princess was no virgin. Arthur Paget, the royal envoy in Berlin, prophetically remarked, "Such a marriage might well draw with it calamities which are unknown, or at least forgotten in England." Another diplomat, Lord St. Helens, referred to the "stain" on Caroline's character, stating, "We must endeavor to make the best of it, and to hush up all bad stories."

A popular rhyme lampooned the royal house of Hanover and the entire scheme:

> The King he said unto his son, You know you're deep in debt, sir,
> So you must have a wife, 'tis vain to pounce and fret, sir.
> I'll have you send to Germany to fetch a pretty cousin. . . .

But the king was not the only person urging the prince to marry Caroline. According to the Duke of Wellington, "Lady Jersey made the marriage simply because she wished to put Mrs. Fitzherbert on the same footing with herself, and deprive her of the claim to the title of lawful wife." So she chose a wife for her royal lover with "indelicate manners, indifferent character, and not very inviting appearance, from the hope that disgust for the wife would secure constancy for the mistress."

Eager to get hold of as much money as possible, and the sooner the better, George circumvented the standard diplomatic channels and sent his own emissary, Major Hislop, to Brunswick with a letter for Caroline and the request that her parents send her to England ASAP. After Hislop returned to London on November 19, 1794, with Caroline's portrait and a packet of correspondence from the Brunswick royals, the prince informed his mother that Caroline was "in hourly and anxious expectation of being immediately sent for . . . so much so that she said if the carriage was ready at the door she would not wait for anybody to hand her into it."

The Earl of Malmesbury, James Harris, had already been dispatched to Brunswick that autumn, charged with bringing the princess back to England for a royal marriage. His diary entry describes her "pretty face—not expressive of softness—her figure not graceful—fine eyes—tolerable teeth, but going—fair hair and light eyebrows, good bust—short, with what the French call '*épaules impertinentes*' [broad shoulders]. Vastly happy with her future expectations . . ."

On December 3, the Duke and Duchess of Brunswick formally consented to the match. The marriage treaty was drawn up in English and Latin and duly executed. George's portrait finally arrived in Brunswick and right after the marriage ceremony, with Malmesbury standing in for the groom, Caroline affixed the miniature to a ribbon, which she immediately began to wear about her neck. Her mother wrote to George, "Caroline is so happy with your picture," adding that the young lady's delight at their impending marriage soothed any regrets she harbored at losing a daughter.

But the "delight" Caroline's mother ascribed to her was tempered by a strong dose of pragmatism and self-awareness. Shortly after Malmesbury's arrival in Brunswick, Caroline confided to an unnamed correspondent:

> You are aware, my friend, of my destiny. I am entering into a matrimonial alliance with my first cousin, George, Prince of Wales. His generosity I regard, and his letters bespeak a mind well-cultured and refined. Estranged from my connections, my associations, my friends, all that I hold dear and valuable, I am about to enter a permanent connection. I esteem and respect my intended husband and I hope for great kindness and attention. But, ah me! I say sometimes I cannot now love him with ardor. I am indifferent to my marriage, but not averse to it; I think I shall be happy, but I feel my joy will not be enthusiastic. . . .

Malmesbury remained in Brunswick for several weeks, endeavoring to instill the most rudimentary basics of decorum and discretion in the twenty-six-year-old German hoyden. But tutoring the future Queen of England even on the simplest matters of attending to her toilette was rough sledding.

In an era when nearly everyone had bad teeth, hers were worse, and Malmesbury had to introduce her to a brush and tooth powder, as well as the joys of soap and water. The earl also discovered that Caroline's undergarments—her "coarse petticoats and shifts and thread stockings"—were not only shabby but were filthy and smelled rank, "never well washed or changed often enough." The earl was astonished that the princess made no apology for their condition, or for her own appalling personal hygiene. And she evinced no hurry to remedy the situation until Malmesbury made a point of telling her that the prince was "very delicate" and expected "a long and very careful *toilette de propreté.*"

As Malmesbury continued to lay the groundwork for the necessary taming of the shrew, he instructed Caroline "never to talk politics or allow them to be talked to her." When she asked the earl, point-blank, about George's purported mistress, Lady Jersey, Malmesbury advised her not to display any jealousy of her husband. If she suspected him of an infidelity, she was to feign ignorance, pretending not to notice it.

"I am determined never to appear jealous," Caroline assured the earl, adding, "I know the Prince is *léger* [light, as in, inconstant], and am prepared on this point."

By December 16, Malmesbury had formed the impression that Caroline "had no *fond* [depth], no fixed character, a light and flighty mind, but means well and well disposed; and my eternal theme to her is *to think before she speaks, to recollect herself.*"

Caroline's departure from Brunswick was scheduled for December 21. On the twentieth, the duchess received an anonymous letter, warning her that Lady Jersey would be a bad influence on Caroline and encourage her to take lovers. The duchess unwisely showed Caroline the letter. But Augusta's bad judgment gave Malmesbury the cue he needed to instruct Caroline on the issue of adultery and how it applied to the future Queen of England. The earl warned Caroline that "anybody who presumed to *love* her was guilty of *high treason* and punished with *death*, if she was weak enough to listen to him; so also was she. This startled her."

On December 29, 1794, Caroline finally set out from her father's palace. "How can I be otherwise than happy?" she rhetorically asked Malmesbury. "Am I not going to be married to the finest and handsomest prince in the world and live in the most desirable country in Europe?"

Meanwhile, in that "most desirable country," the wedding plans were proceeding apace as George's debts continued to mount. Four bridesmaids were selected, since that had been the number of attendants at the last wedding of a Prince of Wales. But their gowns couldn't be made up until the bride's garments were chosen. George declared a preference for royal robes over court dress, but his mind wasn't on the ceremony. Before Caroline's arrival he expressed the fervent desire to serve in the army, begging his father to make him a general. After ignoring his son's requests, the king politely told his heir that he would be "most happy" to see him seriously turning his thoughts to a martial career, but steered him toward a *marital* one instead, adding, "May the Princess Caroline's character prove so pleasing to you that your mind may be engrossed with domestic felicity . . . and that a numerous progeny may be the result of this union, which will be a comfort to me in the decline of my years."

War and weather prevented a speedy journey, and Caroline didn't reach England until Easter Sunday—April 5, 1795. Later that day, in the Duke of Cumberland's rooms at St. James's Palace, the prince and princess met for the first time. Neither one made a good first impression on the other. Caroline had just arrived from Greenwich, where Lady Jersey—who was to be Caroline's Lady of the Bedchamber—had deliberately delayed the arrival of the welcome party by dallying with her toilette. Then she sabotaged the naïve German princess by telling her that her attractive blue and white ensemble wasn't sufficiently fashionable, urging Caroline to don a white satin frock and green mantle festooned with gold trim that made her look dumpier. Telling her she looked too pale, Lady Jersey also persuaded the princess to apply more rouge, thereby obscuring her delicately formed features and clear complexion. Satisfied that Caroline looked sufficiently fat and coarse, Lady Jersey assured her she was ready to meet her future husband.

At St. James's, in accordance with the protocol she had struggled to absorb, Caroline curtsied deeply to George, a florid-faced, heavyset dandy with powdered ringlets. According to Malmesbury, "He raised her (gracefully enough) and embraced her, said barely one word, turned round [and] returned to a distant part of the apartment."

This retreat was followed by the now-famous request for brandy.

Was it Caroline's looks—her plump, squat, no-necked figure and oversized head—or her body odor that had repulsed the Prince of Wales? Malmesbury had cautioned the princess to wash herself thoroughly *all over*.

That night, Caroline's first in London, was an unmitigated disaster. She was hurt that Lady Jersey was present at their dinner table—seated right between her and George—and aimed a few pointed barbs at her, implying that she knew perfectly well that her ladyship was the prince's mistress. She then began asking impertinent questions about the prince's other long-standing inamorata, Maria Fitzherbert.

Years later, Caroline told Lady Charlotte Campbell, "The first moment I saw my *futur* and Lady Jersey together, I know how it all was, and I said to myself, 'Oh, very well!' I could be the slave of a man I love; but one whom I love not, and who did not love me, impossible—*c'est autre chose*."

Over the next few days, as the wedding approached, the monarchs subtly offered their heir an "out." Her Majesty drew the prince aside and told him, "You know, George, it is for you to say whether you can marry the Princess or not."

The king (whose erratic and often bizarre behavior had led to the diagnosis of "madness" during the 1780s) grew uneasy as well. He admitted to his wife, in what may have been his most lucid moment of the decade, that he would accept the responsibility for breaking off what might be a disastrous match. Although his second thoughts were short-lived, he deputized one of George's younger brothers, the Duke of Clarence, to watch the Prince of Wales at all hours in case he did something stupid or ill-advised.

At the London gentlemen's clubs, the betting books were full of wagers as to whether the royal wedding would actually take place.

But His Royal Highness was dreaming of a clean credit report; as distasteful as things were, he was not about to back out. Caroline, too, was ever the pugnacious Brunswicker. She didn't care for the thirty-two-year-old prince any more than he did for her, but she was duty- and honor-bound to hold her head high and see it through. She knew the prize was not George—it was the Queen of England's crown.

Caroline and George—who had started drinking steadily three days earlier—were married in the hot, stuffy, and remarkably ill-illumined Chapel Royal on the evening of April 8, 1795. Clad in silver tissue lace festooned with ribbons and bows and a robe of ermine-lined velvet, the dumpy flaxen-haired bride glittered with diamonds and grinned from ear to ear, almost bursting with happiness. In contrast, the podgy, piss-drunk groom, who had made it down the aisle literally supported by two unmarried dukes, wept through the ceremony when he wasn't ogling Lady Jersey. At one point, the prince rose to his feet in the middle of the service, looking as though he was about to bolt.

But the most potentially embarrassing hitch came when the archbishop set down the book after asking whether "any person" knew "of a lawful impediment." The air was thick with tension. Would someone mention Mrs. Fitzherbert? The archbishop looked long and hard from the prince to the king and back again. The chapel remained silent and the ceremony continued.

At the Drawing Room that the monarchs hosted for guests who were not invited to the wedding ceremony, Lady Maria Stuart thought "the Prince looked like death and full of confusion, as if he wished to hide himself from the looks of the whole world. I think he is much to be pitied. . . ." Caroline, however, whom the guests thought had a pretty face, "though with too much rouge," was in high spirits. And even if the groom wanted nothing to do with her, she did have a few champions within the royal family. George's sister Elizabeth found Caroline to have an "open character" and "perfect good temper," telling him, "I flatter myself that you will have her turn out a very comfortable little wife."

On their wedding night, through a haze of brandy, the prince must have gritted his teeth and thought of £600,000, fantasizing about all the improvements he could now make to Carlton House. Caroline was mortified, humiliated, and disgusted by his behavior. She confided to Lady Charlotte Campbell, "Judge what it was to have a drunken husband on one's wedding day, and one who passed the greatest part of his bridal night under the grate, where he fell, and where I left him."

Both of the newlyweds were miserable. According to Lord Minto, "It appears that they lived together two or three weeks at first, but not at all afterwards as man and wife."

Lord Albemarle wrote in his memoirs, "From the day that this poor princess landed in England she became fully aware that she was beset by persons of her own sex who looked upon her as a rival, and who endeavored to make her an object of disgust to her husband." George's intimates would play tricks on Caroline, informing her that such a thing was all the fashion in England, or that George particularly admired it. In a rush to please him, she accepted their chicanery as gospel, and ended up appalling her husband instead of enticing him.

Caroline's gaucheries and jarring sense of humor were a perpetual embarrassment to the prince. And he could not disguise his physical revulsion, telling Lord Minto in March 1796, "Finding that I had suspicions of her not being *new*, she the next night mixed up some tooth powder and water, colored her shift with it and . . . in showing these she showed at the same time such marks of filth both in the fore and *hind* part of her . . . that she turned my stomach and from that moment I made a vow *never to touch her again*.

I had known her three times—twice the first and once the second night—it required no small [effort] to conquer my aversion and overcome the disgust of her person."

Miraculously, however, during one of George's three drunken and disappointing performances in the bedroom, he had gotten Caroline pregnant. No one was more surprised than she was, given the brief and unhappy saga of their sex life. The princess confided as much to Lady Charlotte Bury, indicating that she hadn't thought her husband capable of it. George never forgave her for that insult.

On January 17, 1796, after a terrible labor lasting more than twelve hours, Caroline gave birth (to George's disgust and disappointment) to "an *immense* girl," Princess Charlotte. The succession now secured, the kingdom rejoiced. Fortunately for George, times had changed since the Renaissance. Although there was nothing in English law that prevented a female from inheriting the throne, the fact that the kingdom had metamorphosed from a near autocracy to a constitutional monarchy mooted the preference for a male heir who could lead his troops into battle and bully any rebellious subjects into submission.

With the possible exception of Caroline, who adored children, the Prince of Wales was more thrilled than anyone by the birth of his heir. His duty done, he assured Malmesbury that "the child just born . . . certainly will be the last as I declare I can never approach her again, for she never washes or wipes any part of her body." A few days later, after being seized with one of his dramatic panic attacks, George made out his will, bequeathing everything, including Carlton House and the Pavilion at Brighton, to Maria Fitzherbert. He left the care of his infant daughter "to the king, my father," adding that "the mother of this child" was to have no hand whatsoever in Charlotte's upbringing, "For though I forgive the falsehood and treachery of her conduct towards me, still the convincing and repeated proofs I have received of her entire want of judgment and of feeling, make me deem it incumbent upon me . . . to prevent by all means possible the child's falling into such improper and bad hands as hers."

Although he displayed no intention of being a decent husband, there were some aspects of *fatherhood* that brought George joy. It gave him pleasure to draw up the rules for the nursery. Staff were required to exercise the utmost discretion, never repeating to anyone what went on inside Carlton House; and Caroline was permitted to see her baby for only a brief time every day.

Everyone expected Charlotte's arrival to reunite the Waleses in a lovefest of domestic harmony and marital bliss, but it didn't happen. On the contrary, George took great pains to avoid seeing his wife. Caroline was instructed to remain more or less secluded in London with a short list of socially appropriate visitors, which included one of her mandated attendants—Lady Jersey. Known as the Carlton House System, it was George's way of keeping his wife "in order lest she should keep me so." Restricting Caroline's movements checked her ability to demand limits on his own freedom.

Left alone with her ladies-in-waiting at Carlton House, the Princess of Wales wrote to a German acquaintance, "I do not know how I shall be able to bear the loneliness. The Queen seldom visits me and my sisters-in-law show me the same sympathy. But I admire the character of the English and nothing can be more flattering than the reception that is given me when I appear in public. . . ."

Her attendants and visitors noticed her unhappiness. Lady Sheffield, who dined with the princess in Brighton in late July, noted that "her lively spirits which she brought over with her are all gone, and they say the melancholy and anxiety in her countenance is quite affecting."

George suggested the idea of a marital separation to Lord Malmesbury, assuring the earl that Caroline had lied about his ill treatment of her, though he did admit that he loathed the very sight of his wife. "I had rather see toads and vipers crawling over my victuals than sit at the same table with her," he declared. Part of his revulsion was Caroline's continued inattention to personal hygiene.

But Caroline had indiscreetly shared her opinions of her husband's failings in the boudoir, causing the Earl of Minto to remark,

"I fancy the *mutual* disgust broke out at that time, and if I can spell her *hums* and *haws*, I take it that the ground of his antipathy was his own *incapacity*, and the distaste which a man feels for a woman who *knows* his defects and humiliations."

There may be some truth to Minto's observation. One reason the prince had so avidly desired to rid himself of Caroline was because she was not as advertised. George told Malmesbury, "Not only on the first night there was no appearance of blood, but her manners were not those of a novice. In taking the liberties natural on these occasions, she said, '*Ah mon dieu, qu'il est gros!*' [oh, my god, it's big!], and how should she know this without a previous means of comparison."

By mid-April 1796, Caroline, lonely and humiliated, had had enough of Lady Jersey, and complained to her husband that she would no longer spend her days being shut in with no other companion but his mistress. Meanwhile, in case she ever needed to defend herself against her in-laws, she was quietly compiling a list of transgressions committed against her by her husband and other members of the royal family, including the separation from her only child—who was being raised in such seclusion that she was ill prepared to become queen, having so little knowledge of the world.

The Waleses mutually agreed to separate in the spring of 1796, never again to sleep together, and to remain man and wife in name only, even if they resided under the same roof. George sent Caroline a letter stating:

> Our inclinations are not in our power, nor should either of us be held answerable to the other because nature has not made us suitable to each other. Tranquil and comfortable society is, however, in our power; let our intercourse be restricted to that. . . . I shall now close this disagreeable correspondence, trusting that as we have completely explained ourselves to each other, the rest of our lives will be passed in an uninterrupted tranquility.

In an effort to sift through the wreckage of his royal marriage, George demanded an interview with Caroline. Anticipating a scene, the prince took a "second"—on this occasion it was Lord Chomondeley—to witness the maelstrom.

No sooner had they entered Carlton House than Caroline assailed her husband in French. "I have been two and a half years in this house. You have treated me neither as your wife, nor as the mother of your child, nor as the Princess of Wales: and I tell you that from this moment I shall have nothing more to say and that I regard myself as being no longer subject to your orders—or to your *rules.*" She spat out that last word in English.

Reminding their son that his entire life was a very public matter and that separation would reflect badly on his popularity, the monarchs tried to reconcile the Waleses, but the marriage was irreparable. By December 1796, the formal separation agreement was finalized, and a few months later Caroline moved to a house in Charlton, near Blackheath, although her husband told her she was welcome to avail herself of Carlton House at any time. Anxious that the settlement arrangements not appear petty or ungenerous, George also made it clear that he had no objections to her attending public entertainments, particularly as he knew she was fond of the opera.

Caroline took full advantage of her freedom. By 1799, she was indulging her flirtatious personality at Montague House, regularly entertaining several of the most prominent Cabinet ministers—including the PM himself, William Pitt. She was rumored to be enjoying a series of lovers from her guest list. "I have a bedfellow as often as I like," she once boasted, "nothing is more wholesome." Her behavior became increasingly shocking. Unwisely, Caroline never seriously credited anyone's warnings that her sexual escapades were treasonous offenses. "Nobody can improve me in morality," she declared. "I have a system quite of my own."

Princess Charlotte would later observe, "My mother was bad, but she would not have become as bad as she was if my father had not been infinitely worse."

Caroline loved children, but after Charlotte had been taken from her and given a separate establishment, the prince sought to exclude her from seeing their daughter with any degree of regularity, and from having any input in the girl's education. To fill the void, Caroline "adopted" a number of children—orphans or the offspring of destitute parents who could not afford to care for them. She placed the children with nearby foster mothers, but they were always welcome to come and play at Montague House.

One of those children was Willy Austin. He had been born on July 11, 1802, to the wife of a cashiered Deptford dockyard worker. Babe in arms, Sophia Austin had sought Caroline's assistance in reinstating her husband's employment. The princess offered to care for the little boy herself, and ten days after this first interview, Sophia returned with little Willikins, as Caroline would call him. Assured that her son would be given the best of everything, Sophia released him to Caroline.

For some years the air was thick with rumors about Caroline's indiscreet conduct, and behind the scenes, the prince had been endeavoring to dig up as much evidence of it as possible. The search culminated in a proceeding called the Delicate Investigation, which commenced on June 1, 1806. At issue was Caroline's alleged adulterous behavior and whether little William Austin was actually her illegitimate son. But the investigators were unable to obtain any incontrovertible proof of Caroline's infidelity, a remarkable failure given her former footman Samuel Roberts's testimony that "The princess is very fond of fucking"; and the statement made by Lady Lisle, one of the Women of the Bedchamber, that the princess was "a terrible flirt."

After the Brownlow Street Hospital records proved that Sophia Austin's testimony regarding little William's birth was entirely truthful, on July 4, 1806, the Lord Commissioners rendered their verdict: "There is no foundation for believing that the child now with the Princess is the child of her Royal Highness, or that she was delivered of any child in the year 1802; nor has anything appeared to us which would warrant the belief that she was pregnant in that

year, or at any other period within the compass of our inquisition."
The bottom line was that the prince had no grounds for a divorce
because his wife had been cleared of committing any specific
crime.

"Are you not glad to see me with my head upon my rump?" a
relieved Caroline asked a visitor. However, while the princess had
been found innocent of giving birth to a bastard, the commission
found enough merit in the allegations of sexual misconduct for her
behavior to warrant further scrutiny.

Although he was fond of his niece, the king determined that it
was for the best to terminate all social intercourse between Caroline
and the royal family, including—or perhaps especially—ten-year-
old Charlotte. Enraged at becoming persona non grata, Caroline
threatened to publish her lengthy list of grievances against the
prince, as well as all the documents pertaining to the investigation,
which cast her husband in an equally unflattering light. The real
danger lay not with the enumeration of George's numerous extramarital affairs and any resultant royal bastards, but with the public
exposure of his relationship with Maria Fitzherbert and *their* two
alleged children. As anticipated, George panicked and Caroline was
swiftly, if awkwardly, restored to the royal fold.

A month or so later, husband and wife met face-to-face for the
last time. According to Lady Bessborough, the sister of Georgiana,
Duchess of Devonshire, "They did not speak, but coming close
together both looked contrary ways, like the print of the spread
eagle."

Another eyewitness claimed that the pair did speak, but briefly.
"They met in the very centre of the apartment—they bowed, stood
face to face for a moment, exchanged a few words which nobody
heard, and then passed on; he frigid as an iceberg, she with a smile,
half-mirthful, half-melancholy, as though she were rejoicing that
she were there in spite of him."

Caroline was in marital purgatory, in her words "a princess and
no princess, a married woman and no husband—never was dere
[sic] a poor devil in such a plight as I." Her words echo nearly ver-

batim the satirical "epitaph" of Maria Fitzherbert that was published in the *World* in September of 1788.

In 1813, financial woes obliged Caroline to quit Montague House for a more modest residence in Bayswater. She endeavored to maintain at least a toehold in society, but it wasn't always easy. In the spring of 1814, when Tsar Alexander of Russia visited England, Caroline was omitted from the guest list for his reception at Carlton House. Princess Charlotte added her mother's name, but her father scratched it out again. Then he thrice prevented the tsar from paying a social call on Caroline by sending messengers to intercept him.

One night at the opera house Caroline arrived to hear the orchestra playing "God Save the King." The people remained on their feet and greeted her with resounding cheers. On her way home, her carriage was mobbed with sympathetic well-wishers. Poking his head into her coach, one man assured the princess, "We will make the prince love you before we are done with him."

George's pettiness even went so far as to prohibit Caroline from worshipping at St. Paul's; he reserved every seat in the cathedral for a service to commemorate the peace and she was turned away. Balls in her honor were cancelled when the prince forbade his friends from accepting invitations to attend them.

After enduring nearly twenty years as a royal pariah, the Princess of Wales made the decision to quit England. At the age of forty-six, she embarked for the Continent on August 9, 1814, attended by an assortment of English retainers and companions. As her ship put out to sea, she was observed to be weeping.

Soon after her arrival in Italy, she was rumored to have commenced a torrid affair with a native member of her entourage. The thirty-two-year-old Bartolomeo Pergami was a stud of a man over six feet tall, with curly black hair and thick dark mustachios. He came from a well-heeled Crema family and had been a quartermaster in the Austrian Viceregal army, serving in the Russian campaign of 1812 as a courier for General Pino, although he'd lost his position, allegedly for killing a higher-ranking officer in a duel.

Caroline, traveling abroad, was not present at the May 2, 1816, wedding of Princess Charlotte to Prince Leopold, the third son of the Duke of Saxe-Coburg-Saalfeld. Not only had Charlotte finally escaped her repressive, infantilizing upbringing, it was a love match. Caroline was also absent from her daughter's bedside when, after fifty hours of agonizing labor, on November 5, 1817, the princess was delivered of a stillborn boy.

Hours later, the twenty-one-year-old Charlotte was dead, most probably from either a postpartum hemorrhage or an infection that was not caught in time and was then mistreated. Her grieving husband, robbed of his chance to become England's king consort, returned to the Continent and remarried. He eventually became King of the Belgians, and was the uncle of Queen Victoria.

Caroline was living in Pesaro, on the east coast of Italy, when she received the sorrowful news. Contrary to the propaganda disseminated by her husband, Caroline was *very* affected by Charlotte's death, as well as her chance to be a grandmother and eventually queen mum. She had fainted when she was told of Charlotte's tragic demise, and from then on suffered severe headaches and bouts of extreme melancholy.

With their daughter dead, George no longer felt it necessary to tolerate his sham of a marriage. In 1818, the regent wrote to his Lord Chancellor illuminating the need for "unshackling myself from a woman who has for the last three and twenty years . . . been the bane and curse of my existence," and who "now stands prominent in the eyes of the world characterized by a flagrancy of abandonment unparalleled in the history of women, and stamped with disgrace and dishonor."

That summer, George dispatched a three-man commission to Milan "for the purposes of making enquiries into the conduct of Her Royal Highness the Princess of Wales since she quitted England in the month of August 1814." In their efforts to collect information for a potential divorce claim, the investigators interviewed more than eighty-five witnesses, most of whom were Italian servants who gave their statements through interpreters. Frightened by the Milan Commission's existence, Caroline correctly surmised that several witnesses were being bribed to give statements, and feared for her safety. "A great body of evidence" was amassed, but the regent was advised that he could not obtain a divorce "except upon proof of adultery, to be substantiated by evidence before some tribunal in this country."

He was also warned that Caroline could raise the issue of *his* numerous extramarital liaisons, including his marriage to (the Catholic) Maria Fitzherbert—which would terminate his right of succession, as well as expose him to a potential charge of bigamy.

On July 13, 1819, the Milan Commission presented its report, and after reviewing it, the Cabinet decided on July 24 that it could not concur with its conclusions that the Princess of Wales and Bartolomeo Pergami were engaged in an adulterous affair. It was the Cabinet's view that the report did not contain enough evidence to assure that Caroline would be found guilty of adultery in an English court of law. She had dodged another bullet.

Caroline was at Leghorn (Livorno) in 1820 when she received a letter from her lawyer, Henry Brougham, advising her of the death of George III on January 29 and urging her to return to England immediately, as she was now Queen of Great Britain. But a subsequent letter informed her that the new king, her estranged husband, would take no action against her *unless* she set foot again on English soil. If she remained on the Continent, she would still be considered Queen of England, but would have to accept the fact that according to George's wishes she would never be crowned.

One of George IV's first acts as king was to insist that Caroline's name be struck from the church liturgy, so that the country was not exhorted to pray for her by name every Sunday. Caroline found this decree to be so intolerable that she decided to come home. Adding insult to injury, she then discovered that she would not be called the queen after all, but simply Caroline of Brunswick.

Leaving her foreign entourage behind, on June 5 she landed at Dover and received an enthusiastic reception from her subjects. The fifty-two-year-old Caroline was cheered all the way to London with shouts of "God Save the Queen" and "No Queen, No King." She had become the people's symbol of an abusive, repressive, and hypocritical monarchy. The press called her "the injured queen."

Because Caroline's alleged lover was a foreigner, and their purported affair took place outside of England, George urged the government to consider a Bill of Pains and Penalties that would punish Caroline for her alleged adultery with Bartolomeo Pergami. However, *Pergami*, being an Italian, could not possibly have committed treason against a king and crown that were not his own; therefore, if *he* was not treasonous, then technically, neither was Caroline.

Nevertheless, on July 5, the Bill of Pains and Penalties was introduced into the House of Lords. The bill sought "to deprive Her Majesty Caroline Amelia Elizabeth of the title, prerogatives, rights, privileges, and exemptions of Queen Consort of this Realm, and to dissolve the marriage between His Majesty and the said [Queen] Caroline."

But from the start, there were problems. The Whig lords were solidly against the Bill of Pains and Penalties. Several Tories, including some of the king's closest friends, didn't think it prudent to proceed, fearing that His Majesty's numerous skeletons would be dragged from his closet by the defense. And many of the clerical lords would only vote for the bill if the divorce clause was removed. Nevertheless, the hearings proceeded, and at the end of the sixteenth day of testimony, much of it graphically prurient, the prosecution rested its case.

But now it was the defense's turn. Caroline's ambitious lawyer, Henry Brougham, demolished the witnesses' testimony, characterizing the prosecution's case as the "tittle-tattle of coffee-houses and alehouses, the gossip of bargemen on canals and . . . cast-off servants," and denouncing the Milan Commission as "that great receipt of perjury—that storehouse of false swearing and all iniquity." He declared that Caroline's so-called affair with Pergami had been nothing but a dumpy middle-aged woman's one-sided attempt to appear beloved.

People and the press talked of little but the queen's trial. Caroline, who had learned how to manipulate public opinion, copied the newspaper editors on a letter she sent to her husband. Probably ghostwritten by Brougham, because Caroline's use of English never became sophisticated, the queen maintained, "From the very threshold of your Majesty's mansion the mother of your child was pursued by spies, conspirators, and traitors. . . . You have pursued me with hatred and scorn, and with all the means of destruction. You wrested me from my child . . . you sent me sorrowing through the world, and even in my sorrows pursued me with unrelenting persecution."

Lord Ellenborough spoke for his fellow peers when he conceded that "the queen was the last woman any one would wish his own wife to resemble," yet he voted against the bill, having acknowledged that Caroline's husband was just as ill behaved and licentious as she was, if not significantly worse. The opinion of many of the lords reflected that of John Bull. In the words of Henry Brougham, "all men, both in and out of Parliament . . . admit everything to be true which is alleged against the Queen, yet, after the treatment she had received since she first came to England, her husband had no right to the relief prayed by him or the punishment sought against her."

The government withdrew the Bill of Pains and Penalties four days later after the third reading of the bill when, at 108 to 99, only nine votes separated the ayes from the nays. The crown conceded that if the outcome was this close in the Lords, the bill would never pass in the Commons, where the king's numerous extramarital infidelities, as well as the Mrs. Fitzherbert issue, would surely sink his case. Fear of mob violence was another reason the government withdrew the bill.

The Lords had decided to punish the king for his hypocrisy rather than condemn the queen for her adultery.

George was so shocked by the withdrawal of the bill that he considered abdicating and leaving for Hanover, where he was Elector, there to remain forever.

Caroline was too exhausted to rejoice. Lady Charlotte Campbell observed that the queen "appeared worn-out in mind and body. The desolateness of her private existence seemed to make her very sorrowful: she appeared to feel the loss of her daughter more than at any previous moment, and she wept incessantly."

So the case was closed. And a popular satirical verse made the rounds of coffeehouses:

> *Most gracious Queen we thee implore*
> *To go away and sin no more,*
> *Or, if that effort be too great,*
> *To go away at any rate.*

Now that her name and character had been formally cleared, the queen was also eager to be crowned alongside her husband. However, the Privy Council informed Caroline that it rested within the *king's* purview to crown his consort and therefore was not a decision she could appeal either to the council or to Parliament, nor could she take her case to the people or the press. Nonetheless, the queen insisted on attending the king's coronation and being rightfully crowned alongside him.

George took every precaution to prevent this event. He hired beefy prizefighters, captained by the champion pugilist Gentleman Jackson, to guard the doors to Westminster Abbey, the palace, and the hall on Coronation Day, July 19, 1821. As the participants and invited guests assembled at six a.m., Queen Caroline, dressed to the nines, arrived in the Dean's Yard and was observed banging on the doors, demanding entry.

At first she was denied admittance because she did not have a peer's ticket. Her chamberlain Lord Hood argued with the door-keep, "I present to you your Queen. Surely it is not necessary for her to have a ticket." When that argument failed Hood immediately produced a ticket signed "Wellington," to which the door-keep replied that the ticket would only admit one, and there were four people standing before him: Hood, the queen, and her two ladies-in-waiting, one of whom was *Lady* Hood.

"The Queen—open!" Caroline shouted. An eyewitness reported hearing her fuming and raging, "Let me pass; I am your Queen. I am Queen of Britain!"

A page opened the door wide enough for Caroline to glimpse sentries with crossed bayonets standing just inside.

The King's Lord High Chamberlain then dispatched his deputy to handle the hubbub, demanding, "Do your duty, shut the Hall door."

After all these years, the fight had finally gone out of her. Demoralized and deflated, Caroline slunk away to jeers of "Shame!" "Go away!" and "Back to Pergami!"

Within days of the coronation, Caroline suffered an obstruction and inflammation of the bowels. She dosed herself with enough calomel and castor oil "to turn the stomach of a horse." Her physicians realized she was dying. She asked to be buried in Brunswick with a simple epitaph on her coffin: *Caroline of Brunswick, the injured Queen of England.* According to Henry Brougham, Caroline had initially chosen the phrase "murdered queen," but had been convinced to mollify it.

With only a few hours of life left, she told Lord Hood, *"Je ne mourrais pas sans douleur, mais je mourrais sans regret"*—I don't die without sorrow, but I die without regret.

Death came to the fifty-three-year-old Caroline at 10:25 p.m. on August 8, 1821. This Queen of England who never reigned was the only monarch in British history to have been subjected to a Bill of Pains and Penalties.

George IV was aboard the royal yacht when he received the news; he retired to his cabin for the remainder of the day. The court was ordered to go into mourning for all of three weeks. The nation was not required to officially mourn their queen at all.

Bartolomeo Pergami, who never saw Caroline again after she returned to England in 1820, died in 1842 after a fall from his horse.

George IV survived his wife by nine years. He died on June 26, 1830, at the age of sixty-seven as the result of a burst blood vessel in his abdomen. He was "a man of as many gifts as frailties," in the words of his dear friend, the statesman Charles James Fox; rarely had someone possessed so much promise and done so little with it. This mini-epitaph reads like a condemnation, but Fox may in fact have been a bit fulsome in his praise of his deceased drinking buddy, because there is little to tally up in the credits column of George IV's reign, other than his decision as regent to continue to ally with Spain in the Peninsular War against Napoleon. Although his aesthetics were impeccable, George squandered his subjects' goodwill with lechery and lavish spending while soldiers and sailors went unpaid, Luddite laborers rioted, and over in Ireland there were threats of civil war.

On July 16, 1830, the *Times* of London editorialized that "There was never an individual less regretted by his fellow creatures than this deceased king." As eccentric and often disliked as Caroline had been, her husband's popularity was even lower. For all his aesthetic sensibilities, throughout his life George IV—overweight, oversexed, and overdressed—was a hypochondriac, a moral hypocrite, an emotional bully, a glutton, a drunkard, a womanizer, and a bigamist—although Princess Lieven, who knew him well, insisted that George was not a bad man, though he was capable of bad actions. A man of great and discerning taste whose behavior was so often tasteless, George IV was buried at Windsor. He was succeeded by his younger brother William, Duke of Clarence, who ruled as William IV.

Often viewed through rosy lenses, the Regency is one of the most popular backdrops for romance novels. The setting for Jane Austen's evergreen stories, it was an age of aesthetics, another renaissance of culture and construction that nowadays is depicted as a kinder, gentler era where manners mattered. In 1815, a veiled hint from the royal librarian James Stanier Clarke that the regent had declared his enthusiasm for Miss Austen's writing left her with no choice but to dedicate *Emma* to him—although she despised his shabby treatment of Caroline of Brunswick.

"Poor woman," Jane wrote, "I shall support her as long as I can, because she is a Woman and because I hate her Husband. . . . [If] I must give up the princess I am resolved at least always to think that she would have been respectable, if the Prince had behaved tolerably by her at first."

Napoleon Bonaparte
1769–1821
Ruled as Emperor of the French: 1804–1814 and 1815

and

Josephine de Beauharnais
1763–1814

married 1796–1810

"Yet God is my witness that I love him much more than
my life, and much more than that throne, that crown
which he has given me!"

—Empress Josephine in 1809

SHE WAS A WOMAN WITH A PAST; HE, A MAN WITH A
future that would become legendary. He considered empire his
destiny. When she was a girl, a fortune-teller read her cards and
informed her that "she would one day be more than queen of
France, but that she would not die a queen."

And when Napoleon Bonaparte and Josephine de Beauharnais
met—each of them ambitious in their own way, each one a
survivor—their initially lopsided relationship was commenced out
of convenience. Yet over time they would come to complement
each other perfectly. As Napoleon told her, "Nature has given me

a strong and resolute character; she has made you of lace and gauze."

Known as "Rose" until Napoleon summarily renamed her Josephine, she was born Marie-Josèphe-Rose Tascher de la Pagerie in Trois-Îlets, Martinique—a Creole whose family owned a sugar plantation. Her own rise from provincial teen to Paris belle began when her paternal aunt Edmée, the mistress of Martinique's governor François de Beauharnais, arranged for Rose's passage to Paris to wed her lover's son, Alexandre, a vicomte.

So in 1779, sixteen-year-old Rose, petite and still carrying a bit of puppy fat, sailed for France. Except for the domestic rudiments taught to girls at the time, she was uneducated and decidedly uncultured. In contrast, Alexandre, a rising military officer, was a pompous, swaggering, sexually precocious youth who had already fathered a bastard child with a married mistress some years his senior. But he would not receive his inheritance until he wed— hence his haste to rush to the altar.

Josephine and Alexandre were married on December 13, 1779, and both parties were immediately miserable. Alexandre left his unsophisticated wife at home as often as he could, while he rejoined his regiment and his mistress. Yet the couple spent enough time together to produce two children—Eugène, born on September 3, 1781, and Hortense, born on April 10, 1783. Fortunately, both of them took after their sweet-tempered, kindhearted mother.

Leaving Rose in Paris, Alexandre sailed for Martinique with his mistress in tow, hoping to secure an appointment there, which of course would conveniently keep him as far from his wife as possible. After absorbing his lover's toxic insinuations that Rose had been a promiscuous slut before he met her, he amassed a collection of false accusations about her sexual conduct, accumulated through bribery. Even as Alexandre hypocritically defended his own acts of infidelity, he wrote to Rose to inform her that he could no longer be wed to a woman who was such a hussy. He therefore considered their marriage to be over, and insisted that she enter a convent.

So, in 1784, at the age of twenty-one, Rose moved into the convent of Penthémont, a haven for upper-class Parisiennes who needed to retreat from the outside world for a while. There, she began to model herself after the chic and sophisticated young aristocrats who were her fellow boarders.

Despite his charges of unladylike conduct, her husband could produce no proof of any infidelities on her part. Disgusted with having her reputation unfairly dragged through the mud, Rose petitioned for a formal separation. The following year, she won a judgment against Alexandre to the tune of five thousand livres a year and the restoration of her honor.

Meanwhile, at Penthémont, Rose had amassed a terrific wardrobe, which was clearly above her means. A shopaholic even in her leanest days, Rose took lovers who paid her bills, a common arrangement in late-eighteenth-century France. With no husband, and of course no employment, she did whatever she could to survive and feed her children. Rose made an extremely desirable mistress, renowned for her sympathetic personality, charm, and graciousness. She was graceful and petite (historians' conjectures on her height range from five feet to five feet four inches) with light brown hair, and amber eyes that often changed color. Her voice, with its lilting island cadences, and her slow, seductive walk were aphrodisiacs. On top of those languorous qualities, she was a good listener.

Having gotten back on her feet, Rose sailed to Martinique to visit her family, luckily avoiding the outbreak of the French Revolution. After spending two years on the island, she returned to France in 1790 to find the entire world as she had known it turned topsy-turvy. The monarchy had been replaced with a republican government formed by the revolutionary faction that had stormed the Bastille a year earlier. And the president of the new Constituent Assembly was her ex-husband, Alexandre de Beauharnais!

Rose became a popular fixture at the fashionable intellectual salons, but admitted that she was "too indolent to take sides" in the heated political discussions of the moment. A friend claimed that Rose's attention "wandered from any discussion of abstract ideas," but she was adept at faking it and knew when to remain silent to avoid revealing her ignorance. Meanwhile, as Alexandre's alimony and child support payments were spotty at best, Rose continued to take lovers as a survival mechanism. Among them were the most prominent and powerful men of the day, including Paul Barras and, possibly, Jean-Lambert Tallien.

But it was a dangerous age, and everyone's position was precarious. Alexandre was imprisoned for committing a perceived military blunder. In April 1794, Rose's apartment was ransacked for sensitive documents belonging to her ex-husband. After the suspicious papers were uncovered, Rose was arrested and imprisoned in Les Carmes. There, amid seven hundred other inmates, she awaited execution.

Alexandre was condemned on July 21 and was felled by the "national razor," Madame Guillotine, a few days later. But shortly after the July 28 execution of Robespierre, one of the most formidable architects of the revolution, Rose and three thousand other political prisoners were released. The period known as the Terror had ended and Paris was quick to resume its gaiety under a new government known as the Directory, or *Directoire*.

Also making the salon circuit was a man known as "Barras's little Italian protégé," a twenty-six-year-old brigadier on half pay, Napoleone Buonaparte. Like Rose, who was born just a few months after France wrested Martinique from British control, Napoleone was an island outsider in the glittering social circles of Paris. Several weeks before his birth, his native Corsica had been taken from the locals by the French, but his family had cast their lot with the conquerors.

He'd trained for a military career since the age of nine, revealing himself (even as a child) to be sharp-tempered, arrogant, self-sufficient, and quick to take offense while preserving a rigid sense of decorum. A report on his conduct as a cadet stated that he was "solitary, haughty, egotistical. . . . Reserved and studious, he prefers study to any kind of amusement. . . . He enjoys reading good au-

thors and has a sound knowledge of mathematics and geography. . . .
He is most proud and ambitious."

At the time they met, the soigné but unintellectual Rose seemed an
ill match for the studious history buff, her elegance an odd foil for the
diminutive (measured in the Parisian foot, which was 12.789 inches,
he was approximately five feet six) career soldier with the gloomy,
introspective personality. His lanky dark hair was "ill combed and
ill powdered"; he wore a ratty oversized overcoat everywhere he
went; and his "complexion [was] yellow and seemingly unhealthy"—
all of which combined to produce a "slovenly look," according to
Laure Permon, a former childhood friend who knew him well. Not
only that, his skin was marked by scabies, which he had contracted
while in Toulon staving off the royalists and the British military
detachment that supported them.

But Napoleone was a rising star, a success at Toulon in 1793
when he was only twenty-four. By 1795 he was commander of the
Army of the Interior and then, through the assistance of his friend
Paul Barras, secured a post within an influential department of the
Committee for Public Safety in Paris. Perfectly placed to move up
in the world in every way, and changing the spelling of his name to
appear more "French," he decided that in his quest for status,
wealth, and power, it was time to find a rich wife.

He'd had his eye on Barras's lover and salon hostess, Rose de
Beauharnais. It was a fluid society as far as liaisons were concerned,
and some historians have conjectured that Barras did not mind
when his Corsican friend took Rose off his hands, whether temporarily or permanently, as her possessive nature was a bit high-
maintenance for him. Rose's rapt attention to his war stories at
dinner one evening cemented Napoleon Bonaparte's desire for her.
He yearned for recognition and her praise had stroked his ego into
a lustful frenzy.

They became lovers—if not that night, then not too much later.
For Rose, the affair was a pleasant diversion, but Napoleon was
smitten. After their first night between the sheets Rose gave him a

sketch of herself as a memento. Only hours after leaving her bed, he scribbled a rhapsodic note headed "seven in the morning":

I awaken full of you. Between your portrait and the memory of our intoxicating night, my senses have no respite. Sweet and incomparable Josephine [by now he had renamed her], what is this strange effect you have upon my heart? What if you were to be angry? What if I were to see you sad or troubled? Then my soul would be shattered by distress. Then your lover would find no peace, no rest. But I find none, either, when I succumb to the profound emotion that overwhelms me, when I draw from your lips, from your heart, a flame that consumes me. . . .

You will be leaving the city at noon. But I shall see you in three hours. Until then, mio dolce amor, I send you a thousand kisses—but send me none in return, for they set my blood on fire.

However, the poet had a pragmatist's soul. Before pursuing a serious involvement with Josephine, Napoleon visited her notary to inquire about her wealth.

Their blossoming courtship was nearly nipped in the bud when he learned that she had substantially bent the truth about her family's plantation income. She scarcely had a *sou* to her name. But she *was* well connected. And he was madly in love, despite her bad teeth, rotted down to black stubs from all the sugar she consumed as a child.

Although she was not conventionally beautiful, a contemporary of Josephine's once commented that "she offered her soul in her eyes." And although Napoleon thought he might have captured her soul even as he took her body night after night, he had not won her heart. Josephine found him "passionate and lively," but "awkward and altogether strange in all his person." His letters were so full of ardor—and so illegible—that she showed them to her sophisticated girlfriends as an example of what a strange duck he was, mocking him behind his back.

Both parties were intensely focused on their own advancement, so in that respect they had something in common. But Josephine was not in love with Napoleon when she agreed to his proposal of marriage. However, she was a thirty-two-year-old mother of two in an age when girls were considered prime wedlock material at sixteen. And she was six years her ardent suitor's senior.

Neither of their families considered the match ideal. Napoleon's large family of parvenus was quick to deride Josephine, although she disliked them just as vehemently. One of his younger sisters, Pauline Bonaparte, referred to Josephine as "the old woman," which was kinder, at least, than what his mother privately called her: *la putana*—the whore.

Nevertheless, on the evening of March 9, 1796, in the dingy mayor's office of the second arrondissement, Napoleon and Josephine were wed in a very small civil ceremony. From the start, the marriage was somewhat inauspicious, if not in fact invalid. Claiming that he had been preoccupied with paperwork, the groom was nearly three hours late. The young officer who witnessed Napoleon's signature was still a minor, and therefore ineligible to serve in that capacity. The official who conducted the marriage ceremony was also not legally qualified. And Josephine had failed to produce her birth certificate, claiming she lacked access to the document because the British now occupied the Windward Islands—so she conveniently shaved a few years off her age. Most biographers claim that she gave her age as twenty-nine. Napoleon, also lacking a legitimate birth certificate, opted to use the birth date of his elder brother Joseph—making him twenty-eight on his wedding day—and lied about his birthplace, claiming that it was Paris, rather than admitting to Ajaccio, Corsica.

But no doubt Josephine looked lovely in her white muslin dress and patriotic tricolor sash. About her neck she wore a medallion that was a gift from her new husband, inscribed with the phrase *To Destiny*.

The wedding night, too, was fraught with excitement of an unusual nature. The bridegroom was appalled that his wife intended to permit her pug, Fortuné, to join them in bed. But the pet was a permanent fixture, no matter the lover. Josephine advised Napoleon to take it or leave it.

"So I resigned myself," Napoleon later wrote.

And as soon as the newlyweds commenced consummation, Fortuné bit his rival.

On March 5, Napoleon had been appointed commander of the republican army in Italy, and two days after the wedding, he departed for headquarters in Nice. He sent passionate letters to Josephine from the front, often writing to her twice a day. He longed to kiss her heart, then her lower anatomy, then <u>much</u> lower as he emphatically double underscored the word, referring to her as his "sweet love . . . the pleasure and torment" of his life. "Never had a woman been loved with more devotion, fire, and tenderness." If she ever left him he'd have lost everything that made life worthwhile. He dreaded losing her and her "adorable person."

On April 3, 1796, Napoleon wrote:

You are the one thought of my life. When I am worried by the pressure of affairs, when I am anxious as to the outcome, when men disgust me, when I am ready to curse life, then I put my hand on my heart, for it beats against your portrait. . . . By what magic have you captivated all my faculties, concentrated in yourself all my conscious existence? It constitutes a kind of death, my sweet, since there is no survival for me except in you.

To live through Josephine—that is the story of my life.

But all the purple prose was still not enough to make her fall in love with him. Josephine tended to be an indifferent correspondent, but the strength of Napoleon's passion may have been too overwhelming, even suffocating, despite their geographical distance. And perhaps, because her husband's romantic ardor was one-sided, it was difficult for her to respond in kind, as she could not bring herself to fill a page with floridly embroidered lies.

Receiving no letters from his wife, Napoleon panicked. "No news from my friend . . . *mi dolce amor.* . . . Has she forgotten me already?" Then he entered another stage of paranoia; the desperate wooer who feared she'd returned to the arms of her former lover, Barras. Napoleon sent her "a thousand kisses on your eyes, your lips, your cunt" and told Josephine "the flame that comes from your lips consumes me."

And still no letters from her. Napoleon's next reaction was rage: "Obviously your pretended love for me was but a caprice."

Finally, full of repentance for being such a boor, he wrote, "Drowning in my sorrow I may have written too harshly."

"My emotions are never moderate," he told his wife. Missing Josephine dreadfully, in June he dispatched a handsome cavalry officer, Joachim Murat, to escort her to Italy.

Napoleon always wore the miniature of Josephine about his neck. The day Murat arrived in Paris, the glass that protected the tiny portrait shattered. Napoleon blanched, announcing that the omen was an indication that Josephine was either dead or was being unfaithful. He was, in fact, frighteningly prescient.

Josephine told Murat she was pregnant and therefore unable to travel. But that excuse merely delighted her husband, who longed to see her "little tummy," which he was certain lent her "a wonderfully majestic appearance."

However, there was no pregnancy. Or, if there was, Josephine lost the baby before she might have begun to "show." In any event, she and Napoleon had only spent two nights together before he'd left for Italy; conception was possible, but not likely. She could have become pregnant as a result of their premarital sex, but if that were the case, her condition would certainly have been obvious by this time. Josephine's subsequent claim that she was too ill to leave Paris wasn't considered satisfactory, either. When Napoleon threatened to desert his post and return to her arms, France's Directory government insisted that Josephine pack her bags for Milan forth-with. Accompanying her was a blue-eyed, black-curled, diminutive and vivacious army captain nine years her junior named Hippolyte Charles. They had been lovers for months.

Josephine was madly in love with Hippolyte and their corre-spondence reflects their mutual ecstasy. Yet they managed to be extremely discreet during the journey from Paris to Milan, and upon their arrival, Napoleon was deliriously happy to see his wife, gushing, "What nights! My happiness is being near you, *ma bonne amie*. . . . Surely, you must have some faults in your character. Tell me."

If he only knew.

Napoleon's effusive passion for his wife embarrassed her. Alter-nately cruel and crude, he would pinch her so hard she would cry, or fondle her breasts in public. Josephine remained in Italy for eighteen months while Napoleon conducted his military campaigns. In the wake of his decisive victories against the Austrians that win-ter, his correspondence expressed his eagerness to show her the proof of his "ardent love"; to be in bed with her and once again see her face, her hair bound into a headscarf à la Creole, and her "little black forest."

"I kiss it a thousand times and wait impatiently for the time when I will be in it. To live within Josephine is to live in the Elysian Fields."

But Josephine remained overwhelmed by her husband's peculiar brand of ardor. "My husband does not merely love me. He abso-lutely worships me. I think he will go mad," she told her friend and society hostess Thérèse Tallien in 1796.

Not only was Josephine still romantically involved with Hip-polyte Charles when Napoleon returned to Paris (and her ostensi-bly waiting arms) on December 5, 1797, but she was actively engaged in business dealings with her lover through the Bodin com-pany, using her influence to obtain contracts for Bodin to supply the army of Italy—her husband's troops. Both Josephine and Hippolyte may have profited from this *Directoire*-era Halliburton by skimming commissions off the top.

Hippolyte Charles was the one bright spot in Josephine's life. In 1798 she wrote to him that "if [Napoleon] wanted a divorce, he only had to ask me . . . I hate all of them [the Bonaparte brood]. You alone have my loving tenderness. . . ." Her husband's quixotic moods, his focus on military affairs, the pressures of public life now that Napoleon was a war hero, and continual derision from her in-laws conspired to make her life hell.

Meanwhile, Napoleon had his eye on the ultimate prize—the government of France—but his old friend Barras was none too keen on helping him take center stage. So Napoleon focused his sights on conquering Egypt. As a military man, his star was still on the rise, and it was a badge of honor that he continued to have the English running scared. Josephine, beginning to realize what a great man she had wed, asked to accompany her husband, but Napoleon thought it best that she remain in France. Even so, on the voyage to Egypt, he spoke of her incessantly. According to his secretary, Louis-Antoine de Bourrienne, "his fondness for her was close to idolatry."

But the idol was about to be shattered.

On July 19, 1798, as Napoleon and General Junot strolled beside an Egyptian oasis, the general told his commanding officer about Josephine's affair with Hippolyte Charles. Napoleon turned deathly pale and immediately exclaimed that he would demand a very public divorce. "I can't bear to be the laughing stock of Paris . . . I love that woman so much I would give anything to have what Junot has told me pronounced untrue."

"I have nothing to live for. At twenty-nine I have exhausted everything," he wrote when his older brother Joseph confirmed the worst. "My emotions are spent, withered, nothing remains but for me to become a complete egoist," he added.

So he exacted his revenge by taking lovers. Zenab, the sixteen-year-old daughter of an Egyptian sheikh, paid a high price for

Napoleon's lust. Following her stint as his unwilling bedfellow, as the French army was departing she was beheaded by religious zealots—the punishment for all native girls who had consorted with foreigners.

Napoleon flaunted his next mistress, Pauline Fouères, the twenty-year-old blond wife of one of his cavalry lieutenants, dispatching the cuckolded husband on a fool's errand in order to maximize his time with Pauline. Napoleon intimated that he would marry her after he divorced Josephine for her infidelity, but the "stupid little slut" wasn't conceiving. "Heavens! It isn't *my* fault!" Pauline defensively exclaimed—one of many intimations made over the years about Napoleon's lack of virility.

By the time he returned to France from the Mediterranean, Josephine's affair with Hippolyte Charles was common knowledge. Nonetheless, she was depressed and missed her husband. She had taken Napoleon's suggestion to find them a quiet country estate, purchasing the Château de Malmaison some ten miles from Paris, lavishly furnishing and redecorating it, although she was already up to her eyebrows in debt.

Counterrevolution was in the air and Napoleon was the man of the moment. He was still in Egypt when prominent government officials began courting Josephine, hoping she would urge her husband to step into the breach. But the first fire to be put out was the marital conflagration.

Upon returning to their Parisian residence in the rue de la Victoire only to discover that his wife was not at home, Napoleon threw her garments and possessions out of the armoires and cupboards and ordered a servant to dispose of them, shouting, "I will never forgive her!"

Josephine was absent because she had wanted to speak with her husband about Hippolyte Charles before anyone else further poisoned the waters. She had tried to intercept his entourage in Lyons but arrived too late. But once she was back in Paris, Napoleon refused to see her. Josephine bombarded his locked door with tearful entreaties, assuring him that she would explain everything. After what his secretary Bourrienne characterized as "three days of marital pouting," Napoleon unbarred the door. The spat continued in his dressing room and Napoleon swore he would never live with his wife again.

But the following morning, when Napoleon's brother Lucien showed up to provide further dirt on Josephine's infidelity, he found the couple cozily in bed.

Napoleon had always been the ardent pursuer and Josephine the indifferent prey. But this quarrel marked a turning point in the relationship. Now it was Josephine's turn to play the wooer. This ugly patch made her realize how much she relied upon—and loved—her husband. Hippolyte Charles was given his *congé*; but their affair had cost Josephine Napoleon's trust. And Napoleon would make her pay dearly for it throughout the rest of their marriage, flaunting his own infidelities while she remained totally faithful, endeavoring to be the perfect wife in every way.

Josephine's skills as a society hostess were indispensable to the rising politician. They were learning how to be partners as she ultimately accepted the hand he'd dealt her. "Bonaparte makes your daughter very happy," Josephine wrote to her mother in Martinique. Now, their only quarrels were about her debts.

On November 10, 1779, Napoleon marched into the Council of Five Hundred, republican France's legislative body, and declared that it was time for change. Although he was shouted down as a military dictator, that week the government reconstituted itself as a tri-person Consulate with Napoleon as one of the three Consuls. Before long he was First Consul and the most powerful government official in France.

As the First Consul's wife Josephine was expected to set the tone for all Frenchwomen, presenting an elegant, refined demeanor. Gone were her flesh-baring diaphanous neoclassic gowns and body stockings, replaced with the high-waisted puff-sleeved frocks that became the fashionable silhouette.

She became invaluable to her husband's "fusion" policy of integrating "a large and important segment of society" (the surviving nobility of the *ancien régime*, with whom she had hobnobbed in her early days in Paris) into the new postrevolutionary culture. Compared to the upstart Bonaparte family, the former vicomtesse de Beauharnais, with her elegant bearing and charming behavior that always put everyone at ease, was a genuine aristocrat.

Napoleon and Josephine moved into the Luxembourg Palace, where he spent long hours drawing up a new constitution. Although they spent just ten days there before moving into the Tuileries, Josephine was never comfortable residing in the same apartments that had housed Marie Antoinette less than a decade earlier. "I was not made for such grandeur . . . I can feel the Queen's ghost asking what I am doing in her bed," Josephine remarked to her daughter, Hortense.

Napoleon, who had no problem adjusting from ratty revolutionary to aspiring emperor, endeavored to cheer his overwhelmed wife. "Come, little Creole, get into the bed of your masters," he coaxed as he romantically carried her over the threshold on their first night at the Luxembourg.

Napoleon considered Josephine his good-luck charm and believed that a sort of "magnetic fluid" flowed between them. And he complained of missing his "sweet little one" while he was defeating the Austrians at Marengo; yet when he triumphantly returned to Paris he took up with a series of mistresses. Josephine was forced to swallow her pride. Her husband adored her, but he wanted an heir. She had thus far failed to conceive with him and her visits to the healing spa waters at Plombières in the hopes of becoming fertile were proving fruitless.

Napoleon's numerous sexual conquests humiliated her. The room adjacent to his office was set aside for trysts, during which he would divest himself of little more than his sword, insisting that "the matter was all dealt with in three minutes."

"Love is not for me," he dismissively claimed. "I am not as other men."

Yet all over France it was whispered that Napoleon was occasionally impotent. At some dinner tables an acceptable topic of discussion was the exceptionally modest amount of the First Consul's ejaculated semen and the size of his penis, disproportionate even to his diminutive stature. Even Josephine was known to jest *"Bon-a-parte, c'est bon à rien"*—Bonaparte is good for nothing.

However, her biggest fear was that her husband would eventually fall in love with one of his paramours, or impregnate the woman (or both) and then demand a divorce. In 1803 Josephine turned forty and was desperate to turn back the clock, dyeing her hair and beautifying her skin with white lead makeup, rouge, and facial masques of raw meat. Josephine was expected to (and did) put up with his "rutting season," as her husband called it, and was anxious to remain his number one in every way. In reply to an affectionate letter Napoleon penned from the Channel coast, Josephine wrote, ". . . I want to be always in your eyes as you would want me to be. . . . All I want is to be your sweet and tender Josephine devoted only to your happiness . . . that is my wish, to please you and to love you—no, to adore you."

But being adoring—and acquiescent—didn't mean Josephine wasn't jealous of her rivals. And Napoleon expected her to understand and accept his infidelity. "It is your place to submit to all my fancies. You ought to think it perfectly natural that I should allow myself amusements of this kind . . . I am a person apart. I will not be dictated to by anyone."

"With every new mistress he would become hard and pitiless toward his wife," wrote Claire de Remusat, one of Josephine's ladies. "He did not hesitate to tell her about the affair, nor to go into details about the perfections and imperfections of her body . . . nor to show an almost ferocious astonishment that she should disapprove of it."

Napoleon made it quite clear to Josephine what her role as his wife required: "I want you to resign yourself to serving my political advantage."

On August 15, 1802, Napoleon was made Consul for Life. He and Josephine moved from Malmaison to the much more formal palace at Saint-Cloud, where Napoleon took to dressing in a red velvet coat embroidered in gold and spent lavishly on home furnishings and décor. Self-conscious about his stature, he walked about on tiptoe, consciously mimicking the swaying gait of Louis XVI and referring to the executed king as his uncle. Gone were the days of the smelly, unkempt revolutionary. Napoleon had become exceptionally fastidious about his personal hygiene, spending hours at a time in terribly hot baths. He'd go through sixty bottles of cologne in a month, and would brush his teeth twice in a row with two different products, followed by the use of a tongue scraper. His scraggly locks were a thing of the past as well. Now, once a week he'd have Josephine's coiffeur cut his hair very short.

He drew up a hefty list of protocol that invoked, or at least mirrored, that of any European court, gradually becoming the very thing—and to the nth power—that had been torn apart and toppled just a decade earlier. At Saint-Cloud not much was different from the Bourbon court except the names and faces, and even some of those, who by some miracle had escaped the guillotine, were comfortably welcome there.

But Napoleon's ascent was far from over. On May 28, 1804, the Senate bestowed upon him the oxymoronic title of "Emperor of the French Republic." Napoleon then granted titles to his brothers and sisters, who were dispatched to reign over some of his conquered territories. Coronation Day, December 2, 1804, was months in the planning. Pope Pius VII was tapped to officiate, but when he learned that Napoleon and Josephine's wedding had only been a civil ceremony and therefore they were not married in the eyes of the Church, he explained that he could not anoint them with holy oil at the coronation. After a private conversation with the pontiff, Josephine was able to convince Napoleon to undergo a religious wedding ceremony if he wanted the Pope's participation at the coronation. So they were hastily married by one of Napoleon's relatives, Cardinal Joseph Fesch. The sacrament cemented Josephine's position as Napoleon's wife; it would now be much harder to divorce her.

Royalists scorned the outsized spectacle of Napoleon's coronation, which was reputed to have cost eight million francs. The emperor was so bedecked with jewels that someone said he resembled "a walking looking-glass." The comtesse de Boigne thought his ceremonial robes—a purple velvet mantle lined in ermine and embroidered with bees, his adopted symbol—looked "terrible on the short, fat Napoleon," who "resembled the King of Diamonds." His pale skin looked even sallower under his coronet of gilded laurel leaves. Josephine's coronation dress and train were of white satin lavishly embroidered with gold and silver. Atop her fashionable updo of curls was a pearl and diamond tiara.

Claire de Rémusat wrote that "the manner of his crowning Josephine was most remarkable. After picking up his smaller crown, he first put it on his own head and then transferred it to hers. . . . His manner was almost playful. He took great pains to arrange this little crown, which was set over Josephine's diadem. He put it on, then took it off, and finally put it on again.

"Tears, which she could not repress, fell upon her clasped hands. Both appeared to enjoy one of those fleeting moments of shared felicity which are unique in a lifetime."

That night the new emperor and empress enjoyed a romantic dinner à deux. Napoleon insisted that his wife wear her crown. "You look so pretty with it," he assured her, adding that "no one could wear a crown with more grace."

By 1805, Napoleon had decided to make himself King of Italy and needed Josephine beside him because "I win battles. Josephine wins hearts." His infidelities continued apace, but there were "no more jealous scenes now," according to Josephine's son, Eugène de Beauharnais. Yet privately, she candidly admitted to Claire de Rémusat that her husband "has no moral principle, he hides his lascivious leanings . . . but if one left him alone to pursue them . . . bit by bit he would give himself up to the most shameful passions. Has he not seduced his own sisters?" Josephine genuinely gave credence to the rumors that Napoleon had slept with his equally nymphomanical sister Pauline, because, as emperor, he considered himself licensed to satisfy "every fantasy." But to preserve domestic tranquility, she refused to let her husband see her bitterness. And now that Josephine was empress, Napoleon had no quarrel with her extravagant expenses. It was imperative that she always look the part. Proud of her forty-something face and figure, he encouraged her to revisit the scanty styles of the *Directoire* with their plunging décolletée. She was still beautiful, but also still barren. And when Josephine defensively reminded her husband that she'd already brought two children into the world, Napoleon countered that she'd given birth many years earlier and that her doctor had informed him that her "menses had stopped."

Nonetheless eager as ever to remain by her husband's side, in September 1806 Josephine accompanied him partway on his journey to the Rhineland, where he planned to attack the Prussians. He penned loving letters, expressing his distress at hearing she was so often in tears, and assuring her that she had "spoiled me for the others" by being so "gentle, sweet-natured, and captivating."

On January 7, 1807, Napoleon wrote to discourage Josephine from joining him in Poland, disingenuously, and rather cruelly, insisting, "I don't know what you mean by ladies I am supposed to be involved with. I love only my dear little Josephine who is so good, though sulky and capricious and loveable except when she is jealous and becomes a little devil. . . . As for these ladies, if I needed to occupy my time with one of them I assure you I would want her to have pretty rosebud nipples. Is this so with the ladies you write to me about?"

Josephine's worst fears, rosebud nipples or not, were perfectly well founded. On New Year's Eve, Napoleon had become instantly smitten by a lovely blond twenty-year-old named Marie Walewska. He demanded that in the interests of diplomacy, her husband, the seventy-year-old Count Anaste de Walewice Walewski, release her to him. Marie was naturally reluctant to participate in this proposed exchange; but her acquiescence was the beginning of a lasting affair, and Marie Walewska bears the rare distinction of being the only one of Napoleon's mistresses with whom he was genuinely in love.

Marie's existence in the emperor's life—and bed—also brought Josephine's status to the forefront. In the fall of 1807, Napoleon concluded that his spouse was bringing him down, that he'd married beneath him. Not only couldn't she conceive, but she had not come from grand enough stock and his imperial status demanded that he acquire a wife from one of the noblest houses in Europe. High on his list of replacements was Anna Pavlovna, the sister of the Russian tsar.

Aware that he was seriously contemplating divorce, Josephine continued to behave like a model wife. Nothing she would do or say would invite comment or censure. "I have no pleasures," she lamented. "People are amazed that I can endure such an existence . . . I can't go out anymore." And yet Napoleon remained ambivalent about divorcing his wife, aware of Josephine's contribution to his success. "If I had been thrown into prison instead of ascending a throne, she would have shared my misfortune. It is right that she should share my grandeur," he told his secretary, Monsieur Roederer. The emperor was also aware that public opinion was against a divorce. "She is a link between me and the people. And she reconciles a part of Parisian society to me which would abandon me if I abandoned her," he explained to Joseph Fouché, his sinister Minister of Police.

When Marie Walewska became pregnant, divorce from Josephine became an even stronger probability; it was proof that the potency problem lay not with the emperor, but with his wife. Napoleon was doubly convinced of his prowess when another mistress, Eléanore Denuelle, also conceived—although Eléanore was concurrently sleeping with one of Napoleon's brothers-in-law, Joachim Murat.

Josephine was well aware that divorce hung over her head like the sword of Damocles, although her husband had yet to specifically demand it. The fact that Napoleon could not bear to discuss the subject frankly with her became her only hope that he would never go through with it. Each of them became physically ill whenever the topic was discussed. She had taken to anxiously inquiring of everyone who saw Napoleon regularly whether he had said anything about it to them. The uncertainty was killing her. Napoleon had asked her children to break the news to her but they pointedly refused. Hortense wrote, "Witness to my mother's constant tears and to the indignities that provoked them, both my heart and my pride rebelled. I found myself wishing that the divorce had been pronounced."

Finally, Fouché informed Josephine that for the sake of "the cohesion of the dynasty," Napoleon required legitimate heirs. By the summer of 1808, Napoleon's empire stretched from the Tagus River on the Iberian Peninsula to the Russian steppes, and from Hamburg and the North Sea to the boot of Italy.

On November 30, 1809, the emperor summoned Josephine to Fontainebleau for a discussion. She found his demeanor chilly. The door that connected their rooms had been permanently locked. Her in-laws pointedly snubbed her. Sensing what was about to happen, Josephine quietly told Napoleon, "You are the master and you shall decide my fate." If he asked her to leave, she hoped he would make the request with dignity. "I am your wife; I have been crowned by you in the presence of the Pope. Such honors demand that they should not be voluntarily renounced. If you divorce me, all France will know that it is you who are driving me out."

That evening, when Josephine tried to pour his coffee, Napoleon turned away and accepted it from a page instead. She swallowed her pride and asked her husband, "Why do you want to leave me? Are we not happy?"

"Happy? Happy? Why the lowest clerk of one of my ministers is happier than I," Napoleon exclaimed. "Are you mocking me?" Pacing and fuming he told Josephine that he might have been happy had not her suspicious jealousy and anger over the years destroyed his peace of mind. And in any event, the interests of France demanded that he choose a fertile womb over marital contentment. He even had the temerity to add that he was more in pain than she because it was his hand that was hurting her.

"No, I can never survive it!" Josephine cried. She shoved her fist in front of her mouth to stifle her tears and followed her husband out of the room. When the servants heard anguished shouts from the adjoining chamber, they burst into the room and found the empress lying on the rug. Above her stood Napoleon, his eyes brimming with tears. "The interest of France has done violence to my heart!" he exclaimed. "I pity her with all my soul," he later added. "I thought she had more character, and I was not prepared for the outburst of her grief."

What had he expected instead?

Hours later, in response to Josephine's devastation, Napoleon told Hortense—his sister-in-law (by virtue of her arranged marriage to Napoleon's brother Louis, King of Holland) as well as Josephine's daughter—"Nothing will make me go back on the divorce. Neither tears nor entreaties."

Although Hortense recognized his right as "the master" to require an heir, she defended her mother's tears. "It would be remarkable if, after a marriage that has lasted for thirteen years, she did not shed them." But Hortense diplomatically added, "She will submit to your will, and we will all go away, taking the memory of your kindness with us." The notion of Josephine's children leaving his court as well nearly cost Napoleon his resolve. But despite all the emperor had done for them, Hortense and Eugène would never consider remaining at Saint-Cloud after he had cast out their mother.

Napoleon was at least magnanimous to Josephine in the divorce settlement. She was able to keep Malmaison, and would have the Elysée Palace as her Parisian residence. He would settle all her debts, plus she would receive an annual allowance of three million francs. Josephine would also get to keep all of her jewels—and most important, she would retain the title of Empress—and would be known as "Empress Dowager" after he remarried. In addition, she would assume an additional title, Duchess of Navarre. In return, the emperor expected her to retreat into the shadows.

On January 10, 1810, Napoleon and Josephine were divorced in a ceremony held in the candlelit throne room presided over by the

Arch-Chancellor and the Secretary of State to the Imperial Household. Nearly the entire court was assembled, attired in formal court dress. The spouses' text was scripted, although Napoleon, speaking first, reiterated that he had only come to this pass because he required an heir and that it had caused him great anguish to sacrifice the woman he loved for the sake of an imperial successor. "Far from ever finding cause for complaint, I can to the contrary only congratulate myself on the tenderness and devotion of my beloved wife." Tears rolled down his cheeks as he added, "the memory of the thirteen years in which she has adorned my life will be treasured by me forever. . . . God alone knows what this resolve has cost my heart. I have found the courage to go through with it only in the conviction that it will serve the best interests of France."

Under the hostile glare of *la famille* Bonaparte, with as much equanimity as she could manage, Josephine read from her script, her fingers trembling so much she could hardly hold the paper. "With the permission of our august and dear husband, I must declare that, having no hope of bearing his children who would fulfill the needs of his policies and the interests of France, I proudly offer him the greatest proof of attachment and devotion ever offered on this earth." She grew so overcome with emotion that she had to hand her speech to an attendant, who read the rest of it.

When the ceremony was over and all the documents had been duly executed, Napoleon kissed Josephine and accompanied her to her apartments. Later that day, she visited his rooms, her hair "disordered and her face contorted," according to Napoleon's valet Louis Constant. The imperial couple began to weep. "Be brave," the emperor counseled his now ex-wife, "I will always be your friend."

The following day Josephine and her household moved into Malmaison. Napoleon visited her there that afternoon, and they were spotted walking hand in hand. It was clearly painful for each of them to let go of what they had shared for so many years. Josephine had been the emperor's rock, confidante, companion, and grand passion. She had grown in the relationship from tepid indifference to utter devotion.

Constant was surprised at Josephine's "care for the man who abandoned her," as she always expressed the greatest concern for the emperor's welfare and safety, particularly before he embarked on his (disastrous) Russian campaign in 1812. "It was as though she was still his most beloved wife," the valet remarked.

Napoleon had wasted no time in remarrying, espousing the nubile Marie Louise of Austria on April 1, 1810, barely two months after he divorced Josephine. And he no doubt felt vindicated in his decision to ditch his first wife after Marie Louise bore him a son, Napoleon François Joseph Charles, almost a year to the day from their wedding.

Josephine had always suffered agonizing migraines. In 1813, after she read about Napoleon's defeat at Leipzig, the pain was compounded by premonitions of foreboding. Endeavoring to console her former husband, she wrote, "Sire, although I can no longer share in your joys, your grief will always be mine, too. I cannot resist the need to tell you that I love you with all my heart."

In 1814 Josephine left Paris for the Château de Navarre just before the allies occupied the city and Joseph Bonaparte surrendered it. Napoleon agreed to abdicate in favor of his young son, but that would have entailed a regency and the proposal was rejected. So on April 11 the emperor resigned without precondition, and at the suggestion of the Russian tsar Alexander, he was named sovereign of the tiny Mediterranean island of Elba. There he was allowed a modest court and all the perquisites of royalty, including a small standing army and cavalry. He was also joined on the island by his mother and his sister Pauline, the only one of his numerous siblings to voluntarily share his exile. "If it were not for his wife I would go lock myself up with him," exclaimed Josephine on hearing the news.

On the advice of Tsar Alexander, Josephine and Hortense returned to Malmaison in the spring of 1814. There, as the bridge between the former imperial court and the new regime, Josephine entertained various foreign rulers and dignitaries with her usual charm and elegance, never hesitating to inform them that if she had still been Napoleon's wife she would have been proud to accompany him to Elba. She maintained his rooms at Malmaison, shrine-like, just as he had left them.

By this time, Josephine was fifty years old. Her skin had become discolored and her usually dulcet voice was raspy and hoarse. She had caught a cold in mid-May after going riding in one of her flimsy white muslin frocks and the chill had metamorphosed into a fever. Her symptoms were those of diphtheria. Yet she refused to remain in bed, hosting a dinner and dance in the tsar's honor on the evening of May 24. Over the next couple of days her condition worsened. On May 27 she became delirious, murmuring snatches of a one-sided conversation: "Bonaparte"—which was how she always addressed him—"Elba . . . the king of Rome" [the title he'd given his son by Marie Louise of Austria].

Josephine's children were beside her gilded swan-shaped bed when she died on the morning of May 29, "as gently and sweetly as she lived," according to her son, Eugène. Mourning etiquette prevented her children from attending their mother's funeral, a quiet ceremony held in the church at Rueil, where they later erected a sculpture of her.

According to Louis Marchand, Napoleon's valet on Elba, when his master received the news of Josephine's death he locked himself in his study for three days. "Why did they let my poor Josephine die?" he lamented to his physician, Dr. Corvisart.

"Sire, I believe she died of a broken heart," the doctor replied.

Actually, Josephine's autopsy revealed that she had died of pneumonia, extreme inflammation of the trachea, and a "gangrenous angina," so in some respect Corvisart was correct.

Napoleon looked at his doctor. "That *bonne* Josephine," he said, adding, "she really loved me, didn't she?"

The deposed emperor penned a cathartic note to his late ex-wife, telling Josephine, "I have never passed a night without clasping you in my arms. . . . No woman was ever loved with more devotion, passion, and tenderness." His years of ill treatment of her had evidently evanesced, replaced with rosier memories and a bit of revisionist history.

Napoleon spoke often of Josephine to his valet Marchand, who distilled those remarks into a description that forms a perfect eulogy: "She had the elegance of a Creole together with infinite grace and charm, and an evenness of temper that never failed. All her clothes were elegant and once worn by her immediately set the fashion. . . . He conceded that she was extravagant and that on several occasions he had to settle her debts, but these debts were frequently incurred through her generosity in giving presents and she exceeded everyone else by the grace of her manner as she gave them. . . . With her kind nature and sensitivity she would pity other people's misfortunes and weep with those who came to tell her of their troubles, which, the Emperor said, often made her the prey of those who took advantage of her generosity."

During his second exile on St. Helena, Napoleon often spoke of Josephine to General Henri-Gratien Bertrand, the manager of his household, although he had a crude way of describing the attraction. "I really loved Josephine, but I had no respect for her. She had the prettiest little cunt in the world. . . . Actually, I married her only because I believed her to be rich. She said she was, but it wasn't true. She was a liar and an utter spendthrift, but she had a certain something that was irresistible. She was a woman to her very fingertips."

NAPOLEON BONAPARTE

❦ *and* ❧

MARIE LOUISE OF AUSTRIA
1791–1847

married 1810–1821

"Never would I believe I could be so happy. My love for
my husband grows all the time and when I can remember
his tenderness I can scarcely prevent myself from crying.
Even had I not loved him previously, nothing can stop me
from loving him now."
—Marie Louise, Empress of France, in 1811

MARIA LUDOVICA LEOPOLDINA FRANCISCA THERESA
Josepha Lucia of Austria, better known as Marie Louise, never felt
comfortable in France, the country that—in the not-too-distant
past—had brutally executed her great-aunt, Marie Antoinette.

But in 1809 Klemens Wenzel von Metternich, Austria's Foreign
Minister and Minister of State, had decided it was better for his
country to sleep with the enemy than to be invaded by it. Metternich
urged Marie Louise's father, Holy Roman Emperor Francis II, and
Emperor of Austria (as Francis I) to sacrifice his eldest daughter to
Napoleon Bonaparte.

Empress Josephine of France had proved unable to conceive and the heirless Napoleon was impatient to divorce her and remarry. His only qualification for a replacement was that she be "a walking womb." His first choice had been Anna Pavlovna, the sister of the Russian tsar, but by the end of the first week of February 1810, when the Russians had still not agreed to the match (rumors of Napoleon's impotence had persuaded Anna's mother that the potential bridegroom was a risky bet), Napoleon moved on, focusing instead on his fallback uterus, Her Serene Highness Marie Louise of Austria.

According to Napoleon's sister Caroline, who would have done anything to see the door of the Palace of Saint-Cloud hit Josephine's derrière on her way out, Marie Louise was quite attractive, with a good figure, "charming blonde hair, hands, and feet, a cultivated mind and dignified bearing; all in all she was very amiable and sweet . . . of course she is very young."

Since Napoleon had always regarded women as "mere machines for making children," the young archduchess seemed like a perfect fit. It wouldn't much matter that she was taller than he, with an ungainly walk; that she was a bit plump, and had inherited the Hapsburg/Bourbon bulging eyes and pouty lower lip in addition to a slightly hooked nose; and that she was *so* innocent that her parents had ensured that all of her childhood pets were female in order to protect her from learning about sex.

There was only one hitch to be overcome: given her great-aunt's unfortunate history in France, Marie Louise was rather disinclined to meet their emperor, much less wed him. With pitch-perfect teenage hyperbole, she wrote, "To see this creature would be a worse torture for me than all the martyrdoms."

In January 1810, when she read a newspaper account of Napoleon's divorce from Empress Josephine, she wrote to Victoria de Poutet, the daughter of her governess, "I pity the unfortunate woman on whom his choice falls; that will certainly put an end to her fine days." She had continued to look for news in the Frankfurt gazette that Napoleon had selected his new bride, but finding nothing, feared that *she* might be the chosen one. Although she steeled herself to do her duty if necessary, she also insisted that "Papa is much too kind to force me."

Francis *had* told the matchmaking Metternich that he would not compel his daughter to wed the Emperor of France. But politics and the safety of nations almost always trump a girl's romantic preferences and this occasion was no different. With her marriage to Napoleon all but a done deal, the eighteen-year-old archduchess endeavored to conceal her disappointment from her father. Instead, she focused on the positives that might come of the match—her ability to visit the incomparable Paris museums, the possibility that her fiancé was musical (he wasn't), and whether he might permit her to have a botanical garden.

However, before giving his final consent to the match Emperor Francis remained concerned about the legal issues surrounding Napoleon's first marriage and divorce. Napoleon's Deed of Separation from Josephine, dated January 14, 1810, was a civil bill of divorcement and carried no ecclesiastical authority. Did that mean that Marie Louise's marriage to him would be bigamous? So Napoleon had his relation, Cardinal Fesch, fix things up. After three weeks of deliberation the cardinal declared their marriage invalid, claiming there had been no legitimate witnesses to the religious ceremony he had performed himself shortly before Napoleon's imperial coronation.

When it came down to the actual proposal, Napoleon got off to a rather tasteless start. His hand-picked emissary, dispatched to the Austrian embassy in Paris with his bid for Marie Louise's hand, was Eugène de Beauharnais—Josephine's son.

But on February 23, 1810, Napoleon used his extraordinary epistolary gifts to pen his first letter to Marie Louise. It contained a proposal so full of tender respect that she could not possibly continue to view him as Boney the bogeyman:

> The brilliant qualities which make you an outstanding person have inspired us to serve and honor you. While addressing ourselves to the Emperor, your father, and begging him to

entrust us with the happiness of Your Imperial Highness, may we hope that Y.I.H. will share the sentiments that prompt us to make this step? May we flatter ourselves that Y.I.H. will not be driven solely by the duty of parental obedience? Should Y.I.H. have even the least amicable feelings for us, we wish to cherish them; and we set ourselves the constant task of pleasing you in every way so that we presume that one day we shall succeed in winning Y.I.H.'s affection . . .

Marie Louise's mother, Maria Theresa of the Two Sicilies, had died in 1807. So it fell to Napoleon himself to behave like an anxious mother of the bride and micromanage the wedding plans. As if he didn't have enough to do trying to take over the world, he commissioned his fiancée's trousseau of sixty-four dresses, dozens of changes of lingerie, shawls, dressing gowns, and copious quantities of jewelry. The Emperor of France even took care of ordering his future wife's pincushions.

On the evening of March 11, 1810, just weeks after Napoleon had formally divorced Josephine, Marie Louise was married to him by proxy at the Hofburg Palace in Vienna. Her uncle, Archduke Karl, stood in for the groom. The following day, she set out for France via the same handover route that Marie Antoinette had traveled exactly forty years earlier, preparing to meet her bridegroom in the medieval forest of Compiègne.

Having received mixed reviews of Marie Louise's looks, Napoleon decided that "So long as she is kind and gives me healthy sons, I will love her as if she were the most beautiful girl in the world." Anxious that *he* might not live up to the mark, he had asked Josephine's daughter, Hortense—Queen of Holland by virtue of her marriage to his younger brother Louis—to teach him to waltz. Unfortunately, he was hopeless and resigned himself to the fact that he was "not intended to excel as a dancer."

Napoleon was so eager for that first glimpse of Marie Louise that he halted her cavalcade of coaches, threw open the door to her carriage, and immediately embraced her.

"Your portrait does not flatter you," she happily declared, instantly winning his affection.

Napoleon then quizzed Marie Louise on how she had been instructed to behave toward him.

"To obey you in every way," was her succinct reply.

The pair continued to ride in their separate carriages to the castle at Compiègne. After perfunctorily presenting her to his family, the forty-year-old emperor led his teenage bride to their bedchamber, ignoring the preplanned events for the evening, as well as his current mistress, Mme. De Mathis, who was also installed in one of the castle's rooms. Hortense described Marie Louise's demeanor as ". . . gentle and sweet, though a trifle embarrassed."

Because of the proxy marriage in Vienna, Napoleon and Marie Louise were technically already wed. Therefore, the emperor saw no need to wait for the formal ceremony to bind them before getting down to the business of begetting an heir. His valet, Louis Constant, recalled "a long conversation" between the bridal couple, after which Napoleon returned to his own room. There he donned his dressing gown, liberally doused himself with cologne, and sneaked back into his wife's boudoir.

The shocked courtiers were heard to murmur to each other, "*Ils sont couchés*"—They are in bed!

Marie Louise, carefully coached by her father to obey her husband in all things, accepted her destiny with alacrity. Napoleon recalled that after he'd taken her virginity, his nubile wife asked him to "do it again."

The following morning, still basking in the afterglow of satiation, Napoleon told his secretary, Méneval, "Marry a German. They are the best women in the world, obliging, innocent, and fresh as roses." Two days after he met Marie Louise, Napoleon wrote to Emperor Francis to inform him that she had fulfilled all his expectations. "I have not failed to give her and receive from her proofs of the tender sentiments which bind us together. We suit each other perfectly."

For her part, Marie Louise described her husband as "attractive and eager," and she soon found herself genuinely falling for him, writing, "There is something very forceful and captivating about [Napoleon], which is impossible to resist."

Soon, the teen was besting him at billiards and sketching his portrait, while Napoleon ordered Josephine's former apartments in the Tuileries to be repainted "virginal white." He even preordered a layette, complete with miniature uniforms and weapons, for the son he was certain Marie Louise would give him.

On April 1, 1810, Marie Louise wed Napoleon in a civil ceremony. At three p.m. the following afternoon the religious ceremony, performed by Napoleon's cousin Cardinal Fesch, took place in a purpose-built chapel in the Louvre.

With a heavy crown atop her upswept hair, the bride, significantly taller than the groom, was clad in a satin dress trimmed in ermine and a diamond-encrusted robe. Napoleon wore a flamboyant Spanish-style white and gold satin ensemble embroidered with golden bees. His black velvet hat was studded with rows of diamonds; among them was an enormous gem that had once been among the Bourbon crown jewels, which clasped a trio of white swan feathers, giving the diminutive autocrat the illusion of additional height.

The four hundred wedding guests included three queens—all married to Napoleon's brothers; one of them was Josephine's daughter Hortense de Beauharnais, whom Napoleon, with his usual lack of tact, had assigned to his new wife's household as Marie Louise's Mistress of the Robes. To ensure that his second nuptials would be a popular event, the emperor had free food distributed throughout Paris.

The wedding reception was hosted by Napoleon's sister Pauline at the Château de Neuilly, which she had turned into a twinkling fairyland. Mimes imitated classical statuary. Craftsmen had manufactured a miniature reproduction of the palace at Schönbrunn in case the new empress was homesick. The delighted groom was spotted cheerfully slapping his bride's derrière and pinching her cheeks. But a second reception, hosted by General Henri Clark, the

Minister of War, was less salubrious, turning to tragedy when the wooden ballroom caught fire. After seeing Marie Louise to safety, Napoleon returned to help direct the firefighters.

Unfortunately, the imperial honeymoon was not the romantic travelogue Marie Louise had anticipated, but a Napoleon-style progress through the low countries. The food was awful; the countryside was dreary; and their sightseeing consisted of tedious inspections of mills and factories. Napoleon was grumpy, mocking his wife every time she mentioned she was hungry, claiming that she ate too much, and in any event, she shouldn't eat in a moving coach. When Marie Louise complained of a headache, Napoleon opened the window of the carriage during a downpour so that her garments became spattered with water. At that moment, the new bride resolved that if she had her life to live over, she would never marry, an oath she didn't keep—twice over.

Upon their return to Paris it was clear that the honeymoon was over in more ways than one. Although he spent his evenings in her company, Napoleon kept Marie Louise as confined as a fairy-tale heroine, making sure her days were filled with reading, needlework, and instruction in music, but otherwise she was isolated from the world. Other men were kept at a safe distance; even tradesmen were forbidden to speak to her.

As Marie Louise began to settle into her new life, the difference between the emperor's two wives emerged, a striking study in contrasts. Where Josephine was headstrong and wildly extravagant, the cautious Marie Louise was judiciously sparing in her purchases. She even refused some of her husband's lavish gifts. Josephine had not been well educated and had learned much of what she knew and did by being an empathetic listener and an astute mimic, but her flirtatiousness and skills as a hostess were legendary. Marie Louise was a gifted musician and exceptionally well read, but was nonetheless shy and reserved, prone to blushing at the slightest display of forwardness, and was extremely uncomfortable when she was expected to mingle with the public or hobnob among courtiers and foreign dignitaries. She was also wildly jealous of Josephine, pitting her own fertile youth against the former's desiccated husk of a body whenever she saw the chance to illustrate the contrast. One day when they were driving past Malmaison, Napoleon asked Marie Louise if she would like to see the château. Marie Louise began to cry and commented to someone in their entourage, "How can he want to see that old lady? A woman of low birth at that." To oblige Marie Louise Napoleon tried to obliterate all traces of his first wife from the Tuileries. Her image was painted out of portraits and her monograms were removed.

As time went on, Napoleon began to pull farther away from Josephine, in whom he had confided even after their divorce, embarrassed at finding himself falling in love with a woman half his age whom he'd all along expected to be no more than a uterus. He was as giddy as a kid at a carnival when Marie Louise became pregnant. Napoleon was particularly fond of Marie Louise's freshness and innocence, a far cry from Josephine's soigné worldliness. To that end, he did everything in his power to prevent the still unspoiled Marie Louise from becoming jaded. It was devilishly attractive to him that she preferred his company to any other diversion. And when she suffered from morning sickness, Napoleon went to great lengths to provide her with all sorts of entertainments that might distract her from fearing a miscarriage.

On the evening of March 19, 1811, Marie Louise went into labor. She fell asleep at around five a.m. on March 20 and the worried *accoucheur* warned Napoleon that he might not be able to save both mother and child. He asked the emperor to choose whose life to spare, should it come down to it. Unhesitatingly, Napoleon replied, "Well, then, save the mother. Think only of the mother."

Out came the forceps. Frightened and weakened by labor pains, Marie Louise stirred and whimpered, "Must I be sacrificed because I'm Empress?" At around eight a.m., her child was born. The infant made no sound for seven minutes, and everyone feared the worst, but finally the baby began to yelp and the cannons commenced to fire. The salute would be only twenty-two guns if Marie Louise had given birth to a girl. On the twenty-third boom, the people of Paris knew that their emperor had an heir.

Napoleon proudly, but rather callously, told Josephine that his son—Napoleon François Joseph Charles—"has my chest, my mouth, and my eyes. I trust he will match up to his destiny." He spoiled the boy rotten, keeping him by his side as often as possible, dandling him on his knee while he worked in his study, and surrounding him with an entourage he considered worthy of such a princeling. Consequently, Marie Louise rarely had the opportunity to bond with her son. She grew anxious whenever she was around him, fearful of dropping him.

Nonetheless, she was quite the blissful wife, writing home, "Never would I believe I could be so happy. My love for my husband grows all the time and when I can remember his tenderness I can scarcely prevent myself from crying. Even had I not loved him previously, nothing can stop me from loving him now."

And after seventeen months of marriage, when Napoleon had to leave her for the first time, journeying to Bologna to inspect his fleet and troops stationed there, she wrote to him, "You cannot imagine my feelings when I pass by your room and see your shutters closed."

The Russian campaign of 1812 marked Napoleon's first devastating losses in years. Ravaged by bitter cold and empty bellies, his men took to eating the corpses of their horses and their own fallen comrades. Abandoning what was left of his troops, Napoleon returned to France, where he hosted numerous galas, despite the dispatch from General Berthier that read, "Sire, your army exists no more."

"I shall always remember one of those dismal balls, at which I felt like I was dancing on graves. I don't feel like dancing any more," Marie Louise confessed to a friend.

She was never crowned empress. Times had become too dire for another lavish coronation. Instead, on March 30, 1813, Marie Louise swore an oath of fidelity to the emperor and to the constitution at a ceremony in the Elysée Palace, during which Napoleon conferred on her the title of Regent. She had not been named regent during any of his other absences from France. In any event, Napoleon had never intended her duties to be much more than ceremonial, believing she possessed "too young" a mind for the ugly and often unpleasant business of state. Instead, the emperor's sixty-year-old Arch-Chancellor Cambacérès handled the actual duties of regent.

Napoleon's empire was in danger. By the Treaty of Chaumont, Prussia, Britain, Russia, and Marie Louise's homeland of Austria had allied their forces to destroy it. But Marie Louise's father hastened to assure her that he bore her husband no personal ill will. The same was true of Napoleon's opinion of Francis. Although Austria had joined the coalition to destroy Napoleon, neither emperor wanted Tsar Alexander to end up holding the best hand and becoming the arbiter for peace.

On January 24, 1814, Napoleon departed Paris in an effort to halt the allied advance. This time when he named his wife to the Regency Council he intended for her to assume a more important role. And she did prove quite competent, providing her husband with detailed reports of government business. In one of her dispatches to him she wrote, "I am growing very brave since your last success . . . I hope I no longer deserve to be called a child—that's what you liked to call me before you went away."

When Napoleon was exiled to Elba in 1814, his twenty-two-year-old wife wished to join him, but her father refused to permit it. Although she was an empress and a mother, Marie Louise remained the pawn of two strong men, enemies on the battlefield, each of whom sought to control her. Rather than allow her to travel to Elba, Emperor Francis insisted that his daughter visit her family in Vienna for a couple of months. From there she could journey to Italy, where she had been created Duchess of Parma according to the terms of the Treaty of Fontainebleau, by which Napoleon abdicated on April 11, 1814.

Marie Louise wrote to her husband, "You know by now that

orders have been given to prevent my joining you, and to use force if necessary. Be on your guard, my darling. We are being duped. I am in the utmost anxiety about you."

On April 13, at Fontainebleau, Napoleon wrote a farewell letter to Marie Louise assuring her that he loved her "more than anything in the world." Then he tried to poison himself with a cocktail of belladonna, hellebore, and opium, but after suffering a fearful stomachache he recovered the following day.

Napoleon sailed for Elba on April 19, 1814, in the aptly named frigate *Undaunted*. After visiting her Austrian relations, in June Marie Louise traveled to Aix-les-Bains for the waters. There she met thirty-nine-year-old Adam Adalbert, Graf von Neipperg. The charming and cultivated Neipperg had been a general in the Austrian army but had also served as his country's ambassador to Stockholm. Having lost his right eye in a saber duel he wore a black cloth tied about his head, which hid the injury and lent him a mysterious air. Personally selected as her equerry by Emperor Francis and Metternich, Neipperg was to see that not only did Marie Louise never reach Elba but that she "forget France and consequently the Emperor."

It didn't take long for him to accomplish his mission, aided and abetted by members of Marie Louise's entourage, who convinced her of Napoleon's numerous extramarital infidelities, assuring her that the imperial marriage itself had been purely political. By September 1814, Marie Louise was Neipperg's lover. She returned to Vienna with him, having abandoned all thoughts of joining her husband on Elba. By then, she declared she would never again set foot in France, "that horrible country, for anything in the world." She even forwarded Napoleon's letters, unopened, to her father, although she asked him to be kind to her husband, writing, "It is the only request I feel I can make and it is the last time I shall concern myself with his fate. I owe him a debt of gratitude for the calm unconcern in which he allowed me to spend my days with him instead of making me unhappy. . . . I hope that we shall have a lasting peace now that the Emperor will no longer be able to disturb it."

Evidently, Napoleon did not blame his wife for her wavering

loyalty. Toward the end of his life he astutely observed, "I believe that Marie Louise is just as much a state prisoner as I am myself . . . I have always had occasion to praise the conduct of my good Louise, and I believe it is totally out of her power to assist me. Moreover she is young and timorous."

On August 28, 1814, Napoleon received a letter from Marie Louise dated April 10, containing a lock of her hair—her gift to him for his forty-fifth birthday and the last he would ever receive from her.

One evening in February 1815, Napoleon made the abrupt decision to return to France. Within twenty-four hours, he had boarded a brig. On March 1, the ironically named *Inconstant* sailed into Antibes and Napoleon's invasion force of approximately one thousand men, forty horses, and two cannon were disembarked. The deposed emperor announced that he had come to attack the King of France—Louis XVIII, the younger brother of Louis XVI—and to conquer his kingdom.

On June 18, Napoleon's army was defeated at Waterloo. By the 1815 Treaty of Paris, Austria took possession of several territories in Northern Italy, making Emperor Francis's empire half again as large as it was in 1812.

Before the decisive battle Napoleon had written to Marie Louise from Belgium asking her once more to meet him there. By then he was ill, suffering from piles. He'd grown rotund and his breathing was labored, causing him to pause on occasion to lick the saliva from his lips. General Thiebault commented that "everything about him seemed twisted, shriveled. The normal pallor of his skin had been replaced by a noticeably greenish tinge."

A fortnight later, Napoleon abdicated. He made plans to dispose of all his wealth and considered moving to America. But on June 27, he found the port at Rochefort blockaded by British warships. In concordance with Britain's allies, the Prince Regent denied his request for asylum in England.

Instead, the Royal Navy's *Northumberland* brought Napoleon to the remote South Atlantic island of St. Helena, a British colonial outpost thousands of miles from any major land mass. He was accompanied by a small entourage, including his chef, Monsieur La Page. Apart from his first few weeks on the island, Napoleon resided at Longwood, a musty and mildewed residence open to the elements and affording no shade from the subtropical sun. Rats swarmed everywhere in packs so thick their bodies often obscured the floorboards, and various species of biting insect tortured the island's inhabitants, who were also subject to violent illnesses, including dysentery, liver infections, and raging fevers.

On St. Helena Napoleon had plenty of time to reflect on his life, writing his memoirs, and taking up horticulture. He confided to General Henri-Gratien Bertrand, the manager of his household, that if Josephine had given him a child, he'd have never divorced her. He'd chosen her out of desire and affection; they'd come up in the world together. He ruefully admitted that marrying Marie Louise was "the greatest mistake of my life," adding, "I should have married a Russian."

By the end of 1819 Napoleon's health was failing. He had headaches and insomnia as well as scabies and dermatitis, and was also plagued by ague, nausea, vomiting, a distended stomach, and the occasional convulsive fit. He had always been derailed by stress-induced petit mals.

After a carriage ride on March 17, 1821, Napoleon suffered continuous vomiting and was certain he was dying of stomach cancer, the same disease that had killed his father. By mid-April, he realized he did not have much longer to live.

In a final version of his will, Napoleon wrote, "My death is premature. I have been assassinated by the English oligarchy and their hired murderer." In this document he also set about making bequests to his family. On his sixteenth birthday his son, "Napoleon II," was to receive his most cherished possessions—the blue cloak he wore at the battle of Marengo, the sword he wielded at Austerlitz, his uniforms and accompanying military trappings. Marie Louise, of whom he had such "tender memories" (despite whatever eleventh hour regrets Napoleon may have harbored about having married her), was to receive a bracelet bound together by his hair, as well as his heart—in a cask preserved by spirits. It was a spirited gesture to give Marie Louise his heart for all eternity, even if it would no longer beat for her, but his British jailers ultimately prevented that final request from coming to fruition.

On April 25 the fifty-one-year-old deposed emperor became violently ill. A Corsican priest administered extreme unction on May 2, despite the protests of Napoleon's valet, who insisted that his master was a freethinker.

At 5:49 p.m. on May 6, 1821, Napoleon Bonaparte died. Purportedly, among his faintly murmured last words was "Josephine." An autopsy revealed a grossly enlarged liver, an ulcerated and perforated stomach, and a large gastric ulcer. Walter Henry, one of the attending doctors, noted that the corpse was hairless with white, delicate skin, and well-defined breasts. "The pubis resembled the Mons Veneris in women," and he had exceptionally small genitalia, "like a boy's." Napoleon had previously boasted of his feminine assets to his physician on St. Helena. "As you can see, doctor, beautiful arms, rounded breasts, soft white skin, not a hair. . . . More than one beautiful lady would glory in a bosom like mine."

The hairlessness of Napoleon's corpse was also consistent with signs of arsenic poisoning. Samples of his hair contained both antimony and arsenic. Of the thirty-one symptoms that present for arsenic poisoning, Napoleon suffered from twenty-eight. Arsenic was widely used at the time to treat many common ailments. It was also an ingredient of rat poison and those vermin were abundant at Longwood. Additionally, arsenic was found in the coloring of the Longwood wallpaper, a popular shade known as Schalers Green, which contains copper arsenite. But the enormous dose of calomel administered shortly before Napoleon's death, plus the accumulation of arsenic in his system, might have combined to produce fatal strychnine poisoning instead.

Five days after his death, Napoleon's body, ensconced in four coffins, was buried in Geranium Valley on St. Helena.

Marie Louise read about her husband's passing on July 18, 1821, in the *Gazzetta Piemontese*. Her matchmaker, Metternich, hadn't even bothered to give her the news. In a letter Marie Louise wrote soon afterward to her childhood friend Victoria de Poutet, she eulogized her royal marriage:

Although I never felt strong sentiments of any kind for him, I cannot forget that he is the father of my son, and far from treating me badly as most people suppose he did, he always showed the deepest regard for me, the only thing one can hope for in a political marriage, so I am very affected, and although I ought to be thankful that his miserable existence is over, I could have wished him many years of a contented life—provided it could have been spent far away from me.

Apart from the late emperor's mother, the one who most mourned Napoleon's passing was the ten-year-old Duke of Reichstadt, Napoleon and Marie Louise's son, known by his Austrian title after 1818. No family member sought to break the news of his father's death; instead, his under-tutor informed him of it, and admitted that he was surprised by his charge's crying jag. Marie Louise was more moved by her son's tears than by her husband's demise; the duke's sorrow had caused her to reconsider her own feelings. "Death wipes out all one's unpleasant memories, as I found on this occasion. I could think only of the good he had done me, of the agony of his death, and of his last unhappy years; and I wept bitter tears for him."

The duke would later write, "If Josephine had been my mother, my father never would have been sent to St. Helena and I would not be languishing here in Vienna."

Soon after Napoleon's death, Marie Louise secretly wed her lover, Adam Adalbert, Graf von Neipperg. She'd already given him two children and was pregnant with their third. The former empress was at the apex of happiness, claiming she deserved it because "God knows all I have suffered in life."

She became an enlightened ruler of Parma, where her subjects referred to her as *la buona duchessa*. But Neipperg died on February 22, 1829, and soon after, disturbances in Parma caused Marie Louise to decamp with her children to Piacenza. Her son by Napoleon, the Duke of Reichstadt, who had been raised in Austria, died of tuberculosis on July 22, 1832, at the age of twenty-one.

On February 17, 1834, Marie Louise wed her third husband, Comte Charles de Bombelles, the majordomo of her court. They were married for thirteen and a half years. Marie Louise died at the age of fifty-six on December 17, 1847, and was buried beside the bodies of her father and the Duke of Reichstadt in the vault of the Kapuzinerkirche in Vienna.

In 1840, Napoleon's body was exhumed and taken to Paris, where it lies entombed beneath the dome of Les Invalides. One hundred years later Adolf Hitler ordered the remains of the emperor's sole legitimate son to be interred alongside his father. The duke's coffin left Vienna for Paris on December 12, 1940, which would have been the hundred and forty-ninth birthday of his mother, Marie Louise.

In a major descent from the sublime to the vengefully macabre, just after his demise Napoleon was emasculated by a Corsican priest surnamed Vignali. Centuries passed and what was allegedly the emperor's organ changed hands, so to speak, until 1977, when John K. Lattimer, professor emeritus and former chairman of urology at the Columbia University College of Physicians and Surgeons, bought it at auction for $3,000. Lattimer passed away in May 2007. Presumably, Napoleon's penis lives on.

QUEEN VICTORIA
1819–1901
RULED ENGLAND: 1837–1901

and

PRINCE ALBERT
OF SAXE-COBURG-GOTHA
1819–1861

married 1840–1861

"When day dawned (for we did not sleep much) and I beheld that beautiful angelic face by my side, it was more than I can express!"
— Queen Victoria's diary entry, February 11, 1840, the morning after her wedding night

*W*HEN SHE WAS SIX DAYS SHY OF HER SEVENTEENTH birthday, on May 18, 1836, Victoria, not yet Queen of England, had the opportunity to meet her two Coburg cousins, Ernest and his younger brother, Albert. Authoritative males were lacking in her young life. Victoria's father, the Duke of Kent, had died of a chill at the age of fifty-two, when she was only a few months old. Her mother, the German-born Princess Victoire of Saxe-Coburg-Saalfeld, deliberately shielded Victoria from her "wicked uncles" so that she could never be tainted with even the slightest whiff of the immorality that was the hallmark of the Hanoverian monarchy. Victoria was to represent a fresh start, the future of England, rather than an extension of its dissolute past.

However, Victoria was always in search of a father figure. When she was growing up, avuncular wisdom was dispensed long-distance by her mother's brother Leopold, King of the Belgians—the former husband of George IV's daughter, the late Princess Charlotte. And it was Leopold who played matchmaker between Albert and Victoria.

Victoria's immediate reaction to her sixteen-year-old cousin was overwhelmingly positive. According to her diary entry, ". . . Albert . . . is extremely handsome; his hair is about the same color as mine; his eyes are large and blue, and he has a beautiful nose and a very sweet mouth with fine teeth; but the charm of his countenance is his expression, which is most delightful; *c'est à la fois* [it's simultaneously] full of goodness and sweetness, and very clever and intelligent."

However, Albert privately nursed some reservations regarding Victoria's suitability as a future spouse. His mother had wed his significantly older father at the age of sixteen, but had run off with a handsome army lieutenant when Albert was just five years old. The incident soured his views on females and sex and undoubtedly helped to form Albert's zero-tolerance policy regarding scandalous women and the men who enabled them. Victoria was ebullient and vivacious; she enjoyed late nights and parties and also delighted in the trivialities and fripperies of court life and etiquette. Albert had also heard she was stubborn, and—perhaps even worse—that she was not terribly fond of nature, which was one of his passions.

Nevertheless, the visit progressed swimmingly. On June 7, Victoria wrote to Leopold with characteristic effusiveness, "I must thank you, my beloved Uncle, for the prospect of great happiness you have contributed to give me, in the person of dear Albert. Allow me . . . to tell you how delighted I am with him, and how much I like him in every way. He possesses every quality that could be desired to render me perfectly happy. He is so sensible, so kind, and so good, and so amiable, too. He has besides, the most pleasing and delightful exterior and appearance you can possibly see."

The stage had been set for a genuine love match, that rarest of occurrences in the history of royal marriages. And how times had changed from the days of Henry VIII. As England was formally an Anglican country and the royal family all Protestants, there was of course no need for the couple to secure a papal dispensation before heading to the altar. Consanguinity, as it once applied to cousins— even first cousins—had become a nonissue.

On June 20, 1837, the eighteen-year-old Victoria acceded to the throne on the death of her uncle, William IV. By all accounts the diminutive sovereign possessed remarkable poise for one so young and with such enormous responsibility on her slim shoulders. Her modest yet regal demeanor quickly won Victoria the praise of her ministers as well as her subjects. And, almost immediately, those ministers began pressuring her to marry. But the queen felt unready to wed right away—if at all. "I said I dreaded the thought of marrying; that I was so accustomed to have my own way, that I thought it was 10 to 1 that I shouldn't agree with anybody," Victoria wrote in her journal on April 18, 1839. "Oh, but you would have it still," the PM, Lord Melbourne, hastily assured the young sovereign.

But Melbourne, nearly sixty years old and as much a father figure for Victoria as he was a parliamentarian, argued against the notion of wedding one of her cousins, adding, "Those Coburgs are not very popular abroad; the Russians hate them."

Her little feet grown even colder at the idea of marriage, Victoria wrote to her uncle Leopold that July, expressing her uneasiness at being older (by a few months) than Albert. Besides, she scarcely knew him and was also worried that they might not suit one another as lovers: ". . . one can never answer beforehand for feelings, and I may not have the feeling for him which is requisite to ensure happiness. I may like him as a friend, and as a cousin, and as a brother, but not more; and should this be the case (which is not likely), I am very anxious that it should be understood that I am not guilty of any breach of promise, for I never gave any. . . ."

So in October 1839 Albert set out once more for England and a second look-see. And upon meeting him again, the reluctant queen became thunderstruck. Her October 10 journal entry records, ". . . It was with some emotion that I beheld Albert—who is beautiful." The following day her diary was full of praise for his waltzing and his horsemanship. On October 13, she admitted in her journal that she had changed her mind about postponing marriage for a few years. Melbourne counseled her not to wait too long; if they presented Parliament with a royal engagement there was little the legislative body could do to find a way of thwarting it if they so chose. And he urged her to inform Albert of her decision without delay.

No one could propose to a regnant queen of England. So the twenty-year-old Victoria was impelled to take the initiative and offer her hand, or ask for Albert's, in marriage. It was one of the few times she took the reins in their relationship. Her diary entry of October 15, 1839, memorializes the proposal: "At about ½ p. 12 [half past twelve] I sent for Albert; he came to the Closet where I was alone, and after a few minutes I said to him that I thought he must be aware why I wished [him] to come here, and that it would make me happy if he would consent to what I wished [to marry me]; we embraced each other over and over again, and he was so kind, so affectionate; Oh! To feel I was, and am, loved by such an Angel as Albert was too great a delight to describe! He is perfection; perfection in every way—in beauty—in everything! I told him I was quite unworthy of him and kissed his dear hand—he said he would be very happy [to share his life with her] and was so kind and seemed so happy, that I really felt it was the happiest, brightest moment in my life. . . . Oh! how I adore and love him, I cannot say!! How I will strive to make him feel as little as possible the great sacrifice he has made . . ."

That evening, before the queen went to bed, she was handed a letter that read, "Dearest greatly beloved Victoria, How is it that I have deserved so much love, so much affection? . . . I believe that Heaven has sent me an angel whose brightness shall illumine my life. . . . In body and soul ever your slave, your loyal ALBERT." After reading this tender and effusive declaration, Victoria burst into tears.

According to Victoria's diary, during Albert's visit the two of them kissed and snuggled and held hands at every available opportunity. Albert accompanied her to a parade review in Hyde Park, where Victoria may have taken more notice of her fiancé's physique than the military marches, observing that Albert was wearing a pair of white cashmere breeches with "*nothing under them.*"

He wielded the blotting paper after she signed state documents. She "gave him a ring with the date of the ever dear to me 15th engraved in it" along with "a little seal I used to wear." And "I asked if he would let me have a little of his dear hair."

"No two lovers could be happier than we are!" she declared on November 1.

They parted from each other with many tears but Albert wrote to Victoria when he reached Calais: "I need not tell you that since we left all my thoughts have been with you and your image fills my whole soul." Two weeks later, he wrote, "Dearly beloved Victoria, I long to talk to you, otherwise the separation is too painful. Your dear picture stands on my table and I can hardly take my eyes off it." Whenever the queen received a letter from Albert, she would melt. "Never, never did I think I could be loved so much," she replied to him on November 28.

Nonetheless, many English disdained the match. A popular satirical verse from 1840 titled "The German Bridegroom" referred to Albert as a gold digger:

> *Here comes the bridegroom of Victoria's choice,*
> *The nominee of Lehzen's vulgar voice;*
> [Baroness L. was V.'s former governess]
> *He comes to take "for better or for worse"*
> *England's fat queen and England's fatter purse.*

But the prospective royal marriage had a few niggling political hurdles to overcome. For example, Parliament was adamant that Albert not be made a peer. There was also some concern that because Albert was German, he might impose their national character and agenda on the British monarchy. It was difficult for Victoria to explain to her fiancé that "The English are very jealous of any foreign interference in the government of the country. . . ."

As their wedding day neared, it was clear how much the typical gender roles were reversed. Albert had griped when he learned that their honeymoon would only consist of a few days spent at Windsor. On January 31, 1840, Victoria wrote to him, patiently reiterating why the magnitude of her responsibilities precluded a lengthy holiday. ". . . dear Albert, you have not at all understood the matter. You forget, my dearest Love, that I am the Sovereign, and that business can stop and wait for nothing. Parliament is sitting, and something occurs almost every day, for which I may be required, and it is quite impossible for me to be absent from London; therefore two or three days is already a long time to be absent. I am never easy a moment, if I am not on the spot, and see and hear what is going on."

According to Melbourne, Albert was "a great stickler for morality" and "extremely strait-laced." To that end, he insisted that Victoria's bridesmaids have thoroughly unblemished characters, and even that the girls' *mothers'* reputations be stainless. In contrast to Albert's strict judgmental nature, Victoria was, at the time, far more empathetic and forgiving, chiding Albert for his narrow view of humanity. "I always think that one ought always to be indulgent towards other people, as I always think, if we had not been well brought up and well taken care of, we might also have gone astray."

On February 10, 1840, three years after becoming queen, Victoria married her first cousin, Albert of Saxe-Coburg-Gotha, in the Chapel Royal, St. James's.

It's difficult to imagine how Victoria found the time to write a journal entry on her wedding day, but her firsthand description of events could scarcely be matched by another. According to the diary, before breakfast her mother brought her a nosegay of orange blossoms and a wreath of orange blossoms was placed atop her hairdo; the wreath would set the bridal fashion for decades, as would the color of her dress. "I wore a white satin gown with a very deep flounce of Honiton lace, imitation of old. I wore my Turkish diamond necklace and earrings, and Albert's beautiful sapphire brooch." Albert wore the uniform of a British Field Marshal, decorated with the Order of the Garter.

"When I arrived at St. James's, I went into the dressing-room where my 12 young Train-bearers were, dressed all in white with white roses, which had a beautiful effect. Here I waited a little till dearest Albert's Procession had moved into the Chapel." His procession, and hers, were both lavish and colorful. But there was a near comical moment when it was clear that Victoria's bridal train wasn't long enough to allow all twelve of her bridesmaids to walk normally; like the women's chorus in a Gilbert and Sullivan operetta, they had to trip forward with precarious, mincing steps, taking care not to bump into each other.

Witnessed by three hundred guests, "The Ceremony was very imposing, and fine and simple, and I think ought to make an everlasting impression on every one who promises at the Altar to keep what he or she promises . . ." Victoria wrote. Afterward, she returned to Buckingham Palace alone with Albert, where they had a half hour of conversation to themselves before it was time to set out for Windsor. Victoria changed out of her formal wedding ensemble into a simpler version of the same, "a white silk gown trimmed with swansdown and a bonnet with orange flowers."

After they reached Windsor and acclimated themselves to their suite of rooms, Albert "took me on his knee, and kissed me. . . . We had dinner in our sitting room; but I had such a sick headache that I could eat nothing and was obliged to lie down in the middle blue room for the remainder of the evening, on the sofa, but, ill or not, I never, never spent such an evening. . . . He called me names of tenderness, I have never yet heard used to me before—was bliss beyond belief! Oh! This was the happiest day of my life!—May God help me to do my duty as I ought and be worthy of such blessings."

With such effusive joy and vitality, it's doubtful—despite the raging headache—that Victoria was gritting her teeth and thinking of England as she and Albert consummated their marriage.

On February 11, 1840, the morning after the wedding night, Victoria awoke in a state of bliss, but she still had time to memorialize her feelings in her journal. "When day dawned (for we did not sleep much) and I beheld that beautiful angelic face by my side, it was more than I can express! He does look so beautiful in his shirt only, with his beautiful throat seen. . . ." Later that day she wrote to her uncle Leopold, gushing, "Really, I do not think it possible for any one in the world to be happier, or as happy as I am. . . . What I can do to make him happy will be my greatest delight. . . ."

Victoria's afterglow remains just as bright in her journal entry of February 12. "Already the 2nd day since our marriage; his love and gentleness is beyond everything, and to kiss that dear soft cheek, to press my lips to his, is heavenly bliss. . . ."

The following day, the woman who after Albert's death stubbornly refused to acknowledge that women had such vulgar appendages as "legs" wrote with a hint of the erotic, "My dearest Albert put on my stockings for me. I went in and saw him shave; a great delight for me."

Victoria and Albert couldn't get enough of each other, either in or out of the bedchamber, and within a few weeks, the queen was pregnant. If she could have enjoyed her apparently terrific sex life without the incumbent duty of childbearing, she probably would have been ecstatic. She and Albert eventually had nine children, but Victoria never had much praise for infants, even her own.

Pregnancy was "the ONLY thing" Victoria dreaded. She had hoped to devote all her personal time to her precious spouse. And when she learned that she was in a delicate condition, she was "furious. It was too dreadful," she told her uncle Leopold. If her "plagues" were to be "rewarded only by a nasty girl," she would drown it. And to the Dowager Duchess of Saxe-Coburg-Gotha the queen wrote, "I am really upset about it and it is spoiling my happiness; I have always hated the idea and I prayed God night and day to be left free for at least six months. . . . I cannot understand how anyone can wish for such a thing, especially at the beginning of a marriage."

Toward the end of 1840, at the christening of her eldest daughter and first child, Princess Victoria, the queen was already pregnant again, and her increasing state depressed her. Later she would insist, "What made me so miserable was to have the first two years of my married life utterly spoilt by this occupation. I could enjoy nothing, not travel or go about with [Albert]. If I had wasted a year . . . it would have been very different." She felt as though her wings had been clipped and considered her gender "a most unenviable one."

Years later, in 1859, she wrote two separate letters to Vicky, now Princess Frederick Wilhelm of Germany, regarding the recent birth of Vicky's first child (the future Kaiser Wilhelm), admitting that she ". . . hated the thought of having children," and ". . . I have no *tendre* for them till they have become a little human; an ugly baby is a very nasty object—and the prettiest is frightful when undressed— till about four months; in short as long as they have their big body and little limbs and that terrible frog-like action. . . ."

Albert, however, was thrilled by his wife's fertility. After Princess Victoria was born, the queen wrote that her adoring and solicitous husband had behaved "just like a mother" to her, "nor could there be a kinder, wiser, or more judicious nurse." Albert would read to the queen, write for her, or simply sit by her side in a darkened room. He came the moment she called, and wheeled her bed or sofa from one room to the next. Beyond Buckingham Palace, he represented his wife at Privy Council meetings. His aim, he told the Duke of Wellington, was to be "the natural head of the family, superintendent of her household, manager of her private affairs, her sole *confidential* adviser in politics, and only assistance in her communication with the officers of the Government . . . her private secretary and her permanent minister." Although Victoria's initial inclination after their marriage had been to avoid discussing affairs of state with her husband and to keep him out of politics and governance—restricting his input to "a little help with the blotting paper," as she put it—Albert eventually became all that he desired and more, even choosing his wife's clothes and accessories.

Much of this was due to King Leopold's advice to his niece. "The Prince ought in business as in everything to be necessary to the Queen. He should be to her a walking dictionary for reference on any point which her own knowledge or education have not enabled her to answer."

The royal couple had their first real fight over the upbringing of their children. Victoria had insisted on retaining her former governess, Baroness Lehzen. But Albert saw the baroness as "a crazy, stupid intriguer . . . who regards herself as a demi-God, and anyone who refuses to recognize her as such is a criminal." Harsh words indeed, and intended to wound his wife as well as her representative in the nursery, neither of whom he felt gave his input any credence. "Victoria is too hasty and passionate for me to be able often to speak of my difficulties," Albert complained to his mentor, Baron Stockmar. "She will not hear me out but flies into a rage and overwhelms me with reproaches of suspiciousness. Want of trust, ambition, envy, etc, etc. . . . All the disagreeableness I suffer comes from one and the same person," he added, referring to Baroness Lehzen. He would frequently lament, "I am only the husband and not the master of the house."

But Victoria could be as hotheaded and stubborn as her spouse. She offered her side of the story to Stockmar, insisting that she didn't wish to quarrel with Albert, but he "must tell me what he dislikes and I will set about to remedy it, but he must also promise to listen to and to believe me; when (on the contrary) I am in a passion which I trust I am not very often in now, he must not believe the stupid things I say like being miserable I ever married and so forth, which come when I am unwell. . . ."

Victoria suffered from severe postpartum depression each time she gave birth. As she described it in her journal, "there is often an irritability in me which . . . makes me say cross and odious things which I don't myself believe and which I fear hurt A., but which he should not believe . . . but I trust I shall be able to conquer it. Our position tho' is very different to any other married couples. A. is in my house and not I in his.—But I am ready to submit to his wishes as I love him dearly."

The Baroness Lehzen was eventually dismissed, and Albert assumed control of the children's upbringing, proving to be an exceptionally doting father. From then on, the royal household was managed, and their offspring raised, according to his strictures—pragmatic, prudent, efficient, and disciplined. Together, he and Victoria worked diligently to promote the royal family as the archetype of English domestic bliss, a model for the middle classes to emulate.

Their children remained the only object of their quarrels. Another flare-up occurred in April 1853, after the queen had given birth to her eighth child, Prince Leopold, who suffered from hemophilia—a blood disorder recessively linked to the X chromosome. Prince Leopold's case is traditionally believed to have been caused either by a mutation in Victoria or in the sperm of her father, the Duke of Kent. From there, the disease spread through virtually every royal house of Europe as Victoria arranged political marriages for her daughters—three of whom were carriers of the disorder.

Victoria's stress over her delicate newborn exacerbated her usual postpartum melancholia. Albert made things worse by infantilizing his wife, calling her "dear child" or "dear, good little one." Although he was aware of the larger, more troubling matters that were the catalyst, he would accuse her of starting rows over trifles. When the spoken word failed, he defended his conduct to her in a letter:

> . . . When I try to demonstrate the groundlessness and injustice
> of the accusations which are brought against me I increase

your distress. . . . But I never intend or wish to offend you. . . . If you are violent I have no other choice but to leave you . . . I leave the room and retire to my own room to give you time to recover yourself. Then you follow me to renew the dispute and to have it all out. . . . Now don't believe that I do not sincerely and deeply pity you for the sufferings you undergo, or that I deny you do really suffer very much. I merely deny that I am the cause of them, though I have unfortunately often been the occasion. . . . I am often astonished at the effect which a hasty word of mine has produced. . . .

Despite these squabbles, the royal marriage was an indispensable partnership. The first time Victoria became pregnant, a bill was passed in Parliament giving Albert the full powers of regent. He was also appointed a Privy Councilor. Under Prime Minister Robert Peel's government (1841–46) he had keys to the cabinet and red dispatch boxes and was sent all important government papers to review with the queen. Peel made it possible for Albert to be present when Victoria's ministers had audiences with her; and on some occasions the consort met alone with ministers on his wife's behalf. As far as Victoria was concerned, any presentations made to Albert had the same force and effect as if they were made directly to her.

His influence in every aspect of her life was enormously felt. Although he was not a tactful man, Albert was able to reform the royal household, coordinating departments, eliminating redundancies, and cutting waste. Caricaturists lampooned him counting scrub brushes at Windsor Castle, because it was rumored that Albert had told servants to provide their own soap, brushes, and mops. Candles were restricted to two per room; even the consumption of toilet tissue was restricted, as Sir Arthur Ellis discovered, observing that the lavatories at Windsor were supplied with newspaper.

Throughout their marriage Victoria lamented that the natural order of things had been reversed. She firmly believed that man was meant to master woman. And as Queen of England, she was answerable to no man. She had probably heard the popular quip about her and Albert that made the rounds during their engagement:

> *She is lovely, she is rich,*
> *But they tell me when I marry*
> *That she will wear the* britsch.

To find a way of rectifying this anomaly, after sixteen years of marriage, in May of 1856, the queen issued a formal Memorandum, declaring, "It is a strange omission in our Constitution that while the wife of a King has the highest rank and dignity in the realm after her husband assigned to her by law, the husband of a Queen regnant is entirely ignored by the law. This is the more extraordinary, as a husband has in this country such particular rights and such great powers over his wife, and as the Queen is married just as any other woman is, and swears to obey her lord and master, as such, while by law he has no rank or defined position. . . ."

The following year, after Parliament refused to grant Albert the title of Prince Consort through legislative channels, Victoria angrily overrode them by issuing letters patent awarding the title to her husband.

In his diary Charles Greville—Clerk of the Council in Ordinary under three successive sovereigns, including Victoria—wrote: "The Prince is become so identified with the Queen that they are one person, and as he likes business, it is obvious that while she has the title he is really discharging the functions of the Sovereign. He is King to all intents and purposes. I am not surprised at this, but certainly was not aware that it had taken such definite shape."

Albert's intrusion into every aspect of English life had won him many enemies, particularly among the aristocracy. The prince's talents—his horsemanship, his grace as a dancer and ice skater, his strengths as a swimmer and sportsman, his musical gifts and most certainly his prudery and his awkwardness around all women other than his wife—earned him contempt rather than praise. Even the cut of his coat and the manner in which he shook hands was derided as being too arrogantly German.

As a result, Albert became homesick, once to the point of tears. Victoria found him weeping in a hallway after he'd said good-bye to his father, who had paid them a visit. Moved by her husband's rare display of emotion, the queen wrote in her journal, "God knows how great my wish is to make this Beloved being happy and contented."

For such a happily married woman, Victoria harbored highly negative views of wedlock—at least as it affected her own brood. The queen's matchmaking efforts for her nine children would earn her the nickname "grandmother of Europe," but it nonetheless broke her heart when she had to sacrifice one of them, particularly a daughter, on the matrimonial altar. On May 16, 1860, having been Albert's wife for a little more than two decades, and having recently wed their eldest child, Vicky, to Prince Frederick Wilhelm of Germany, she admitted, "All marriage is such a lottery—the happiness is always an exchange—though it may be a very happy one—still the poor woman is bodily and morally the husband's slave. That always sticks in my throat. When I think of a merry, happy, free young girl—and look at the ailing, aching state a young wife is generally doomed to—which you can't deny is the penalty of marriage."

The year 1860 also marked the beginning of a decline in Albert's health. That November he was seriously ill with violent shivers he called the "English cholera." For the past couple of years he'd been gloomy and irritable, with premonitions of a premature death. By 1861 he was suffering from frequent headaches and pains in his limbs.

Victoria would always insist that their eldest son, the Prince of Wales, Albert Edward (known as Bertie) was responsible for hastening her husband's demise. Bertie had been sent to Dublin, attached to the Grenadier Guards at the Curragh Military Camp. Just for kicks and giggles one night his mates installed a vivacious and willing young actress, Nellie Clifden, in the young prince's bunk. So Bertie spent the night with her. The scandal engendered by the Nellie Clifden affair sent the already ailing Albert rushing up to Cambridge to smooth things over with the university dons. Compounding matters, discussions were already under way with the King of Denmark to wed Bertie to his daughter, Princess Alexandra, which compelled Albert to do some damage control with the Danish royal family.

On November 25, father and son trudged through the Cambridge rain as Albert endeavored to sort Bertie out. Albert was nursing a cold he had caught three days earlier, which had taken a turn for the worse, manifesting itself as neuralgia (acute nerve pain) and catarrh (an upper respiratory inflammation). Within a few days' time he was gravely ill, and became bedridden at Windsor Castle.

Victoria's daily journal entries and her letters to Vicky express her immense concern for Albert's health, and chart both the progress and the relapses of his illness, expressing joy at the tiniest signs of improvement. She melted when he was pleased to see her and uttered German terms of endearment, such as *"Fraüchen"* (little woman) and *"gütes Weibchen"* (excellent wife).

On December 14, 1861, the queen paid her customary seven a.m. visit to her husband's sickbed. In her journal, she wrote, "Never can I forget how beautiful my darling looked lying there with his face lit up by the rising sun, his eyes unusually bright gazing as it were on unseen objects and not taking notice of me." The doctors viewed it as a "decided rally" and gave the queen permission to take a very brief walk as long as she remained close at hand. Victoria stepped out onto the terrace with their daughter Alice, but soon burst into tears and reentered Albert's room.

"The breathing was . . . so rapid . . . I think 60 respirations in a minute. I bent over him and said to him *'Es ist Kleines Fraüchen'* [it is your little wife] and he bowed his head; I asked him if he would give me *'ein Kuss'* [a kiss] and he did so. He seemed half dozing, quite quiet . . . I left the room for a moment and sat down on the floor in utter despair . . . Alice told me to come in . . . and I took his dear hand which was already cold, though the breathing was quite gentle and I knelt down by him. . . . Two or three long but perfectly gentle breaths were drawn, the hand clasping mine and . . . all, all was over. . . . I stood up, kissed his heavenly forehead and called out in a bitter and agonizing cry, 'Oh! My dear darling!' "

The official cause of Albert's death was listed as typhoid fever, but given his symptoms, some twentieth-century historians have posited that he had suffered from stomach cancer for some time and the disease had weakened his resistance to the catarrh he contracted that November.

When Albert died at the age of forty-two, "cut off in the prime of life," in Victoria's words after twenty-one years of marriage, part of the queen died with him. Stricken to the point of collapse, she slept with his coat on top of her, clutching his nightshirt like a lover. The Blue Room at Windsor where Albert spent so much time became a shrine, his personal effects maintained exactly the way he had left them. Victoria turned the entire kingdom into a memorial to her late husband, declaring, "*His* wishes—*his* plans about *every* thing, *his* views about *every* thing are to be *my law*! And no *human power* will make me swerve from *what he* decided and wished."

Everyone at court wore black mourning for a full year. After 1864 the queen permitted her maids of honor to wear shades of purple, mauve, gray, and white. Victoria's mourning remained permanent. For the first few years after Albert's death, her only desire was to sit and weep or erect various shrines to his memory. According to Lord Clarendon, "She believes that his eye is now constantly upon her, that he watches over every action of hers and that in fact, she never ceases to be in communication with his spirit." Although she'd gained everyone's sympathy at the outset, by 1864 Victoria's ongoing absence from public life was severely criticized by her subjects, her ministers, and the press, as was her appearance at Parliament only when she needed to request treasury money for her expanding family.

Lord Halifax, the Lord Privy Seal, told the queen's private secretary Henry Ponsonby, "It is impossible to deny that H.M. is drawing heavily on the credit of her former popularity, and that Crowned Heads as well as other people must do much that was not necessary in former days to meet the altered circumstances and altered tone of modern times . . . the mass of the people expect a King or a Queen to look and play the part. They want to see a Crown and Sceptre and all that sort of thing. They want the gilding for the money. It is not wise to let them think . . . that they could do without a sovereign who lives at Osborne and Balmoral as any private lady might do."

During these semi-reclusive years, Victoria's intimate friendship with a Scottish gillie, John Brown, created a national scandal. Brown was a connection to Albert, someone who had known her husband well in happier times. Blunt and outspoken, the devoted Brown saw to her every need, and never took a single day off in eighteen and a half years of service. By 1866, word had gotten out that Victoria and her personal Highland servant had a special relationship, leading to a crop of salacious and unchecked rumors about the queen's inappropriate affection for John Brown, including the intimation that Victoria and her gillie were secretly married, thus inspiring her nickname, "Mrs. Brown." Proof of a sexual affair remains elusive, although Victoria once told a granddaughter, "do you know my dear, I sometimes feel that when I die I shall be just a little nervous about meeting Grandpapa for I have taken to doing a good many things that he would not quite approve of." However, she was more likely referring to the séances she attended in an effort to commune with Albert's spirit.

Brown died on March 27, 1883, at the age of fifty-seven. Victoria, now sixty-three, was distraught. As she wrote to Henry Ponsonby on April 3, it was like losing Albert all over again. She would endure many more years of life without them.

Victoria was the longest-reigning monarch in British history, lending her name to an era that spanned two-thirds of the nineteenth century. During her sixty-three years, seven months, and two days as queen, the British Empire reached its zenith, covering a quarter of the world. But imperial expansion exacted its price, notably the 1857 Sepoy Massacre in India and the two South African Boer Wars.

Trade was so extensive, and the available goods so exotic, that the English became an acquisitive population, packing as much bric-a-brac into their gaslit homes as humanly possible. The Industrial Revolution, the steam engine, and the invention of the telegraph changed the way people lived, worked, communicated, and traveled, transforming the British economy.

And yet Victoria hated change. She was unnerved by the numerous shifts of government during her reign—twenty prime ministers, although some of the same men went in and out of office over the years. The modifications to her household, with her daughters' eventually wedding and moving far away from home, put her off balance as well. During her own marriage she had secretly wished to retreat from the world to enjoy a normal, untrammeled life; and after Albert's death she might have become a permanent recluse and abdicated the throne, but she did not trust the Prince of Wales to rule responsibly.

In her final years, Victoria's eyesight began to fail. She complained of the ailments of aging—sciatica, neuralgia, lumbago, insomnia, indigestion, gastric pain, and trouble with her false teeth. On January 16, 1901, she suffered a cerebral hemorrhage. On January 22, with a crucifix resting in her hands, Queen Victoria died at the age of eighty-one, marking the end of the House of Hanover. Examining her postmortem, her physician, James Reid, noticed that she had a ventral hernia and a prolapsed uterus. According to generally observed medical protocol of the era governing male doctors and their female patients, he had never physically examined her while she lived, but had treated her purely through verbal communication.

Her coffin reposed in the Albert Memorial Chapel at Windsor, and on February 4, 1901, it was placed in their mausoleum at Frogmore in Windsor Great Park. Above the door was inscribed, "His mourning widow, Victoria the Queen directed that all that is mortal of Prince Albert be placed in this sepulcher A.D. 1862. *Vale desideratissime* [Farewell most beloved]. *Hic demum conquiescam tecum, tecum in Christo consurgeam* [Here at length I shall rest with thee, with thee in Christ I shall rise again]."

Victoria was succeeded by their eldest son, Bertie, the Prince of Wales, who was crowned Edward VII at the age of fifty-nine.

Franz Joseph I
1830–1916
Ruled Austria: 1848–1916

❧ *and* ❧

Elisabeth Amalie Eugenie,
Duchess in Bavaria, Princess of Bavaria
1837–1898

married 1854–1898

"I cannot understand how people can look forward to marriage so much and expect so much good to come of it. It is a ridiculous institution."
— Elisabeth (Sisi), Empress of Austria

"MARRY IN HASTE, REPENT AT LEISURE" WOULD BE an apt way to describe the relationship between Emperor Franz Joseph of Austria and his child-bride, his Bavarian cousin Elisabeth.

"Sisi" was one of eight children born to Duke Max in Bavaria, a charming bohemian eccentric, and his pragmatic wife, Ludovica, whose family, the Wittelsbachs, had long ruled Bavaria.

From childhood, it was her father who Sisi most resembled, enjoying such decidedly unroyal activities as excursions to circuses and country fairs, where they would disguise themselves as strolling players. Sisi inherited Max's peripatetic streak and his passion for horseback riding. Both of them chafed at the regimented lifestyle expected of a royal, where their poetic natures were suffocated and stifled by centuries-old etiquette and protocol.

In 1853, Ludovica's sister, Archduchess Sophia, the mother of the Austrian emperor Franz Joseph, decided to pay her a visit for the purposes of inspecting the Wittelsbach girls as potential marriage material for the emperor. Sophia quickly settled on Sisi's slim, dark, and serious older sister, Helen, determining that the girl possessed the proper temperament to become an empress. The only problem with the eighteen-year-old "Nené" was her lack of interest in riding, because "there was nothing the Emperor admired more in a woman than an elegant seat on a horse."

The astonishingly beautiful fifteen-year-old Sisi, with her sweet round face, almond-shaped eyes, and masses of wavy auburn hair that grazed the backs of her knees, was already an accomplished equestrienne, but Sophia didn't even pause to consider her. The archduchess could tell in a heartbeat that Sisi was not the right candidate—not only too young, but too emotionally sensitive.

Sophia extended an invitation to Ludovica, Max, and Nené to visit her summer home, Villa Eltz, in Bad Ischl in August—the only time her busy son could take a vacation from his imperial duties. But Duke Max, who disliked his sister-in-law as much as he disdained court etiquette, took a pass, which left an empty seat in the carriage. There was no reason to deny it to Sisi, with her perennial thirst for travel.

Once everyone was formally introduced at Bad Ischl, however, it became abundantly apparent that Archduchess Sophia had misjudged her son. Franz Joseph evinced no interest in Nené's moribund demeanor and chiseled features. Instead, opposites attracted. Guided by his hormones, the twenty-two-year-old emperor was immediately smitten with Sisi, a girl whose temperament could not have been further from his own. Franz Joseph was critical, punctilious, and detail-oriented, a stickler for etiquette and a slave to duty. His long hours of paperwork, far from being a tedious

chore, gave him something to focus on. As things eventually transpired, just about the only thing that Sisi and Franz Joseph shared
in common was a natural shyness that was often mistaken for
aloofness or arrogance. And the emperor would soon discover that
Sisi suffered from a strange psychosomatic ailment, becoming physically ill when she grew restless or bored. In stark contrast to Franz
Joseph's solidity, Sisi was an elusive, ethereal will-o'-the-wisp.

Additionally, Sisi's childhood seemed not to have an expiration
date; while from boyhood, the rigid and disciplined Franz Joseph
had been educated in statecraft, and therefore never had much of a
chance to be a kid. By the age of eighteen, the tall, mustachioed
ruler with his soft, full lips and Hapsburg high forehead reigned
over an empire of 38 million people. At seventeen he had gone to
war and experienced its carnage, crushing the 1848 uprising in
Italy under Field Marshal Radetzky. Fearless in battle, the young
emperor wore a uniform every day for the rest of his life, unless he
was out hunting.

The emperor's intense gazes made Sisi blush. His envious younger
brother Charles Ludwig assured their mother that "Franzl likes Sisi
better than Nené. You will see, she is the one he will want to
marry." Sophia dismissed the comment: "What utter nonsense! As
if he would look at that little monkey!"

But the following morning, an uncharacteristically cheerful Franz
Joseph burst into his mother's boudoir and peppered her with questions about Sisi. How did she like her? Wasn't she enchanting?—
"So modest and yet so completely at ease—so gay and yet so
touching in her simplicity—as fresh and unspoilt as a green, half-
opened almond, with such a sweet look in her eyes, and lips as soft
and inviting as ripe strawberries. Even that dreary black dress
couldn't spoil her pretty figure. . . ."

Sophia tried to get Franz Joseph back on track, reminding him
that the pious Nené was "such a good-looking girl with her slim,
straight figure, and intelligent as well—a girl who would grow into
a handsome woman." That evening, to further convince her son
that he was backing the wrong horse, she placed Sisi between her-

self and the old Prince of Hesse, with whom the girl could not possibly hold her own in conversation. Sophia was right, but it didn't stop her son from staring at the girl all throughout the meal.

And at the ball that Sophia hosted on the eve of her son's twenty-third birthday, which was meant to present Nené and her son to the Viennese aristocracy as their future rulers, Franz Joseph upset his mother's plans by turning the event into the Sisi sideshow, giving each of his bouquets to her, while Nené—his intended fiancée, as least as far as Sophia was concerned—stood by and watched the emperor dance as often as possible with her little sister.

Franz Joseph ultimately convinced Sophia to approve of Sisi. And on Sunday morning, August 19, 1853, Ludovica accepted his marriage proposal on her daughter's behalf, thrilled to be uniting Sisi to the biggest catch in Europe. Sisi, too, was over the moon, assuring her mother, "Of course I love him, how could I help but love him?" Then she burst into tears, sobbing, "If only he were not an emperor."

Almost from the moment the royal betrothal was announced, Sisi demonstrated the qualities that would make her as unfit for her new role as Sophia had predicted. The throngs of delirious well-wishers in the streets crushing up against her carriage to catch a glimpse of their future empress utterly unnerved her and left her on the verge of tears. "It is a pity that Sisi is so delicate," the archduchess commented, as if to say to her son, "I told you so."

Nearly every convent in Bavaria was kept busy stitching Sisi's trousseau, which included fifty dresses of varying weights and formality, dozens of undergarments and pairs of silk stockings, 113 pairs of shoes, and sixteen hats. Unfortunately, what was fashionable in the comparatively laid-back Bavaria was scoffed at by the sophisticated Viennese. A worried Franz Joseph wrote to his mother to say, "I have difficulty believing that it will be pretty."

In April 1854, Sisi renounced her claim to the Bavarian throne and began her journey to Vienna. Just a few miles from the city, at the imperial palace of Schönbrunn, she got her first taste of what lay in store for her, and what had been a matter of course for the emperor all his life—the complete lack of privacy and a fanatical devotion to protocol. Her new Mistress of the Household, the pinch-faced Countess Esterházy-Liechtenstein, handed her a thick sheaf of papers, which she was expected to memorize verbatim, titled "Order for the Ceremonial of the Public Entry into Vienna of Her Royal Highness the Most August Princess Elisabeth." It was the "script" for her role as a Hapsburg bride.

On April 23, the morning of her official entry into Vienna, Sisi broke down and wept in her mother's arms. But by the time she climbed into the glass coach with its painted panels by Peter Paul Rubens, her eyes were dry and she wowed the crowd in her pink and silver gown embroidered with roses. Atop her abundant auburn tresses sat a diamond crown. "On show like a freak in a circus," Sisi muttered to her mother.

The following day, April 24, 1854, illuminated by the glow of ten thousand candles, a thousand people packed the Church of the Augustinians within the parish of the Hofburg to witness the Cardinal Prince-Archbishop of Vienna's joining of Franz Joseph and Sisi in holy matrimony. A papal dispensation had been necessary because Sisi and Franz Joseph, both Catholics, were first cousins. Significantly taller than her husband, Sisi looked every inch the empress in a wedding gown of white and silver strewn with myrtle blossoms, and a crown of opals and diamonds. She shyly glanced at her mother before murmuring her "I dos"—barely opening her mouth because the Archduchess Sophia had criticized her yellow teeth. In contrast to Sisi's whisper, the enchanted bridegroom's assent resounded to the farthest pew.

Sermon after tedious sermon followed the ceremony. The bridal party didn't leave the church until evening, and made straight for the Hofburg, where the newlyweds spent another two hours sitting stiffly and accepting the formal congratulations—involving much curtsying and genuflecting—of countless dignitaries. Almost pathologically shy and fearful of meeting strangers, Sisi didn't realize that no one could speak to her unless she addressed them first. She was utterly tongue-tied, with no gift for the inspired small talk in which most royals are raised from birth to excel.

After the wedding supper finally ended, Sisi was led to her bed-chamber by a dozen pages bearing gilded candelabra. Her mother and Countess Esterházy helped her undress and put her to bed. A half hour later, the eager bridegroom—still in full military uniform—knocked on her door, accompanied, according to Haps-burg tradition, by his mother, who had come to present him to his nubile new wife.

But Sisi behaved as though she heard nothing. Exhausted by the day's ordeal, and terrified of sex, she buried her head in the pillow and pretended to be fast asleep.

Two days after the wedding the royal marriage was consum-mated. Sophia had the news by eight that morning. Having such deeply personal information shared with her mother-in-law as Sisi was still enjoying the afterglow was just one of the drawbacks of spending the honeymoon in the Hofburg. During the days immedi-ately following their nuptials, Franz Joseph spent six to seven hours at his desk, reminding his bored new bride that "World politics will not wait on our honeymoon."

Although he was one of the most famous workaholics of all time, Franz Joseph still had enough of a libido to take the necessary breaks. His sex drive had made Sisi his empress; and once his pa-perwork was shelved and night fell, he couldn't get enough of her. A tender, ardent, and patient lover, he must have been shocked to discover that his sixteen-year-old bride was frigid. Carnality not only left Sisi cold, it disgusted her.

The empress's revulsion was corroborated by her two confi-dantes—her cousin, Countess Marie Larisch, and her lady-in-wait-ing, Marie Festetics—who both claimed that Sisi was neither sexual nor passionate. Countess Larisch wrote, "the empress regarded the excitement of being adored as a tribute, which her beauty had a right to demand . . . the grossness of life repelled her just as much as its beauty attracted her."

She had gotten her heart's desire, but hated every minute of it. Almost literally from the moment she married, Sisi was profoundly unhappy. Craving freedom, she penned maudlin poetry, referring to her regimented new life as a "prison cell."

She could go nowhere and do nothing alone, and was not even permitted to walk about solely in the company of her husband, as it was deemed undignified behavior. Not allowed to confide in anyone because it would have compromised her position as empress, "I felt so abandoned, so lonely," Sisi told Marie Festetics. Her husband's imperial duties kept him away for long hours at a stretch, and as he never confided in her about them, she felt even more excluded. "I was completely alone all day long and was afraid of the moment when Archduchess Sophia came. For she came every day, to spy on what I was doing at any hour. I was completely *à la merci* of this completely malicious woman. Everything I did was bad. . . ."

Sophia, with a lifetime of experience in the Hapsburg court, had the teenage girl's best interests at heart, but Sisi was inclined to see her mother-in-law as a monster who attempted to control every aspect of her life. The ugly clash of wills between the "proper" way of doing things and Sisi's desperate need for freedom lasted until Sophia's death in 1872.

The emperor probably thought he was doing Sisi a favor by not troubling her with things she'd likely find tedious or wouldn't comprehend. Yet the result was a self-fulfilling prophecy: deciding that Sisi was either too naïve or too uninterested in the complexities of governing an empire, his family and their advisers never bothered to school her in them.

Yet Sisi did have an indirect influence in her husband's policies. To the delight of many, wedlock had turned Franz Joseph into a far more compassionate ruler. Queen Victoria's brother-in-law, Duke Ernest of Saxe-Coburg, noticed that "the young emperor's marriage has changed him very much for the better. . . . In spite of the dark outlook and the political frost, one feels a sort of joyous excitement about him . . . and the more I see him the more convinced I am that he has a remarkable talent for governing and will give the old Hapsburg state a great position."

A few weeks after their wedding, Sisi became pregnant. Naturally, Archduchess Sophia wanted to control the next nine months as well. She counseled her son to treat Sisi with particular patience, tenderness, and understanding. As for her daughter-in-law's passion for certain pets, she cautioned Franz Joseph, "I do not think Sisi ought to spend so much time with her parrots, for if a woman is always looking at animals, specifically during the earlier months, the children may grow to resemble them. She had better look in her looking-glass or at you. That would have my complete approval."

According to Countess Larisch, Sisi "loathed the whole business of childbearing." Obsessed with her own beauty, she was so concerned that pregnancy was ruining her figure and making her ugly that she refused to be seen in public. Plagued with morning sickness and depression, she no longer wished to share her husband's bed. On March 5, 1855, the seventeen-year-old Sisi gave birth to a daughter. According to Archduchess Sophia, as the labor pains increased, the emperor had remained by his wife's bedside, holding her hand and comforting her; and that after the birth Sisi lovingly held her newborn, exclaiming, "Oh, now everything is all right, now I don't mind how much I suffered!" as she and the emperor erupted in joyous tears. Three weeks after her daughter was born, Sisi wrote to a Bavarian relative that "at first it seemed strange to me to have a baby of my own; it is like an entirely new joy. . . ."

Yet years later, Sisi described the event quite differently, claiming that before she awoke after giving birth, her infant was taken from her by her mother-in-law, who named her Sophie. The empress added that although Franz Joseph was utterly delighted with his baby girl, she had been utterly despondent. Little Sophie's birth meant that she "would have to go through the whole dreary business again" in order to try for a son and Hapsburg heir.

Archduchess Sophia immediately assumed all responsibility for her grandchild's care, choosing every attendant and demanding that the royal nursery be placed on the same floor as her own suite of rooms at the Hofburg, while Sisi was compelled to head upstairs within the vast palace to visit her own daughter.

Sisi gave birth to another girl, Gisela, in the summer of 1856. By this time, the empress and her mother-in-law were at war with each other over the upbringing of the imperial children.

Meanwhile, behind the scenes at the Hofburg, there were rumblings about Sisi's failure to produce an heir. One day, a yellowed pamphlet dated 1784 (originally an anti–Marie Antoinette screed) was anonymously left on her desk, ominously opened to a particular section, where certain passages were heavily marked.

The destiny of a queen is to give an heir to the throne . . . if the queen is so fortunate as to provide the state with a crown prince this should be the end of her ambition. . . . If a queen has no sons she is merely a foreigner in the state and a dangerous foreigner at that—for fearing to be sent back from whence she came will always be seeking to win back the king by other than natural means. She will struggle for power and position by intrigue and the sowing of discord to the mischief of the king, the nation, and the empire.

On the one hand, Sisi was not terribly maternal; on the other, she wanted to wrest control of her children from her mother-in-law. So, in spite of Sophia's protests that little Sophie was a sickly child who couldn't tolerate too much activity or excitement, Sisi insisted on bringing her daughters on a state visit to Hungary.

Both Sophie and Gisela came down with the measles during the imperial couple's tour. But Sophie's symptoms proved fatal. Dashing back to Budapest, Sisi spent over eleven hours at the little girl's bedside, helplessly watching her slip away. On May 29, 1857, the two-year-old archduchess died.

The death of their firstborn child widened the rift between Sisi and Franz Joseph. The emperor erected a protective wall of paperwork around himself. Having softened under Sisi's caresses, he now became a chilly bureaucrat who never seemed to have a moment to spare for his grieving wife. But Sisi, too, seemed not to want to see her spouse, shutting herself in her rooms and weeping inconsolably. She took out her anger on tiny Gisela; for the rest of her life she blamed the girl for giving her older sister the measles and would have as little to do with her as possible.

Sisi was also pregnant again. When her condition was confirmed, she tried any number of quack remedies "guaranteed" to produce a boy. On the afternoon of August 21, 1858, the twenty-one-year-old empress went into labor. By midnight, Franz Joseph was weeping tears of joy as a 101-gun salute announced to the people of Vienna that the Hapsburgs had an heir, the Crown Prince Rudolf.

But the bloom was long gone from the marriage. Sisi was no longer the child-bride to be constantly wooed and cosseted; now she was just the neurotic mother of the crown prince. Franz Joseph no longer dismissed their attendants so they could enjoy a romantic horseback ride together. Although he assured Sisi that he loved her even more than he did when they wed, he preferred going hunting to her company.

The emperor also had more on his mind than his needy wife; he had a thorny political crisis to contend with—France's open support of Italy's bid for unification. In 1859, Franz Joseph made good on his threat to wage war against the Italian states of Piedmont-Sardinia if they refused to toe the Austrian line. Ironically, although they had little to say to each other when Franz Joseph was home, while he was off making war and losing at Magenta and Solferino, Sisi and the emperor enjoyed a loving correspondence—absence evidently making the heart grow fonder, while proximity increased and exacerbated their individual quirks and made it impossible for them to communicate with each other.

During her husband's absences, Sisi focused all her energy on herself. Obsessed with her appearance, if she weighed more than 110 pounds (at a height of somewhere between five feet six and five feet seven and a half), she would starve herself with a liquid diet of orange juice and milk, or orange juice and fresh-squeezed veal juice. Sisi's personal cult of beauty included vigorous daily exercise, particularly extensive horseback riding, and gymnastics. Tending to her hair was also a near mystical ritual, and it was observed that she spent far more hours on her coiffure than with her children.

It was during this period that Sisi was neither sleeping nor eating, and sending desperate letters to her husband at the front. "What shall I do without you? Have you forgotten me in all these events? Do you love me still? If you did not, then I would not care what happens to me."

And yet when Franz Joseph would write that he was coming home, Sisi wanted him to say that it was because he could not wait to embrace her, not because imperial duty called. If he had to stay in Italy, she convinced herself that he was having an affair. Regardless of her paranoia, when her husband actually did return to her, she usually froze him out, emotionally and physically.

The emperor particularly needed her support when he came back to Vienna a disillusioned man, having been compelled to sign a treaty with France that divided several of the northern Italian states between the two powers. To his surprise and delight, this time Sisi welcomed him with open arms, and at first the imperial couple enjoyed a renewed tenderness. But something happened over the following fifteen months to trigger Sisi's complete distaste for her husband, her callous disregard for his feelings, and the wanderlust that would characterize the rest of her days. Some thought her behavior showed signs of the Wittelsbach dynasty's hereditary madness.

Mental illness, or a chemical imbalance that could not be diagnosed by nineteenth-century medicine, may have played a part in Sisi's behavior, but something far more pedestrian might have been responsible for pushing her so far away from her husband that she had to leave the country and place half of Europe between them. She'd heard through the grapevine that Franz Joseph had enjoyed a rendezvous with a Polish beauty, a countess he had known before his marriage. It was rumored that the mystery woman was one of his mother's ladies-in-waiting, or part of her household in some way—yet another reason for Sisi to despise Sophia, whom she now regarded as a procuress.

In the autumn of 1860, Sisi suffered a total physical and mental breakdown. Although no written records survive, rumors have persisted for the past hundred and fifty years that Sisi had received from her adoring husband the gift that keeps on giving—an utterly devastating blow—not merely proof of his infidelity, but a strange disease that left her with swollen wrists and knees. The court physicians refused to give her a diagnosis; so, heavily veiled and incognita, she visited a private doctor in Vienna, who gave her the awful truth. If his diagnosis of venereal disease was accurate, it was likely the catalyst that sent her fleeing from a place she already detested and a marriage that she considered "hell on earth"—a phrase that brought tears to Franz Joseph's eyes whenever she said it to his face.

The "mysterious illness" was publicly billed as tuberculosis, which provided enough of an explanation as to why she was wasting away. Touted to her subjects as a "rest cure," she toured Madeira and Corfu, places where she would be unlikely to meet any Austrians, who gleefully equated the empress's flight with her inability to win the love of the people. There, she took Hungarian lessons, devoured Shakespeare, and received lovesick letters from Franz Joseph. Certainly if he knew by then he had given her a venereal disease (were that indeed the case), his guilt would have been overwhelming.

No sooner did Franz Joseph persuade Sisi to come home than her emotional symptoms returned, manifesting themselves in melancholia (what is now called depression, in addition to what we might diagnose as anorexia). She developed a mania for visiting local lunatic asylums and began to champion better treatment for madness. Edgy and restless, she insisted on resuming her foreign travels, returning to the welcoming throngs of Viennese in August of 1862. Baron Hübner, an eyewitness to the imperial couple's interactions at the time, observed that they were as loving as ever; but Sisi's ladies-in-waiting described her as frequently in tears, spending hours alone in her bedroom sobbing. She was sometimes so irritable that she could not bear to have them around, nor could she tolerate being alone with her husband. This time her mystery ailment was diagnosed as anemia, which had also led to dropsy. As a result, Sisi's feet were painfully swollen with fluid.

The most frequent point of contention in the imperial household seemed to be the upbringing of their children. Their health was always delicate, yet no one seems to have credited their physical, as well as mental, instability with the fact that they were the inbred offspring of a pair of first cousins. Gisela was turning into a plodding creature with none of her mother's beauty or imagination. Crown Prince Rudolf was precociously bright, but possessed a cruel and willful streak and a fascination with pistols—thanks to his brutal tutor, who was always trying to frighten him by shooting them off in his bedroom.

In 1865, the twenty-eight-year-old Sisi presented Franz Joseph with a written ultimatum: "It is my wish that full and unlimited powers should be reserved to me in all things concerning the children . . . I alone must decide everything up to their majority." She added that from then on, "I further desire that everything concerning my own personal affairs, my place of residence (all changes in domestic arrangements) should be left for me alone to decide."

One of those places Sisi chose to reside was Castle Gödollo in Hungary. She had fallen in love with the country—its people, its music, and its picturesque aspect. She actively championed the rights of the strong, proud Magyars, often to the chagrin of her husband, who had brutally subdued their rebellion in 1848–49. In 1867, after many months of negotiations, a political compromise was reached between Austria and Hungary, restoring the latter's 1848 constitution and creating a dual monarchy, the Austro-Hungarian Empire. And on June 8, 1867, with tremendous pageantry, the Emperor and Empress of Austria were crowned King and Queen of Hungary. Sisi's coronation gown, created by Worth of Paris, was a couture version of the traditional Hungarian national costume: an embroidered and bejeweled skirt and train of silver and white brocade, and a black velvet bodice laced entirely with pearls.

It was her beloved Hungary where the thirty-year-old Sisi insisted on bearing her fourth child. But even that decision sowed the seeds of a potential political crisis. If she gave birth to a boy on Hungarian soil, it would mean that he (rather than his older, Austrian-born brother) would be the eventual King of Hungary. It would also mean that upon this hypothetical son's eventual succession, the Hungarian crown lands would be separated from Austria.

Much to the relief of the Austrians, who were coming to despise their empress, on April 22, 1868, Sisi gave birth to a daughter, the Archduchess Marie-Valerie. As neglectful as she had been of her first three children, Sisi would dote so much on "Valerie" throughout the girl's life that she nearly smothered her.

By the 1860s Sisi's renowned beauty had made her an international celebrity, yet it brought her no joy. Hungarian countess Marie Festetics, the lady-in-waiting who became Sisi's closest confidante for years, wrote in her diary, "The Empress is sweet and good, but she makes everything a burden for herself, and what to others is a source of happiness becomes for her a source of discontent. She seems to me like a child in a fairytale. The good fairies came, and each of them laid a special gift in her cradle, beauty, sweetness, grace . . . dignity, intelligence, and wit. But then came the bad fairy and said 'I see that everything has been given you, but I will turn these qualities against you and they shall bring you no happiness. I will deprive you of something which a man bears within him unconsciously—moderation in your actions, occupations, thoughts and sensibilities. Nothing will bring you happiness, everything will turn against you . . . and you will never find peace.'"

Sisi's favorite daughter, Marie-Valerie, turned a critical eye on her mother's manias. "How often I ask myself whether the relationship between my parents might not, after all, have turned out differently if in her youth Mama had had a serious, courageous will for it—I mean, a woman can accomplish anything—And yet she may be right that, given the circumstances, it was impossible to become more intimately one."

It was no secret to anyone at the Austrian court that the emperor was a slave to Sisi's manipulative moods and to her numerous physical indispositions, which she invoked whenever she didn't want to do something that invariably involved professional appearances and the discharging of the formal duties expected of an empress. However, she was always perfectly healthy when it came time to indulge in her brisk exercise regimens, to spend the entire day riding one of her horses at breakneck speed, or to travel for hundreds of miles.

But in a world where her role was so prescribed, where protocol was king and ceremony queen, Sisi's behavior—including her fanatical dieting and exercising—was her way of gaining a measure of control. If all that was hers was her own body, she could at least control *that*—by withholding it from her husband, from their subjects, and by taming it into an enviable, if eventually wraithlike, physique.

After twenty-one years of marriage, Sisi began to spend the better part of her time abroad. She expressed the wish that Franz Joseph could join her, yet at the same time reveled in the opportunity to get away from him. When he explained that his responsibilities kept him from leaving his empire at a moment's whim, she accused him of having the soul of a petty bureaucrat. Tragically, both Franz Joseph and Sisi were desperately lonely—within the marriage as well as when geographical and emotional distance separated them—yet neither could fill the other's needs as spouses and as lovers.

Meanwhile, the imperial brood was growing older and slipping dangerously away from their parents' control—which was weak to begin with. Apart from her obsession with her youngest child, Marie-Valerie, Sisi was absent—emotionally, literally, or both—from their children's lives.

Sisi spent more time worrying about herself than about anyone else. At the age of forty-six, desperate to stave off old age, she took up fencing and mastered it. She continued her gymnastics exercise regimen, as skilled on the trapeze as many circus performers. Terrified of wrinkles, she slathered herself with facial masks made from raw veal or crushed strawberries, frequently invoking her credo, "Life will be worthless to me when I am no longer desirable."

And yet her husband's desire for her went unappreciated. It was only a matter of time before Franz Joseph would seek to replace the emotional void that Sisi had left by her prolonged absences. In 1884 he developed an interest in the theater, and in particular in an actress twenty-three years his junior named Katharina Schratt, also known as Frau von Kiss. Ironically, it was Sisi who had been to see her on the stage and became convinced that the young woman had all the requisite qualities to make the emperor happy.

The May-December relationship between Katharina Schratt and Franz Joseph may not have been a sexual one, although the emperor did fall in love with her. Madame Schratt was tender and solicitous, and a good listener; their liaison would last more than thirty years. Often she would travel with the imperial couple, and Sisi would make a point of being seen walking alone with her in public gardens to stave off any speculation that Franz Joseph was having an affair. For years, Franz Joseph and Sisi would refer to Madame Schratt as their "good friend."

But Archduchess Marie-Valerie was appalled and embarrassed by her father's extramarital relationship. She wrote in her diary, "Oh! Why did Mama bring about this acquaintance, and how can she say to boot that it is a reassurance to her! . . . How can it be that two such noble natures as my parents can be so mistaken and can so often make each other unhappy."

By 1888, Sisi was off on her travels again, returning to Corfu, where she decided to build a villa. She had become obsessed with Homer and the ancient Greeks, when she should have been minding her son's behavior instead. Rudolf had married the homely sixteen-year-old Princess Stephanie of the Belgians in May of 1881, but had hardly been faithful to her, in addition to becoming an alcoholic and a morphine addict—the latter as a result of the pain he incurred when he took a bad fall from a horse. Rudolf had become obsessed with the notion of suicide, and when Stephanie told the emperor that he had asked her to make a suicide pact with him, Franz Joseph stiffly informed his daughter-in-law that she was merely giving way to fantasies.

On the morning of Wednesday, January 30, 1889, Sisi received the awful news that the crown prince had been found dead at Mayerling, his hunting lodge. Beside him was the corpse of his latest fling, seventeen-year-old Mary Vetsera—nude but for the single stemmed rose clasped between her fingers, the victim of a single shot to the head. The imperial couple spun the event, claiming that Mary had poisoned their son and then herself, but no one could ignore the bullet hole in each of their brains. It was later revealed (and most historians still believe) that Rudolf had killed Mary; and, coward that he was, he spent the next six to eight hours sitting on the bed beside her corpse, guzzling brandy until he had the gumption to fulfill their bargain and shoot himself.

"Where did we fail?" the imperial couple asked themselves. Sisi was tortured by her son's death, not so much because she had neglected him for years but because she was convinced that she had passed him "tainted blood" through the Wittelsbach line. Rudolf was related both to Sisi's cousin "Mad King Ludwig" of Hesse-Darmstadt and to Ferdinand and Isabella's daughter "Joanna the Mad."

Rudolf's death and the manner in which it transpired haunted Franz Joseph as well as Sisi, but he dealt with it differently. Their daughter Marie-Valerie wrote to her fiancé, Franz Salvator, Archduke of Austria-Tuscany, "My mother causes me great anxiety. Now that agitation has given way to everyday life, and Papa at least appears outwardly the same, and works as he always did, life seems to her oppressive and cheerless. Besides, she is afraid that her ever-increasing grief may become a burden to Papa and lead to misunderstandings between them."

In 1890, after Marie-Valerie's wedding, Sisi resumed her wanderings once more, returning to Vienna only to quell rumors of her husband's affair with Katharina Schratt. The imperial couple was otherwise estranged and had been so for years. According to the emperor's *valet de chambre*, Eugene Ketterl, "At Gödollo, the Emperor was only rarely allowed to see his wife, even though they were living under the same roof. . . . It could happen that the Emperor might try to see her in vain for ten days running. How embarrassing that was in front of the staff, anyone can imagine; I often felt endless pity for my sovereign lord."

After Rudolf's suicide, Sisi became a black-clad, wraithlike figure who inspired more pity than awe. Sciatica and neuritis plagued her fifty-something body, which she still strove to keep youthful with seaweed wraps and massages. And yet she longed for death, wishing it to "take me unawares," and to do so far from her family.

The empress got her wish in September 1898. During a visit to Switzerland, Sisi had been walking in the woods at Caux with her financial adviser and her attendants when they were accosted by an unemployed twenty-five-year-old Italian workman asking for alms. He was curtly rebuffed by Sisi's controller, who kept the purse shut tightly.

The beggar, Luigi Luccheni, was a wannabe anarchist looking to make a name for himself by assassinating a monarch. His weapon was a sharp-edged file with a rough-hewn firewood handle that he'd purchased in the market at Lausanne. For the next few days, he stalked the sixty-year-old empress.

On the afternoon of September 10, as Sisi and Countess Irma Sztáray strode along the quay, about to board the steamship for Montreaux, Luccheni suddenly collided with them, raising his fist and striking at Sisi. She fell to the ground and hit her head. At first it wasn't quite clear what had happened. The empress was carried to the deck of the steamship, where the captain tried to revive her with water and sugar soaked in alcohol.

"What is it?" she murmured.

The countess noticed a bloodstain on her chemise and a puncture in the fabric. Over the roar of the engines, she cried, "The Empress of Austria has been murdered!"

The captain ordered the boat turned for Geneva, but by then Sisi's breath had become a death rattle. The piercing of Luccheni's file was so small that she very gradually bled to death internally, with only a single drop of blood staining her stays and batiste camisole. She had been Empress of Austria—however reluctantly—for forty-four years.

Franz Joseph had been in the process of writing his estranged wife a letter when he received a telegram from Geneva with the tragic news. "Is nothing to be spared me on this earth?" he wept. Broken and distraught, he gazed at the portrait of Sisi hanging opposite his desk. "No one will ever know how much I loved her," he murmured to himself.

Luccheni pleaded guilty and was sentenced to life in prison. On October 19, 1910, he hanged himself in his cell.

Four years later, on June 28, 1914, Archduke Franz Ferdinand of Austria and his wife were assassinated in Sarajevo as they traveled in an open car, sparking the First World War. The archduke was Franz Joseph's nephew, and (thanks to Crown Prince Rudolf's suicide) the heir to the Austro-Hungarian Empire.

Eighteen years after Sisi's death, on November 21, 1916, at the age of eighty-six, Franz Joseph died, allegedly singing "God Save the Emperor." He had enjoyed one of the longest reigns in history—sixty-eight years—surpassing even Queen Victoria's. But the Age of Empire was over. The Austro-Hungarian imperial monarchy was dissolved after the end of the First World War.

For all Sisi's self-centeredness and emotional remoteness, and Franz Joseph's rigid workaholism, they're a pair of royals we can oddly relate to even though they may not be particularly likeable as individuals. The more eccentric Sisi grew, the more pedantic her husband became; and where the empress gave free rein to her hypersensitivity, he clung to stubborn obstinacy. Their marriage was fraught with tribulations, some of which seem strikingly "modern"—the sort of things you'd expect from an HBO hit series: miscommunication, eating disorders, manic depression, infant death, a problem child who got mixed up with bad company and substance abuse, suicide, frigidity, extramarital dalliances, and ultimately, estrangement. Yet never once did either Franz Joseph or Sisi seem to have contemplated divorce—possibly because they were devout Catholics—and to the last, at least from Franz Joseph, what remained bobbing just beneath the current, amid all the ugly emotional flotsam, was Love.

TSAR NICHOLAS II

1868–1918

RULED RUSSIA: 1894–1917

❧ *and* ❧

ALEXANDRA FEODOROVNA

1872–1918

married 1894–1918

"At last, united, bound for life, and when this life is ended, we meet again in the other world and remain together for eternity. Yours, yours."

—Alexandra's entry in Nicholas's diary on their wedding night, November 26, 1894

QUEEN VICTORIA HAD A PREMONITION. ON DECEMBER 29, 1890, four years before Nicholas and Alexandra were wed, when their love was little more than a long-distance crush, the Queen of England wrote to her eldest daughter expressing her misgivings about the potential union:

. . . there must be no more visits of Alicky to Russia—and . . . you and Ernie [Alexandra's brother] must insist on a stop being put to the whole affair. . . . The state of Russia is so bad, so rotten that at any moment something dreadful might happen . . . the wife of the Thronfolger [heir to the throne] is in a most difficult and precarious position. . . . It would have the very worst effect here and in Germany (where Russia is not liked) and would produce a great separation between our families.

When Victoria finally met Nicholas, she claimed to have "never met a more amiable, simple young man, affectionate, sensible, and liberal-minded." Having married for love herself, Her Majesty also recognized that her granddaughter's relationship with Nicky was a passionate and devoted love match. Her rationale for dissuading Alexandra from making a huge marital mistake was wholly political.

Alicky, as Alexandra was known among the family, was only six years old in 1878 when her mother, Alice of Hesse-Darmstadt, died of diphtheria. Nicholas's youth had also been colored by the death of a close relative; at the tender age of twelve he saw his grandfather, Tsar Alexander II, blown apart by an assassin's bomb.

Nicholas's father was Tsar Alexander III, an imposing, six-foot-six-inch bear of a man who could bend metal bars with his bare hands. His mother was the Empress Marie Feodorovna, known as Minnie, a former Danish princess and the sister of the Princess of Wales. Minnie was as adamantly against a marriage between Alicky and Nicky as was Queen Victoria, but for different reasons: in her view, a daughter of tiny and undistinguished Hesse-Darmstadt was unworthy of becoming the next tsarina of Russia. Minnie was also convinced that Alicky was not enough of a people person for the job. She was too nervous; a shy, badly dressed *parvenue* with a clumsy, schoolgirl manner. But no amount of family pressure from either side could induce either Nicholas or Alexandra to consider wedding anyone else.

Alexandra and Nicholas first met in 1884 when Alicky, only twelve, had journeyed to St. Petersburg for the wedding of her older sister Ella to Nicholas's uncle, the Grand Duke Serge. All week, she exchanged furtive glances with the sixteen-year-old Nicholas. And when he gave her a brooch, she felt so uncomfortable about accepting it that she returned it, wounding his feelings. But they kept in touch over the years, their mutual attraction increasing with each reunion.

In 1892, the same year Alexandra was orphaned by the death of her father, Duke Louis of Hesse, Nicholas made the following entry in his diary: "My dream is to some day marry Alix H. I have loved her a long while and still deeper and stronger since 1889 when she spent six weeks in St. Petersburg. For a long time I resisted my feeling that my dearest dream will come true."

If only Alexandra would lay aside her misgivings about converting to Russian Orthodoxy—a sacrifice required of every tsar's consort—life would be perfect! Alicky was already the subject of much gossip within her family. By then she was nearly twenty-two, tall and slender with red-gold hair and gray-blue eyes, but was still unwed, holding out hope for Nicky, yet all the while maintaining that their different religions posed an insuperable barrier to their happiness.

In April 1894, several of the crowned heads of Europe gathered in Coburg for the wedding of Alicky's homosexual brother Ernest to his cousin Victoria Melita, the daughter of Victoria and Albert's son Alfred. Nicholas and Alexandra were able to spend a good deal of time together, but Alicky burst into tears whenever the subject of religious conversion was raised. So Ella was dispatched to have a nice long talk with her younger sister. Ella had converted when she wed Serge, and somehow she managed to convince Alicky that Russian Orthodoxy and Lutheranism were really quite similar!

As soon as Alicky made her peace with the issue, the young couple was in perfect harmony. And with no further impediment to their union, she joyfully agreed to give her hand to the equally exultant Nicholas, who wrote in his diary, "A marvelous, unforgettable day. Today is the day of my engagement to my darling, adorable Alix. . . . The whole family was simply enraptured."

And to his mother, Nicholas wrote, "We were left alone and

with her first words she consented . . . I cried like a child and she did, too, but her expression had changed. Her face was lit by a quiet contentment. . . . The whole world is changed for me: nature, mankind, everything, and all seems to be good and lovable . . . she is quite changed. She is gay and amusing, talkative and tender."

When she discovered that her fiancé kept a diary—in which his entries were written in English—Alexandra began to scribble romantic notes in it, which usually began with the words "Many loving kisses." One such comment read, "I dreamed that I was loved, I woke and found it true and thanked God on my knees for it. True love is the gift which God has given, daily, stronger, deeper, fuller, purer."

An early love note from Nicky to Alicky reads, "I love you my own darling as few persons can only love! I love you too deeply and strongly for me to show it; it is such a sacred feeling, I don't want to let it out in words, that seem too meek, and poor and vain."

Alexandra promised her beloved that "I am yours, you are mine, of that be sure. You are locked in my heart, the little key is lost and now you must stay there forever."

For the time being life was sunshine and roses. They were reveling in being in love.

But on November 1, 1894, after a brief illness, Tsar Alexander III died. The twenty-six-year-old Nicholas, unschooled in statecraft and riddled with chronic indecision, was now the Tsar of all the Russias. The task ahead of him was enormous. A hundred million subjects inhabited imperial Russia; three-quarters of them were peasants who dwelled in the countryside. Among the population were native Russians, Germans, Orthodox Jews, Slavs, Uzbeks, Tartars, Georgians, and Armenians. The tsar ruled from St. Petersburg, but the empire's center of commerce was Moscow, a lengthy rail journey thousands of miles to the southeast.

Suddenly, Alexandra, already out of her element and disdained by her formidable mother-in-law, was about to become bride and empress all at once.

The wedding date of November 26 had been chosen because it

was also the birthday of the now dowager empress Marie, who was still deep in mourning for her husband. On the day of the ceremony, poor Alexandra, who had been nicknamed "the funeral bride," was laced into a heavy, old-fashioned court dress of silver brocade with a sumptuous robe and train made of cloth of gold lined with ermine. The diamond nuptial crown was all ready to be placed atop her upswept hair. Meanwhile, inside the Uspensky Sobor Cathedral within the Kremlin, guests were shifting from foot to foot and muttering to themselves as the 11:30 commencement time for the ceremony time came and went. Nicholas, in his crimson uniform and boots of the Lifeguard regiment of the Hussars, may have feared that his bride had developed a case of cold feet.

The delay was due to the detention of the hairdresser by a skeptical security detail, and only after an hour of frantic explanation was the sweating and agitated man admitted to Alexandra's presence.

Nonetheless, she made a radiant bride, and the royal couple was pronounced man and wife shortly before one p.m. Alix had converted to Russian Orthodoxy and henceforth would be known as Alexandra Feodorovna.

From the start, the imperial marriage was the picture of the Victorian ideal: outwardly placid, privately passionate. On their wedding night Alicky took the time to write in Nicky's diary, "At last, united, bound for life, and when this life is ended, we meet again in the other world and remain together for eternity. Yours, yours." The following morning she added, "Never did I believe there could be such utter happiness in this world, such a feeling of unity between two mortal beings. I love you, those three words have my life in them."

Although their love life was a study in compatibility, Alexandra might have wished for one significant change on the domestic front. In Russia, a dowager empress took social precedence over the current one and Nicky's mother, Minnie, was no exception. She refused to hand over the crown jewels to her successor until Alexandra eventually got up the courage to make an embarrassing fuss about it. Minnie took dinner beside her son every night, as Alicky uncomfortably watched her infantilize him. Minnie had even chosen the newlyweds' suite of rooms at the Anitchkov Palace, which were small, cramped, and markedly inferior to her own apartments, although Nicholas and Alexandra were now the tsar and tsarina. Their quarters were the ones Nicky and his brother Georgy had shared as children, never intended for adults with vast formal wardrobes. Consequently, Alexandra had no space to hang and store her clothes. And she soon discovered that their servants, also handpicked by Minnie, were spying on her every word and deed and reporting the details to the dowager. Evidently Minnie didn't think her daughter-in-law was showing Nicholas enough respect by addressing him with pet names like "Boysy" (Alix was "Girlsy").

But Alexandra's concern for her beloved Nicky trumped any worries about her own reputation at court. She recognized all too well the magnitude of his responsibilities. Nicholas remained in utter awe of his office, referring to it as "that awful job I have feared all my life." He picked up nervous tics like chain-smoking and stroking his beard.

Early in their marriage Alexandra wrote, "I weep and I worry all day long because I feel that my husband is so young and inexperienced . . . I am alone most of the time. My husband is occupied all day and he spends his evenings with his mother."

Alix begged her husband to assert himself, but he was congenitally incapable of it, and petrified of conflict, particularly with Minnie. Alexandra's attempts to fight back backfired in a big way. In an effort to remind everyone that *she* was now the empress, she dressed opulently and appeared dripping with jewels, but was mocked for overdoing it; and her fashion sensibilities and designer clothing from the best Paris couturiers were criticized for being both tacky and extravagant. Alexandra was never accepted as one of their own by the Russian aristocracy, who disliked and mistrusted her. And for all her language lessons, she never learned to speak Russian well.

Adept with pen and ink, however, Alix amused herself by sketching caricatures of her imperial in-laws. A particularly acerbic one depicted her husband as a baby sitting in a high chair being scolded by his mother. But when her drawings were discovered, the Romanovs failed to see the humor.

A few months later, however, tensions between Alexandra and her in-laws began to ease. Perhaps they realized that she was there to stay, made Nicky desperately happy, and there was nothing they could do about it. "Half a year now that we are married. How intensely happy you have made . . . [me]," wrote Alexandra in her husband's diary.

On May 26, 1895, Nicholas and Alexandra were crowned in the Ouspensky Cathedral in Moscow. Seven thousand guests partook of the coronation banquet, but the festivities were marred by tragedy when an outdoor event at Khodynka Field offering free food and beer to the half million subjects gathered there turned fatal, earning the tsar the nickname "Bloody Nicholas." A rumor that they were running out of beer fomented a stampede, and several dozen people, if not hundreds, were trampled to death or wounded. Their mangled bodies were quickly cleared from the field and promptly disposed of in mass graves, so as not to spoil the gaiety. Because it was widely (and falsely) reported that Alexandra, impervious to the tragedy, danced the night away at a ball hosted by the French, she became known as "the German bitch," an epithet that would dog her all her life. In 1895 it was merely insulting; in 1918, it would be lethal.

The stress of all the coronation activities caused Alexandra to miscarry the male fetus that would have become the tsarevich, the heir to the imperial throne. Eventually, Alexandra and Nicholas would have five children. Between 1895 and 1901 four daughters— Olga, Tatiana, Marie, and Anastasia—were born; and on August 12, 1904, Alexandra gave birth to the tsarevich, Alexis Nicolaevich.

By then, the tsarina, who had initially been so loath to convert to Russian Orthodoxy, had embraced the religion with the fervor of a zealot. She read church history, collected icons, and dabbled in the occult practices that were popular among the Russian aristocracy. However, to many people, particularly her in-laws, she remained an outsider, grim and thin-lipped when she was expected to greet and mingle with guests, her hands red and spotted from some sort of nervous reaction. No one cut her any slack. She'd barely been in Russia a month and could hardly speak the language before she had suddenly become their empress. Her lofty status and title made it impossible for her to make friends because everyone was beneath her. And during her first years of marriage she was so often in the throes of a difficult pregnancy, confined to months of bed rest, that she had attended few social or state engagements.

The early years of Nicholas's reign saw a flowering of culture known as the Russian Renaissance or the Silver Age. Theater and literature sparkled with Stanislavsky, Chekhov, Gorky, and Sholom Aleichem. Pavlov conducted his canine experiments. The canvases of Kandinsky, Chagall, and Bakst brought painting into the modern age, while the artistry of Petipa, Nijinsky, Diaghilev, Fokine, and Pavlova turned the stage of the imperial ballet into one unrivaled among its peers. Prokofiev, Rimsky-Korsakov, Vladimir Horowitz, and Jascha Heifetz made glorious music. It was an embarrassment of riches, especially in a world where many of the tsar's subjects were starving and unemployed.

By 1905, when the empire had lost the Russo-Japanese war, the seeds of revolution had been sown from within. In early January, waves of protests began to sweep across the country; workers struck en masse. On January 22, an activist workers' movement secretly led by the police marched peaceably on the Winter Palace in the capital city of St. Petersburg. Nicholas's infantry fired into the mob, massacring men, women, and children. The day became known as "Bloody Sunday," shattering the illusion that the tsar was one with his people.

Although Alexandra was exceptionally distraught over the carnage of Bloody Sunday, she defended her husband. "My poor Nicky's cross is a heavy one to bear, all the more as he has nobody on whom he can thoroughly rely and who can be a real help to him . . . he tries so hard, working with such perseverance, but the lack of what I call 'real' men is great. . . ."

And to her sister Victoria, Alix wrote of the 1905 uprising and the increased demands for a parliamentary form of government: "All over the country it is spreading. The Petition had only two questions concerning workmen and the rest was atrocious: separation of the Church from the Government, etc. . . . How I wish I were clever and could be of real use. I love my new country. It's so young, powerful and has so much good in it, only utterly unbalanced and childlike. . . ."

In mid-October 1905, Russia was paralyzed by a general strike. Overnight a new workers' organization sprang up, led by a fiery Marxist orator named Leon Trotsky.

Nicholas had two choices: become a dictator or write a constitution. He chose the latter for expediency's sake, although he didn't believe in either a constitution or a parliamentary body. The Imperial Manifesto of October 30, 1905, transformed Russia from an absolute autocracy into a semi-constitutional monarchy.

On paper.

Nicholas was neck-deep in political upheaval but he still found time for his family, and especially for the infant tsarevich, a chubby golden-haired cherub, named for Nicky's favorite tsar, the seventeenth-century Alexis the Peaceful. It had taken ten years for Alexandra to give him a son; a male heir was of paramount importance ever since Tsar Paul I, the son of Catherine the Great, had changed the rules of succession. Paul so detested his mother for her role in the murder of his father, he decreed that no woman could ever again inherit the imperial throne.

But the joys of finally begetting an heir were short-lived. Within weeks of his birth, little Alexis began to bleed from his navel. The flow was stanched but after a day or two it began again. Alexandra's worst fears were confirmed. Alexis had the Bleeding Disease, better known to us as hemophilia. Her uncle and baby brother had died from it and several of her male relatives also suffered from it.

Alix was certain that her son had inherited the fatal trait through her and cursed herself for passing it to him. The empress's guilt overwhelmed her, and in time, her desperate search for a cure would play a significant role in the collapse of the Russian empire and the execution of the Romanovs.

Hemophilia is an inherited blood-clotting deficiency where blood fails to coagulate properly after a cut, puncture, or wound. Even the slightest bruise can cause blood to fill the joints, resulting in severe swelling and extreme pain. The trait is passed through the female line on a recessive gene. Women are carriers but are rarely sufferers of the disease. Queen Victoria was a carrier, as were three of her daughters, including Alexandra's mother, Alice.

At the deliberate wish of his parents, Alexis's disorder was the best-kept secret in the empire. Even the boy's tutors were unaware of the diagnosis. After all, what would be the heir's fate—or that of the empire—if the people were to learn that their future tsar was an invalid who might not survive to adulthood?

The nuclear imperial family was a tight-knit one. In the private wing of the thousand-room Alexander Palace in Tsarkoe Selo (the Tsar's Village)—a Disneyesque version of all that was opulent and exotic about Russia—the family would dress up for afternoon tea and enjoy postprandial parlor games and genteel activities, such as pasting photos into scrapbooks and albums and quietly reading in each other's company. The imperial children were raised like dutiful Victorian bourgeoisie with respect for their elders, charity toward the poor, and a strong sense of duty and usefulness.

Unlike many royal couples, Alexandra and Nicholas shared a bed. The tsar liked to read before putting out the light, but on the occasions when he tried to fall asleep right away, he was sometimes kept awake by Alix, still engrossed in her book, noisily crunching English biscuits. They always spoke and wrote to each other in English. To the tsarina her husband was always "Nicky." He called his wife "Sunny" or "Sunshine." And they shared a secret signal for nookie time: Nicholas would whistle, imitating the warbling of a bird. Early in their marriage, Alix would blush crimson when she heard his signal, drop whatever she was doing, such as needlework or correspondence, grasp her heavy skirts and hasten to heed her husband's sexual summons.

But as the years wore on Alexandra began to suffer from migraines, shortness of breath, and sciatica, and was often confined to a wheelchair. Alexis's disease had turned her further inward. She prayed for hours a day asking God to send someone who could heal her son. When none of the doctors were successful, she never doubted His mercy; she merely resigned herself to accepting her own unworthiness of it.

Finally, in 1905 a savior arrived in the form of a big, burly, lanky-haired peasant. Born Grigory Efimovich in Pokrovskoe, a village in Western Siberia, Rasputin was a smelly, shaggy man with a long black beard and mesmerizing pale blue eyes. He called himself a *starets*—one of the Russian men of God who lived in poverty with the asceticism of a hermit. All Russians, regardless of rank or birth, listened to such holy men and gave them credence. And among the *startsky* of Russia, Rasputin was a rock star. According to his patients, through his hypnotically charismatic gaze Rasputin had the power to bewitch the blood, controlling its flow from one part of the body to another and stanching wounds mesmerically. They overlooked his utter inattention to personal hygiene, his filthy, coarse garments, and his unkempt appearance. No one cared that the holy man was a hedonist—half saint, half satyr, with a sexual appetite the size of Russia itself. In fact, the name "Rasputin"— bestowed on him by his Siberian neighbors for his outsized habits of drinking, fighting, and fornicating—means "dissolute." But titled women dripping in jewels fell over themselves to bed him, and men who should have known better considered it a privilege to sacrifice their wives' bodies to Rasputin's libidinous advances.

Alexandra never succumbed to Rasputin's questionable physical charms. But that didn't stop tongues from wagging, especially after he became her personal *starets*. Alix was so dependent on him to cure Alexis that the British geneticist J. B. S. Haldane believed "Rasputin took the empire by stopping the bleeding of the tsarevich." Late-twentieth-century medical historians have hypothesized that Rasputin's meditative, mesmeric techniques and reassuring presence were calming influences that lowered Alexis's blood pressure, thereby enabling clotting to begin. But at the time, many skeptics considered him to be nothing but a mountebank. Nevertheless, the tsarina would credit none of the *starets*'s detractors and welcomed Rasputin into the Alexander Palace with open arms.

It was the beginning of the end for the imperial family.

Alexandra believed only what she wanted to see. When Rasputin made sexual advances toward her eldest daughter, Olga, and the girls' governess complained of his impropriety, it was she who got sacked. When Alix's sister Ella ventured to declare that Rasputin was a fraud, her remark fractured the sisters' relationship irreparably. Nicholas was of a similar mind, but he knew that dismissing Rasputin would ruin his wife's emotional health. Nicholas would never have forgiven himself if the self-important Rasputin were sent away from Tsarkoe Selo and Alexis were to die soon after his departure.

In 1912, after Alexis suffered a dreadful bleeding episode at Spala and Rasputin was able to cure him long-distance from Siberia, Alexandra wrote to him gratefully, with the same effusiveness she employed in addressing all her intimate friends:

My beloved, unforgettable teacher, redeemer and mentor! How tiresome it is without you! . . . I only wish one thing: to fall asleep, forever on your shoulders and in your embrace. What happiness to feel your presence near me. Where are you? Where have you gone? Oh, I am so sad and my heart is longing. . . . Will you soon be again close to me? Come quickly, I am waiting for you and I am tormenting myself for you. I am asking for your holy blessing and I am kissing your blessed hands. I love you forever.

She signed it *Yours, M* (for "Mama").

This letter sparked rumors that the tsarina and the *starets* were lovers. Those rumors bred others that he had slept with all four grand duchesses as well.

Alexandra was passionately in love with her own husband, was wildly religious, and found the Russian court's moral laxness unforgivable. So it's highly unlikely that she was Rasputin's mistress. Nevertheless, her connection with the *starets*, even if it wasn't sexual, imported corruption into the highest circles of Russian society. And their relationship hastened the downfall of the Romanov dynasty: while Nicholas was leading the Russian army during World War I, Alexandra was in St. Petersburg acting as regent. Her chief adviser—the man who convinced her to suggest specific troop movements to her husband, and who also strongly influenced the selection of ministers responsible for the governance of the empire while Nicholas was at the front—was Rasputin.

Alexandra and Rasputin were believed to be secret German sympathizers or even enemy spies, and their actions in the tsar's absence were viewed as an attempt to bring Russia to its knees so that the Kaiser's troops could march right in.

Although Alix heeded Rasputin's political advice with disastrous results, neither of them had anything but tremendous patriotic devotion to Mother Russia. During the Great War Alix worried constantly for Nicky's welfare, writing often to assure him of her love and support, her unshakable loyalty, and her fear for his well-being. In one of her 1914 letters, Alexandra gushed:

> I bless and love you as no man was rarely been loved before. I long to lessen your weight, to help you carry it—to stroke your brow, press you to myself . . . I long to hold you tight in my arms and let you rest your weary head upon my old breast. We have lived through so much together in these twenty years and without words understand each other.

She perfumed her letters to Nicholas or slipped pressed lilies or violets between the pages. Nicky would scent his replies with jasmine petals, Alix's favorite bloom.

"Good morning my darling," her letters to the front would begin, and they would end with exhortations to "Sleep well, my treasure," assuring him that "I yearn for your kisses, for your arms and shy Childy [Nicholas] gives them to me [only] in the dark and wify lives by them." Alexandra could not conceal her anguished concern each time Nicholas had to depart for the front:

Oh, my love, it was hard bidding you goodbye and seeing that lonely, pale face with big sad eyes at the . . . [train] window—my heart cried out, take me with you . . . I gave my good-night kiss to your cushion and longed to have you near me. . . .

These are not the words of a woman having an extramarital affair with a smelly peasant, no matter how indispensable his presence was to her son's health. Alexandra's passion for Nicholas remained that of a young lover:

32 years ago my child's heart already went out to you in deep love. . . I know I ought not to say this, and for an old married woman it may seem ridiculous, but I cannot help it. With the years, love increases and the time without your sweet presence is hard to bear. Oh, could but our children be equally blessed in their married lives.

Alexandra's letters were her husband's salvation during the tensest months of his life. Nicholas would read them just before he nodded off to sleep. His emotions were no less touched than hers by the deep and loving bond they shared and his words paint a tender picture of domestic tranquility in a world of chaos:

My beloved Sunny, when I read your letters my eyes are moist . . . it seems that you are lying on your sofa and that I am listening to you, sitting in my armchair by the lamp . . . I don't know how I could have endured it at all if God had not decreed to give you to me as a wife and friend. I speak in earnest. At times it is difficult to speak of such things and it is easier for me to put it down on paper owing to stupid shyness. . . . Goodbye, my beloved sweet Sunny. . . . I kiss you and the children tenderly. Ever your old hubby, Nicky.

In another letter he confessed that "I drink them and savor every word you write, and often bury my nose and press my lips to the paper you have touched."

Love notes aside, knowing her husband's distaste for confrontation Alexandra urged Nicholas to be more of an autocrat. Giving away too many rights to the people would only jeopardize Alexis's legacy. She wrote to remind Nicky that "We're not a constitutional country and dare not be, our people are not educated for it . . ." and, "For Baby's sake we must be firm, as otherwise his inheritance will be awful, as with his character he won't bow down to others but be his own master, as one must in Russia whilst people are still so uneducated."

Nicholas humored her, replying, "Tender thanks for the severe scolding. I read it with a smile because you speak to me as though I was a child. . . . Your poor little weak-willed hubby, Nicky."

But there was tension behind the mask. Nicholas wore Alexandra's portrait about his neck day and night as an emblem of her indispensable presence. Without her, he admitted to being an emotional and physical wreck. He was ailing and exhausted, but the cocaine he took to revive him and ease his heart pain was rapidly aging him. Only forty-nine years old, his eyes were sunken and "stony," his pupils faded, and his nose had grown fat while the rest of his face had become wrinkled, thin, and hollow. His beard and mustache were described as "tobacco yellow" by one observer, and his melancholy expression was one of utter helplessness and resignation. In the summer of 1915, he remarked, "perhaps a sacrificial victim is needed to save Russia. I will be that victim."

And back in the capital city of St. Petersburg, renamed "Petrograd" when the war with the Germans began in 1914, Alix was chain-smoking and dosing herself with Veronal to help her sleep.

After the revolution of 1905, it had been clear to the rest of Europe that the tsarist monarchy was on shaky ground. By the end of 1916, change at the top of the food chain was inevitable. The only question was whether it could be achieved without violence.

Alexandra was at the nadir of her popularity. Because she was a first cousin of the Kaiser—although she despised him and his militaristic posturing—she was presumed to be part of a pro-German cabal at the very pinnacle of Russian government and society. Behind her back her detractors called her *Nemka*, the "German woman," just as Marie Antoinette had been derided as *L'Autrichienne*, "the Austrian bitch." Nicholas was warned by one of his own relations that Alexandra could not be trusted: ". . . What she tells you is not the truth; she is only repeating what has been cleverly suggested to her. If you are not able to remove this influence from her, at least protect yourself."

It was Rasputin's malignant presence that had to be eliminated for the health of the empire. He disappeared from Tsarkoe Selo in the last days of December 1916, lured away by the wealthy Prince Felix Youssoupov, the husband of Nicholas's niece Irina. With Nicholas's tacit, top-secret approval, the plot's mastermind, Youssoupov, along with a handful of coconspirators, invited Rasputin to his palace with the promise that the beautiful Irina would be there; in fact, she was miles away, in the Crimea at the time. Always a sucker for sex, Rasputin fell for it, resulting in one of the most famous murders in Russian history. He managed to survive being poisoned, shot, bludgeoned, and kicked, until finally he was bound and drowned in the Neva River. Even so, he managed to slip some of his ropes after he was tossed into the dark and icy water. On January 3, 1917, his body was buried in a corner of the Imperial Park. The devastated empress placed Romanov family mementoes and a personal letter to the deceased inside his casket.

However, Rasputin's death changed nothing in the way the Russian government functioned. Revolution remained imminent. Nicholas was warned by Mikhail Rodzianko, the chairman of the fourth Duma, Russia's legislative body, to do something about his wife's interference in politics. "Alexandra Feodorovna is fiercely and universally hated, and all circles are clamoring for her removal." He added that "all Russia is unanimous in claiming a change of government and the appointment of a responsible premier invested with the confidence of the nation. . . . Sire, there is not a single honest or reliable man in our entourage; all the best have either been eliminated or have resigned. It is an open secret that the Empress issues orders without your knowledge, that Ministers report to her on matters of state. . . . Indignation against and hatred of the Empress are growing throughout the country. She is looked upon as Germany's champion. Even the common people are speaking of it."

"Give me facts," Nicholas demanded.

Rodzianko could present him with none. But he pointedly warned the tsar, "To save your family, Your Majesty ought to find some way of preventing the Empress from exercising any influence on politics. . . . Your Majesty, do not compel the people to choose between you and the good of your country."

But the politician's personal attacks on his wife, coupled with the demand that he send her away, only served to rile Nicholas's anger and stoke his chivalry. "The Empress is a foreigner. She has no one to protect her but myself. I shall never abandon her under any circumstances."

On March 7, 1917, Nicholas departed once more for army headquarters, ignoring his eleventh-hour opportunity to create a responsible ministry that would save his government. On March 8, he remained unaware of the violent riots taking place in the capital because the news was slow to reach him; and in any event his ministers did him a fatal disservice by sugarcoating the truth and downplaying the seriousness of the upheaval.

Petrograd was ground zero for the Russian Revolution of 1917. The first bread riots began on March 8, while Nicholas was en route to army headquarters. Factories had closed and there was a tremendous shortage of fuel and bread because so much of it was consumed by the troops. On March 12, the imperial government in Petrograd collapsed, and legislative power passed into the hands of the Duma. The mob marched in the streets. Bakeries were sacked and looted; arsenals were opened; prisons were stormed and the inmates released. But the imperial guard refused to fire on the crowd, summarily deserting their posts and joining the revolutionaries, swelling their ranks to 66,000 by nightfall.

Three days later, in his private rail car en route to Petrograd, Nicholas abdicated in favor of his twelve-year-old son, Alexis, but rescinded his decision a few hours later, only to re-abdicate in favor of his younger brother, Michael. But Michael didn't want the job and handed back the crown. After three centuries, the Romanov dynasty had ended with a whimper.

Alexandra was hysterical when she learned of her husband's abdication, sobbing and muttering, "The poor dear . . . all alone down there . . . what he has gone through. . . . And I was not there to console him." On March 17, Nicky, detained by the revolutionaries, was finally allowed to telephone Alix. She rushed to the phone like a young lover. Nicholas said simply, "You know?" Alexandra replied, "Yes," and they continued the conversation with a discussion about their children, aware that people were in the room at both ends of the line. In the days preceding her husband's return Alexandra burned her diaries and many of her letters, including years of correspondence with her grandmother, Queen Victoria. The letters she chose to save were those that contained proof of the imperial couple's Russian patriotism.

Alexandra, dressed in her nurse's uniform, was placed under house arrest at Tsarkoe Selo on March 21. That day, Nicholas was apprehended at Mogilev while he was visiting his mother and brought to Tsarkoe Selo, where he was reunited with his family. Alone in the children's room, they fell into each other's arms. Alexandra was quick to assure Nicholas that he was infinitely more important to her as a husband and a father than as the tsar whose throne she had shared. Nicholas laid his head against Alix's breast and sobbed like a baby.

As the Bolshevik Revolution raged, the imperial family remained under house arrest for five months at the mercy of the insurgents, hoping for rescue or for the opportunity to escape to a friendly nation. But on August 13, 1917, the day after Alexis's thirteenth birthday, the family was transported to Tobolsk in Siberia, where they resided for eight months under guard, living on credit and forced to economize. On April 26, 1918, a detachment commanded by Commissar Vasily Vaslevich Yakovlev arrived in Tobolsk to convey the entire family to Ekaterinberg. There, the imperial family was lodged in the two-story home of a merchant who had been given twenty-four hours' notice to vacate the premises. The residence, which had been ominously renamed "the House of Special Purpose," had been turned into a prison. The windows in the five rooms on the top floor had been sealed and painted white so that no one could see outside.

Toward the end of June the family received two letters that told them to be prepared to be rescued. They sat up all night with their suitcases packed, but no one came. Hope turned to fear on July 4 when their usual guard unit was replaced with another led by the icy and sinister Jacob Yurovsky. At least five of the men were foreigners; some historians describe them as Latvians, others as Magyar former prisoners of war from the Austro-Hungarian army—the kind of men assigned to duties a Russian would balk at performing.

On July 16, the entire family and their small entourage, which included their physician, valet, and cook—as well as the Grand Duchess Tatiana's dog—were ushered into the residence's semi-basement on the pretext that the advancing German army had made it necessary to move them. In the sixteen-by-eighteen-foot room with an iron grille covering the window, they waited for the imaginary automobiles to arrive. One of the guards posed them in a tableau, explaining that he needed a photograph to prove they hadn't been kidnapped by the Whites, the Bolsheviks' rival revolutionary faction. But it was a ruse to get the family into a cluster.

Moments later, they were told that the tsar's family had failed to save them and they would all be shot.

Nicholas, his arm protectively placed about his son's shoulder, had just enough time to say "What—?" before he was killed by a single revolver bullet. Alexandra made the sign of the cross as she, too, was felled by a single shot. Olga, Tatiana, and Marie, standing behind their mother, also died quickly. But Anastasia, who had only been wounded, regained consciousness and screamed as she saw her brother kicked in the head and two bullets fired into his ear. Seconds later, she was brutally bayoneted to death. Tatiana's dog was killed by a rifle butt to the head. The family's retainers were assassinated as well.

On July 17, the corpses were disposed of fourteen miles from Ekaterinberg in a mine shaft near Koptyaki, close to a quartet of pine trees nicknamed "Four Brothers." They had been dismembered and chopped into little pieces, doused with gasoline and sulfuric acid to hasten decomposition. But the following morning, as rumors spread regarding their location, Yurovsky, desperate to avoid a backlash against his actions that might result in the unintentional martyrdom of the imperial family, moved as much of the remains as he could to a sealed and concealed pit on Koptyaki Road.

The bodies of most of the Romanovs and their attendants were found in 1991, easily identified because the executioners hadn't bothered to hack up Tatiana's very recognizable pet. Alexis's and Anastasia's remains, which for some reason had been dumped near the pit, rather than within it, were finally found and identified in 2007. On March 11, 2009, the results of the DNA testing on the fragments conclusively proved that they were indeed those of the missing Romanov siblings. As of this writing the remains of Anastasia and Alexis have not yet been interred.

In 1991, the murdered imperial family were recognized as martyred saints by the Russian Orthodox Church outside Russia, although it took until the year 2000 for the synod of the Russian Orthodox Church to arrive at a similar conclusion; but because the last of the Romanovs had not died for their faith, as traditional martyrs have done, they were canonized as "Passion Bearers," or "people who met their deaths with Christian humility."

On July 17, 1998, a ceremony of Christian burial was held and the remains of the family (with the exception of Alexis and Anastasia) were laid to rest with state honors in the St. Catherine Chapel within the Fortress of St. Peter and St. Paul in St. Petersburg, reposing among the bodies of all other Russian emperors since Peter the Great.

Nicholas II, the last of the tsars, was not a good ruler; there's no way around it. During his reign his subjects grew increasingly disillusioned. They were tired of being hungry, and were angered by the rampant corruption in his government, particularly after Rasputin began to meddle in politics and guide Alexandra's hand. And it can certainly be argued that by giving way to Alexandra and not dismissing Rasputin from court, thereby permitting the *starets*'s influence to permeate and infect his government, and by turning a deaf ear on all pleas for responsible leadership, Nicholas made revolution—and Lenin's eventual triumph—possible.

But focusing instead for a moment on their private lives, Alexandra and Nicholas did achieve something that was progressive and modern for a royal household: They were exemplary spouses and parents who lovingly raised their five sweet-natured children in a cozy domestic environment. Neither partner dallied in extramarital affairs, although they both came from families where infidelity was *de rigueur*. From the day they met to the day they died, Nicholas and Alexandra adored each other, their relationship progressing from puppy love to grand passion. Each was the other's rock and best friend, and together they weathered the kind of heartbreak that would cause weaker unions to crumble under the weight of such adversity.

Theirs was much more than a love match. Nicholas referred to Alexandra as his "heart, brain, and soul," a rare compliment in the world of royal marriages.

EDWARD VIII
1894–1972
RULED ENGLAND: 1936

❦ *and* ❦

WALLIS WARFIELD SIMPSON
1895 or 1896–1986

married 1937–1972

"If ever there was a marriage that started off inauspiciously, resented and vilified, with many hopes and probably prayers for its failure, it was ours."
—Wallis Simpson, Duchess of Windsor

EDWARD VIII WILL FOREVER BE KNOWN AS "THE KING WHO abdicated for love." What gets lost in the romantic shuffle is that had he *not* done so, the face of the world in the mid-twentieth century might have become extremely different, with England a puppet nation of Nazism.

For Western civilization everything worked out for the best; but Edward's love affair with Wallis Warfield Simpson didn't have to cause a national crisis. In fact, the twice-divorced American had made it clear, even to Edward, that she would prefer to remain his official mistress than see him renounce his throne for her. In February 1936, when he had been king for just a few weeks, Wallis wrote to Edward, "I am sad because I miss you and being near and yet so far seems most unfair. . . . Perhaps both of us will cease to want what is the hardest to have and be content with the simple way."

Even decades later, Wallis insisted, "I told him I didn't want to be queen. . . . All that formality and responsibility . . . I told him that if he stayed on as king, it wouldn't be the end of us. I could still come and see him and he could still come and see me. We had terrible arguments about it. But he was a mule. He said he didn't want to be king without me, that if I left him he would follow me wherever I went."

Their royal marriage, and the arduous road that led to the altar, made some of the most notorious headlines of the 1930s.

Born only seven months after her parents' marriage, Bessie Wallis Warfield—who eventually ditched her first name because it sounded bovine—came from modest Baltimore beginnings. During leaner years, in an effort to make ends meet, her entrepreneurial mother turned their apartment into an impromptu restaurant, serving up lavish meals to the building's fellow tenants. Yet Wallis behaved like a genuine Southern belle, with an overdeveloped sense of entitlement, and somehow she managed to receive just about everything she demanded.

She was no real-life Daisy Buchanan, though. For one thing, her looks were anything but conventionally attractive. Her nose was lumpy, with a bulbous tip; her jaw resembled carved granite; there was a large mole on her chin below her lower lip; her hands, which an English aristocrat once referred to as "peasant paws," were large and ugly, with stubby fingernails. Meeting her in London in the 1930s, Cecil Beaton, a distant relative by marriage of Wallis's second husband, Ernest Simpson, took her measure immediately. Beaton is probably best known to Americans as the designer of the fabulous black and white costumes for the Ascot scene in *My Fair Lady*. His description of Wallis sounds like the low-class flower girl Henry Higgins bets he can pass off as a duchess. "She looked coarse. Her back was coarse and her arms were heavy. Her voice had a high nasal

twang. She was loud and brash, terribly so—and rowdy and rau-
cous. Her squawks of laughter were like a parrot's." Of course, when
Wallis *did* become a duchess, Beaton revised his opinion and found
many charming things to say about her features.

In 1927, Wallis divorced her first husband, bisexual navy pilot
Earl Winfield ("Win") Spencer. He was a depressive and moody
alcoholic, and a sexual sadist who would tie her to the bedposts
and beat her. According to U.S. State Department files, during this
marriage, as a naval wife she couriered sensitive documents to
various parts of the world, including China, where she enjoyed
extramarital affairs with dashing Italian Fascist ambassadors. She
allegedly became pregnant by one of them, Count Galeazzo Ciano,
and a botched abortion left her with gynecological problems for the
rest of her life. And according to a U.K. Secret Intelligence Service
(SIS) report on Wallis known as the China Dossier, she couriered
drugs during her Asian sojourn. However, some historians believe
the China Dossier may never have actually existed because the
documents alleged to have been contained in it have never been
made public.

Wallis was still married to Win Spencer when she commenced a
passionate affair with the man who would become her second husband, the Anglo-American businessman Ernest Aldrich Simpson.
She wed Simpson in London on July 21, 1928, and it was he who
provided her entrée into the royal enclave.

Wallis Simpson bears the distinction of being the woman who
introduced hot hors d'oeuvres to British society and is also credited
with the credo "You can never be too rich or too thin." She met the
world's most eligible bachelor, Edward, Prince of Wales, at a house
party in Leicestershire given on January 10, 1931, by the prince's
then mistress, Lady Thelma Furness. Thelma and Edward had an
odd relationship, to say the least. They did needlework side by side
on the sofa, and played infantile sexual games. Wearing a diaper,
Edward enjoyed being pushed around in a baby carriage. Thelma
disparagingly (and publicly) referred to him as "the Little Man," a
reference to his woefully undersized male anatomy. The unfortu-

nate nickname stuck, and was candidly used by others in their social set, including, eventually, Wallis Simpson.

Edward, whom the family called "David" (the last in a string of
his seven first names), was the eldest son of the bearded and brusque
former Royal Navy officer King George V, and the grandson of the
portly, priapic, and hard-partying "Bertie," King Edward VII. His
mother was the quiet and remote English-born Princess May of
Teck, who had inherited her German father's courtesy title and was
known in England as Queen Mary.

Shortly after the Great War, George V and his wife had made
a friendly pact with Hitler to wed the Prince of Wales to the
granddaughter of Kaiser Wilhelm, thereby repairing the relations
between the cousins (they were all descendants of Queen Victoria),
which had eroded during and after World War I. This arranged
marriage would create a permanent Anglo-German alliance from
which each nation would benefit. Hitler would get to do whatever
he wanted in continental Europe; in exchange, he would never
wage war on England. The British aristocracy was ecstatic. But the
idea was mooted when the German princess chose to marry into
the royal family of Greece instead.

Edward had attended Oxford, but left the university in 1914 at
the start of the First World War. Although his role was a noncom-
bative one, his life was often in danger during his service. For this
reason, former soldiers would always regard him as one of their
own, even though he had become a dapper, charming, somewhat
fey-looking bon vivant who spent the better part of his life working
hard to convince people that there was more to him than the frivolous playboy whose days consisted of golf, naps, and cocktails,
followed by long evenings cavorting at nightclubs with the "bright
young things" of Café Society. An anti-intellectual, while the rest
of the world was suffering the effects of the Great Depression, the
prince chartered a friend's yacht, had the library removed to make
room for all the alcohol he brought on board, and hosted a floating
house party headed for Fascist Italy—until someone talked him out
of the destination.

The ambitious Wallis, who was very much like the prince in every way, and as ardent a supporter of both the Fascists and the Nazi party, saw in him what she wanted to see, and was bowled over by the power he wielded. "His slightest wish seemed always to be translated into the most impressive kind of reality. Trains were held; yachts materialized; the best suites in the finest hotels were flung open; airplanes stood waiting." What woman's head wouldn't be turned?

The heir to the throne soon became a regular visitor to the Simpsons' home, and the thirty-five-year-old Wallis, rail-slim and seductive, set her cap for him. She blithely ignored the fact that he was already involved with Thelma Furness and took advantage of Lady Furness's holiday in New York to make her move. To Wallis, Edward was the ultimate fairy-tale prince. But people wondered what *he* saw in *her*. Like Anne Boleyn and Camilla Parker Bowles, Mrs. Simpson was no classic beauty, but her self-confidence and "metallic elegance" translated into a highly alluring sexuality.

There was also another attraction. In Edward's own words, "I admired her forthrightness. If she disagreed with some point under discussion, she never failed to advance her own views with vigor and spirit. That side of her enchanted me. . . . From the first, I looked upon her as the most independent woman I had ever met."

And when she quizzed him about his duties, his interest in reform, and his plans for his future reign, the charmed prince admitted, "Wallis, you're the only woman who's ever been interested in my career."

The Prince of Wales fell in love with Wallis in 1934, later writing in his memoirs that one day she "began to mean more to me in a way that she did not perhaps comprehend. My impression is that for a long time she remained unaffected by my interest."

Edward's good friend Walter Monckton, who had known him since they were at Oxford together, felt that it was "a great mistake to assume that he was merely in love with her in the ordinary physical sense of the term. There was an intellectual companionship and there is no doubt that his lonely nature found in her a spiritual comradeship. . . . No one will ever really understand the story of the King's life, who does not appreciate . . . the intensity and depth of his devotion to Mrs. Simpson."

Winston Churchill, a deep admirer of Edward's, although they would end up politically at odds with each other, also noted that the prince was changed for the better by his relationship with Wallis. "He delighted in her company and found in her qualities as necessary to his happiness as the air he breathed. Those who knew him well and watched him closely noticed that many little ticks and fidgetings of nervousness fell away from him. He was a completed being instead of a sick and harassed soul. This experience which happens to a great many people in the flower of their youth came late in life to him [Edward was in his mid-thirties when he met Wallis], and was all the more precious and compulsive for that fact."

Wallis fell in love with the prince during a Mediterranean cruise aboard Lord Moyne's yacht, the *Rosaura*. She, too, experienced the sudden realization that something had shifted in their relationship, that her emotions were now engaged, passing "the undefinable boundary between friendship and love." Soon the lovers developed a private language, referring to themselves as WE (for Wallis and Edward) in their love notes.

Edward and Wallis became nearly inseparable, while Ernest Simpson took frequent business trips to New York. But Ernest was no *mari complaisant*, willing to swallow his humiliation and discreetly keep up appearances. He had plenty of affairs of his own, and understandably, his marriage to Wallis disintegrated.

With the complicity of both Wallis and the prince, Ernest Simpson staged the classic charade where a woman is discovered *in flagrante* in a hotel room with the husband. The Other Woman (who signed the hotel register as "Miss Buttercup"), happened to be Mary Kirk Raffray, a mutual friend, with whom Ernest was already having an affair, and who eventually became his third wife. Although nearly everyone in their intimate circle knew that Wallis and the king were lovers, the pair had to give the impression that they were no more than "good friends." If the court were to learn that Wallis and Edward had been sleeping together, it was a near certainty that her divorce would never be granted.

There was much speculation at the time that Wallis was divorcing Ernest in order to marry Edward—which would have put the king in collusion, a situation that was unethical, if not strictly illegal. Yet from the start, Edward had been working behind the scenes, consulting with the best lawyers, and even convening with Wallis and Ernest, where they discussed a large sum of money that would be paid to Ernest to cheerfully go away. Wallis was eventually granted a divorce on October 27, 1936, although her decree would not become absolute until the following spring.

So she was still married to Ernest Simpson when King George V died on January 10, 1936. But the new king had little interest in keeping their affair under wraps, blithely breaking royal protocol by watching the proclamation of his accession from St. James's Palace with his paramour at his side, and traveling with her everywhere, including his formal visits to foreign countries.

For all his frivolity as Prince of Wales, once Edward became king, he displayed the common touch that John Bull had craved for decades. Edward VIII was the hero of the middle and working classes, of former servicemen, and of impoverished miners.

However, the king was an embarrassing headache to the Establishment because his political sympathies lay with the poor, and he balanced his aristocratic pastimes with charitable works and official ventures to impoverished areas that no other royal dared visit. Touring the economically devastated South Wales Black Area early in his reign, and observing the awful conditions in which the miners dwelled and worked, the shocked and appalled Edward famously remarked, "Something must be done." That sentence would eventually become a catchphrase for the politicians who wanted him out of the way once he announced his intention to marry Mrs. Simpson.

Edward VIII had ascended the throne on January 20, 1936, and almost immediately found himself faced with a constitutional crisis. His prime minister, Stanley Baldwin, informed him that if he insisted on wedding Wallis Simpson, he would have to choose between the lady and the crown. By then, Baldwin and the cabinet also knew that the Secret Intelligence Service files, including the infamous (and dubious) China Dossier on Wallis, contained concrete documentation that she had been a Nazi contact—and a highly promiscuous one, at that. "If the king wants to sleep with a whore that's his private business. But the empire is concerned if he now makes her queen," Baldwin thundered.

Although the wealthy and the middle classes were solidly against his marrying Mrs. Simpson, many compassionate letters from the poor were addressed to Edward's attention, calling him "the People's King," and voicing their approval of his relationship with Wallis. But it's more than likely that Edward never saw this correspondence, or he might not have been so hasty to abdicate. Archival boxes containing thousands of supportive letters and telegrams were not released by the crown until 2003. They emphatically illustrate that Edward's desire to marry the woman he loved—whether she became queen or some other form of consort—was overwhelmingly endorsed by the working classes, by former servicemen who admired Edward's courage during the Great War, and by most British subjects under the age of fifty. They all loved the king because they felt he understood their concerns, and they firmly supported the "modern" view that Edward could marry whomever he bloody well liked! Some Britons even felt that Wallis was simply the government's excuse to get rid of a king who was determined to behave like an individual. Of course, those supporters knew nothing of the SIS files or anything about Wallis's political activities. But there were other, equally vocal proponents of Edward and Wallis—those who knew very well where their sympathies lay. Clad in the black shirts of the Fascist party, they staged rallies in front of Buckingham Palace and the government offices at Whitehall.

Yet, at the time, Baldwin was able to convince the king that his subjects would never accept the twice-divorced American (a double stigma) as their queen. Whether or not that was entirely true, there were certainly rumblings to that effect from more distant corners of the empire. Prime ministers of several of the British Dominions or commonwealth realms, including Canada and Australia, were emphatically against Wallis's having any role or status whatsoever in their empire. But there was doubt in some of the dominions whether abdication was the appropriate alternative to a royal marriage.

Edward proposed the idea of a morganatic marriage. But Baldwin rejected the suggestion, informing his majesty of the dominions' position and citing a lack of parliamentary precedent for the existence of a king's wife who was not the queen, nor had any other official role or title. Despite public opinion, in order for such a compromise to be viable, new legislation would have to be enacted in England, as well as in each of the empire's dominions, requiring constitutional changes in each venue. It would have been a lengthy process, but in any event, Parliament was unwilling to undertake it; therefore, the proposal of a morganatic marriage was not a feasible solution.

The prime minister's position was absolute: if Edward insisted on wedding Wallis *and* remaining king, Baldwin would have no alternative but to resign, leading to a mass mutiny of cabinet ministers and the collapse of the government. For all his Fascist sympathies, Edward was very concerned with upholding the sanctity of the democracy. Keen to avoid "the scars of civil war," he buckled under the pressure of his government.

On December 3, 1936, Wallis and Edward had shared a tearful farewell before she departed for the Continent on a well-advised holiday. In the arched doorway of Edward's home, Fort Belvedere, the king told her, "You must wait for me no matter how long it takes. I shall never give you up."

Wallis didn't have to wait too long. Three days later, Edward made the decision to abdicate. Having done so, he said he felt a tremendous sense of relief and happiness. The formal Instrument of Abdication was executed at ten a.m. on December 10, 1936. And on December 11, at 1:52 Greenwich Mean Time, Edward VIII renounced his throne, the first English monarch to voluntarily relinquish the crown. In a radio broadcast that day, the sovereign told his former subjects, "I have found it impossible to carry the heavy burden of responsibility, and to discharge my duties as King as I would wish to do, without the help and support of the woman I love. . . . The other person most nearly concerned has tried, up to the last, to persuade me to take a different course. . . ."

Listening to the wireless from where she was staying in France, Wallis sobbed uncontrollably. She had been adamant that Edward remain on the throne at all costs, even if it meant that she would have to make the greatest, most painful sacrifice of all and renounce him; however, there is also a substantial amount of correspondence between high-level Nazis to the effect that Wallis was desperate to become Queen of England. This contradiction would indicate that despite her personal ambitions, Wallis may have recognized that the only way for Edward to accomplish the political agenda they so fervently supported was for him to stay on the throne and for her to back away. Additionally, on December 6, Wallis had written to Edward confiding her fear that if he did choose to abdicate, she would be put "in the wrong light to the entire world because they will say I could have prevented it."

Made public in the year 2000, though signed by Mrs. Simpson shortly before Edward's abdication, was a statement Wallis had written with the aid of two friends and advisers—Herman Rogers and Edward's lord-in-waiting, Perry Brownlow—to the effect that she was willing "to withdraw forthwith from a situation that has been rendered both unhappy and untenable."

There was a good reason for the government to suppress Wallis's declaration. Although journalists in the United States and on the European continent had kept their readers informed of "Windsor and Wally's affair," the English press did not publish the story of the king's impending abdication until a week before the event. Their intention was to prevent an informed (and consequently sympathetic) public from upsetting the Establishment's intention to replace Edward with his younger brother Albert, the more pliant Duke of York.

The Church's opinion of a royal's exercising his duty over his desire was crystal clear. Deriding Edward's decision, the Archbishop of Canterbury, Cosmo Gordon Lang, intoned over the wireless, "From God he had received a high and sacred trust. Yet by his own will he has abdicated—he has surrendered the trust. With characteristic frankness he has told us his motive. It was a craving for private happiness. Strange and sad it must be that for such a motive, however strongly it pressed upon his heart, he should have disappointed hopes so high and abandoned a trust so great."

One person close to the throne who never forgave Edward for choosing love over duty was the former Elizabeth Bowes-Lyon, who was married to the shy, stammering Duke of York. Because Edward had no children, his abdication meant that her husband, next in the line of succession, was now the monarch. The new queen consort blamed Edward for ruining his brother's life as well as his health with his appalling act of selfishness.

On December 12, 1936, the day after his abdication, Edward sailed for France. In accordance with an alleged "agreement" with the new king, George VI (formerly Albert, Duke of York), Windsor and Wally would never again reside in England. Edward wrote in his memoirs, "HMS *Fury* slid silently and unescorted out of Portsmouth Harbor. Watching the shore of England recede, I was swept by many emotions. If it had been hard to give up the throne, it had been even harder to give up my country. . . . The drawbridges were going up behind me."

Edward's own mother set the tone for the way the royal family would treat him from then on. In response to a question about when the former king might return to his homeland, Queen Mary replied, "Not until he comes to my funeral."

Wallis was concerned about how Edward would fare in exile. She also despaired of the fact that a mention of their impending marriage would be pointedly omitted from the Court Circular and that the royal family was intent on denying her the use of the title "Her Royal Highness." On January 3, 1937, she wrote to Edward, "It is all a great pity because I loathe being undignified and also of joining the countless titles that roam around Europe meaning nothing."

On March 8, the former King Edward VIII was granted the title Duke of Windsor. It never sat well with the other royals that— HRH or no—Wallis would now be a duchess.

Wallis obtained her decree absolute on May 3, and their formal engagement was announced eight days later. She married Edward on June 3, in a tiny French town at the home of Charles Bedaux, an entrepreneurial expat American businessman who was developing a workforce production system for Adolf Hitler. The bride wore a silk crepe suit by Mainbocher with a floor-length skirt and long-sleeved jacket in a shade of grayish robin's-egg blue that would henceforth be known as "Wallis blue." Her wedding ring, similar to that worn by several queens of England, was fashioned of Welsh gold by a loyal former subject. Edward was dressed in the traditional striped trousers and black morning coat, with a white carnation, his favorite flower, in his lapel.

Unfortunately for the bridal couple, who were both Protestant, the Church of England (of which Edward, when king, had been the Supreme Governor) prohibited a religious wedding ceremony to someone who had been divorced, as long as their former spouses still lived, and Wallis clearly fit the profile. But the Reverend Robert Anderson Jardine of a tiny parish near Durham believed that Edward should not be denied the blessing of God on this terribly special day, and traveled to France of his own accord to conduct the ceremony. On his arrival, however, he was forbidden to officiate by the Bishop of Durham as well as by the Archbishops of York and Canterbury. Although someone had fetched a Protestant cross from the neighboring village, the civil ceremony was conducted in French by the mayor of Monts, Charles Mercier.

No member of the royal family or the court was present at the wedding, on instructions of George VI. Edward felt very hurt by this edict, and up till the last minute maintained hope that *any* of his relations might turn up after all.

Wallis would later write, "If ever there was a marriage that started off inauspiciously, resented and vilifed, with many hopes and probably prayers for its failure, it was ours."

The newlyweds and their 266 pieces of luggage honeymooned on the Orient Express in a private railway car coupled to the train, which had been loaned to them by Benito Mussolini. Among other destinations, they visited Munich, where Hitler warmly received them, chatting with the newlyweds for two hours. When Hitler had learned of Edward's abdication, he lamented, "I have lost a friend to my cause!"

The Windsors now enjoyed the life of expatriates in France and Austria, discreetly exiled from England for their pro-Nazi sympathies at a time when Hitler's rise to power was becoming more ominous by the day and an increasing threat to Britain. When they traveled—and many of their visits were in pro-Fascist towns—word came down from the highest level in England that only a third-string minister or administrator (at best) be sent to meet them, and that they should be honored with no more than "a bite of luncheon."

With specific regard to Germany, British consular officials stationed there were instructed not to meet the Windsors. "The Embassy must scrupulously avoid in any way giving the appearance that His Majesty the king and His Majesty's government countenance the proposed tour." It was bad enough that a member of the royal family was publicly expressing his personal political views, which he or she is expressly forbidden to do; but it was also feared both at Whitehall and Buckingham Palace that Edward was trying to regain his throne with the help of the Third Reich. Letters from Hitler himself, as well as others in his government, fully confirm that conjecture.

Although Wallis had been the one to waver when it came to tying the knot, by all accounts, she was the one who took command of their marriage, ordering Edward about as if he was a lackey. Even when he was still King of England, after she commanded him, in front of a group of their friends, to "take off my dirty little shoes and bring me another pair," Edward fell to his knees and removed her footwear, relishing every moment of his humility. No wonder that their social set referred to him as Wallis's "lapdog."

One evening during a dinner party the Duke of Windsor asked the butler to deliver a message to the chauffeur regarding his plans for the following day. Wallis raised her hands and slammed them on the table. "Never—never again will you give orders in my house!" the duchess shouted. Then in a belated effort to smooth things over, Wallis explained to the mortified guests, "You see, the duke is in charge of everything that happens outside the house, and I on the inside."

Utterly cowed by his wife's outburst, Edward mumbled his apologies.

Philip Ziegler, Edward VIII's official biographer, wrote that the king was an utter sadomasochist where Wallis was concerned. "He relished the contempt and bullying she bestowed on him." And in a rare move for an official personal attendant, Edward's friend and equerry Edward Dudley "Fruity" Metcalfe (to whom he was intimately attached, and with whom he may have had a full-blown sexual affair) openly shared his opinion of Wallis with their mutual friends: "God, that woman's a bitch! She'll play hell with him before long."

But to Edward, it had been worth exchanging his kingdom for this former Baltimore colt, despite the oft-repeated joke that the king, who had once been Admiral of the Fleet, had become "the third mate on an American tramp."

"No one will ever know how hard I work to try to make the little man feel busy," Wallis once confided to a friend during their post-abdication peregrinations. Nevertheless, her life was a balancing act. After what had begun (from her point of view) as merely a thrilling fling, Wallis had come to care for Edward deeply. And although she often felt suffocated by his relentless adoration, she could not forsake him once he had abandoned his throne for her.

Wallis had another feather in her cap, which may have kept her husband intrigued. According to the MI6 file on Wallis known as the China Dossier—the existence of which is still disputed among historians and biographers—during her Asian sojourn in the 1920s she had allegedly visited a number of high-end brothels called "singsong houses," where she learned some of the local prostitutes' more exotic sexual practices, and indulged in them herself. According to sources close to the couple, the duke and Wallis enjoyed sexual role-playing and he was an avid foot fetishist.

The Windsors' Nazi and Fascist connections were also common knowledge for years. Both the British Secret Intelligence Service and the U.S. State Department were aware that Wallis was the source of various leaks to prominent diplomats with close ties to Hitler and Mussolini. Wallis and Edward partied with several other pro-Nazi and/or Fascist sympathizers among the English aristocracy. And during World War II, the British government was convinced that the duke and duchess were disseminating crucial information to their contacts in Paris. Edward and Wallis met openly with Third Reich officials at the highest level, passed sensitive information to them regarding British maneuvers, and were actively scheming to return to England, where they would run a shadow court from the Duke of Westminster's estate until such time as Edward could, with Nazi assistance, regain his throne.

Rudolph Hess reported to Hitler, "The Duke is proud of his German blood. Says he is more German than English. There is no need to lose a single German life in invading Britain. The Duke and his wife will deliver the goods."

In 1939, Edward was assigned to the British military mission in France. But when the English government suspected him of communicating with the enemy (an act of treason) and possibly conspiring with the Germans to arrange a negotiated peace—which was in opposition to the British government's agenda, and for which Edward had no authority—the duke and duchess were informally exiled to a place where their pro-Nazi sentiments could do little to harm British policy.

George VI put an ocean between the crown and his older brother, sending Edward to Nassau, as Governor and Commander in Chief of the Bahamas. Wallis in particular was miserable there. In an attempt to feel more at home, she had Government House, their official residence, redone at tremendous expense, hiring an interior decorator from New York City and installing air conditioning, much to the anger of the Bahamians. Although the Windsors endeavored to demonstrate that they had a social conscience, and Wallis actively involved herself in several charitable war efforts there, they were bored out of their minds in the Bahamas and managed to spend as little time there as possible, taking off for shopping sprees in Manhattan or Palm Springs, and living large while their countrymen and -women endured the dangers and deprivations of wartime. It was reported that Wallis's annual clothing budget at the time was somewhere in the neighborhood of $25,000 (well over $383,000 today).

Wallis once told the legendary society hostess Elsa Maxwell, "My husband gave up everything for me. I am not a beautiful woman. I'm nothing to look at, so the only thing I can do is dress better than anyone else. If everyone looks at me when I enter a room, my husband can feel proud of me. That's my chief responsibility."

The duchess was always fashion-conscious for her husband as well. Wallis had been telling him for years that white dinner jackets at black-tie parties were passé, but the duke insisted on remaining unfashionable—high treason to his wife. One night, at a Palm Beach soiree during their post-Bahamian years, Wallis grabbed a tray of hors d'oeuvres from a passing waiter, shoved them into Edward's hands, and exclaimed, "Here! If you're going to dress like a waiter, you might as well act like one!"

Edward never seemed put off by his wife's insults; no matter what she said or did, he worshipped the ground her "dirty little shoes" had trod upon. But his devotion was occasionally taken for granted. During the course of their marriage Wallis did not remain faithful to her "lapdog," though their contemporaries never believed that *sex* was the glue that kept the couple together. Although their courtship and marriage were seen as the "romance of the century," the duke and duchess always maintained separate bedrooms.

While she and Edward were engaged, Wallis was also sleeping with Guy Marcus Trundle, a pro-Nazi gigolo who was an employee of the Ford Motor Company. And shortly after her royal marriage, she took another lover, William Christian Bullitt, the U.S. Ambassador to France—a closet bisexual who worshipped Hitler and who had strong connections to Mussolini. The prominent fashion designer Elsa Schiaparelli allowed Wallis to use her atelier for her clandestine trysts with both Trundle and Bullitt, finding ways to distract Edward by securing invitations for him to society events while his beloved Wallis was having one of her "fittings."

Thirteen years after Wallis wed Edward, she embarked on an odd sort of affair with Jimmy Donahue, a gay American playboy twenty years her junior, who was also fond of liquor and pills. Donahue often traveled with the Windsors as a threesome, and the duke didn't seem to mind when Wallis and Jimmy, their heads conspiratorially inclined toward each other, giggled like a pair of schoolgirls. Edward also didn't much object to his wife's traveling alone with Donahue, despite Jimmy's provocative endorsement of Wally's talents. "She's marvelous! She's the best cock sucker I've ever known!"

Their affair lasted into the mid-1950s, until the night when a drunken Jimmy kicked Wallis so hard in the shin that she bled. The duke ordered him to pack his bags immediately and never to darken their doorstep again. Donahue eventually committed suicide.

From the postwar years until Wallis and Edward grew too frail and infirm to travel, they enjoyed the peripatetic lifestyle of the bon vivant. Still personae non grata with the royal family, they did little but attend parties and galas, shop, and play golf. Sometimes her husband's frustration at having nothing of import to do took its toll on Wallis, who keenly felt the burden of having to constantly stroke the royal ego and keep him cheered. "You have no idea how hard it is to live out a great romance!" she once lamented to a friend.

In 1967, a commemorative article published in syndicated newspapers, celebrating the Windsors' thirtieth wedding anniversary, included the semi-serious "Duke's Formula for a Happy Marriage," in which each of the Windsors contributed their respective recipes for happiness, beginning with Edward's advice:

Don't ask questions. If you got the right answer it might hurt. If you didn't, it surely would. If she absentmindedly calls you Ernest or Winfield, don't comment; at least she has your role fixed in her thoughts. . . . Don't let marriage interfere with your old customs. Step out to an occasional nightclub, but with your wife just to keep in practice. This will make her feel that whatever pleasures you used to have in such frivolities were incomplete until you met her. If she shows an inclination to go with you to your tailor, ignore it. This is a major encroachment upon your freedom. A minor menace is the selection of your ties, socks, and pyjamas. There is nothing you can do about this. . . . Always praise the way she wears her hair. If possible, like it. She will wear it that way anyway.

Wallis then contributed her witty but telling suggestions:

Be first to decide any question, no matter how trivial. After you've made the decision, ask your husband what he thinks. All men like to be deferred to. . . . Praise any little accomplishments he may have, such as skirling bagpipes. At least you know where he is when he is playing. Tell him how strong he is, and praise him for his character. But suggest that all decisions be mutual. . . . Make him think this love, the only real one of your life, will last forever.

So in some ways they behaved like a long-married couple, whether royal or commoner. The British Royal Family's credo that they should (no matter how hypocritical the picture) represent the epitome of domestic virtue, unsullied by marital infidelity or divorce, was a convenient excuse for their ostracism of Edward and Wallis. The duchess spent decades endeavoring to be accepted by Edward's parents, siblings, and nieces, and never recovered from all the official snubs she received instead. George VI's queen consort

Elizabeth's refusal to allow Wallis to use the title Her Royal Highness would be echoed decades later when her daughter, Elizabeth II, would effectively strip Diana of her HRH following her divorce from Prince Charles.

After battling several illnesses, including throat cancer, probably caused by a lifetime of cigarette smoking, in the predawn hours of May 28, 1972, Edward died, one month shy of his seventy-eighth birthday. He lay in state in Windsor, but not in Westminster Hall, where British monarchs are traditionally honored before burial. It was at Windsor that Wallis paid her respects to his bier on June 3, their thirty-fifth wedding anniversary. Her escort, Lord Mountbatten, recalled that "in the saddest imaginable voice," the duchess said, "He was my entire life. I can't begin to think what I am going to do without him. He gave up so much for me and now he's gone. I had always hoped that I would die before him." The former Edward VIII was interred in the royal burying ground at Frogmore, where he often played as a boy.

By this time Wallis had reached her mid-seventies as well, and her health was also deteriorating. In 1973, at the age of seventy-eight, she fell and broke her hip. A few months later, she suffered a number of fractured ribs in a second fall. Doctors had difficulty inserting the anesthesia tube down her throat because it was so tight from her numerous cosmetic surgeries.

Wallis spent the last five years of her life in complete seclusion, as dementia or Alzheimer's continued to claim her lucidity. Near the end of her life she went blind, and by the beginning of 1984 she was completely paralyzed. On April 24, 1986, Wallis died of heart failure at her Parisian home in the Bois de Boulogne. She was ninety years old. Several members of the royal family, including her surviving sister-in-law Queen Elizabeth the Queen Mother, and Queen Elizabeth II, attended the funeral service and the burial, as they witnessed Wallis, Duchess of Windsor interred beside her beloved Edward. Maybe they just wanted to be sure that the Fascist fashionista was really out of their lives.

RAINIER III,

PRINCE OF MONACO

1923–2005

RULED MONACO: 1949–2005

❦ *and* ❦

GRACE KELLY

1929–1982

married 1956–1982

"You have no idea what hard work fairy stories can be."
—Grace Kelly to journalist Michael Thornton in 1976

*H*E NEEDED TO REVIVE A SAGGING ECONOMY AND wanted to restore the luster to Monaco, his postage-stamp-sized principality sandwiched between France and Italy on the Côte d'Azur.

She, an Oscar winner by the age of twenty-five, was fairly certain that Hollywood could offer her no more than what she had already achieved and was searching for The Next Thing.

Does that sound like "once upon a time"?

In 1955, Grace Kelly, the Philadelphia-born beauty and recent winner of the Best Actress statuette for her role in *The Country*

Girl, was invited to be the guest of honor at the Cannes Film Festival. *Paris Match* editor Pierre Galante was determined to fulfill his assignment to arrange a photo op between the cool blond Hollywood heroine and the ruler of Monaco, who was at the time a royal nobody, and whose realm—roughly the size of New York's Central Park—was a Mediterranean backwater characterized by Somerset Maugham as "a sunny place for shady people." It took a good deal of persuading; Galante's success in effecting the Hollywood-Royal meet was aided by the fact that his wife, Olivia de Havilland, happened to be Grace's favorite actress.

Over the centuries, Monaco's ruling family, the Grimaldis, had weathered several reversals of fortune. By the early 1950s, they were sitting at the low end of the financial teeter-totter, and to the disgust of Prince Rainier, the shipping tycoon Aristotle Onassis held the majority of shares in Monte Carlo's casino. Money speaking louder than any royal title, it meant that Onassis was theoretically the most powerful man in Monaco. His plan was to turn the little seaside principality into a highly exclusive resort community for the world's wealthiest citizens.

Then Monte Carlo's largest bank crashed. The economy, as well as Rainier's personal income, plummeted. When Rainier swallowed his pride and turned to Onassis for advice, the shipping magnate suggested that the realm's financial woes might be solved, the economy turned around, and Monaco's lost luster restored if Rainier were to wed an American movie star—an event that, naturally, would garner enormous press coverage. So the prince compiled a list, comprised mainly of pulchritudinous blondes, including Marilyn Monroe, who evidently self-eliminated when she kept referring to His Serene Highness as "Prince Reindeer."

The five-foot-seven-inch Grace Kelly, twenty-five years old, slim, elegant, and poised (as well as appropriately Catholic), made it onto the short list; and the serendipity of her visit to Cannes in the spring of 1955 ended up setting the stage for twentieth-century continental Europe's most famous, and glamorous, royal marriage.

Grace was the third of four children born to the handsome and athletic Irish immigrant bricklayer, entrepreneur, bon vivant, and sometime politician Jack Kelly. His wife was Margaret Majer, of German descent, although her background was hushed up during an era when the Germans were highly unpopular in the United States and Grace was being touted to movie audiences as the quintessential American beauty.

The morning of May 6, 1955, the day Grace was scheduled to meet Prince Rainier, began inauspiciously. The electricity went out across France due to a labor strike. Grace couldn't dry and style her hair because the hair dryer wouldn't work, nor did the iron, so she was compelled to wear the only dress in her trunk that wasn't wrinkled—a bold floral print with a fitted, drop-waisted bodice and a pouffy taffeta skirt that rustled with every step. Appraising her appearance in the hotel mirror, with the loud frock and the wet hair she had smoothed into a chignon, she declared, "I look a fright." Grace also discovered at the last minute that royal protocol demanded she wear a hat in the presence of the prince. She never much liked them, so she hadn't packed one and had to make do with a friend's headband, a broad crescent of faux flowers.

Ironically, Grace and Rainier's relationship would begin and end with an automobile accident. En route to the Palais Princier, Grace and the publicist and photographer she was traveling with got into a fender bender with a Studebaker. By the time they arrived in Monaco, she was visibly shaken and even less eager to meet Rainier, who—much to the embarrassment of all concerned—was not at the palace to greet them.

Although Grace was known for thoroughly researching her roles, she had not done her homework before this annoying publicity stunt. As the minutes mounted and she impatiently waited for the prince to arrive, she wanted to know whether he spoke English. How would she be expected to address him? And, by the way, how old was he? After forty-five minutes with Rainier still a no-show, the starlet had had it. "Let's get out of here," she announced.

No sooner had Grace risen to her feet than the barrel-chested thirty-one-year-old chain-smoking monarch entered the room. He poured on the charm, and the Monegasque dog-and-pony show began—literally—as he led off the grand tour of his realm with a visit to the palace zoo. Then they shared a laugh over the fact that neither of them had been eager to agree to this meeting. Whatever else Rainier did or said that day produced the desired effect; during the limo ride back to Cannes, Grace couldn't stop murmuring, "He is so charming, so very charming."

By the time she returned to the United States, royalty was on her brain, and not merely because she had dived into the role of a continental European princess in *The Swan*. Grace and Rainier had become pen pals. Although there appeared to be no erotic spark between them, in some ways Grace's whirlwind royal romance was unsurprising, given her penchant for older men. While many of the roles she played on the silver screen were coolly composed ice maidens and "good girls," she'd earned an off-screen reputation as a home wrecker for her numerous love affairs, usually with her leading men, including (according to her biographers) the very married Ray Milland, William Holden, Gary Cooper, and Bing Crosby.

During their stroll around Monaco, Grace had dropped the prince a hint that anytime he found himself in America, he should not hesitate to look her up. Naturally, he found a reason to do so within weeks. She brought Rainier to meet her family, and finally Jack and Margaret Kelly approved of her beau: this one wasn't married, he wasn't an alcoholic, and best of all, he was Catholic.

But Grace's kid sister, Lizanne, was a bit more skeptical; in fact, she was utterly surprised to hear that Grace and Rainier were already engaged. According to Kelly's recent biographer Wendy Leigh, Lizanne said, "She didn't have time to be really in love . . . I don't know why she decided to marry him so quickly."

Grace had agreed to wed a man she hardly knew except through their correspondence, and to become princess of a place where she had barely spent a couple of hours and where she didn't speak the language. Had she thought it all through? Monaco was no temporary location shoot; it was going to be where she'd commit to spending the rest of her life.

Acting was her true passion, and would always remain so, but evidently Grace had concluded that after her mid-twenties it would be downhill in Hollywood from then on. Perhaps it was merely a temporary disenchantment with the profession that caused her to lament that "Each year my makeup call is a lot earlier. And when I look at the other ladies who've been there since dawn, do I want to live like that? Get me out."

So when the one-of-a-kind opportunity arose to exit with a bang and a flourish, Grace grabbed it. However, she did bump into a few men who were still waiting, and hoping, in the wings.

Shortly before Grace and Rainier were introduced, she had been engaged to the fashion designer Oleg Cassini, a French-born Jew who could trace his lineage to the Russian nobility. The pair had enjoyed a whirlwind courtship, and their decision to rush to the altar was precipitated by Grace's discovery that she was pregnant. Torn between her Catholic, though relatively nonreligious, up-bringing, her career ambitions, and her love for Cassini, she ended up having an abortion. Their raison d'être for marriage mooted, she called off the wedding, but she hadn't quite ended the engagement. Believing he was still her fiancé, Oleg was shocked and hurt when Grace told him, during a meeting on the Staten Island Ferry, that she was planning to marry Rainier. When he asked her why she was doing it, her terse reply was not exactly brimming with enthusiasm. "I will learn to love him," she told the designer. "I have made my destiny."

An interesting choice of words.

Behind the scenes, a relationship between Rainier and Grace was heating up, primarily through their correspondence, although each of them coyly downplayed all rumors of a royal romance. Coached by his confessor-confidant, Delaware native Father Francis Tucker, Rainier hit all the right notes in his media interviews, telling the press that his greatest difficulty lay in "knowing a girl long enough and intimately enough to find out if we are really soul mates as well as lovers. I consider it a duty to my people to get married." The Grimaldis were no strangers to family dysfunction. Spouses and siblings had a history of detesting one another; parents couldn't abide their children, and vice versa. Rainier's own parents had split acrimoniously when he was a small boy and he craved familial intimacy. Nearly twenty years later he told a journalist, "I think the experience of my parents' separation when I was only six subconsciously made me very much want my own marriage to succeed. The Princess and I tried to minimize any disagreement between us in the interest of keeping the family together—so that the children would not suffer."

On the subject of soul mates and marital harmony, Grace, a Scorpio, had always placed a lot of faith in astrology and the occult, and was keenly aware that one of her worst possible matches would be with a man born under the sign of Gemini. She nearly kicked herself for not asking Rainier's birthday before agreeing to be his princess bride. It was a question she'd always asked very early in a relationship. How could she have been so remiss? The fact that Rainier was a Gemini was no small matter to Grace. She suffered serious misgivings about going ahead with their wedding plans. According to friends and family members, Grace's primary reason for soldiering on was the intense desire to please her father, who never thought she would amount to much and continually downplayed her successes, including her Academy Award.

Rainier visited the States in December 1955, accompanied by a secretary and a French doctor, amusingly named Robert Donat, whose job it would be to supervise the obligatory, though mortifying, fertility test that would prove there was no impediment to Grace's bearing an heir for Monaco. Grace took it in stride (although she refused to inform her parents about the test), telling a friend she was due for a checkup anyway, and heck, the prince was paying for it!

On December 28, 1955, Grace and Rainier enjoyed a romantic dinner at Manhattan's Waldorf-Astoria Hotel. "If you are to be at my side, then you may need this," the prince told Grace and handed her a gift-wrapped copy of a "coffee-table" book about the history of Monaco. He planned to pop the question over dessert, but when the conversation turned to his family's unfortunate marital history, and Grace grew visibly anxious, he thought better of it.

Plan B was a seductive stroll in Central Park, but on the way down to the lobby, they met Dr. Donat and his nurse Leanne Scott in the elevator and Grace invited the other couple to join them.

There was no plan C. As soon as they exited onto Park Avenue, the frustrated monarch grabbed Grace by the wrist and yanked her through uptown traffic to the median. There he proposed to her, offered her the ring, and curious bystanders overheard Grace's yelps of delight, followed by an "Of course I will marry you!" Their public kiss right in the middle of Park Avenue received a round of applause.

The original engagement ring was exceptionally modest; the prince was told that he'd have to do a lot better if he wanted Grace to say "yes," so he replaced it with a twelve-carat diamond surrounded by rubies, red and white being Monaco's national colors. And Rainier's bank account was a comedown from the nouveau riche lifestyle Grace had enjoyed growing up and the luxe trappings of movie stardom. Jack Kelly was expected to kick in an old-fashioned dowry—$2 million—before the prince would have his daughter. Cynics watching from the sidelines claimed that the bricklaying entrepreneur had merely brokered another business deal.

Additionally, Grace was expected to be an equal contributor to the expenses for the palace upkeep, but was to forgo any financial assets in her own right. Jack was worried that Rainier appeared to be dismissive of his daughter's concerns. "It's killing me that I can't protect her," he lamented.

In the end, Grace, a shrewd negotiator who'd managed to get her own way at Metro-Goldwyn-Mayer, took the mediation out of the hands of the lawyers and sat down with Rainier alone, hammering out her own deal with him.

But one enormous point of contention remained unresolved.

Grace believed she was *temporarily* giving up acting to become Princess of Monaco. Rainier was adamant that she close the door forever on her career. Still convinced that she could eventually change his mind, Grace embarked, literally, upon her new life.

On April 4, 1956, at 9:55 a.m., from the deck of the glamorously appointed SS *Constitution*, Grace waved good-bye to the paparazzi popping their flashbulbs on Manhattan's Pier 84. Also enjoying first-class cabins were seventy-eight Kelly relatives and friends, as well as a number of journalists, including a married photographer for *Paris Match* named Walter Carone. Grace permitted Carone an exclusive photo shoot—and a good deal more, according to her fellow travelers: she more than likely engaged in a shipboard fling with him. Carone died in 1982, but his widow told Kelly's biographer Wendy Leigh that her husband felt Grace "wasn't full of the joy of getting married. He said that she didn't seem to be happy. She didn't seem to be in love with Rainier."

A few days later, during a conversation Grace had with her friend Charlotte Winston, she unfavorably compared Monaco to "taking all of the city of New York and squeezing it onto the head of a knitting needle." When Charlotte asked what Grace was going to do about it, the future princess testily retorted, "What do you think I'm going to do? The whole goddamn world is waiting for me to get married. I can't very well not do it now, can I?"

Grace's first taste of the life that lay in store for her was a bitter one. No sooner did the ship reach the Riviera than the typical in-law rivalry associated with most families' wedding plans began to surface. The snooty Grimaldis found the fun-loving Kellys a boisterous bunch, ignorant of royal protocol. Rainier's mother, Charlotte, and his sister Antoinette gave Grace a particularly chilly reception. The Kelly girls—Grace's older sister, Peggy, and younger sister, Lizanne—found the Monegasques pretentious. On observing the soon-to-be-newlyweds, neither of them believed they were enjoying a genuine romance. "It was never a fairy tale come true," according to Peggy, and Lizanne felt that "it was just a very nice agreement."

On April 18, 1956, Grace and Rainier's eleven a.m. civil ceremony was broadcast across the globe thanks to the magic of tech-
nology and Metro-Goldwyn-Mayer. Long before the era of reality
television, Rainier and Grace had sold the rights to their wedding
ceremonies. Their arrangement with the studio included a percentage of the post-distribution profits, a 30 percent share that the
couple donated to the Monaco Red Cross. Grace, who had broken
her contract with MGM in order to become Princess of Monaco,
had agreed to the filming in order to fulfill its outstanding terms.
The prince, or more accurately, the principality, desperately needed
the publicity to help tourists locate it on a map.

At the civil ceremony, held in the throne room of the Palais Princier, the thirty-two-year-old groom wore the classic ensemble for a
morning wedding: cutaway coat, pearl-gray vest, striped trousers,
and silk top hat. His twenty-six-year-old bride was clad in a rose-
beige lace-over-taffeta suit with matching pale pink gloves and silk
pumps. Grace's vows, as recited by the Minister of State, would set
a twenty-first-century feminist's teeth on edge. As Rainier's wife,
she was by law required to obey him in all things and to reside with
him wherever he chose. If things didn't work out (and Monegasque
princes enjoyed a staggeringly high rate of divorce), Grace was
free to leave—but would not be permitted to take her children
with her.

The following morning, April 19, amid a sea of white blossoms
and gold candelabra, six hundred guests attended the religious ceremony in Monaco's Romanesque cathedral. Billed as "the wedding
of the century," it, too, was literally an MGM extravaganza, funded
by the studio and Jack Kelly's checkbook.

A red velvet carpet undulated all the way up the stone steps.
Grace's eight-thousand-dollar ivory *peau de soie* satin gown, embroidered with seed pearls and nineteenth-century Brussels lace, was
designed by Helen Rose, the woman who had also created the
sumptuous costumes for *The Swan*, Grace Kelly's cinematic swan
song. It took six bridesmaids to carry the nine-foot train; Grace's
updo, enhanced by a cap that matched her gown, accentuated with

a white tulle veil, was styled by Virginia Darcy, the studio's principal hairdresser. And the MGM PR machine handled the publicity. Thirty million people watched it worldwide.

At 10:41 a.m. Grace and Rainer, whose black jacket was bedecked with medals and ribbons, golden epaulettes, and a diagonally worn red and white sash—the Order of St. Charles—were pronounced man and wife by the Bishop of Monaco.

Grace Kelly was the second American to become Princess of Monaco. The first was Alice Heine, a Catholic convert who was the widow of the duc de Richelieu and niece of the Jewish German poet Heinrich Heine. On October 30, 1889, she became wife number two of Rainier's great-grandfather, Prince Albert I. But Alice's existence in Monaco was officially expunged after she committed adultery. When Albert denounced her in public in front of the first-night opera audience and slapped her across the face, Alice left the building—and the principality—never to return.

The stocky, muscular Prince Rainier III, whose ancestors included James IV of Scotland and Prince William "the Silent" of Orange, descended from the offspring of an extramarital affair. His grandfather, Prince Louis II of Monaco, had fathered a daughter named Charlotte with the stepdaughter of an Algerian laundress. Because Charlotte was illegitimate, the girl's grandfather, Prince Albert I, refused to recognize her as Louis's daughter, so she was not formally legitimized until Albert's death.

In 1920, Charlotte married a minor European royal, Pierre de Polignac, and two years later she became the hereditary Princess of Monaco, making Pierre a prince. But because a woman could only inherit Monaco's throne if she were married to a man named Grimaldi, Prince Pierre adopted the surname. Their son, Prince Rainier Louis Henri Maxence Bertrand, was born in 1923.

Rainier was educated in England and Switzerland, where he was considered intelligent and a good student. Not one to use his noble birth to shirk military duty, he was an artillery officer during World War II. The prince bravely fought the Germans in Alsace, winning both the Légion d'Honneur and the Croix de Guerre.

On Rainier's accession to the throne in 1949, gambling accounted for 95 percent of his principality's annual revenue. A decade later, Grace's personal luster, her commitment to cultural and educational projects, and her arsenal of famous and glamorous friends combined to achieve Rainier's Riviera Shangri-la. During the second half of the twentieth century, Monaco became a jet-setter's Mecca, a haven for high-rolling playboys and the so-called glitterati. Gambling revenues now total a mere 3 percent of Monaco's economy, with much of the balance from tourism and banking.

Grace's passion for culture was a tremendous asset to her adopted home, but there was little else she shared in common with the Monegasques or with their monarch. He slumbered through the ballet, but adored oceanography; she was seasick for most of their honeymoon aboard the royal yacht.

Their lack of common interests might have been surmountable, but their dissimilar temperaments strained the royal marriage from the start. Grace was lively and spontaneous, while Rainier "was singularly lacking in joie de vivre," according to American society columnist Dorothy Kilgallen. Rainier's nephew, Christian de Massy, described him as "totally autocratic. You couldn't contradict him." In an effort to smooth the inevitable ruffled feathers, Grace employed the serenity for which she was famous long before she became Her Serene Highness. Playing the peacemaker, she would invent excuses for her husband's rudeness. But it didn't take long before there was marital trouble in the Mediterranean playground.

In 1957, after she'd been married to Rainier for only a year, Grace entertained Cary Grant at the palace. The prince had not been amused to see a photograph in the local paper, *Nice Matin*, of his wife greeting her former costar from the Hitchcock thriller *To Catch a Thief* with a kiss. Although her numerous affairs during her single days had been well publicized, now that she was Princess of Monaco even the slightest semblance of sexual impropriety was not *comme il faut*. Rainier was visibly jealous. Grace's other friends from her former life met with the same ill-tempered mopey treatment from her husband. Their shared showbiz lingo, and experiences from a past that he had never been a part of, made the prince feel like an outsider in his own realm. Fully aware of this dynamic, and apparently a bit frightened of her husband, Grace was always conscious of trying not to upset him.

Whatever she had imagined her new life would entail, Grace had been singularly unprepared for the role of royal consort. Gwen Robyns, a New Zealand native who became Grace's biographer and then a close friend, in part from excising much of her original text regarding Grace's pre-Rainier romances, told Kelly's most recent biographer, Wendy Leigh, that the new princess "was in a trap. From being a movie star with absolutely the whole world at her feet, she dropped to second place. Grace had always been able to twist men around her little finger. But not Rainier. He was His Serene Highness, and she was just a girl from Philadelphia. She was miserable from day one."

One reason for Grace's unhappiness in the marriage was the double standard to which female royal consorts have been held for centuries. Three months after their lavish wedding, Grace began hearing rumors of not one but several royal mistresses. Her father, who had also been known to "step out," had expressed his concerns about this very issue during Grace's engagement, reminding her that all royal men were notorious philanderers. Now Jack Kelly's prophecy was proving true. Two years into the marriage, in a phone call with a dear friend and former Hollywood hairdresser, Grace confided, "I know he has affairs with other women. That's very frustrating to me, and it makes me very, very unhappy." Once, she had been The Other Woman in a handful of Hollywood marriages. Now she was the shunned wife who was expected to bear her spouse's infidelities in silence and with dignity. She was in danger of becoming her mother.

Instead, she reverted to her old ways and became a mistress. Whether it was initially for solace or for a bit of revenge, in 1958, when her former *High Society* costar Frank Sinatra came to Monte Carlo to promote his film *Kings Go Forth*, they commenced a passionate affair that would last for years. He referred to her as his "dream girl" and affectionately called her "Gracie"; the princess called him by his given name, Francis.

She would enjoy other extramarital affairs as well. But Grace fulfilled the royal consort's primary duty three times. On January 23, 1957, she gave birth to her first child, Princess Caroline, in the palace library—without the aid of anesthetic. She bore Rainier two more children: Albert, on March 14, 1958, and Stephanie, on February 1, 1965. With Caroline's birth, Monaco's continued sovereignty was secure, although as a male Albert would displace his older sister in the line of succession. It was during Grace's pregnancy with Caroline that she was frequently photographed sporting a large Hermès handbag, a gift from her husband, which she held in front of her belly to obscure the bulge. The accessory, which still remains popular, became known as the "Kelly Bag."

While Rainier seemed torn between the desire to limit media access to their children and the awareness that feeding the publicity machine would insure continued notoriety for his tiny principality, Grace, who turned out to be the stricter disciplinarian, endeavored to instill as much normalcy as possible in their children's lives.

The royal family sought peace and quiet at Roc Agel, their sixty-acre estate located approximately two hours from Monaco in the Maritime Alps. Dotted with fruit trees, the property also boasted a working dairy; and Grace decorated their farmhouse in the latest American fashion in interior design, indulging her nostalgia for Hollywood by papering the powder room with her old movie stills. It was something of an ironic place for them. Rainier, who for several years of their marriage had forbidden the screening in Monaco of any of his wife's films, may have been secretly pleased to have proof positive that Grace's career was in the toilet.

In 1966, after a decade of marriage, and at least three miscarriages that left her emotionally devastated, the princess granted an interview to Barbara Walters, who pointedly asked her if she was happy. Grace replied, "I've had happy moments in my life, but I didn't think happiness—being happy—is a perpetual state that anyone can be in. Life isn't that way. But I have a certain peace of mind, yes. My children give me a great deal of happiness [this was years before her daughters ended up as tabloid darlings while still in their teens]. And my life here has given me many satisfactions in the last ten years."

But in 1978 the princess confessed to Gwen Robyns, "You know, I have come to feel very sad in this marriage. He's not really interested in me. He doesn't care about me." By then, Rainier's numerous infidelities were an open secret. A few minutes later, Grace confided, "I so appreciate those times in my life when I was madly, desperately, and hopelessly in love. *Those* were the best of times. I don't know that I ever had that with Rainier."

Back in 1973, Grace had made her first public appearance without her husband, and as the decade progressed the Grimaldis spent increasingly more time apart. Grace put down roots in Paris. And on June 7, 1975, an article titled "Princess Grace's Marriage on the Rocks" was published in the *National Star*. Topics in supermarket tabloids tend to strain credulity, but in this case, the article contained enough truth to spawn a spate of hasty denials, even though it never saw the light of day in either France or Monaco because of laws restricting negative press of local royals.

In 1977, over lunch in Manhattan with her old friend Charlotte Winston, Grace ruminated on what might have been had she not made the decision to wed Rainier, admitting that she had allowed herself to be pushed into the royal union "by my own mother," caving in to Margaret's strenuous objection to marrying Oleg Cassini. Oleg, of course, would have cheerfully supported Grace's decision to remain an actress. "How many wonderful roles might I have played by now?" she asked Charlotte rhetorically. "How might my life have turned out? That one decision changed my entire future."

And to a former show-business pal, Grace confided the peace she had made with her marital unhappiness, saying, "Some of us sign on for a run of the play contract—no options."

But what Grace admitted to her friends is not what she said to the press.

In 1979, looking back on her decision to quit Hollywood and wed Rainier, Grace told the *Sunday Mirror,* "All I ever wanted was to be someone's wife, the wife of a particular man. I needed someone with a strong personality to hold his own against the fame of an actress. . . . I wasn't happy in my personal life. I wanted to be married, so I made my decision and I've never regretted it." However, she also found the transition from actress to royal consort a bumpy one. That same year, she told an interviewer, "After my days as an actress I had to become a normal person again, and at the beginning I suffered a personality crisis. My husband was determined to turn me into a real princess and it was with so much patience and understanding that he showed me the way."

On March 9, 1981, Grace had a brief encounter with another young royal who was in for the same treatment from her future husband and his chilly family. In the ladies' room at London's Goldsmith Hall, where she was participating in a poetry reading, Her Serene Highness ran into Lady Diana Spencer. It was Diana's first public appearance as Prince Charles's fiancée. Spilling indecorously out of a black gown that was two sizes too small because the dress she intended to wear hadn't arrived in time, Lady Di confided her terror at the life that lay in store for her. Grace embraced her, and cupping Diana's face in her hands bluntly replied, "Don't worry, dear, it will get worse."

Personality differences and rampant extramarital infidelities notwithstanding, the Grimaldis did as most royal couples of theirs and earlier generations did, and stayed married, celebrating their twenty-fifth wedding anniversary on April 19, 1981. Although they played the happy couple in the presence of their guests, they remained estranged. Two months earlier, Grace's older sister, Peggy, speaking to the *Sun,* had observed, "They like separate things. When they are apart they have individual lives. They are even financially independent of each other. It's a nice agreement."

During 1981 and 1982, friends who had long known the prince and princess noticed that their relationship seemed to be enjoying a renaissance. Although the Monegasques never conscienced

Grace's decision to resume her career, the prince had finally come to terms with Grace's passion for acting and was comfortable confessing that in the beginning of their marriage he had probably been too impatient for Grace "to fit in and to feel at ease. Often I didn't understand her outlook on things; I have to be honest and admit that much." The Grimaldis had mellowed, individually, and as a couple, and had finally developed a mutual respect for one another, a level of comfort ironically aided, perhaps, by so much time spent apart.

Looking back on the state of Grace and Rainier's relationship in 1982, Barbara Tuck Cresci, the widow of Rainier's longtime Consul-General Frank Cresci, observed, "In the end, despite all of the separations over the years, they were getting back on the same track again and truly thinking like a married couple with a future."

Throughout the early months of 1982, Grace admitted to her friends that she had been battling numerous ailments, from heart trouble to a particularly difficult menopause to issues of body image. The once-lithe princess, who, during her acting career, got naked on more than one first date with confidence and ease, confessed to her friend Gwen Robyns, "I'm so fat, and I feel so horrible about myself. I just don't want to show my body to anyone, it's so awful."

On the morning of September 13, 1982, the fifty-two-year-old Grace and her seventeen-year-old daughter, Stephanie, who at the time harbored dreams of becoming a professional race car driver, were motoring along a winding road in the ten-year-old Rover 3500 that had been a gift from Rainier. Grace was at the wheel. In those days she rarely drove—and just a few weeks earlier, Rainier had expressly forbidden her to do so. Grace suffered severe recurring migraines, could not see well without her glasses, and had recently been involved in a near collision. That morning, she was supposed to have been chauffeured back to the palace in the prince's Rolls-Royce, but had a demanding schedule during the coming week and first needed to see her couturier; so she took off for

Monte Carlo on her own. For whatever reason, she never fastened her seat belt.

Thirty minutes into the precipitous snaking drive along D37, Grace lost control of the car. In an utter panic, she exclaimed to Stephanie that the brake wouldn't work. Stephanie tried to yank the hand brake, but succeeded only in putting the automobile in park. The Rover swerved across the narrow two-lane road, broke through the retaining wall that hugged the precipice, and spiraled dozens of feet down an embankment, decapitating a tree, and coming to rest upside down near a vegetable garden.

Eerily, in *To Catch a Thief*, director Alfred Hitchcock filmed Kelly speeding along the same winding corniche. Grace never liked to drive, petrified of losing her ability to control the vehicle. Apparently, she loathed that specific bend in the road, and had long held the presentiment that she would die in an automobile crash. Hitchcock took advantage of that fear on camera.

At first it was believed that Grace's injuries were relatively minor, not much more than a broken leg. But tests conducted during the hours that followed the crash determined that the princess had suffered extensive internal bleeding, a collapsed lung, and two brain lesions—one that might have represented a minor stroke that caused her to lose control of the vehicle in the first place and the other as a result of the accident.

At noon on September 14, a sorrowful Rainier consented to the disconnecting of Grace's life support, and at 10:35 p.m., Her Serene Highness Princess Grace-Patricia de Monaco was pronounced dead. Eight hundred people attended her funeral, held on September 18 in the same cathedral where Grace and Rainier had married. Notably absent was Princess Stephanie, who remained in the hospital recovering from her injuries.

In 2002, on the twentieth anniversary of her death, Rainier invoked Grace's memory, saying, "she is always present in our hearts and in our thoughts," and praising her for "carrying out to perfection her role as wife and mother." Despite the prince's many extramarital liaisons, his French biographer, Philippe Delorme, believed that he "never really got over her death. It was an irreparable loss. It would have been very hard to replace her." After Grace's death, however, Rainier was romantically linked to his cousin Princess Ira von Fürstenberg, a Fiat heiress and the former sister-in-law of the fashion designer Diane von Furstenberg.

Prince Rainier outlived his wife by nearly twenty-three years. During the last three years of his life, he struggled with numerous health issues and was hospitalized for coronary problems in 2004. He died on April 6, 2005, at the age of eighty-one, and was succeeded by their only son, Prince Albert.

Charles, Prince of Wales

B. 1948

❧ *and* ❧

Lady Diana Spencer

1961–1997

married 1981–1996

❧ *and* ❧

Camilla Parker Bowles

b. 1947

married 2005–

"There were three of us in this marriage, so it was a bit crowded."
—Diana to Martin Bashir, *Panorama* interview, November 1995

ON JULY 29, 1981, THE ENTIRE WORLD WATCHED AS nineteen-year-old Lady Diana Spencer walked down the carpeted aisle of St. Paul's Cathedral to wed the thirty-two-year-old Prince of Wales, heir to the English throne.

The bride was wearing a puff-sleeved, full-skirted ivory confection that would be copied for years to come by wannabe princesses, even though the designers apparently forgot that Diana's twenty-five-foot train would somehow have to be stuffed into the glass coach that brought her to the cathedral.

Nor did anyone realize at the time that when Prince Charles spoke the words "forsaking all others till death us do part" before the Archbishop of Canterbury, his family, friends, and much of the rest of the known universe—he never intended to keep his vow.

So who was the tall shy blonde inside the voluminous, and somewhat wrinkled, dress? And what journey had her life taken before that fateful trip to the altar and—to all but the key players—a storybook wedding?

Born the Honorable Diana Spencer, she boasted a better pedigree than Prince Charles. The House of Windsor is a twentieth-century creation that evolved from the German houses of Saxe-Coburg-Gotha and Hanover. The first Hanover to sit on the English throne was George I, whose reign began in 1714.

Diana, however, could trace her aristocratic lineage to the reign of James I (1603–25), who created the 1st Baron Spencer. The title was upgraded to an earldom by George III in 1765. She was the third daughter of Viscount Althorp, who became the 8th Earl Spencer on the death of his father in 1975, and his wife, the former Frances Roche, the younger daughter of the 4th Baron Fermoy. Their 1954 nuptials had been considered "the society wedding of the year." But when Diana was six years old her parents' marriage collapsed after Frances fell in love with a married businessman, Peter Shand Kydd, and left her young family, eventually marrying her lover on May 2, 1969. Frances and Johnnie Althorp endured an acrimonious divorce battle. Because Johnnie was a powerful nobleman, he gained custody of their four children; however, Johnnie was not exactly a hands-on father, and the two youngest Spencer children, Diana and Charles, often cried themselves to sleep, missing their mummy.

Diana was educated at various boarding schools, never excelling academically. She twice failed her O levels, the most basic high school exams. But she was praised for her artistic talents, and won awards for her impeccable care of various guinea pigs. She also had a natural aptitude for relating to seniors, younger children, and the infirm, which formed part of the schools' community outreach programs.

During her teenage, pre-Charles years, Diana's chums described her as "A strong character, buoyant and noisy." She also loved to eat.

A stint at a Swiss finishing school proved a bust because Diana got nothing out of it, so she convinced her parents they were wasting their money and returned to England. By then, she was beginning to blossom. According to her brother, "Suddenly the insignificant ugly duckling was obviously going to be a swan."

She tagged along with her oldest sister's social set, harboring crushes on Sarah Spencer's cast-off boyfriends, never really having one of her own. Her innate sense of destiny told her that she "had to keep myself tidy for what lay ahead."

The Spencer children's step-grandmother was the romance novelist Barbara Cartland, and, according to the princess's biographer Tina Brown, the teenage Diana devoured Cartland's books, especially the ones where the plot revolved around marrying a prince or a king. As ambitious as she was naïve, Diana craved the same fate. Ironically, even though most of Sarah's former beaux didn't give her a second look, Diana would eventually end up wedding one of them.

Charles Philip Arthur George, His Royal Highness The Prince of Wales, Earl of Chester, Duke of Cornwall, Duke of Rothesay, Earl of Carrick, Baron Renfrew, Lord of the Isles, and Prince and Great Steward of Scotland was born on the night of November 14, 1948, to the Princess Elizabeth, who stood next in line to the English throne. His father is Elizabeth's fourth cousin, the Greek-born Prince Philip, Duke of Edinburgh, the title he was granted on his wedding day. Queen Elizabeth made her husband a Prince of the United Kingdom in 1957, and although he is Her Majesty's consort because he is her spouse, and is styled "His Royal High-ness," he does not bear the title "King Consort" or "Prince Consort." Philip's mother, a descendant of Queen Victoria, was known as Princess Alice of Battenberg, but in 1917 the family anglicized its name to Mountbatten, and England's current ruling family is occasionally referred to as the Windsor-Mountbattens, or even as the Mountbatten-Windsors, although by royal decree they are the House of Windsor.

When Charles was just three years old, his mother acceded to the throne on the death of his fifty-six-year-old grandfather, George VI, in February 1952. This left the twenty-five-year-old queen with little time to devote to her young family.

Prince Philip was a stern figure and rebuked Charles for what he perceived to be a lack of rigor and robustness. As a child, Charles attended the Cheam preparatory school, where he would cry himself to sleep. And at thirteen, in 1962, he was enrolled in his father's alma mater, Gordonstoun, a rigid academy on Scotland's northeast coast. Charles was utterly miserable there. His schoolmates made sucking noises whenever he walked by. Anyone who befriended him was considered a brownnoser and teased mercilessly, so the young heir found himself utterly alone. He begged to come home, but his father was intent on making a man of him.

At Gordonstoun Charles had been deliberately kept extremely sheltered from the opposite sex, lest there be any embarrassing scrapes involving unsavory or overly ambitious young ladies. No surprise then that according to Penny Junor, one of his biographers, Charles "had a number of girlfriends" after he reached adulthood, ". . . but the relationships were mostly platonic. Not a natural womanizer, he was far more likely to present a girl with some hideous practical joke—like the envelope he gave to one which exploded with rubber bands when she opened it—than a single rose."

On July 1, 1969, the twenty-year-old heir was formally invested as Prince of Wales. After a tour of his new realm he returned to university, eventually completing four terms at Trinity College.

In 1970 a seemingly insignificant event took place; however, it was the proverbial tremble of a butterfly's wing that culminates in a tsunami. Charles met the woman who would become his great love—Camilla Shand.

Camilla was the daughter of the Hon. Rosalind Cubitt and Bruce Shand, a World War II hero and an educational films representative who spent the better part of his time playing the country squire, indulging his passion for horses and hounds. Unlike Charles, who had to greet his mother with a handshake, and Diana, whose parents were both absentees, Camilla grew up in a loving family environment.

Camilla bravely toughed out Dumbrells, a boarding school known for its Spartan atmosphere and positively Victorian deprivations. And as she navigated the shoals of adolescence Camilla also proved herself quite sexually precocious, according to royal biographer Christopher Wilson. Homely, but voluptuous, she was a daring athlete who cheerfully wore dowdy tweeds and twinsets when her girlfriends flashed their thighs in Mary Quant miniskirts. She had a confidence, an "inner glow" as her friends described it, that made her extremely attractive and very likable among her posher pals—as well as with the boys.

But Camilla's real claim to fame was the *way* in which she introduced herself to Prince Charles. At a party at Smith's Lawn following a polo match at the Royal Horse Guards' Polo Club in Windsor, Camilla sauntered up to the prince and purportedly announced, "My great-grandmother and your great-great-grandfather were lovers—so how about it?"

Camilla's scandalous ancestress was Alice Keppel, nicknamed "La Favorita" by royal insiders. For the last dozen years of his life she was the royal paramour of Queen Victoria's son "Bertie," the Prince of Wales and later King Edward VII. She was even at his bedside, much to the annoyance of his wife, Queen Alexandra, when he died in 1910. Mrs. Keppel remained married throughout her royal affair; her husband, George, was thought to be completely at ease with the arrangement, the ultimate *mari complaisant*.

According to Kevin Burke, to whom Camilla lost her virginity in 1965, her debutante year, she was obsessed with following in Mrs. Keppel's footsteps. "She was always mentioning it, as if it were something almost talismanic." So when her path crossed Prince Charles's, Camilla seized what she considered to be her birthright. With the tenacity of one of her Jack Russell terriers, she never let go. People who saw Camilla and Charles during that first meeting described their attraction as a *coup de foudre,* a blazing spark of passion and sexual chemistry. The intense magnetism they shared, even from across a room, was apparent to even the most casual of onlookers.

There would be three people in that relationship as well.

Before she met Charles, Camilla had dumped Burke for *her* Grand Passion. She had fallen hard for Andrew Parker Bowles, a Roman Catholic army officer eight years her senior who was handsome, dashing, and, according to biographer Christopher Wilson, as much of a rake as Camilla was boy crazy. But when Andrew was posted to Germany, Camilla consoled herself at home by hanging out at the Guards' Polo Club at Windsor. Fate and proximity combined to place her in the right venue at the right time to continue what her ancestor had begun.

In the autumn of 1971, duty called and Charles began his career with the Royal Navy, embarking on five years of military service that precluded his presence on English soil for many months at a stretch. Camilla got on with her life, finally marrying Andrew Parker Bowles in July 1973.

So, if the Prince of Wales was so passionately enamored of Camilla's charms, why did he never pop the question when he had the chance? The answer is that he *couldn't* ask Camilla to be his bride.

It might have been the early 1970s in the rest of the world, but the House of Windsor was stuck in a time warp, partly of its own making and partly because even if it wanted to, it was bound by existing laws governing the monarchy. Tradition dictated that the Prince of Wales had to marry a virgin. And Camilla had a sexual past that could not be overlooked. Also working against her was the fact that she wasn't quite blue-blooded enough, although she had attended some of the best schools and her father was a courtier, in service to the crown. There was another factor, too. The suits at the palace knew that Camilla's looks would be a very tough sell to the British subjects, who wanted a beautiful "fairy-tale-princess" face to adorn their commemorative plates, shot glasses, and tea towels.

But Charles and Camilla were not ready to part ways. And in the future his relationship with her would be termed "nonnegotiable," whether Charles was dealing with Machiavellian palace courtiers ("the men in gray," as Diana called them), his mother, or his wife.

From 1972 to 1980, while he was supposed to be seeking a bride, the prince enjoyed a romantic rootlessness, dating several women, some of whom from time to time were heralded by the Fleet Street press as the future Princess of Wales. But something always happened. The sexually experienced women self-eliminated. The virginal aristocrats had plans for their own futures that did not include gilded cages and tiaras or grew quickly disenchanted with Charles's self-centered manner born of privilege and honed with noblesse oblige. Yet for all his playing the field, the prince didn't seem to be having much fun. Women who knew him then and bothered to take his measure described him as lonely and melancholy.

Camilla, meanwhile, was keen to have it all. As desperate as she had been to marry Andrew Parker Bowles, she wanted to retain her status as royal mistress. She and Charles rekindled their affair soon after the Parker Bowleses wed.

Occasionally, members of the press caught Charles and Camilla together during the mid-1970s and printed tart implications about their relationship, but it never became a subject of much scrutiny. At the prince's request Camilla brazenly accompanied him as his "official escort" when he traveled on business overseas. Referring to the prince's tour of Zimbabwe, a Foreign Office source conveyed his utter disgust that everyone there knew "the royal family's envoy had brought his popsy along with him. The lack of tact was inde-scribable. It just made a joke out of the whole thing."

Camilla was the prince's confidante in every way, privy to his most intimate frustrations, joys, and sorrows. She vetted his girl-friends as future princess material and knew what moves Charles intended to make long before the hapless women did.

Resigned to his responsibilities, Prince Charles told the media, "I think one must concentrate on marriage being essentially a ques-tion of mutual love and respect for each other. . . . Essentially you must be good friends, and love, I'm sure will grow out of that friendship. I have a particular responsibility to ensure that I make the right decision. The last thing I could possibly entertain is getting divorced."

He neglected to mention that his married lover was helping him choose someone who would never prove a threat to their liaison.

Her Majesty was not the slightest bit amused by Charles's adul-terous philandering, and despite her son's protests, refused to meet Camilla or ever to be in the same room with her. The monarch is also Supreme Governor of the Church of England, which does not condone adultery. By 1980 Prince Philip, too, had had enough. Charles had agreed to settle down and choose a bride when he turned thirty, a milestone he'd passed two years earlier. What was he waiting for? They were running out of well-bred Protestant vir-gins. It was time to grow up and do his duty.

The Prince of Wales first met Diana Spencer in 1977 on the Al-thorp estate when he was dating her older sister, Sarah. His first impressions of her were that she was "a very jolly and amusing and attractive sixteen-year-old, full of fun."

Yet Diana's gut reaction to the prince was less salubrious. "What a sad man," she observed. She "kept out of the way" at a dance the Spencers hosted that weekend. "I remember being a fat, podgy, no make-up, unsmart lady, but I made a lot of noise and he liked that."

Charles fancied Diana's boisterous behavior enough to ask her to give him a tour of the Spencers' illustrious picture gallery, but the competitive Sarah edged her out of the way. Lest readers form the impression that Charles would carnally know two of the three Spencer girls, in interviews Sarah insisted that her relationship with Charles had been "totally platonic. I think of him as the big brother I never had."

Sarah was scratched from the royal scorecard, but Charles kept her younger sister in his sights. In 1978, Diana was surprised to receive an invitation to the prince's thirtieth birthday party. And in February 1979, when she was living in a flat in London's Colherne Court with a passel of female roommates and working as a kindergarten teacher and part-time cleaning lady (whose clients included Sarah), Diana was invited to join a royal house party at Sandringham.

Lucinda "Beryl" Craig, one of Diana's roommates, teased her about the possible outcome of the event. "Gosh, perhaps you are going to be the next queen of England."

Diana, who at the time was on her hands and knees scrubbing the floor, looked up from her rag and replied, "Beryl, I doubt it. Can you see me swanning around in kid gloves and a ballgown?"

Well, yes, actually.

It was a classic Cinderella moment.

In July 1980, Diana was invited to a house party by Philip de Pass, the son of two close friends of Prince Philip. At the last minute, she was told that Prince Charles would be there as well. "You're young blood, you might amuse him," Philip de Pass told her.

Charles had been devastated by the recent assassination of his great-uncle and mentor, Lord Mountbatten, whose sailboat had been blown apart by an IRA bomb. After a polo match that weekend, sitting on a hay bale beside the prince, the intuitive Diana ventured to share her reaction when she saw him at his "uncle Dickie's" funeral. "My heart bled for you . . . it's wrong, you're lonely, you should be with someone to look after you."

For a brief moment Charles forgot about Camilla Parker Bowles, and saw the solicitous Diana Spencer in a new light.

In Diana's words, Charles "was all over me" that weekend.

"I thought, 'Well, this isn't very cool'—I thought men weren't supposed to be so obvious. . . . The next minute he leapt on me practically . . . and I wasn't sure how to cope with it."

But pawing her at the de Passes was one of the few times that Charles ever did make an effort to romance Diana.

Over the next few months the prince embarked on a whirlwind, if tepid, courtship. Diana was put through the gauntlet of royal trials—including the obligatory visit to Balmoral and the sailing excursion to Cowes aboard the royal yacht, *Britannia*. The starry-eyed press, eager for a royal wedding, practically had them married already. Although Diana admitted in Andrew Morton's revised biography that her experience of men was practically nil, she was certainly aware that she was not being wooed in anything resembling the customary fashion; she and Charles were never alone. They were always accompanied by members of his family or his closely knit circle of friends several years her senior, which invariably included Camilla and Tom Parker Bowles. Camilla was convinced she had found the perfect royal bride, cheerfully telling a friend, "She's like a mouse."

At least one move ahead in this bizarre chess game, Camilla always seemed to know everything that transpired between Diana and Charles, and during these pre-betrothal "tests" she counseled Diana on how to behave with her royal beau. "Don't push him into doing this; don't do that," Diana later recalled.

The naïve teen was confused by it all, particularly by Charles's indifference to her physically, even as he appeared to be rushing her at breakneck speed toward the altar. She commented that as a suitor ". . . there was never anything tactile about him. It was extraordinary, but I didn't have anything to go by because I never had a boyfriend."

For weeks she puzzled over the Camilla-Charles dynamic. But finally, the penny dropped. "Eventually I worked it all out and found the proof of the pudding and people were willing to talk to me."

Was that why Diana laughed in his face when Charles proposed marriage to her on February 6, 1981, at Windsor Castle? Surprised at her reaction, Charles was "deadly serious," according to Diana, reminding her that "you do realize that one day you will be Queen."

She let it sink in and told Charles "Yes," adding, "I do love you so much. I love you so much," to which Charles replied, "whatever love means." He would later repeat the line on international television. But when Charles said it directly to Diana, she chose to put an utterly different construct on it, interpreting the words to mean *I love you, too.* "So I thought that was great." Admitting her naivete, she added, "I thought he meant that."

Looking back on it as she made the secret tapes that would be smuggled to biographer Andrew Morton, Diana realized that Charles had "found the virgin, the sacrificial lamb and in a way he was obsessed with me. But it was hot and cold, hot and cold. You never knew what mood it was going to be. Up and down, up and down."

Ironically, Charles would repeatedly charge his wife with the same behavior.

Diana was still only nineteen years old on February 24, 1981, when the royal engagement was officially announced. That day, at a press conference, Charles and Diana were asked if they were in love. It was supposed to be a puffball question. "Of course," Diana replied. Charles dragged out his stock "whatever love means" response, which immediately threw a wet blanket over the already faint romantic spark.

Charles's doubts about their compatibility were expressed privately as well. According to Christopher Wilson, only a month before the royal wedding he confided to a friend, "She is exquisitely pretty, a perfect poppet . . . but she is a child. She does not look old enough to be out of school, much less married." True: she was still a teenager. And Diana may have lived in large houses with plenty of servants and extensive art collections, but she'd never had a demanding job, never managed a staff, never run an office or been a slave to a punishing schedule. In fact, she'd always gotten out of anything she found unpleasant or demanding. In no way was she prepared for the full-time, real-life demands of being a royal and sharing her husband with the rest of Britain—including Camilla Parker Bowles. Charles aired his misgivings with his parents as well, but was met with an acrimonious scolding.

For years people have questioned why Diana said yes to Charles's proposal of marriage, knowing how much Camilla Parker Bowles was in the picture. There are several possible reasons. By then, Diana was in love with Charles—or had convinced herself she was. Somewhere deep down she knew it was a lopsided match, but she believed it would blossom into a mutual True Love. If it could happen in Barbara Cartland romances, why not in real life? Since their wedding vows contained the promise of eternal fidelity to each other, Diana may have thought Charles would take them seriously, as he did so many of his other responsibilities to his subjects, and Camilla would be snipped out of the romantic picture.

Also, Diana was ambitious. Although she had cold feet in the days before the wedding, and despite her premonition that she would never be queen, she also knew instinctively that something big had always been in store for her, the chance to do something for the people and to do her duty. She passionately wanted to be Princess of Wales.

Yet she nearly called it off. Journalists and paparazzi had dogged her everywhere she went, and she claimed to have been given no advice on how to cope. Diana maintained her cool with the members of the press, but inwardly she was panicked and falling apart. She began to suffer bouts of bulimia that would plague her for practically the rest of her life, bingeing and purging, bingeing and purging. Three weeks before the big day and scarcely twenty years old, she bolted to Althorp after a party where Charles utterly ignored her. After a heart-to-heart talk, her father, Earl Spencer, convinced her to go ahead with it. She nearly collapsed from the strain just a few days in advance of the wedding, and her sisters tried to buck her up, teasing, "Too late, Duch [Diana's family nickname]; your face is on the tea towels."

Although Charles's biographer Penny Junor refutes these claims, according to Diana the royals and palace staffers were cold to her. She insisted that none of her future family was there to greet her when, on the day before her engagement was announced, she was told that she had to move out of her Colherne Court flat and into the Queen Mother's residence, Clarence House. Instead Diana discovered a letter on her bed from Camilla Parker Bowles inviting her to lunch—written days before Diana *herself* found out where they were going to send her. In the innocuous guise of an avid equestrienne, Camilla, keen on marking her territory, intended to suss out whether Diana intended to accompany her future husband on the hunt.

"The Camilla thing rearing its ugly head the whole way through our engagement" stressed out Diana immensely. She was a wreck in the final days leading up to the wedding, but was gladdened by a sweet gift Charles sent to her after the rehearsals. It was a signet ring embossed with three feathers (the Prince of Wales's crest) and "a very nice card that said 'I'm so proud of you and when you come up I'll be there at the altar for you tomorrow. Just look 'em in the eye and knock 'em dead.' "

On July 28, 1981, "her last night of freedom," Diana was "very, very calm, deathly calm. I felt like I was a lamb to the slaughter." Diana may have later regretted her hyperbole; even the most nervous of brides don't look upon their trip to the altar as a journey to the abattoir.

The following day, all the world was ready for a royal wedding, except for two and a half people. Diana spotted Camilla in St. Paul's as she walked down the aisle. "Let's hope that's over," she thought, with renewed self-confidence. Diana recollected that during the ceremony she was "so in love with my husband that I couldn't take my eyes off him. I absolutely thought I was the luckiest girl in the world."

Seven hundred fifty million people in seventy countries watched them exchange their vows—vows Charles apparently never intended to keep. In a way, he was committing perjury in the most public of witness boxes.

During his engagement to the virginal Diana, Charles had continued to sleep with Camilla, and they even made love within days of the royal wedding. Charles's valet Stephen Barry told the *Daily Mirror*'s royal watcher James Whitaker, "Sir had always been infatuated with Camilla since they first knew each other in the early 1970s. But when he took her to bed in the very week of his wedding it seemed incredible. Certainly incredibly daring, if not incredibly stupid."

"I was told one thing, but actually another was going on," Diana said of the universal campaign to "gaslight" her when it came to Charles and Camilla's relationship. "The lies and the deceit. For example my husband sending Camilla Parker Bowles flowers when she had meningitis. 'To Gladys from Fred.' "

"Fred" also gave "Gladys" a gold and enamel bracelet with an entwined F and G. Diana discovered the gift shortly before the royal wedding and went ballistic. It was just one of many vociferous rows they had over the Camilla issue. But the angrier and more emotional Diana became, the more Charles shut down, fighting her fire with frost. His insensitivity only served to turn her shrewish.

Their honeymoon aboard the royal yacht was anything but romantic. Every night they were expected to dine with the *Britannia*'s officers, hosting parties instead of doing as newlyweds should. One day, as the prince and princess compared appointments, photos of Camilla fluttered out of Charles's diary. Diana's devastation sparked yet another quarrel. And one evening Charles sported cuff links embossed with interlocking Cs. Diana guessed their provenance, but instead of being sensitive to her dismay, Charles snarled that Camilla was a dear friend and would always remain so, and yes the cuff links were a gift from her—but what of it?

What of it? He phoned Camilla every day during his honeymoon with Diana, to complain about how difficult she was, intimating that he had made a dreadful sacrifice for his country. Diana was convinced that her husband was "obsessed with Camilla"—and she was right. This fixation on Mrs. Parker Bowles was just about the only thing the newlyweds had in common. Diana admitted that "at night I dreamt of Camilla the whole time. . . . I had tremendous hope in me [for our marriage] which was slashed by day two." She confessed to "crying my eyes out on our honeymoon. I was so tired, for all the wrong reasons . . ."

In October 1981 the Waleses' first child, William, was conceived, and finally Diana had something positive and joyous to focus on. But it was a difficult pregnancy. Her horrendous morning sickness was compounded by her bulimia. The grueling pace of her schedule didn't help. The doctors prescribed pills, when according to Diana all that was required was a little *patience*, from the royal family in general and from her husband in particular. She had a huge learning curve to master in a brief space of time with no coaching, while they'd been doing it all their lives.

"I learned to be 'royal' . . . in one week," Diana said, petulant that no one had ever told her "Well done!" when she got something right, as if she were a schoolgirl who'd aced an exam or brought home an excellent report card. "My husband made me feel so inadequate in every possible way that each time I came up for air, he pushed me down again." Yet during their public appearances, she was the one they scrambled to see. Charles knew that people on his side of the cordon during a walkabout were disappointed that they didn't get the princess instead, and it made him angry, bitter, and jealous. He couldn't see that his wife was an *asset*, said Diana's friends.

In the face of her husband's rejection, Diana acted out, in desperate, troubled bids for his attention. She threw herself down a flight of stairs when she was pregnant with William, and later admitted to a doctor who began to treat her bulimia that she had attempted suicide four or five times. One evening when Charles dismissed her complaint about something as "crying wolf," she grabbed his pen knife from his dressing table and "scratched myself heavily down my chest and thighs. There was a lot of blood."

Instead of embracing Diana and endeavoring to understand her pain, Charles behaved as he usually did: he absented himself—either emotionally, literally, or both.

Diana claimed that the worst day of her life was when she realized that Charles had gone back to Camilla—the woman she privately called "the rottweiler." Soon after Prince William's birth, the princess, already an emotional basket case from severe postpartum depression, overheard Charles's end of a romantic telephone conversation with Camilla while he lounged in his bath. "Whatever happens, I will always love you," the prince told his lover. Diana confronted him and yet another "filthy row," as she termed it, ensued. She was convinced that her postnatal blues were exacerbated by Charles's ongoing affair. Many was the night that he rang up with some excuse about working late, or didn't come home at all. In November 1983, Diana suffered a miscarriage at Balmoral. When she most needed her husband's support, Charles left to join the prestigious Beaufort Hunt—and Camilla.

The queen was convinced that her son's marital problems stemmed from Diana's bulimia. Although Her Majesty was perfectly aware that (to her disgust) Camilla remained in the picture, she refused to dignify the subject by raising it.

Small wonder, then, that Diana and Charles no longer shared a bed after their second son was conceived, although, ironically, Diana admitted that she and Charles "were very, very close to each other the six weeks before Harry was born . . . then suddenly, as Harry was born it just went bang, our marriage, the whole thing down the drain. . . . By then I knew he had gone back to his lady but somehow we managed to have Harry."

To Diana's chagrin, "We had to find a date where Charles could get off his polo pony for me to give birth." After Prince Harry was born on September 15, 1984, instead of making sure that his wife and child were well and healthy, according to royal biographer Christopher Wilson, Charles's first reaction was a slightly dismissive "Oh, it's a boy" (he had hoped for a girl), followed by "And he's even got red hair"—as do so many Spencers, but no Windsors. Charles then departed the hospital in a huff, off to play polo.

It was another turning point in the Waleses' already troubled marriage; but this time it seemed that the breach was irrevocable. "Something inside me died," Diana told her friends.

Seeking solace, explanations, or simply affirmations, Diana began to rely on astrological analyses, crystals, aromatherapy, Eastern medicine, such as acupuncture, and holistic approaches to healing.

And in 1989 she began to focus on charitable causes, finding her calling by combining her royal duty with her nurturing instincts. "Anywhere I see suffering, that is where I want to be, doing what I can," Diana told a conference of church leaders. She cared about the underprivileged and the undernourished, lepers, sexually abused children, teens with substance abuse issues, and the homeless. She visited hospitals giving "a cuddle" to AIDS patients at a time when much of the world considered them contagious untouchables.

Yet despite her grueling schedule of personal appearances, Diana had plenty of time for her sons. In addition to the Waleses' other incompatibility issues was the subject of child rearing. It was important to Diana to be a hands-on parent—something both she and Charles had missed out on. She strongly felt that their boys should grow up as "normal" as possible, and attend school with other children. Charles wanted his own former nanny Mabel Anderson (who some have said bore a striking resemblance to Camilla) to educate the children at Kensington Palace.

As Charles continued to find solace and enjoyment in Camilla's arms, Diana took a string of lovers as well. One of them, James Gilbey, observed of the Waleses, "Their lives are spent in total isolation [from each other]. It's not as though they ring each other and have sweet chats each evening and say: 'Darling, what have you been doing?' It simply doesn't happen."

By the autumn of 1990, it was Charles who was on the verge of a nervous breakdown. He began to spend more and more time at

Highgrove, his Gloucestershire estate located within a brief drive from Bolehyde, where the Parker Bowleses resided. According to journalist James Whitaker, "Camilla was now regarded by their friends as Charles's official hostess in Gloucestershire. She boasted about the roses she was growing in the Highgrove garden, she threw dinner parties for Charles, and she sunbathed in the gardens in a bikini while Charles pottered in the garden nearby. Set against the standards of most civilized people this behavior was outrageous. A neighbor told me, 'It was as if neither cared who saw what was going on. They were, to all intents and purposes, living as man and wife.' "

When the prince took it upon himself to return to Kensington Palace, where Diana remained with their sons, it became the scene of such tension and acrimony that one of Diana's friends nicknamed it "the Mad House." Staffers felt compelled to choose sides. According to another of her friends, all the positive reinforcement Diana had done on her self-image during Charles's absences was decimated when they were back under the same roof.

Charles had tried to dissuade his wife from attending the fortieth birthday party for Camilla's sister Annabel Elliott on February 2, 1989, but Diana insisted on putting in an appearance. After her husband and Camilla disappeared from the party for hours, Diana, although cautioned not to do so, decided to search for them. She found Charles and his mistress deep in conversation with another man and announced that she had something private to say to Camilla. The men beat a hasty retreat and an anxious Camilla braced herself.

Diana told her, "I would just like you to know that I know exactly what is going on between you and Charles, I wasn't born yesterday. . . . I'm sorry I'm in the way, I obviously am in the way and it must be hell for both of you, but I do know what is going on. Don't treat me like an idiot."

As this anecdote was related by Diana, Camilla's reaction is unrecorded. But Diana later told Charles, "You may ask her. I just said I loved you—there's nothing wrong in that. . . . I've got nothing to hide, I'm your wife and the mother of your children."

That part of Diana wanted to hold on to Charles, even if by the skin of her teeth; another part of her wanted to snip at least some of the ties that bound them. She told Andrew Morton, "If I was able to write my own script, I'd say that I would hope that my husband would go off, go away with his lady and sort that out and leave me and the children to carry the Wales name through to the time William ascends the throne." She may have known that for some time Charles had harbored the pipe dream of chucking it all and moving to Tuscany with Camilla.

In the summer of 1989 Diana was encouraged by her own family and by her in-laws to try to make a fresh start of things with Charles. At this stage, divorce was considered unthinkable by all parties, even though the Waleses couldn't stand to be in the same room with each other. They took a much publicized trip to India in early 1992, and while Charles addressed a group of business leaders in Delhi, Diana stole the limelight by having herself photographed posing alone in front of the Taj Mahal, the ultimate monument to love.

For years the British public had learned little about Charles's ongoing affair with Camilla Parker Bowles. But that year, the prince's best-kept secret for two decades would be blasted to the four corners of the earth. Diana decided to go public. For months she recorded tapes that were secretly couriered by Dr. James Colthurst from Kensington Palace to the biographer and journalist Andrew Morton. When Morton's offices were burglarized, it seemed that the thieves were on the hunt for something quite specific, and from then on Diana relayed her thoughts into a device fitted with a scrambler.

On June 7, 1992, the first installment of Morton's sensational tell-all, *Diana, Her True Story*, was serialized in the *Sun* and Diana's allegations of her husband's marital infidelity were published. The cathartic but self-serving text conveniently glossed over the princess's own extramarital liaisons.

No sooner had the news hit the stands than Charles sped up to Windsor to discuss the consequences of divorce with his mum and dad.

Faced with an explosion too loud to ignore, the following day the Waleses sat down in Kensington Palace to talk about their marital future and the potential repercussions of a separation. Diana later said that she felt a "deep, deep, profound sadness. Because we had struggled to keep it going, but obviously we ran out of steam."

The Morton exposé had instant, and seismic, repercussions. Camilla, who had gotten away with much for decades, was finally subjected to the painful sting of tabloid headlines and the harsh glare of paparazzi flashbulbs. It also ended up creating a thick set of battle lines within the royal ranks. Diana (and Morton) immediately felt the backlash from the palace and the Establishment. Publicly airing one's royal unmentionables was just not done. The already radioactive Diana had now committed the ultimate transgression. Adultery: okay. Talking about it: taboo.

Diana's and Charles's friends formed armed camps around their principals. Charles's circle, who described *Diana, Her True Story* as "the longest divorce petition in history," advised him to go through with it. And in the summer of 1992, Diana herself asked her husband point-blank, "Why don't you go off with your lady and have an end to it?"

But duty triumphed over hypocrisy. The subject of Charles's divorce was (as his marriage had been) in the hands of a higher authority: his mother the queen.

After another meeting at Windsor Castle, Charles's parents declared that any notion of a formal separation was off the table. The Waleses were sent home to try again, and Diana and Charles reluctantly agreed to spend the next few months endeavoring to iron out their differences. But the palace didn't hold up its end; Prince Philip pointedly snubbed his daughter-in-law when she passed him in the royal box at Ascot and sent Diana four extremely vicious letters during the following few weeks. Even courtiers were frosty to her.

Diana had long thought her phones were tapped, but by now she was not the only royal to have become paranoid. The Firm, as the upper echelon of the ruling family called themselves, were extremely concerned about conspiracies and wondered almost daily what fresh hell awaited them. There was suspicion not only about tapped phones but about purloined documents and MI5 involvement.

Perhaps the paranoia was not so unfounded. What happened next made Diana's published confessions regarding a sham marriage and the royal family's rampant hypocrisy and insensitivity appear banal.

December 1989 had been a banner month for the recording of compromising phone conversations. Transcripts and voice recordings were made from what were believed to be two separate calls, one between Charles and Camilla and the other between Diana and her lover at the time, James Gilbey. The tapings were traced to, or pinned on, individual ham radio operators; but investigators later substantiated that it would have been nearly impossible for these individuals to have made such sophisticated recordings. In fact, the purported call between Diana and Gilbey turned out to be a seamless patch of two different conversations conducted at two entirely different times. The exchange between Charles and Camilla was also revealed to be a clever collage of several phone calls made in the months around December 1989.

More frightening was the discovery that numerous calls involving many members of the royal family had been recorded, including twenty-eight conversations between Charles and Camilla and a phone call made from Prince Andrew to his wife, the Duchess of York, while he was aboard his ship, the HMS *Camperdown*. It's phenomenally unlikely for a ham amateur to have been able to record Andrew's call, but to date, no culprit has been discovered.

The first transcribed phone call to make the presses was the one between Diana and Gilbey, ostensibly conducted on New Year's Eve 1989. The scandal became known as "Squidgygate" because Gilbey affectionately called Diana either "Squidge" or "Squidgy" several times during the conversation. It cost the princess whatever public relations points she had won by "outing" Charles's relationship with Camilla in the Andrew Morton book.

But in January 1993, any sympathy Charles might have gained from the Squidgygate tarnishing of Britain's goddess was utterly lost when the transcript of an eleven-minute fragment of a phone call allegedly made to Camilla on December 18, 1989, made its way into tabloids worldwide. Rife with sexual innuendo and mutual, passionate declarations of love, the conversation includes a joke about reincarnation in which Charles would come back in his next life as his lover's tampon. This episode, which embarrassed the House of Windsor more than any of Diana's betrayals and transgressions, whether actual or imagined, was dubbed "Camillagate."

The mockery of a royal marriage had to stop. The queen consulted with Prime Minister John Major and the Archbishop of Canterbury regarding any potential barriers to Charles's eventual accession should he divorce Diana. The PM assured Her Majesty that there were no legal ramifications and it would have no effect on the governance of the kingdom.

Diana was most concerned about how a formal separation would affect their sons, who, after Charles, stood second and third in line to the throne. The line of succession would remain unchallenged, she was told, but the boys would have to be raised within the court, according to centuries-old royal protocol. That meant that any plans Diana might harbor to live abroad in the future would not include her sons.

On December 9, 1992, an official statement was released announcing the Waleses' formal separation. Princes William and Harry were in school but Diana made sure they were informed a week earlier to prepare them for what was ahead.

From the highest levels, pressure was applied on Charles to give up Camilla, but he stubbornly made it clear that their relationship was "nonnegotiable." Diana might be out of the picture, but Camilla remained firmly in the foreground, at least as far as the prince was concerned.

Like any separating couple, Diana and Charles divided their

possessions and immediately set about redecorating their homes. All traces of Diana's existence disappeared from Charles's beloved Highgrove. She got rid of her husband's military and architecture paintings and added a woman's touch to Kensington Palace— soothing pastoral landscapes and images of dancers and flowers. Then she decorated the bathroom with satirical cartoons about Charles.

Having remade her residence, it was time for the princess to re-invent herself. She wanted to become a roving ambassador for in-ternational causes, but the Firm still regarded her as a ticking time bomb and suddenly she found her public appearance requests cur-tailed. On Friday, December 3, 1993, at a charity luncheon, Diana announced that she was retiring from public life. From then on, her first priority would be her children. Charles's first reaction was that his estranged wife—still a royal—was selfishly indulging in an ap-parent dereliction of duty.

Diana compromised by making the official appearances that were required of her, but it was evident that the Waleses' marital separa-tion would never end in a rapprochement. Eventually, Charles and Diana brought their respective cases to the press, each of them eager to sway the tide of public opinion.

In an interview on June 29, 1994, with the BBC's Jonathan Dim-bleby, Charles admitted his infidelity during their marriage. But he immediately issued a disclaimer, telling Dimbleby, "Until it became irretrievably broken down, both of us having tried."

The reaction of the *Daily Mirror* was, "He is not the first royal to be unfaithful, but he is the first to appear before 25 million of his subjects to confess."

On November 20, 1995, journalist Martin Bashir's interview with Diana was broadcast on a current affairs television program called *Panorama*. The princess aired the royal couple's dirty linen and accused the Windsors, and most pointedly Her Majesty, of being out of touch with the times. It was then that Diana, her eyes uncharacteristically rimmed with thick black liner sure to smear ostentatiously at the first sign of tears, uttered her famous line,

"There were three of us in this marriage, so it was a bit crowded." She also cast aspersions on her husband's fitness to be king.

The palace had had enough. After securing the concurrence of the prime minister and the Archbishop of Canterbury, the queen sent a separate letter to each of the Waleses, commanding them to divorce.

On Wednesday, February 28, 1996, Diana agreed to an uncontested divorce. Although she would walk away with a "compensation package" worth more than £17 million, she described it as "the saddest day of my life." The Waleses' marriage was dissolved on August 28, 1996, with the issue of the decree absolute.

Diana chose to retain her involvement in just five charities and reintroduced her idea of becoming an international humanitarian ambassador. As she began to find her footing as a newly single woman, her self-confidence returned and she even saw her rival in a rosier light, gradually coming to admire Camilla Parker Bowles's loyalty to her former husband and the discretion she exercised when it came to their affair. It was Charles who had rubbed her face in it, not his lover. "He won't give her up and I wish him well," Diana once confided to a friend. "I would like to say that to his face one day."

Camilla and Tom Parker Bowles had divorced in 1995, in part due to the fallout from the Waleses' television interviews. They had been living apart for the previous three years, but during their marriage Tom was as unfaithful as his wife had been, even rekindling his own royal romance with Princess Anne around the time of her 1992 divorce from Mark Phillips.

Finally, the press began to pay attention to the Charles and Camilla story and the public was appalled to learn from a former valet of the prince's that he had to scrub the grass stains from the knees of His Highness's pajamas after he'd spent the night shagging his lover on the lawn at Highgrove, and that on some nights Charles had even bedded Camilla as Diana slept upstairs. The Britons were even more disgusted to discover that their tax dollars had been footing the bills for the Prince of Wales's mistress.

In 1995, Camilla's grocery shopping for her new Wiltshire estate was performed by Charles's Highgrove butler. The invoices were sent to the Prince of Wales's account. And after Charles divorced Diana and Camilla was acknowledged as his paramour, he awarded her a wardrobe allowance. Charles eventually covered her £130,000 debt at Coutts bank and gave her an annual stipend of £120,000, which over time increased to £180,000 per annum. In a particularly sentimental and romantic gesture, he also made a point of tracking down and purchasing the jewelry that his great-great-grandfather Edward VII had given to his lover, Camilla's royal mistress-ancestress Alice Keppel, so that he could repeat the gesture by bestowing it on Alice's descendant.

During the summer of 1997, Diana embarked on a relationship with Emad "Dodi" Al-Fayed, the forty-two-year-old son of the Egyptian-born Harrods department store owner Mohamed Al-Fayed. Dodi was known primarily as an international playboy with a few choice credits as a film producer. Their romance blossomed with astounding velocity; after knowing him for just a few weeks, Diana gave Dodi an extraordinarily sentimental gift—a pair of cuff links that had belonged to her father. Dodi's friends, and his father, were convinced they would soon be headed for the altar.

But on August 30, 1997, after a six-week courtship, the couple perished in a speeding sedan during an attempt to evade a hellish cavalcade (two motor scooters, three motorcycles, and five automobiles) of aggressive paparazzi. Ironically, that which made Diana so famous and so iconic—her talented collusion with the press—is what ultimately killed her, although who knows what might have happened had their chauffeur's blood not been filled with a lethal combination of liquor and pills.

Diana's death shocked the world, eliciting an unprecedented outpouring of public grief. Her September 6, 1997, funeral may have been watched by as many people as witnessed her royal wedding, but even then the Windsors and the Spencers argued down to the final hour about who would walk behind her coffin and where Diana would be laid to rest. Diana had wished to be placed in the family crypt near her father and beloved paternal grandmother, whom she believed had always watched over her from Heaven. Instead, her younger brother, Earl Spencer, insisted that her body be interred on a remote island on the Althorp estate, where she reposes like a character out of Tennyson's *Idylls of the King*.

Diana's tragic end put the spotlight once more on Charles's infidelity. Many people believed that if only he had been kinder to Diana, had loved her the way she loved him, hadn't cheated on her and then rubbed her nose in it, had dumped Camilla for good and really tried to make the royal marriage work, then Diana would never have been in that sedan with Dodi Fayed.

After learning of Diana's death, the thought had even occurred to Charles himself. The prince told his private secretary, Stephen Lamport, "They're all going to blame me."

People had also found a way to condemn Camilla as the temptress and interloper who didn't do the noble thing by allowing her former lover to be a faithful husband. After the Camillagate tapes were released in 1993, she was pelted with rolls outside a Sainsbury's supermarket, lobbed by angry women who thought she was evil incarnate and who blamed her for the destruction of the prince's marriage.

To the mortification of the House of Windsor, Diana's death effectively deified her. And in the months following the tragedy Camilla receded from the spotlight. Public opinion, never in her favor, was even more strongly against a potential marriage to Charles, and Britons vehemently opposed the idea of her ever becoming his queen.

Although there is no doubt Charles mourned Diana, he discreetly continued his affair with Camilla until the negative light in which her fellow Britons perceived her had noticeably waned.

In 1997 Charles finally "outed" his relationship with Camilla when he hosted a fiftieth birthday party for her, but the event was a private affair. Not until 1999 did she and Charles appear together publicly as a couple. It took another year for the queen to acknowledge Camilla's relationship with her son by attending an event at which Mrs. Parker Bowles was also present—and that was only because the occasion was the queen mum's one hundredth birthday celebration. Three years later, in 2003, Camilla moved into the prince's residence, Clarence House.

In 2002, the Church of England finally ended the centuries-old practice of prohibiting divorced persons with surviving ex-spouses from being married in the Church. Now Camilla would be able to marry her prince—so long as Charles received permission from his mum the sovereign, in accordance with the Royal Marriages Act of 1772. In the intervening years since Diana's tragic death, the tide of public opinion had begun to flow in Camilla's favor, with the dawning acknowledgment that the real Cinderella story belonged to her and Charles. He had loved her passionately for thirty-five years. Poor Diana had been savaged by it, but now her memory could remain immortal and beloved while Camilla and Charles became the poster children for Love Conquering All, giving hope to dowdy middle-aged singletons in every corner of the earth.

On April 9, 2005, the romance that Diana viewed as a nightmare and Charles saw as a fairy tale had a happy ending for him when he wed Camilla in a civil ceremony at the Guildhall in Windsor. At the time, public sentiment remained very much against the title of Princess of Wales being bestowed on the woman who shattered Diana's hopes for wedded bliss. So Camilla became Her Royal Highness The Duchess of Cornwall.

Charles's mother was not present at the Guildhall ceremony; for the queen to attend a civil wedding is not in keeping with her position as Supreme Governor of the Church of England. Later that day Her Majesty did put in an appearance at the blessing of their union in St. George's Chapel.

If Charles becomes king, because she is his wife Camilla will in fact be Queen of England. However, according to a statement from Clarence House, it has been agreed upon that Camilla's official title would be HRH The Princess Consort.

In the spring of 2008, Charles and Camilla purchased a three-bedroom country residence in Wales, Llwynywormwood Estates, surrounded by 192 acres of organic farmland. The three-feathered crest of the Prince of Wales hangs over the fireplace. Eco-friendly washing powder was spotted by an ecorazzi.com reporter on the kitchen draining board and the residence boasts a number of green elements both inside and out. And for those who want to live like a prince, the building is also registered as a B&B and is available for rental when its owners are not in residence.

As Prince of Wales, Charles has involved himself over the decades with a number of nonprofit charitable entities, and has spoken extensively on his two passions: architectural preservation and organic farming. The Prince's Trust, primarily known for sponsoring pop concerts, funnels dozens of millions of pounds into improving the futures of Britain's underprivileged youth.

But all of Charles's philanthropic work, his advanced views on agriculture, and his retrograde opinions of British architecture will likely represent a fragment of his legacy as Prince of Wales. What people will remember most is his personal life and how he chose to live it. Time and history will tell whether he (and Camilla) will be forgiven for their moral turpitude and for the years of emotional and psychological pain they inflicted on the Princess of Wales. Charles's ludicrously ineffective characterization of his marriage to Diana as a "business arrangement," where she knew the score from the start, neither excuses nor condones his behavior.

However, because the princess engendered so much sympathy, even after airing the Waleses' dirty linen in *Diana, Her True Story*, an action she later regretted, her extramarital affairs—with James Gilbey, James Hewitt, Dr. Hasnat Khan, and others—seem to have been accepted, or at least forgiven, by much of the general public as the acts of a woman desperately in search of the love, affection, and positive reinforcement that were missing from her childhood, and more important, from her marriage.

The marriage of Charles and Camilla has been something of an anticlimax. As a couple they visit foreign dignitaries and have rarely made headlines. Camilla, now over sixty years old, lacks Diana's beauty, élan, and passion for hot-button causes. But she may be suffering from some of the same disappointments as her predecessor.

In April 2008, the *Daily Mail* reported that the couple "are said to argue in front of aides, and Camilla sometimes prefers to spend time alone" at Ray Mill in Wiltshire, the country hideaway she purchased after her divorce from Andrew Parker Bowles. As flippant as Charles was when it came to Diana's needs, he is "very dismissive of Camilla's views and lifestyle," according to a staffer, who noted, "He is ever more fussy, ratty and irascible."

"The rows have been escalating over the past three months," according to one "well-placed source," embarrassing their staff, who can't help overhearing them. As of the 2008 *Daily Mail* article, the Waleses had attended thirty-three domestic engagements as a couple, although Camilla had appeared alone at as many of them, while Charles had put in solo appearances at ninety events.

As glamorous as Diana was as Princess of Wales, the prince and his second wife have been dubbed by courtiers "the Glums." So what happened to all the mutual interests, in addition to passion and sexual chemistry, that drew Charles and Camilla together in the first place—the fondness for the hunt, for Italy and its rich history, for architecture?

It would appear that Camilla is finding out that life as a royal is a lot harder than she might have anticipated from the other side of the sheets; she, too, has chafed against its limitations. According to another aide interviewed by the *Daily Mail*, "the problem is, Camilla isn't really pompous or conscious of status and hierarchy but he is and always has been. She finds that very confusing and restricting. She had a free life before, having fags [cigarettes], drinking, going to riding holidays, and she can't do any of those anymore. She doesn't even have regular contact with all her chums. . . . He is more pedantic, more over-mannered. At Windsor recently, I was talking to him and when he finished his drink he just held it out to the side and waited for a flunky to take it. Camilla would never do that. She would find someone to give it to."

Both Diana and Camilla had been confident that they could slip into the role of a royal with ease. Diana came from a wealthy and illustrious family and had managed to survive the ordeal of dealing with both the paparazzi and her future in-laws during the months of her engagement. Camilla had been Charles's mistress for decades, a soft shoulder and a sympathetic ear when he confided his difficulties in performing the duties expected of him.

Naturally Clarence House denied any rift, while the couple's friends stress that "the problem is far from insurmountable."

Evidently, being a royal mistress was cake compared to being a royal consort. Perhaps Camilla can plumb the recesses of her soul and mine some empathy for Diana.

Charles will likely soldier on, doing his duty while gritting his teeth and thinking of England. He will draw on the centuries of "strength training" that enables British royals to maintain their famously stiff upper lips in times of crisis and pain, a talent that he once jested was ". . . 1500 years of breeding. It comes from being descended from Vlad the Impaler!"

Acknowledgments

Thanks as always are due to my terrifically astute editor, Claire Zion, and my superagent, Irene Goodman, for their astounding literary midwifery. I am also appreciative of the entry suggestions made by Dr. Mona Garcia and for the gift of her time. And I can never express enough gratitude to my husband, Scott, for his perpetual and unflagging love and support, both of me and my creative, but often uncertain, métier—especially in these times of economic insecurity.

Selected Bibliography

BOOKS

Aram, Bethany. *Juana the Mad: Sovereignty & Dynasty in Renaissance Europe*. Baltimore: The Johns Hopkins University Press, 2005.

Aronson, Theo. *Napoleon & Josephine: A Love Story*. New York: St. Martin's Press, 1990.

Baldwin, David. *Elizabeth Woodville: Mother of the Princes in the Tower*. Thrupp, Stroud, Gloucestershire: Sutton Publishing, Ltd., 2002.

Birmingham, Stephen. *Duchess: The Story of Wallis Warfield Simpson*. Boston and Toronto: Little, Brown & Company, 1981.

Brooks, Polly Schoyer. *Queen Eleanor, Independent Spirit of the Medieval World: A Biography of Eleanor of Aquitaine*. Boston: Houghton Mifflin Company, 1999.

Brown, Tina. *The Diana Chronicles*. New York: Doubleday, 2007.

Cawthorne, Nigel. *Sex Lives of the Kings and Queens of England*. London: Prion, 1994.

Coxe, Howard. *The Stranger in the House: A Life of Caroline of Brunswick*. London: Chattus and Windus, 1939.

David, Saul. *Prince of Pleasure: The Prince of Wales and the Making of the Regency*. New York: Atlantic Monthly Press, 1998.

Denny, Joanna. *Katherine Howard: A Tudor Conspiracy*. London: Portrait/Piatkus Books, Ltd., 2005.

Edwards, John. *Ferdinand and Isabella: Profiles in Power*. Great Britain: Pearson Education Limited, 2005.

Erickson, Carolly. *Alexandra: The Last Tsarina*. New York: St. Martin's Press, 2001.

————. *Josephine: A Life of the Empress.* New York: St. Martin's Press, 1998.

Feuchtwanger, Edgar. *Albert and Victoria: The Rise and Fall of the House of Saxe-Coburg-Gotha.* London: Hambledon Continuum, 2006.

Fraser, Antonia. *Marie Antoinette: The Journey.* New York: Anchor Books, 2001.

————. *Mary Queen of Scots.* New York: Bantam Dell, 1969.

Fraser, Antonia, ed. *The Lives of the Kings & Queens of England.* Berkeley, Los Angeles, London: University of California Press, 1999.

Fraser, Flora. *Pauline Bonaparte: Venus of Empire.* New York: Alfred A. Knopf, 2009.

————. *The Unruly Queen: The Life of Queen Caroline.* New York: Alfred A. Knopf, 1996.

Frieda, Leonie. *Catherine de Medici: Renaissance Queen of France.* New York: HarperCollins Publishers, Inc., 2003.

Gies, Joseph and Frances. *Life in a Medieval Castle.* New York: Harper & Row, 1974.

Gomez, María A.; Juan-Navarro, Santiago; and Zatlin, Phyllis, eds. *Juana of Castile: History and Myth of the Mad Queen.* Cranbury, New Jersey: Associated University Presses, 2008.

Graham, Roderick. *An Accidental Tragedy: The Life of Mary, Queen of Scots.* Edinburgh: Birlinn Limited, 2008.

Guy, John. *Queen of Scots: The True Life of Mary Stuart.* New York: Houghton Mifflin Company, 2004.

Hamann, Brigitte [trans. Ruth Hein]. *The Reluctant Empress: A Biography of Empress Elisabeth of Austria.* Berlin: Ullstein, 1998.

Haslip, Joan. *The Lonely Empress: Elizabeth of Austria.* London: Phoenix Press, 1965.

Herman, Eleanor. *Sex With the Queen.* New York: HarperCollins, 2006.

Hibbert, Christopher. *Napoleon: His Wives and Women.* New York: W. W. Norton & Company, 2002.

————. *Queen Victoria: A Personal History.* New York: Basic Books, 2000.

————. *Queen Victoria in Her Letters and Journals.* New York: Viking Penguin, Inc., 1985.

Higham, Charles. *The Duchess of Windsor: The Secret Life.* Hoboken: John Wiley & Sons, Inc., 1988.

Holme, Thea. *Caroline: A Biography of Caroline of Brunswick*. New York: Atheneum, 1980.

Irvine, Valerie. *The King's Wife: George IV and Mrs. Fitzherbert*. London: Hambledon and London, 2005.

Ives, Eric. *The Life and Death of Anne Boleyn*. Oxford: Blackwell Publishing, 2004.

James, Susan. *Catherine Parr: Henry VIII's Last Love*. Stroud, Gloucestershire: Tempus Publishing, Ltd., 2008.

Junor, Peggy. *Charles: Victim or Villain*. New York: HarperCollins, 1998.

King, Greg. *The Duchess of Windsor: The Uncommon Life of Wallis Simpson*. New York: Citadel Press, 2000.

Leigh, Wendy. *True Grace*. New York: Thomas Dunne Books, 2007.

Leslie, Anita. *Mrs. Fitzherbert*. New York: Charles Scribner's Sons, 1960.

Lever, Evelyne [trans. Catherine Temerson]. *Marie Antoinette: The Last Queen of France*. New York: Farrar, Straus and Giroux, 2000.

Liss, Peggy. *Isabel the Queen*. New York: Oxford University Press, Inc., 1992.

Massie, Robert K. *Nicholas and Alexandra*. New York: Ballantine Books, 1967.

Mattingly, Garrett. *Catherine of Aragon*. New York: Book-of-the-Month Club, 1941.

Morton, Andrew. *Diana, Her True Story* [A Commemorative Edition with New Material Including *Her Own Words*]. New York: Simon & Schuster, 1997.

Munson, James. *Maria Fitzherbert: The Secret Wife of George IV*. New York: Carroll & Graf Publishers, 2001.

Palmer, Alan. *Napoleon & Marie Louise: The Emperor's Second Wife*. New York: St. Martin's Press, 2001.

Plowden, Alison. *Caroline and Charlotte: Regency Scandals*. Thrupp, Stroud, Gloucestershire: Sutton Publishing, Ltd., 2005.

Princess Michael of Kent. *The Serpent and the Moon: Two Rivals for the Love of a Renaissance King*. New York: Touchstone, 2004.

Richardson, Walter C. *Mary Tudor: The White Queen*. London: Peter Owen Limited, 1970.

Rounding, Virginia. *Catherine the Great: Love, Sex, and Power*. New York: St. Martin's Press, 2006.

Shaw, Karl. *Royal Babylon*. New York: Broadway Books, 1999.

Starkey, David. *Six Wives: The Queens of Henry VIII*. New York: HarperCollins, 2003.

Taraborrelli, J. Randy. *Once Upon a Time: Behind the Fairy Tale of Princess Grace and Prince Rainier*. New York: Warner Books, 2003.

Weir, Alison. *Eleanor of Aquitaine: A Life*. New York: Ballantine Books, 1999.

Williams, Susan. *The People's King: The True Story of the Abdication*. New York: Palgrave Macmillan, 2004.

Wilson, A. N. *The Rise & Fall of the House of Windsor*. New York and London: W. W. Norton and Company, Inc., 1993.

Wilson, Christopher. *A Greater Love: Prince Charles's Twenty-Year Affair With Camilla Parker Bowles*. New York: William Morrow and Company, Inc., 1994.

———. *The Windsor Knot: Charles, Camilla and the Legacy of Diana*. New York: Citadel Press, 2002.

Zweig, Stefan [trans. Cedar and Eden Paul]. *Marie Antoinette: The Portrait of an Average Woman*. New York: Grove Press, 1933.

ARTICLES

Beer, Barrett L. "Jane [Jane Seymour] (1508/9–1537)." In *Oxford Dictionary of National Biography*, edited by H. C. G. Matthew and Brian Harrison. Oxford: OUP, 2004, www.oxforddnb.com/view/article/14647.

Bernard, G. W. "Seymour, Thomas, Baron Seymour of Sudeley (*b.* in or before 1509, *d.* 1549)." In *Oxford Dictionary of National Biography*, edited by H. C. G. Matthew and Brian Harrison. Oxford: OUP, 2004. Online ed., edited by Lawrence Goldman, January 2008, www.oxforddnb.com/view/article/25181.

Davies, C. S. L. and John Edwards. "Katherine (1485–1536)." In *Oxford Dictionary of National Biography*, edited by H. C. G. Matthew and Brian Harrison. Oxford: OUP, 2004. Online ed., edited by Lawrence Goldman, January 2008, www.oxforddnb.com/view/article/4891.

Gibbs, G. C. "George I (1660–1727)." In *Oxford Dictionary of National Biography*, edited by H. C. G. Matthew and Brian Harrison. Oxford: OUP, 2004. Online ed., edited by Lawrence Goldman, October 2007, www.oxforddnb.com/view/article/10538.

Goodare, Julian. "Mary (1542–1587)." In *Oxford Dictionary of National Biography*, edited by H. C. G. Matthew and Brian Harrison. Oxford: OUP, 2004. Online ed., edited by Lawrence Goldman, May 2007, www.oxforddnb.com/view/article/18248.

Greig, Elaine Finnie. "Stewart, Henry, duke of Albany [Lord Darnley] (1545/6–1567)." In *Oxford Dictionary of National Biography*, edited H. C. G. Matthew and Brian Harrison. Oxford: OUP, 2004. Online ed., edited by Lawrence Goldman, January 2008, www.oxforddnb.com/view/article/26473.

Gunn, S. J. "Brandon, Charles, first duke of Suffolk (*c.*1484–1545)." In *Oxford Dictionary of National Biography*, edited by H. C. G. Matthew and Brian Harrison. Oxford: OUP, 2004. Online ed., edited by Lawrence Goldman, January 2008, www.oxforddnb.com/view/article/3260.

Hicks, Michael. "Elizabeth (*c.*1437–1492)." In *Oxford Dictionary of National Biography*, edited by H. C. G. Matthew and Brian Harrison. Oxford: OUP, 2004. Online ed., edited by Lawrence Goldman, May 2008, www.oxforddnb.com/view/article/8634.

Horrox, Rosemary. "Arthur, prince of Wales (1486–1502)." In *Oxford Dictionary of National Biography*, edited by H. C. G. Matthew and Brian Harrison. Oxford: OUP, 2004.

———. "Edward IV (1442–1483)." In *Oxford Dictionary of National Biography*, edited by H. C. G. Matthew and Brian Harrison. Oxford: OUP, 2004. Online ed., edited by Lawrence Goldman, January 2008, www.oxforddnb.com/view/article/8520.

Ives, E. W. "Anne (*c.*1500–1536)." In *Oxford Dictionary of National Biography*, edited by H. C. G. Matthew and Brian Harrison. Oxford: OUP, 2004, www.oxforddnb.com/view/article/557.

James, Susan E. "Katherine [Katherine Parr] (1512–1548)." In *Oxford Dictionary of National Biography*, edited by H. C. G. Matthew and Brian Harrison. Oxford: OUP, 2004. Online ed., edited by Lawrence Goldman, January 2008, www.oxforddnb.com/view/article/4893.

Kilburn, Matthew. "Sophia Dorothea [Princess Sophia Dorothea of Celle] (1666–1726)." In *Oxford Dictionary of National Biography*, edited by H. C. G. Matthew and Brian Harrison. Oxford: OUP, 2004, www.oxforddnb.com/view/article/37995.

Levy, Martin J. "Fitzherbert, Maria Anne (1756–1837)." In *Oxford Dictionary of National Biography*, edited by H. C. G. Matthew and Brian Harrison. Oxford: OUP, 2004, www.oxforddnb.com/view/article/9603.

Loades, David. "Mary (1496–1533)." In *Oxford Dictionary of National Biography*, edited by H. C. G. Matthew and Brian Harrison. Oxford: OUP, 2004. Online ed., edited by Lawrence Goldman, January 2008, www.oxforddnb.com/view/article/18251.

Marshall, Rosalind K. "Hepburn, James, fourth earl of Bothwell and duke of Orkney (1534/5–1578)." In *Oxford Dictionary of National Biography*, edited by H. C. G. Matthew and Brian Harrison. Oxford: OUP, 2004, www.oxforddnb.com/view/article/13001.

Matthew, H. C. G. and K. D. Reynolds. "Victoria (1819–1901)." In *Oxford Dictionary of National Biography*, edited by H. C. G. Matthew and Brian Harrison. Oxford: OUP, 2004. Online ed., edited by Lawrence Goldman, January 2008, www.oxforddnb.com/view/article/36652.

Reynolds, K. D. "Diana, princess of Wales (1961–1997)." In *Oxford Dictionary of National Biography*, edited by H. C. G. Matthew and Brian Harrison. Oxford: OUP, 2004. Online ed., edited by Lawrence Goldman, October 2006, www.oxforddnb.com/view/article/68348.

Warnicke, Retha M. "Anne [Anne of Cleves] (1515–1557)." In *Oxford Dictionary of National Biography*, edited by H. C. G. Matthew and Brian Harrison. Oxford: OUP, 2004, www.oxforddnb.com/view/article/558.

———. "Katherine [Katherine Howard] (1518x24–1542)." In *Oxford Dictionary of National Biography*, edited by H. C. G. Matthew and Brian Harrison. Oxford: OUP, 2004. Online ed., edited by Lawrence Goldman, January 2008.

Weikel, Ann. "Mary I (1516–1558)." In *Oxford Dictionary of National Biography*, edited by H. C. G. Matthew and Brian Harrison. Oxford: OUP, 2004. Online ed., edited by Lawrence Goldman, January 2008, www.oxforddnb.com/view/article/18245.

Web Sites

www.englishhistory.net
www.lordbothwell.co.uk/macbeth.html

www.gracekellyonline.com/wedding/
www.madmonarchs.nl
www.dailymail.co.uk
www.ecorazzi.com
Lawrence H. Officer, "Purchasing Power of British Pounds from
1264 to 2007," MeasuringWorth, 2008, www.measuringworth.com/
ppoweruk.

NB regarding relative monetary values: during the writing of this book
the American dollar fluctuated widely against the British pound, with
an average conversion rate of £1 to $1.50. Financial calculations from
British pounds in a given year to American dollars as of 2008 (which
is as far as the Web site goes as of this writing) were obtained from
www.measuringworth.com. The sums I provided "in today's economy" and similar wording are rounded numbers, not intended to be
an exact calculation but to give readers a general sense of the monetary
values then and now.

Photo by Ron Rinaldi

LESLIE CARROLL is the author of several works of women's fiction and, under the pen name Amanda Elyot, is a multipublished historical fiction writer. She and her husband, Scott, reside in New York City. *Notorious Royal Marriages* is her second foray into the field of historical nonfiction. Meet the author at www.lesliecarroll.com.

Let's Dish the Dirt on Notorious Royal Marriages!

For *Royal Affairs*, my maiden voyage into nonfiction, I set up a blog at www.royalaffairs.blogspot.com, and I see no reason why we can't chat on that blog about the couples profiled in *Notorious Royal Marriages* in addition to the lovers and adulterers found in *Royal Affairs*—particularly since there tends to be a crossover cast of usual suspects.

Please visit the blog to chat with me about the fascinating lives and tempestuous unions I've covered in both books, as well as juicy tidbits about other notorious royal marriages that didn't make the final cut. I welcome book club leaders to set up a "tryst," choosing a blog day all to yourselves, where I'll discuss the book interactively with your members. Alternatively, we can set up an interactive speakerphone chat during your meeting. To do so, please contact me through my Web site.